FASHION SKETCHBOOK

FASHION SKETCHBOOK

sixth edition

BINA ABLING

Fairchild Books | New York

Executive Director & General Manager: Michael Schluter
Executive Editor: Olga T. Kontzias
Senior Associate Acquiring Editor: Jaclyn Bergeron
Assistant Acquisitions Editor: Amanda Breccia
Associate Art Director: Sarah Silberg
Development Editor: Beth Cohen
Production Director: Ginger Hillman
Senior Production Editor: Elizabeth Marotta
Ancillaries Editor: Amy Butler
Associate Director of Sales: Melanie Sankel
Copyeditor: Susan Hobbs
Cover Design: Carly Grafstein
Cover Art: illustrations by Bina Abling, photography by Giovanni Giannoni (Gianfranco Ferre Spring 2012 RTW)
Text Design and Composition: Carly Grafstein
Photo Research: Avital Aronowitz
Videographer and DVD Developer: Katie Fitzsimmons
Camera Assistants: Frank Marino and Jay Catlett

Library of Congress Catalog Card Number:
ISBN: 978-1-60901-228-1
GST R 133004424
Printed in Canada
TP 14

Contents

Extended Contents   vii

Preface   xi

Tools and Equipment Hints   xiii

Chapter 1   Fashion Figure Proportions   1

Chapter 2   Basic Figure Forms   37

Chapter 3   Model Drawing   61

Chapter 4   Fashion Heads   81

Chapter 5   Garments and Garment Details   107

Chapter 6   Drawing Flats and Specs   141

Chapter 7   Basic Rendering Techniques   181

Chapter 8   High-End Rendering Techniques   223

Chapter 9   Drawing Knits   265

Chapter 10   Design Focus and Layout   295

Chapter 11   Drawing Men   329

Chapter 12   Drawing Children   377

Chapter 13   Accessories   411

Fashion Archive   443

Credits   475

Index   477

Extended Contents

Preface   xi
Acknowledgments   xii
Tools and Equipment Hints   xiii

CHAPTER 1
Fashion Figure Proportions   1
Figure Elongation and Stylization   2
Guidelines   4
Heads Tall, Figure Grid   6
Figure Map, Grid System   8
Consistent Proportions   10
Fashion Figure Objectives   12
Croquis Templates   14
Drawing the Figure Freehand   16
Subjective Height   18
Posing Dynamics   20
The Balance Line   22
Center Front   24
Back Views   26
The Profile Pose   28
The Fuller Figure   30
Fashion Maternity Figures   32
Early Illustrations for Womenswear   34

CHAPTER 2
Basic Figure Forms   37
Torso Definition   38
Drawing Legs: Form and Shape   40
Posing Legs   42
Foreshortening: Legs   44
Drawing Feet   46
Drawing Arms: Form and Shape   50
Foreshortening: Arms   52
Drawing Hands   54
Figure Tips   56

CHAPTER 3
Model Drawing   61
Model Drawing Poses   62
Balance Line   63
Angles in a Pose   64
Torso in a Pose   66
Gesture Components   68
Interpreting Anatomy   70
Fashion Runway and Showroom Poses   72

CHAPTER 4
Fashion Heads   81
Drawing Heads and Fashion Faces   82
Drawing Heads   84
The Diamond Technique   86
Drawing a Full-Front Head   87
Drawing a Three-Quarter-Turned Head   88
Drawing a Profile Head   89
Fashion Faces, Sketching Features   90
Posing the Head   92
Sketching Features   94
Stylizing the Face   96
Rendering Hair Color   98
Fleshtone and Pencil   100
Period Looks   101
Fashion Heads, Runway Looks   102

CHAPTER 5
Garments and Garment Details   107
Sketching Necklines and Collars   108
Sketching Sleeves   110
Sketching Blouses and Dresses   112
Sketching Skirts   114
Sketching Flares and Gathers   116
Sketching Pleats   118

Blouses, Skirts, and Dresses 120
Sketching Pants 122
Drawing Pants 124
Shorts and Pants 126
Sketching a Blazer 128
Drawing Jackets 130
Drawing Coats 132
Jackets and Coats 134

Guest Artists
Aram Sung 136
Carmen Chen Wu 138

CHAPTER 6
Drawing Flats and Specs 141
Flat Figure Templates 142
Figure Formulas for Flats 144
Tops: Templates for Shirts, Blouses,
    and Dresses 146
Bottoms: Templates for Shorts,
    Pants, and Skirts 148
Structure for Flats 150
Swimwear and Lingerie Flats 152
Comprehensive Flats 154
Women's Outerwear Flats 156
Presentation or Portfolio Flats 158
Croquis Mixed with Flats 160
Flats and Figures Mixed 162
Specs 166
Measuring and Detailing for Specs 168
Analyzing a Garment for Flats or Specs 170
Flats and Specs 172
Spec Sheets 174

Guest Artists
Christina Kwon 176
Jodie Lau 178

CHAPTER 7
Basic Rendering Techniques 181
Rendering Fleshtones 182
Gouache 184
Mixing Colors for Watercolor 185
Rendering Fabrics in Watercolor 186
Reducing a Print 188
Finished versus Partial Rendering 190
Fabric Practice Templates 192
Color Testing 194
Color Nuances 196
Stripes 198
Checks, Gingham, and Plaids 200
Geometric Patterns 202

Fall Fabrics 204
Animal Prints 208
Fashion Designer Color Challenges 210
André Courrèges 211
Emilio Pucci/Carolina Herrera 212
Rudi Gernreich 213
Geoffrey Beene/James Galanos 214
Arnold Scaasi 215

Guest Artists
Raya Clements 216
Eduarda Salmi Pereira 218

CHAPTER 8
High-End Rendering Techniques 223
Sketching Ruffles 224
Sketching Cascades 226
Sketching Cowls 228
Sketching Smocking and Shirring 229
Gathers, Gores, Cowl Drape, and Pintucks 230
Changing Proportions 232
Bridal Looks 234
Bridal Trains 236
Dress and Gown Flats 238
Drape and Volume 240
Luxe Fabric Rendering 244
Black Fabric Rendering 246
Beading, Satin, Chiffon, Crystal Pleating,
    and Tulle 250
Feathers, Fringe, and Lace 252

Guest Artists
Elizabeth Kennedy 254
Chi Lo 256
Carmen Chen Wu 260

CHAPTER 9
Drawing Knits 265
Knit Essentials 266
Knitwear Flats 268
Basic Knit Stitches 270
Repeat Patterns 272
Cables and Combinations 276
Complex Knits 278
WWD Photo Reference 282

Guest Artists
Anthony Manfredonia 284
Jodie Lau 286
Christina Kwon 288
Joseph Singh 290
Jose "Juni" Salgado 292

CHAPTER 10
Design Focus and Layout   295
Design Direction   296
Attitude in a Pose   298
Design Emphasis   300
Stylization for Designers   302
Design Objectives   304
Design Journal Pages   308
Design Journal Thumbnail Sketches   310
WWD Designer Fitting Photos   311
Maximizing Design Impact   312
Composition Direction   314
Grouping Figures   316
Layout or Line Up   320

Guest Artists
Julian Guthrie   324

CHAPTER 11
Drawing Men   329
Menswear Figure Basics   330
Proportions for Menswear Figures   334
Runway Poses for Men   336
Elongation for Menswear   338
Drawing Men's Legs   340
Drawing Men's Arms and Hands   342
Drawing Men's Heads   344
Drawing Men's Hair   345
Clothing the Male Figure   346
Menswear Pants   348
Menswear Tops   350
Sketching a Suit   352
Menswear Flats   354
Design Journal Roughs   358
Marker Rendering for Menswear   360
Fashion Runway and Showroom Poses   362

Guest Artists
Sascha Flowers   366
Neha Bhatia   368
Matthew Conmy   370
Julian Guthrie   372
Early Menswear Illustrations: 1900 to 1930   374

CHAPTER 12
Drawing Children   377
Children's Age Groups   378
Childrenswear Proportions   380
Infant   381
Toddler   382
Younger Child   383

Child   384
Tween Boy   385
Tween to Teen   386
Teen Boy   387
Drawing Children's Heads   388
Drawing Children's Arms and Hands   390
Drawing Children's Legs and Feet   392
Design Roughs for Childrenswear   394
Rendering Childrenswear   396
Flats for Children   398

Guest Artists
Eri Mikami   400
Serena Chang   402
Callista Wolff   404
Anika Sushil Gupta   406
Early Childrenswear Illustrations:
   1920 to 1930   408

CHAPTER 13
Accessories   411
Jewelry Croquis   412
Jewelry Templates   414
Sunglasses   416
Hats and Gloves   418
Drawing Men's Hats   420
Drawing Women's Hats   421
Belts   422
Hardware for Belts and Bags   423
Handbags and Purses   424
Shoes   425
Footwear Design Roughs   426
Sporty Shoes   428

Guest Artists
LaToya Leflore   430
Jason Buchanon   432
Julian Guthrie   434
Malinda Franklin   436
Felice DaCosta   438
Early Accessories Illustrations: 1950s   440

Fashion Archive   443
Credits   475
Index   477

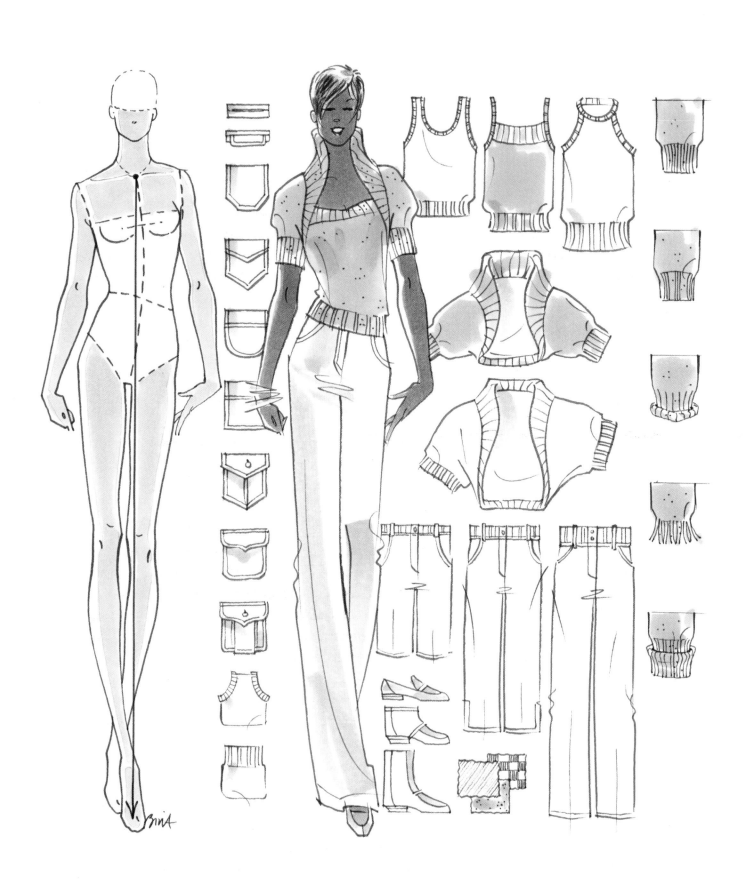

Preface

The sixth edition of *Fashion Sketchbook* is in full color. It is completely revised, with updated drawing instructions and new images in every chapter. Many of the photos are *Women's Wear Daily* fashion runway and showroom photos that inform and maximize lesson goals. The photos will inspire as well as fuel your fashion illustrations, with a stronger connection to the fashion design studio or classroom experience. The goal is to accelerate comprehension, application, and diversification of your drawing skills.

Most chapters are infused with *WWD* photographs of design silhouettes, fabric examples, or muslin shapes for greater reference value. Color rendering, now integrated thoughout the textbook, includes photographic examples of current designer reference with more in-depth, mixed media illustration techniques to explore. The first two chapters, on basic figure drawing, have been expanded with trendier, elongated fashion forms. Chapter Three, Model Drawing, in all new layouts, now reflects your classroom experience, with more figure analysis and new runway poses. The fashion heads chapter provides more concise sketching methods and new *WWD* fashion faces to draw. The chapters on fashion design garment detail incorporate all of the previous edition's successful sketching techniques but now have been updated to include *WWD* pictoral reference that supplements your designer image research. Chapter Seven, with a full component of *WWD* images, focuses on specific types of fabrics matched to their colored pencil and marker rendering solutions. The menswear and childrenswear chapters, both updated, have been revised to offer more stylistic sketching options. The chapter on flats and specs has been changed to create a broader base of more detailed drawing instructions. This textbook's unique Fashion Archive, containing more than 400 garment and accessory references for fashion nomenclature, has been updated and (drawing) Problem Spots has been completely redone to reflect new sketching issues. Throughout this sixth edition, there are over a dozen new guest artist spreads, which serve as guides and goals for all of your drawing skills. A DVD is also included. There are six video segments that demonstrate mixed media rendering techniques. It provides a broader platform to help you fully develop your fashion design illustrations.

What can be more fun than drawing for a living? The more I know about fashion, the more I want to sketch. I approach drawing and teaching, in this ever-changing field of expertise, with the same enthusiasm as my first day in class. I was thrilled then and feel the same sense of excitement today. I love my career choice. I can't imagine ever being bored by my job. Drawing for me is as important as breathing   it's that vital to my being. I sincerely hope and encourage you to feel the same way about your career. Enjoy each page, and every moment of learning, reach for your full potential, and believe in your talent as much as I do and did to create this sixth edition.

Acknowledgments

My revisions for this sixth edition were extensive. So much hard work, time, and talent have gone into this book's success and for that I thank the entire creative and sales teams at Fairchild Books. Appreciation, applause, and accolades to Jackie, Sarah, Liz, Amy, and Carly. Their time, talent, and tenacity in making all things possible for this edition were amazing. This sincere thanks includes Beth, Avital, and Katie for their talents and teamwork. More thanks to all of the gracious designers, photographers, and exquisite models whose work here will inspire so many future fashion talents. Special thanks to Felicia DaCosta for her insight, for beautiful knit samples, and for coordinating the guest artists. I am very grateful to Joseph Pescatore for the exquisite muslin samples and the fashion shoot of the heritage designer garments. I thank all of the talented fashion designers whose motivating design illustrations are featured in this book, encouraging the next generation and helping them to develop their style and potential. Thanks to all of this book's reviewers for their generous support and suggestions. To my colleagues and students I offer special thanks. It is always an honor to work with you.

Tools & Equipment Hints

Paper

The variety in paper is at once wonderful and daunting. You have to read the covers of the pads carefully to find out what kind of paper it is. Most regular sketching papers come in two surfaces: "vellum," which is slightly rough, and "plate," which is smooth. They perform differently, so test each kind to find out what works for you. Smooth paper can be fast to sketch on and is great when working with pens. Rougher paper is slower and its surface is great for pencil. Marker papers come in varying degrees of transparency, whiteness, and workability. You need to try out at least two separate brands and then test strip your markers on them. Always use the top or front of the paper because the back of it will probably perform differently. Watercolor papers come in pads or in single sheets. For fashion use, the watercolor paper with a slightly pebbled surface, as opposed to the very rough surface, works better. Rough papers are too "thirsty" and take too long to paint.

Tracing Paper

As with other paper, each paper company makes unique tracing paper. Some are more transparent than others; they can also vary in thickness. A few varieties are quite smooth and can handle all media; others, of lesser quality, will not stand up to extensive use. Most tracing paper is used as a cover for your work or as a preliminary test run for conceptual planning. All tracing paper is limited in use except for its see-through abilities. It is also great for corrections and useful as overlays on a sketch.

Graphite/Ebony Pencils

Graphite pencils look like regular writing pencils that are sheathed in wood. Ebony pencils can be all lead with just a plastic coating. The difference is that these drawing pencils come in hard or soft leads that vary from H for hard to B for soft. You will need to test these leads to see how light the Hs are and how dark the Bs are. All of these leads are delicate, however. If you drop them, the lead in the wood casing can crack and will be difficult to sharpen because the lead will continue to break all the way down the shaft of the pencil. There are also mechanical pencils. These are holders into which you place leads, which you buy separately. Again, these leads come in H (hard) and B (soft) designations.

Colored Pencils

There are three types that you will need: (1) Those that have hard leads; (2) the kind that have soft leads; and (3) the type that are water-color based. As a rule, the thicker the lead in the pencil, the softer and darker the pencil will be. Harder leads in the pencil will give you a crisper line quality. Watercolor pencils fall in between hard and soft leads. You want to learn control techniques for each type of pencil because they can perform very differently in the rendering process.

Pens

Pens come in as many types of points or nibs as markers do. There are fine, chiseled, broad, and medium. Some have felt tips, while others have metal or plastic tips. Some are supposed to be waterproof or permanent, which means that they will not run or bleed when you use them with other media. Be skeptical and always test the limits of your pens.

Brush Pens

These are pens with a tip similar to a brush—a paintbrush. Some brush pens come in different-width tips which are equal to a #2- or a #7-size paintbrush. In addition to black, they also come in colors. Test the black brush pens because some of them have a reddish cast while others tend to be more grayish than pure black.

Markers

There are many different types of markers. Each manufacturer uses different chemicals that act as the coloring agent. Before you buy any marker, test it to ensure that it is "wet"—not dried out—and to see if it can be used in conjunction with another brand of marker. Most markers are compatible. There are different options for refills, many types of points, and a vast array of colors. Some markers are toxic. Remember to always put the cap back on tightly after each use and keep markers out of the reach of children.

Water-based Paints

Both gouache and watercolors mix with water; gouache is opaque, while watercolor is transparent. These paints are used to create washes. Experiment with both types to find which will work for you. There is an incredible range of possibilities for using these paints, varying from intense to delicate for any single color. Practice blending the ratio of water to your paints slowly so you do not create bubbles. Gouache and watercolor paints are very different, but they can be used together in your rendering. Inks can be used, too. Inks are much brighter colors and work well in conjunction with watercolors.

Brushes

Brushes come in various sizes. They range roughly from size 0 to size 12. Beyond the size of their tips (which can be pointed or flat), you will notice they are available in different hairs or fibers. Some brushes are made with natural animal hairs. These are usually the best; they last the longest without becoming permanently stained or losing their shape. Find a brush that has body or resistance to pressure with just enough "give" to suit your needs. When you buy a good brush, always treat it well. Clean it after each use and stand it upright on its wooden base or lay it down on its side so the tip will not become bent.

FASHION SKETCHBOOK

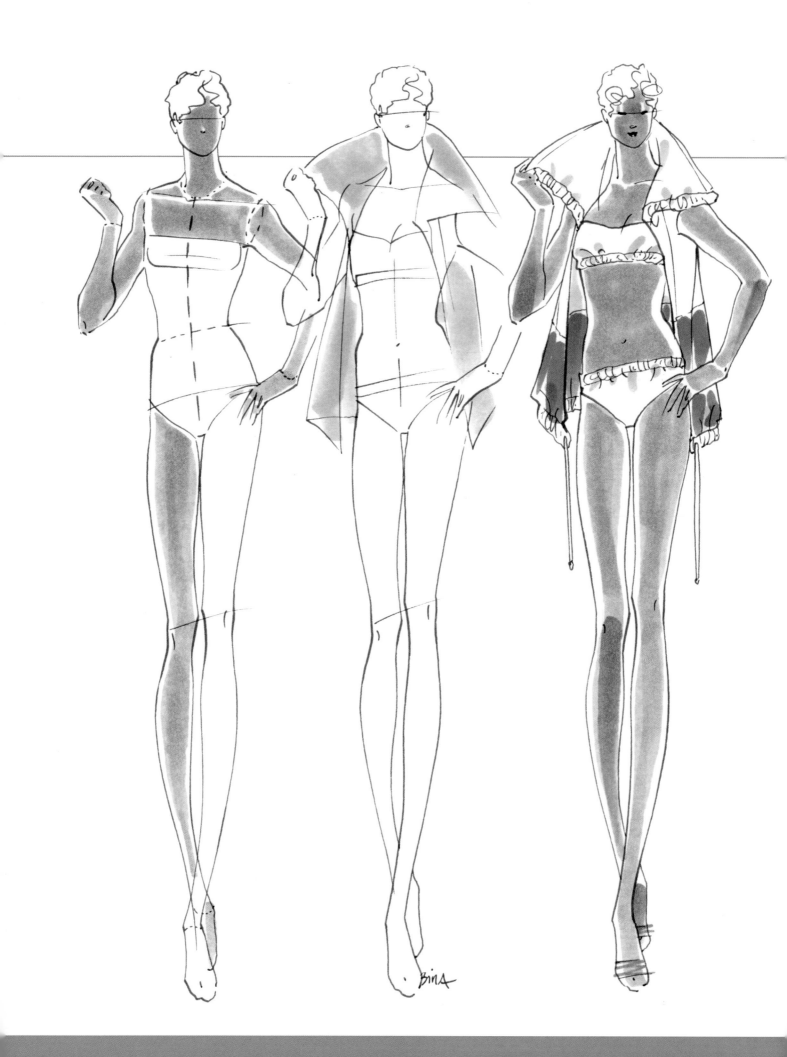

1

Fashion Figure Proportions

The classic approach to drawing the human figure in the fine arts includes anatomy: bones, muscles, and the natural form of the body. In fashion art, the classic approach is mimicked but often precludes the natural form because realism gets filtered through fashion idealism. For example, with realism, the artist sketches the female figure with a naturally sized, thicker torso and wider hips. Conversely, with idealism, the artist sketches the female figure with an unnaturally long, thin torso and hips that are much too narrow to be real. This exaggeration is what separates fashion sketching from fine arts drawing. The painter Modigliani is one of the few exceptions. His long slender forms outdo almost all of current fashion exaggerations in figure length.

Chapter 1 will take you through all of the basic steps of drawing the fashion figure, from the initial basic static poses, all the way through to intermediate level-fashion design poses. To understand this type of figure sketching we will take it apart, map out the fashion figure (and its labels of sewing lines), and put it back together—one body unit at a time. This chapter has been designed to simplify the process of studying fashion proportions so that you can learn how to draw, develop, and interpret this fashion figure through your own style and direction.

Figure Elongation and Stylization

Working on the premise that the average height for a woman is 7 to 8 heads tall, here are examples of how the business of fashion interprets the design figure.

Petite: This figure is drawn to an average-sized height and can include the plus-sized figure.
Model: Here the fashion version of a figure has a taller, slightly elongated frame.
Elongated: Now the fashion figure is exaggerated, stretched longer in its fantasy height.

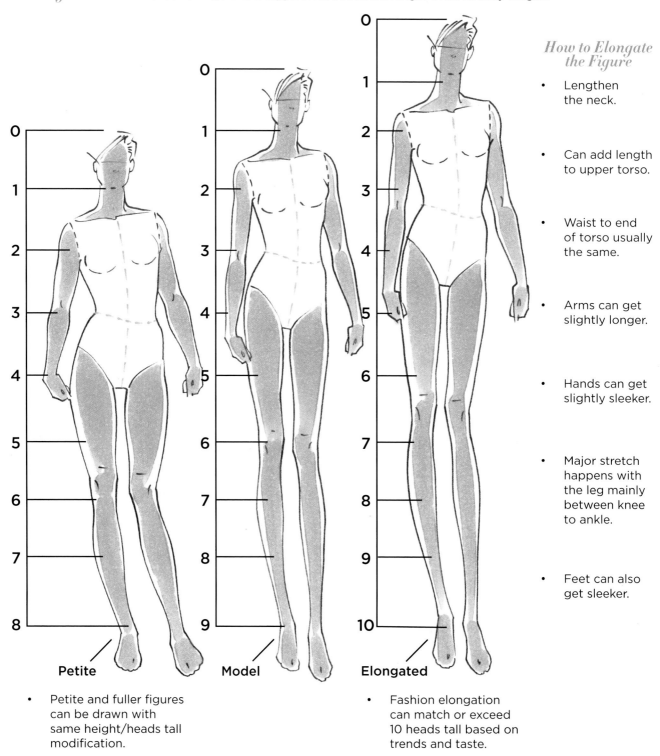

Petite

Model

Elongated

How to Elongate the Figure

- Lengthen the neck.

- Can add length to upper torso.

- Waist to end of torso usually the same.

- Arms can get slightly longer.

- Hands can get slightly sleeker.

- Major stretch happens with the leg mainly between knee to ankle.

- Feet can also get sleeker.

- Petite and fuller figures can be drawn with same height/heads tall modification.

- Fashion elongation can match or exceed 10 heads tall based on trends and taste.

Stylized: At this point the figure is maximizing fashion fantasy, hinting at normal.
Demi-Stylized: This figure can be a hybrid, somewhere in between truth and dare.
Realistic: Here the figure is a bit classic, a conservatively drawn fashion fantasy.

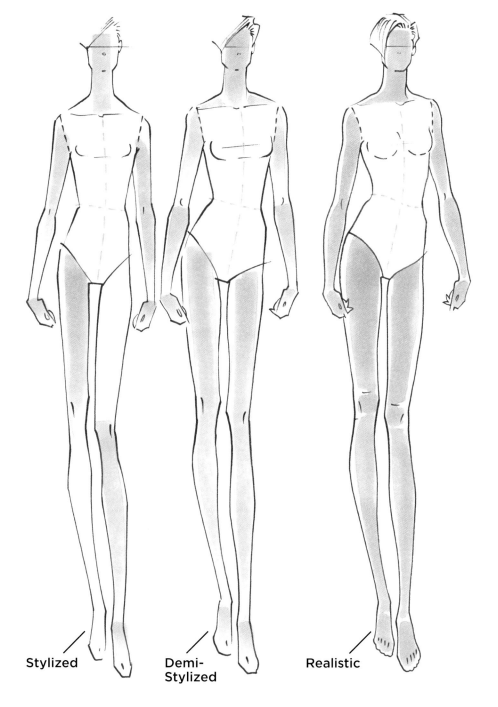

Stylized

Demi-
Stylized

Realistic

- Stylized means more impressionistic, less realism in the figure.

- Stylized figures minimize the posing but then maximize the fashion elongation.

- Stylized figures are often related to the designer's signature design focus or look, while realistic figures show the designer's fit and fabrication.

- Stylized figures also add stronger individual styling and customer features in a sketch.

- Stylized figures can take less time to draw.

Guidelines

As shown on these figures, there are specific guidelines on the fashion figure that divide the form into sections. These guidelines serve two purposes: First, the lines define and label sections of the fashion figure that you can use as a guide for drawing a particular pose. Second, the lines roughly imitate a few of the sewing lines that can be found on a dress form or mannequin. In this case, the guidelines can help you dress the figure so that design detail in a garment is properly drawn on the figure.

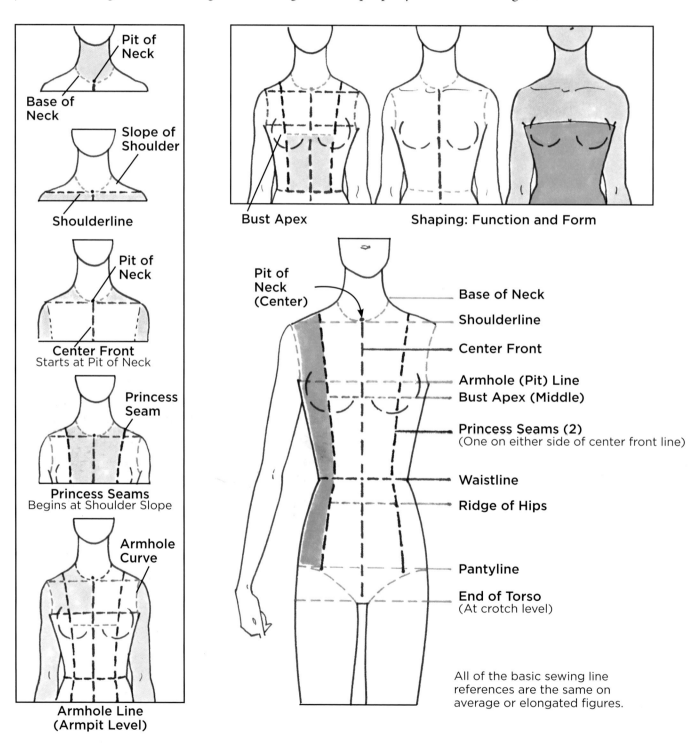

Pit of Neck

Base of Neck

Slope of Shoulder

Shoulderline

Pit of Neck

Center Front
Starts at Pit of Neck

Princess Seam

Princess Seams
Begins at Shoulder Slope

Armhole Curve

Armhole Line
(Armpit Level)

Bust Apex

Shaping: Function and Form

Pit of Neck (Center)

Base of Neck

Shoulderline

Center Front

Armhole (Pit) Line
Bust Apex (Middle)

Princess Seams (2)
(One on either side of center front line)

Waistline

Ridge of Hips

Pantyline

End of Torso
(At crotch level)

All of the basic sewing line references are the same on average or elongated figures.

The sewing lines on the facing page apply to all views of the figures. This page illustrates how they fit on the front, back, and profile poses, helping to create the interior curves of the torso.

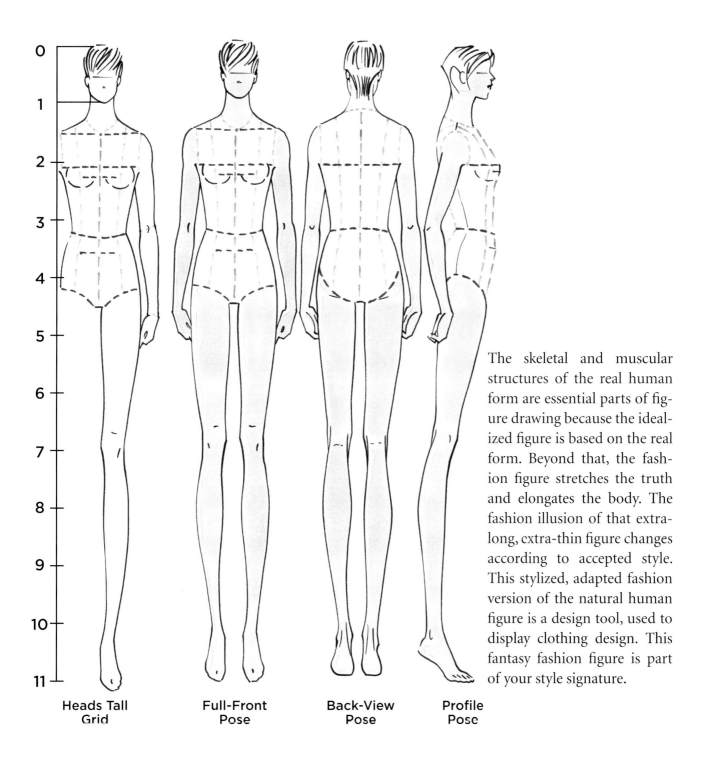

0
1
2
3
4
5
6
7
8
9
10
11

Heads Tall Grid

Full-Front Pose

Back-View Pose

Profile Pose

The skeletal and muscular structures of the real human form are essential parts of figure drawing because the idealized figure is based on the real form. Beyond that, the fashion figure stretches the truth and elongates the body. The fashion illusion of that extra-long, extra-thin figure changes according to accepted style. This stylized, adapted fashion version of the natural human figure is a design tool, used to display clothing design. This fantasy fashion figure is part of your style signature.

Figure Map, Grid System

General weights and measurements have the real figure at about 7 to 8 heads tall. The fashion figure generally starts at a model's height: 10 heads tall. This is where you can start your figure study, map out the body, and learn how to draw a static, full-front fashion pose. Static means standing straight, not posed. This map, for the static figure, is a grid, sectioning the body into literally 10 heads tall to create the set of study proportions for an elongated fashion form.

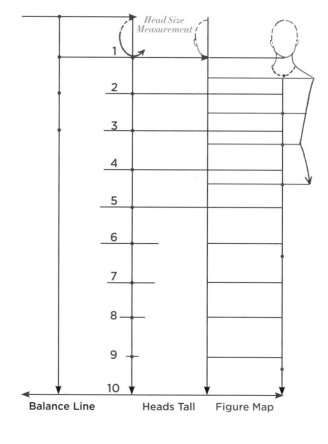

Balance Line   Heads Tall   Figure Map

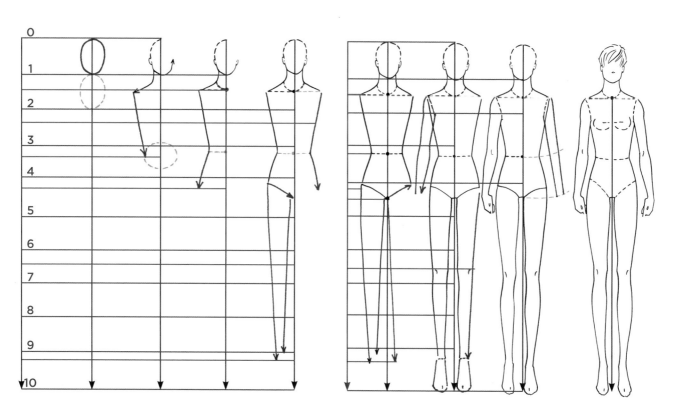

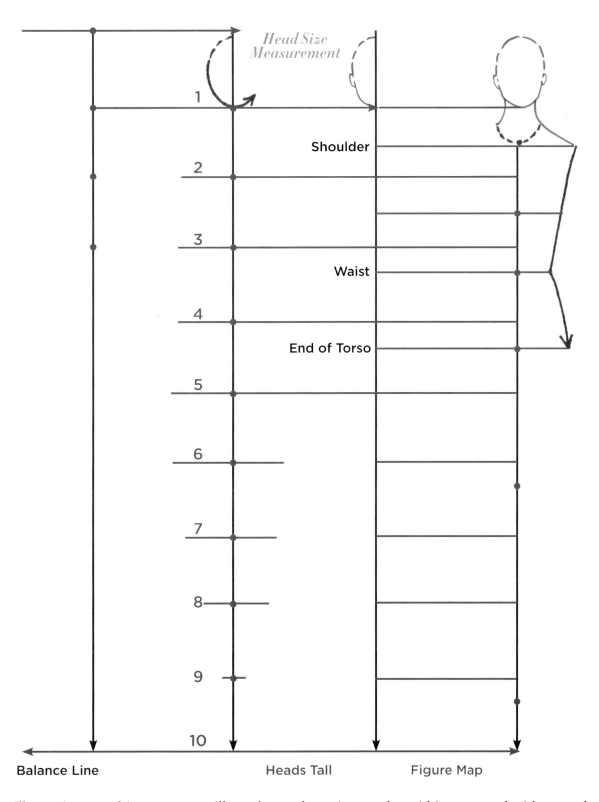

Head Size Measurement

1

Shoulder

2

3

Waist

4

End of Torso

5

6

7

8

9

10

Balance Line   **Heads Tall**   **Figure Map**

In the illustrations on this page, you will see that each section on the grid is partnered with a number. These numbers represent the approximate heads tall position for what will become fashion proportions or a figure map for the body. Example: The shoulder, waist, and end of torso all fall in between lines as their proportions are mapped in.

Figure Map, Heads Tall

1. Draw a vertical line that is the desired length of your figure. Next, draw a short horizontal line at the top and bottom or at the beginning and at the end of your line.

2. Divide the line evenly into 10 sections and label each line consecutively in numbers from 0 to 10. These are your units of heads-tall proportions.

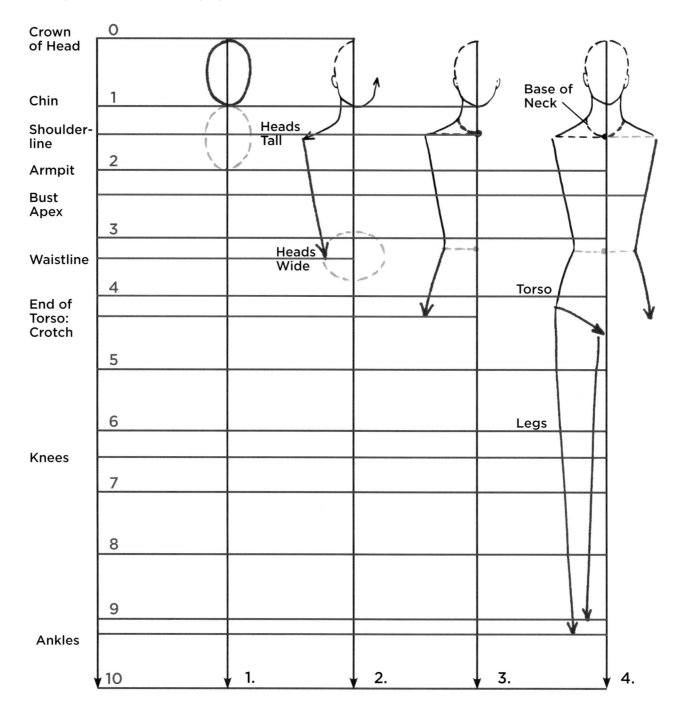

3. Make notes on your grid as to the locations for all of the measurements for dividing the figure into body units. These will be your units of heads-wide proportions.

4. Now work on drawing in the major parts of the body. Start with the head, neck to shoulderline, and then get started on drawing the torso and legs.

5. Draw in each leg, carefully planning for its length and standing position. You want to practice getting both legs to match in size, then add the feet.

6. Now that the figure has been established, you can work on the arms. Here, too, you have to practice getting matching arm lengths and widths.

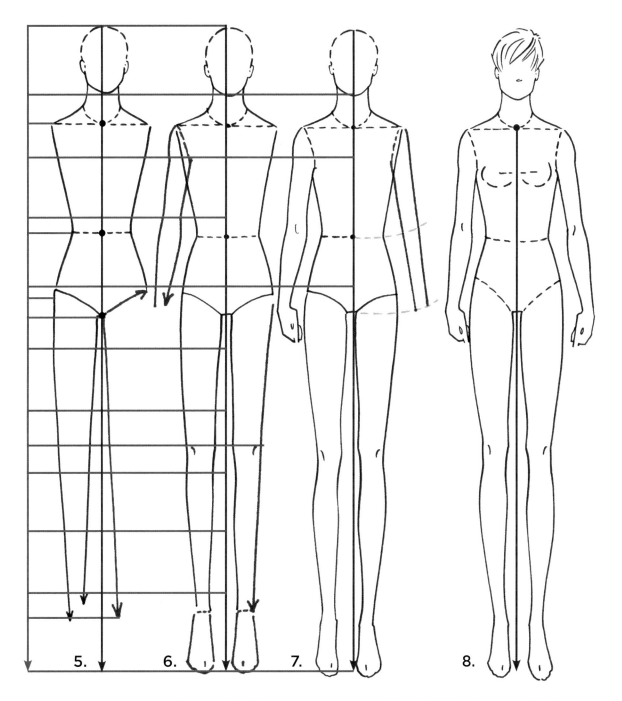

7. This is the time to start rounding out the figure's contours, to work on defining the curves for the torso, legs, and arms.

8. The final step is to work on the interior of the torso. After the natural curves of the bustline and waistline, you may want to add in the sewing lines for more definition.

Consistent Proportions

Torso

The upper torso, your figure's chest, is drawn longer than the lower torso, your figure's hips. The waistline is the natural dividing line between the chest and hip units.

Legs

The thigh, your figure's upper leg, can be equal in length to the calf, your figure's lower leg. The knee is the middle of the leg, in between the thigh and the knee units.

Arms

The upper arm is equal to the length of the lower arm. The elbow is centered, in between the shoulder cap and the wrist, in the middle of the arm.

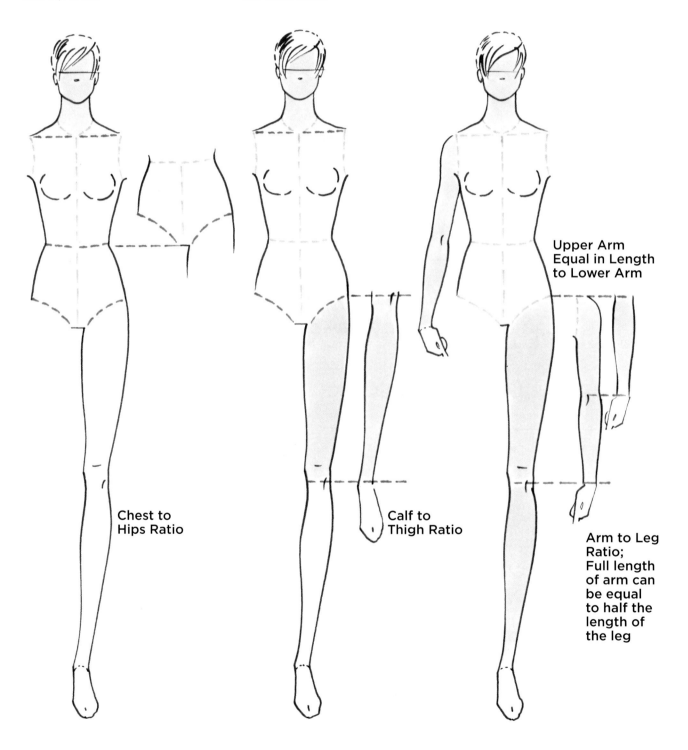

Chest to Hips Ratio

Calf to Thigh Ratio

Upper Arm Equal in Length to Lower Arm

Arm to Leg Ratio; Full length of arm can be equal to half the length of the leg

Body Units

The figure can be deconstructed, divided into its body units, to further analyze figure sketching and to study fashion proportions. This figure breakdown illustrates how to build a pose.

Comparisons

The upper arm is shorter than the upper leg. The head can match the length of the hand or foot. This is your study guide.

Profile Studies

Proportions are sometimes more obvious in this figure position. It makes it easier to access arm to leg ratios.

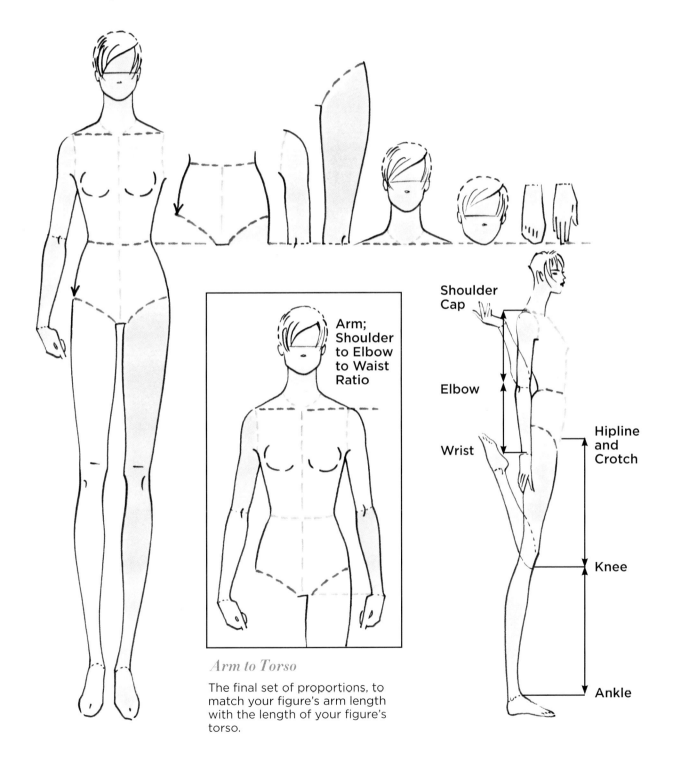

Arm; Shoulder to Elbow to Waist Ratio

Shoulder Cap

Elbow

Wrist

Hipline and Crotch

Knee

Ankle

Arm to Torso

The final set of proportions, to match your figure's arm length with the length of your figure's torso.

Fashion Figure Objectives

Once comfortable with drawing the preliminary fashion figure, you should explore adapting that static pose. The next phase is to re-pose that figure in a design-appropriate stance like a runway-type pose. These examples of working out the dynamics of re-posing the static figure create a less stiff, more fluid, fashion pose.

Transforming Static Poses and Extending Figure Elongation

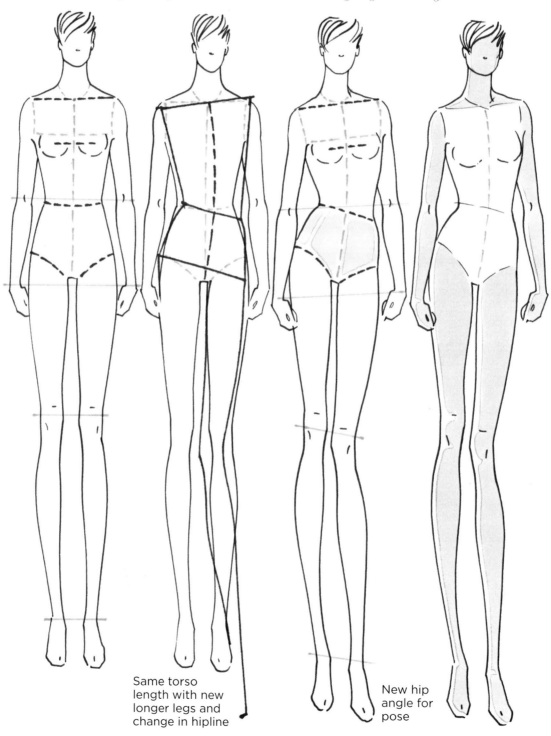

Same torso length with new longer legs and change in hipline

New hip angle for pose

You can also adapt a fashion runway-type pose by opening it up a bit to accommodate a wider fashion design silhouette (for pants or sleeve design details). The point here is to put more space between the arm and torso and the legs.

Opening Up Any Given Pose and Adapting Poses to Accommodate Fuller Garment Shapes

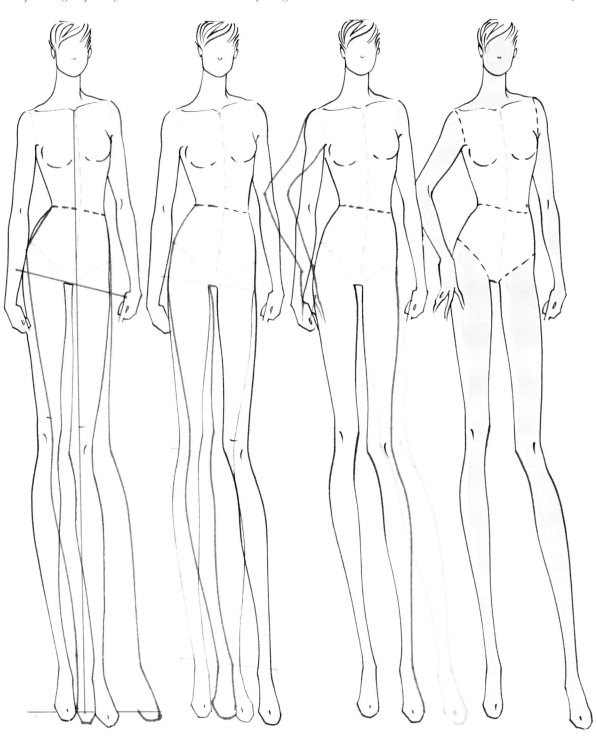

Croquis Templates

Lublu

Often, to make deadlines, the fastest drawing solution is to use one simple pose. A pose that's quick and easy to repeat, in any number when one size fits all, gets the project going. Completing a project on time can preclude spending valuable time working on more specific posing variety when you should instead be focused on design variety.

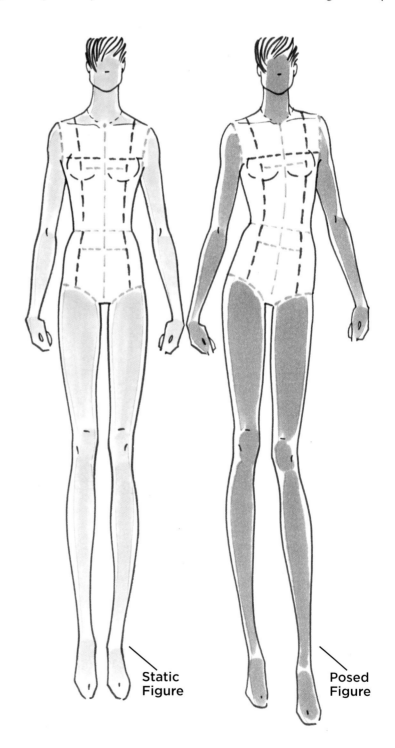

Static Figure

Posed Figure

Croquis Templates

You can use any simple pose, such as the photo or sketch examples here, adapting that pose to accommodate design options, and trace over it for the required number of figure groupings per project.

The static pose is often the easiest to adapt, moving an arm or leg to open up the pose for wider fashion silhouettes. This type of three-figure, static-pose setup is one of the easiest posed figure groupings to create, trace, and repeat.

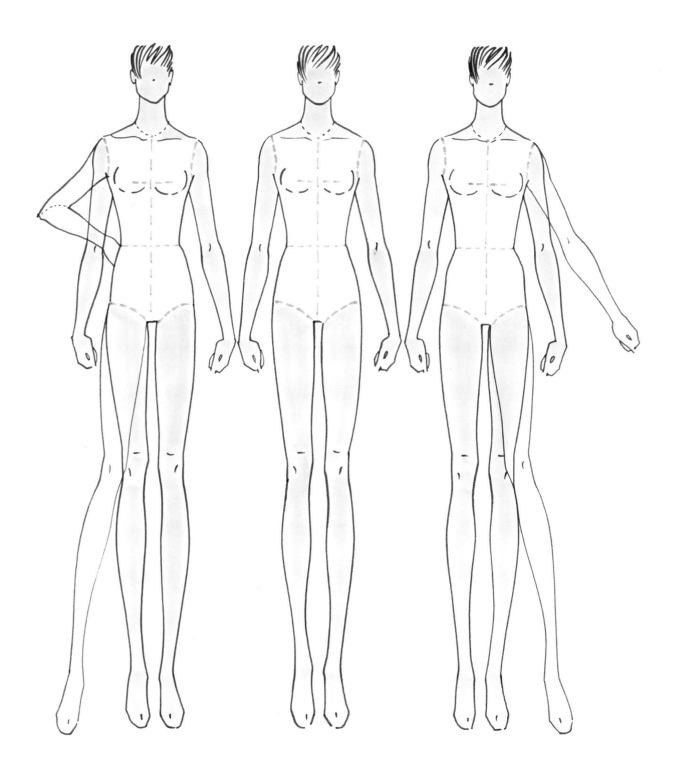

Drawing the Figure Freehand

1. Start your sketch with action angles through the torso. Get the length and width of the torso set in its pose.
2. Drop the balance line down to the "floor." Establish the height of the figure. Find the direction and curve for center front.
3. Center front will divide the hipline at the crotch into left and right thigh areas. Draw the supporting leg first.
4. Begin the extended leg. Start from the crotch into the inner thigh.

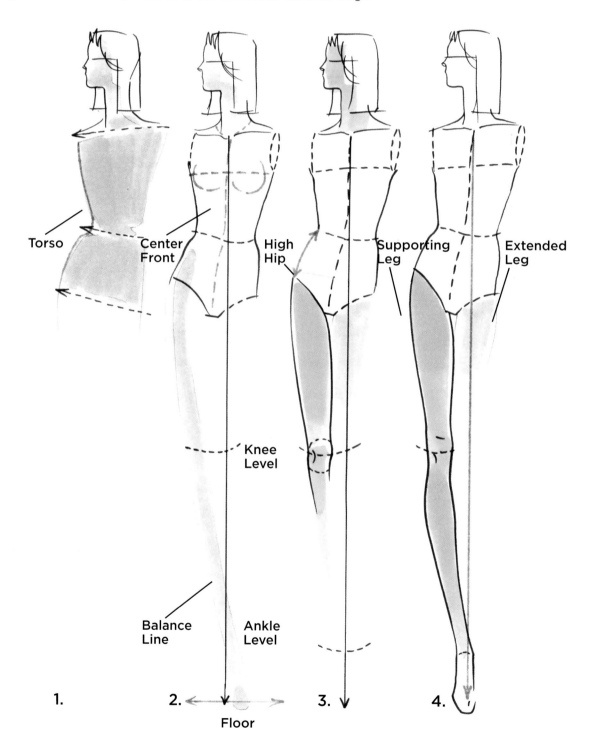

5. Finish drawing the extended leg. This time drop the foot lower than the supporting leg's foot.

6. Draw the other arm behind the chest on the far side of the pose.

7. On the side of the torso closest to you, sketch the arm that rests on or over the chest. This is the filler side, so all of the shoulder cap is visible.

8. To give definition to the form and contours, finish the figure with the interior sewing lines.

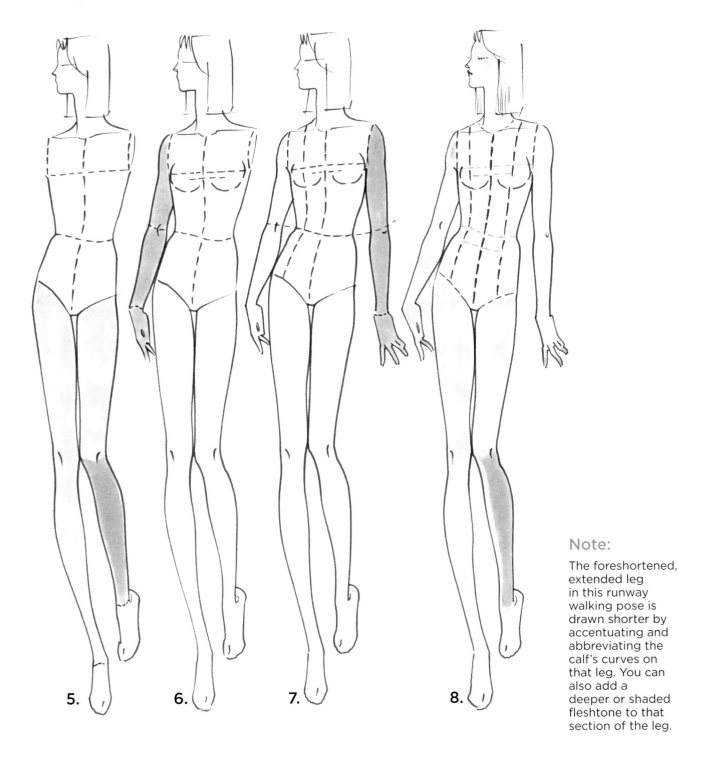

Note:

The foreshortened, extended leg in this runway walking pose is drawn shorter by accentuating and abbreviating the calf's curves on that leg. You can also add a deeper or shaded fleshtone to that section of the leg.

Subjective Height

The fashion figure can be enlarged systematically and still be the same heads tall at any size you need to draw it in. All of the same basic rules for proportions will still be true.

Tall and long is the fashion fantasy figure, but just what size figure you need is up to your design project's parameters. The figure height that fits your page, and feels artistically comfortable to design on for croquis or finished sketches, is your choice. The grid system, the heads-tall method for building a pose, works at any size.

Quickly analyze the differences among these figures. Look for both the subtle and the obvious changes in each figure's proportional relationship to the others on this page. Only the head sizes remain constant.

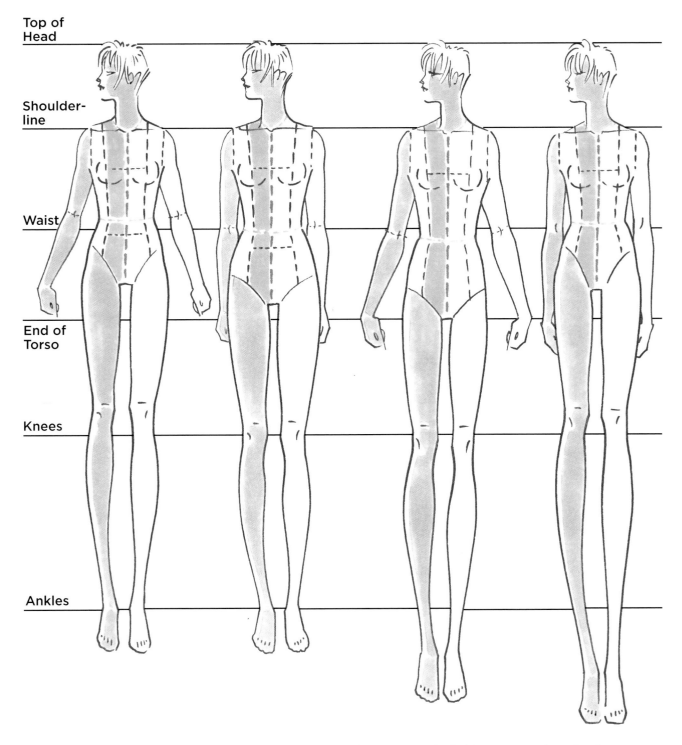

The figures on this page illustrate a range and variety that can exist in fashion proportions for the torso or legs. Excluding the heads, each figures' fashion elongations have been interpreted differently. These stylistic figure nuances are fine as long as they don't interfere with design construction and garment details.

Posing Dynamics

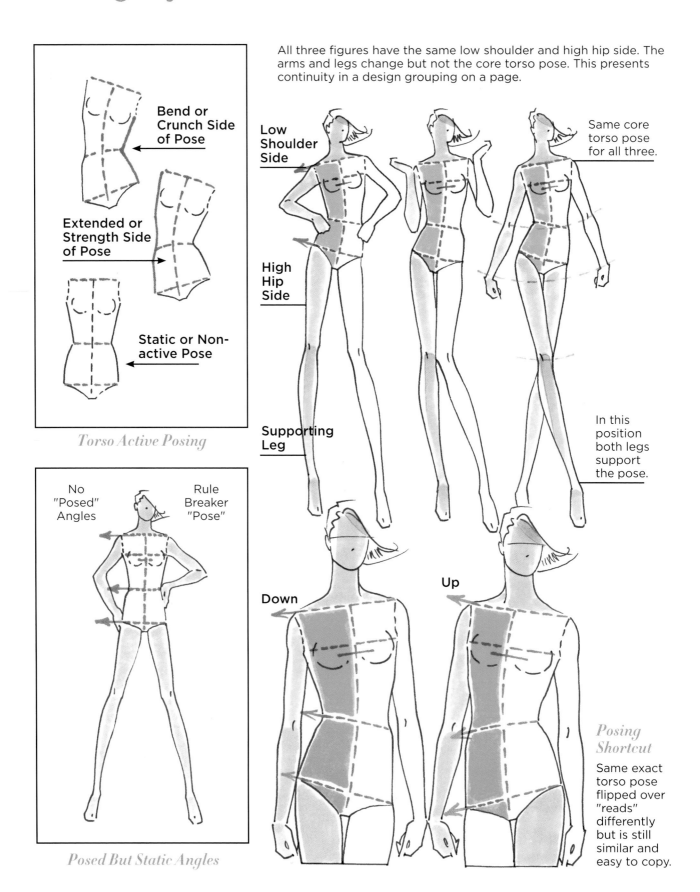

All three figures have the same low shoulder and high hip side. The arms and legs change but not the core torso pose. This presents continuity in a design grouping on a page.

Bend or Crunch Side of Pose

Extended or Strength Side of Pose

Static or Non-active Pose

Torso Active Posing

No "Posed" Angles

Rule Breaker "Pose"

Posed But Static Angles

Low Shoulder Side

High Hip Side

Supporting Leg

Same core torso pose for all three.

In this position both legs support the pose.

Down

Up

Posing Shortcut

Same exact torso pose flipped over "reads" differently but is still similar and easy to copy.

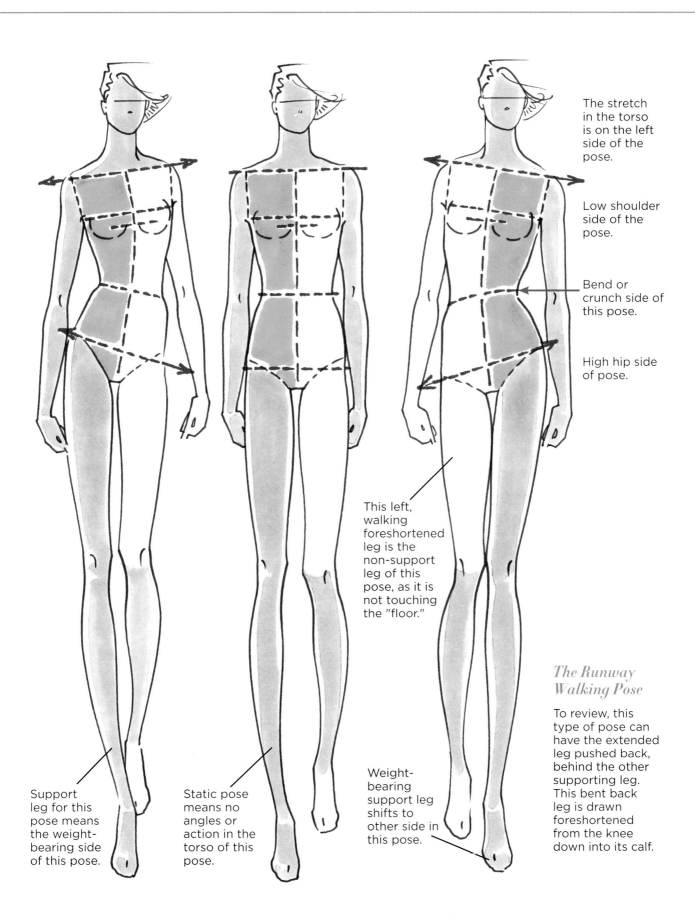

The stretch in the torso is on the left side of the pose.

Low shoulder side of the pose.

Bend or crunch side of this pose.

High hip side of pose.

This left, walking foreshortened leg is the non-support leg of this pose, as it is not touching the "floor."

The Runway Walking Pose

To review, this type of pose can have the extended leg pushed back, behind the other supporting leg. This bent back leg is drawn foreshortened from the knee down into its calf.

Support leg for this pose means the weight-bearing side of this pose.

Static pose means no angles or action in the torso of this pose.

Weight-bearing support leg shifts to other side in this pose.

The Balance Line

The balance line is a line that runs perpendicular to the floor. When held (or drawn) against the figure, this line will keep the body from tipping over. For example, if both feet are to the right or to the left of the balance line, then the figure will not be standing upright. The poses shown here place the feet on different sides of the balance line or place one of the feet directly on the balance line. There are exceptions to the rule. In fact, when drawing the fashion figure, all the rules are made to be broken. It is, after all, a figure fantasy, an idealization of the body.

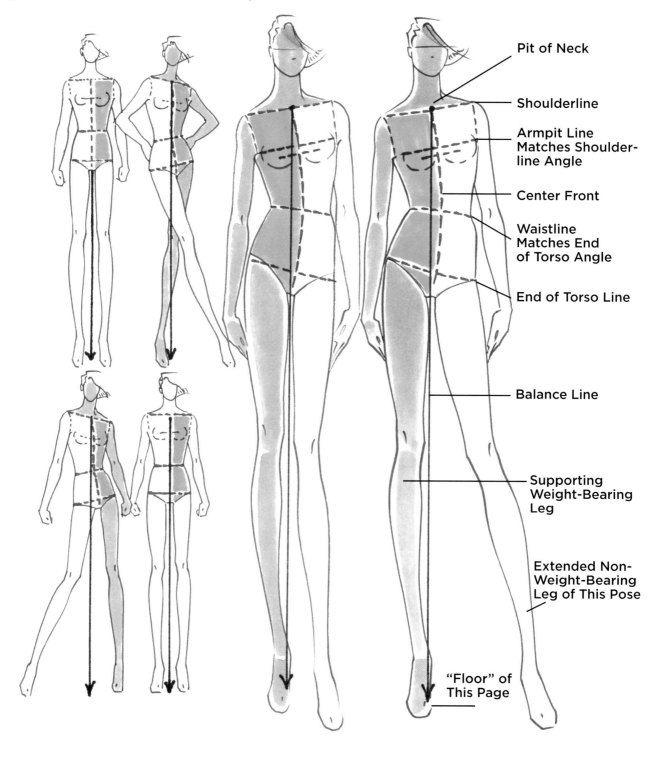

Pit of Neck

Shoulderline

Armpit Line Matches Shoulder-line Angle

Center Front

Waistline Matches End of Torso Angle

End of Torso Line

Balance Line

Supporting Weight-Bearing Leg

Extended Non-Weight-Bearing Leg of This Pose

"Floor" of This Page

- These three poses have the same torso angles. For this pose both high hip and high shoulder are on the same side.

- With all of the pose angles lining up it is easy to follow the swing of the arms and legs in this type of fashion pose.

- In a pose like this the supporting leg remains fixed—only the non-weight-bearing or relaxed leg can change or move.

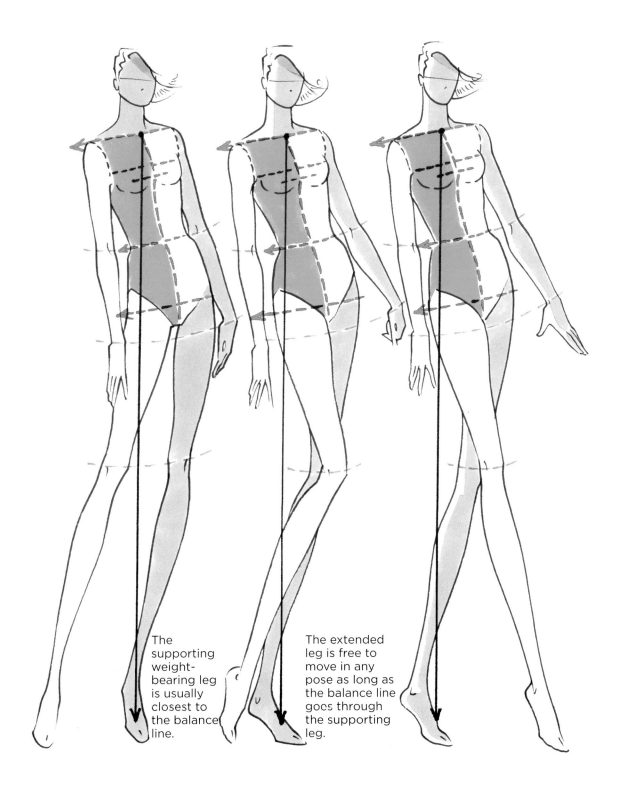

The supporting weight-bearing leg is usually closest to the balance line.

The extended leg is free to move in any pose as long as the balance line goes through the supporting leg.

Center Front

Center front is in the middle of the torso. Additionally, the spine is the center back regardless of where or how the figure is posed. Center front moves independently of the balance line. Center front also does not depend on the position of the supporting leg. The main focus of center front in your drawing is to help you move the rib cage and the pelvis in a pose.

On this page the motion is the same in each pose as the figure turns possibilities away. Center front is between the two princess seams, which also move. They follow the direction of movement that center front takes. On the facing page, four poses emphasize the center back and center front and highlight the supporting leg in a variety of possibilities. These poses draw your attention to the flow of the pose through the middle of the figure.

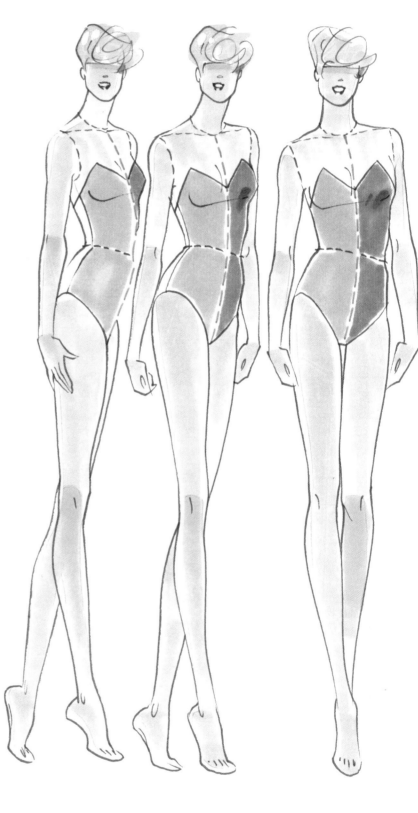

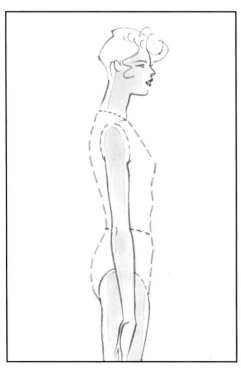

Center Front and Center Back (Her Spine) in Rigid Profile Pose

Profile
Twist and View

Three-Quarter-
Turned View

Full-Front
View

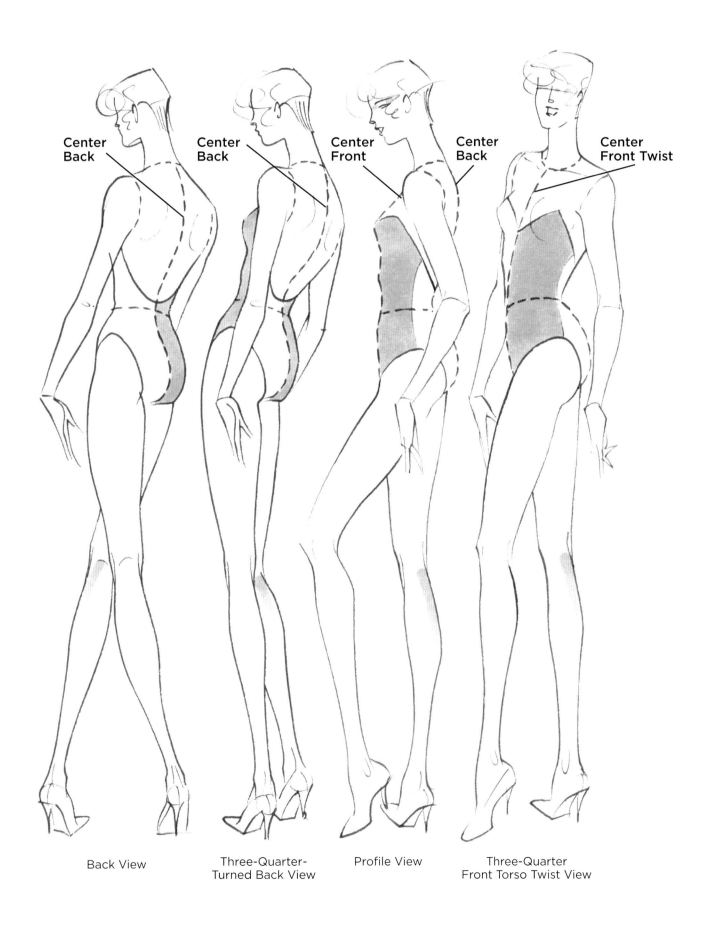

Center
Back

Center
Back

Center
Front

Center
Back

Center
Front Twist

Back View

Three-Quarter-
Turned Back View

Profile View

Three-Quarter
Front Torso Twist View

Back Views

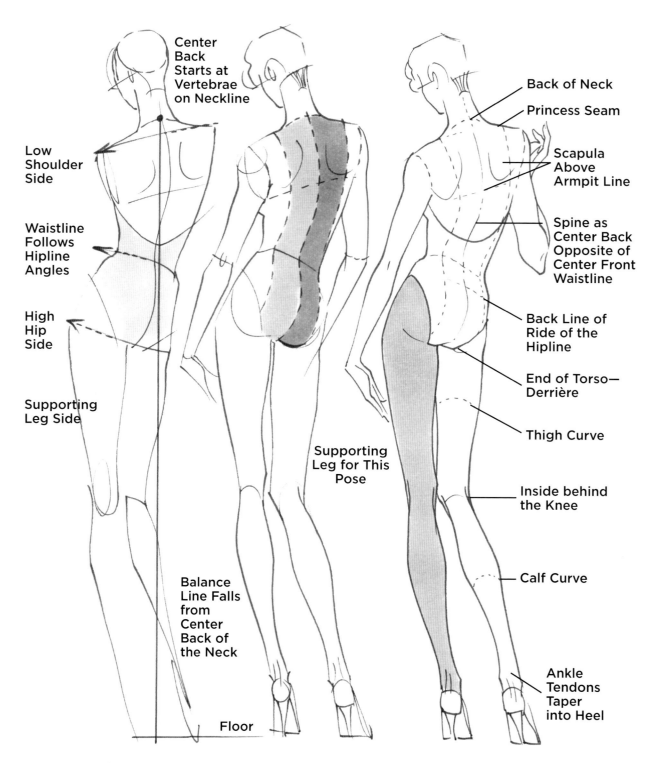

Center Back Starts at Vertebrae on Neckline

Low Shoulder Side

Waistline Follows Hipline Angles

High Hip Side

Supporting Leg Side

Balance Line Falls from Center Back of the Neck

Floor

Supporting Leg for This Pose

Back of Neck

Princess Seam

Scapula Above Armpit Line

Spine as Center Back Opposite of Center Front Waistline

Back Line of Ride of the Hipline

End of Torso— Derrière

Thigh Curve

Inside behind the Knee

Calf Curve

Ankle Tendons Taper into Heel

The back view pose gets the same action angles—high hip, low shoulder, and balance line—as the front view pose. In the back view pose the spine becomes center back, along with the parallel lines of princess seams running down the back. The subtle curves of the scapula, just above the armpits, are not always drawn; however, the curves across the derrière are drawn. There is just a hint of definition for the back of the knee and for the Achilles tendon between the ankles.

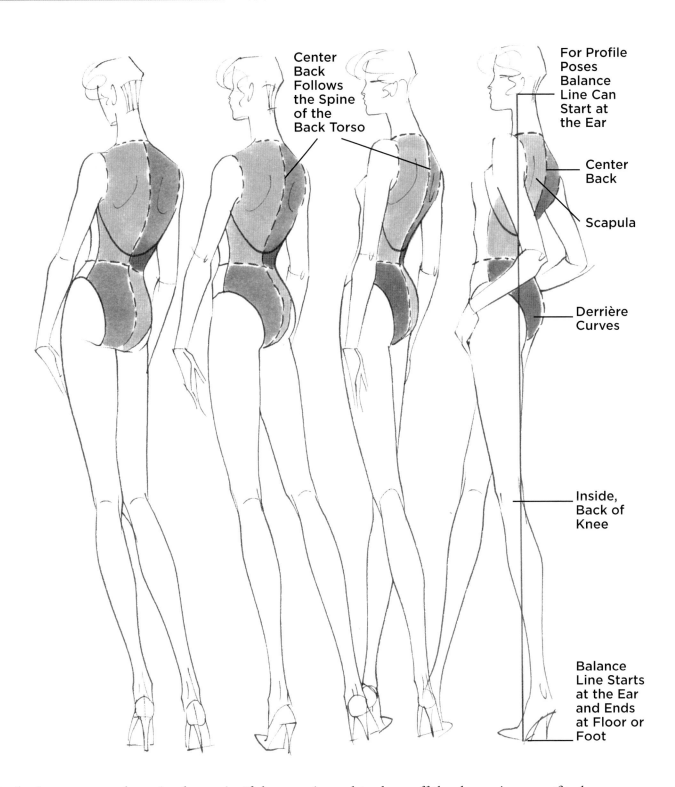

Center
Back
Follows
the Spine
of the
Back Torso

For Profile
Poses
Balance
Line Can
Start at
the Ear

Center
Back

Scapula

Derrière
Curves

Inside,
Back of
Knee

Balance
Line Starts
at the Ear
and Ends
at Floor or
Foot

Back view poses can be quite dramatic. If the pose is used to show off the drama in an outfit, dress, or gown, then keep the back view pose simple to focus on the garment's detail. These poses are fairly simple until they become almost profile, showing as much of the side of the body as the back. These poses are harder to dress due to side seams, unless that is where the main focus of the garment is displayed.

The Profile Pose

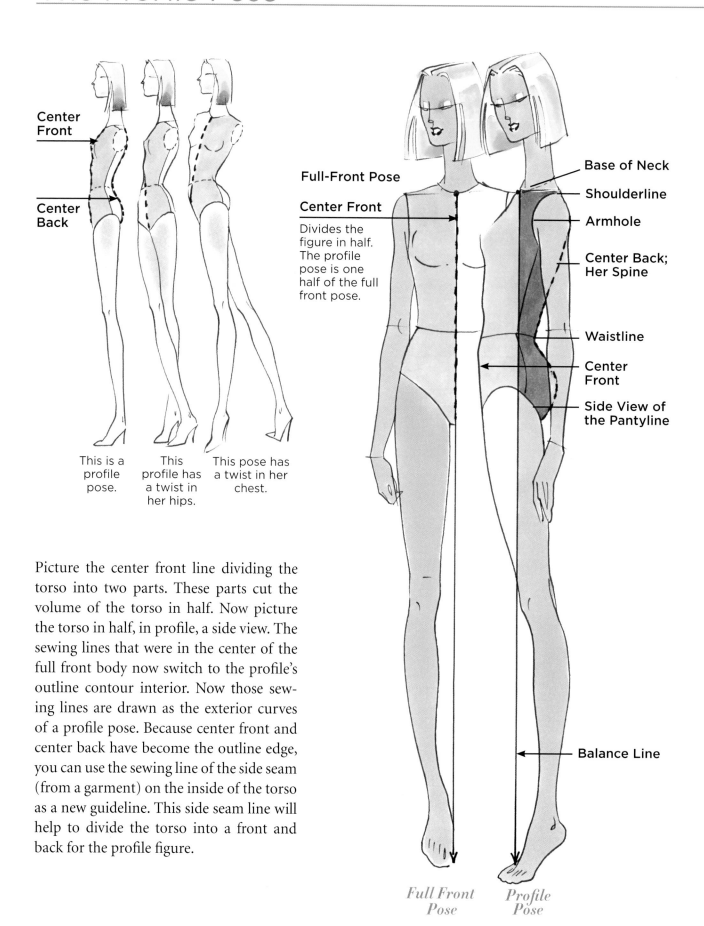

Center Front

Center Back

This is a profile pose.

This profile has a twist in her hips.

This pose has a twist in her chest.

Full-Front Pose

Center Front
Divides the figure in half. The profile pose is one half of the full front pose.

Base of Neck

Shoulderline

Armhole

Center Back; Her Spine

Waistline

Center Front

Side View of the Pantyline

Balance Line

Full Front Pose

Profile Pose

Picture the center front line dividing the torso into two parts. These parts cut the volume of the torso in half. Now picture the torso in half, in profile, a side view. The sewing lines that were in the center of the full front body now switch to the profile's outline contour interior. Now those sewing lines are drawn as the exterior curves of a profile pose. Because center front and center back have become the outline edge, you can use the sewing line of the side seam (from a garment) on the inside of the torso as a new guideline. This side seam line will help to divide the torso into a front and back for the profile figure.

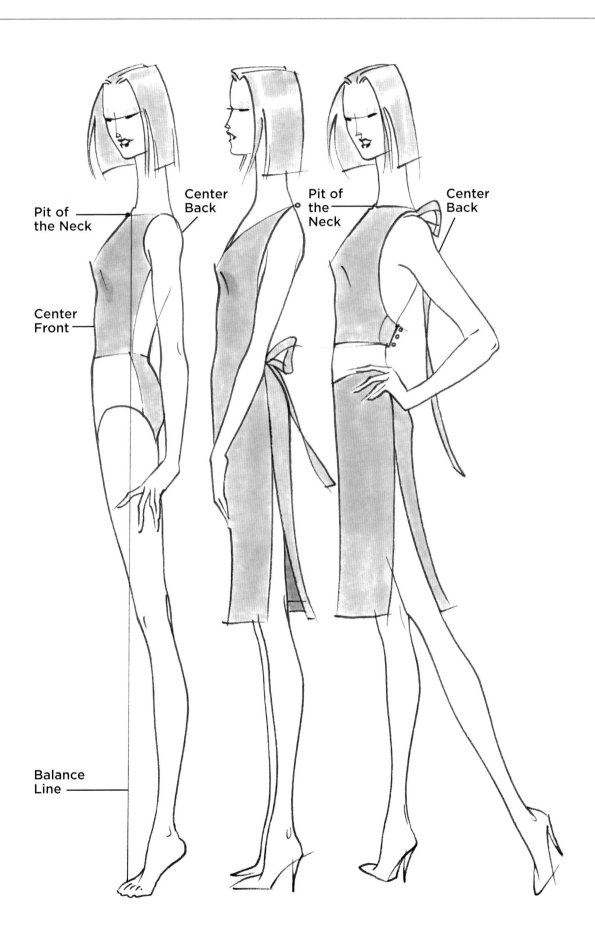

Pit of
the Neck

Center
Back

Center
Front

Pit of
the
Neck

Center
Back

Balance
Line

The Fuller Figure

A new and integral part of fashion is the average, fuller-sized woman. What is new is not the actual size but the fashion industry's attention to style in this category. Designer companies have started specialized divisions as well, recognizing the potential of this market. Many department stores even have entire floors devoted to this size category.

This growing venue in the industry needs its own separate figure illustration, as it should not be drawn in the usual elongated manner, because the fuller figure is often considered an extension of the petite market sizing. This figure, which should have as much fashion flair, attitude, and style as any other fashion illustration, is drawn more realistically as 8 heads tall or less with a slightly thicker, shorter body.

Fashion Maternity Figures

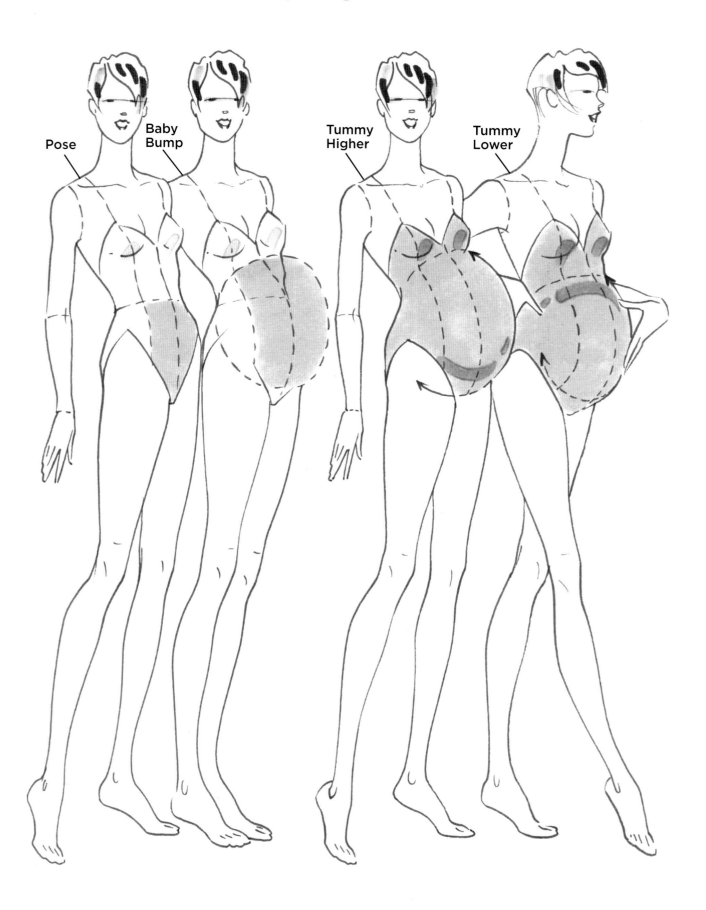

Pose

Baby Bump

Tummy Higher

Tummy Lower

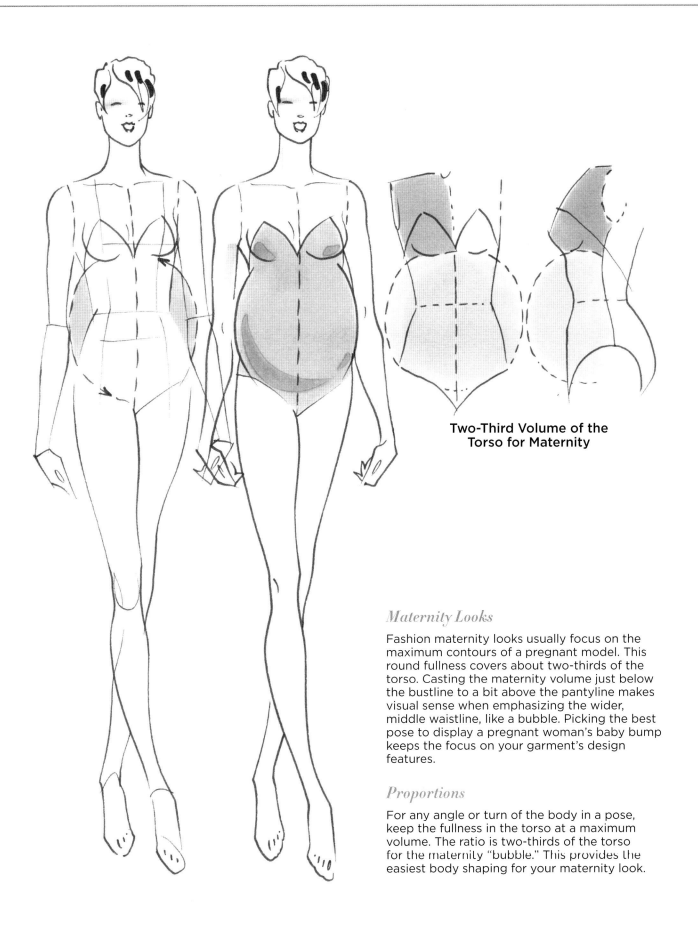

Two-Third Volume of the Torso for Maternity

Maternity Looks

Fashion maternity looks usually focus on the maximum contours of a pregnant model. This round fullness covers about two-thirds of the torso. Casting the maternity volume just below the bustline to a bit above the pantyline makes visual sense when emphasizing the wider, middle waistline, like a bubble. Picking the best pose to display a pregnant woman's baby bump keeps the focus on your garment's design features.

Proportions

For any angle or turn of the body in a pose, keep the fullness in the torso at a maximum volume. The ratio is two-thirds of the torso for the maternity "bubble." This provides the easiest body shaping for your maternity look.

L'Escarpolette

Georges Barbier

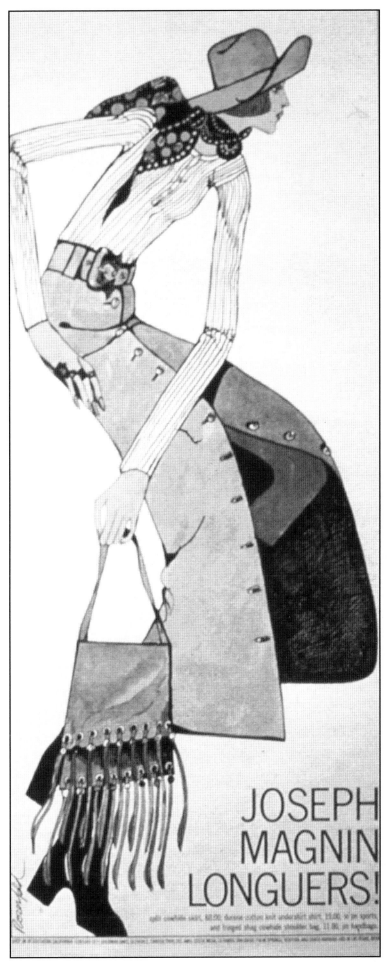

JOSEPH
MAGNIN
LONGUERS!

Richard Rosenfeld

2

Basic Figure Forms

Generally, fashion drawing is concerned with interpretation of the figure, its outside edge, and the outline contour of body curves and angles in a pose. For extra practice, let's disregard the pose for a moment to concentrate on the abbreviated form of the arms and legs. Next, we'll focus on the hands and feet. While those forms are exaggerated in length, they are simplified in shape and style. This type of drawing is not as much a formula as it is a method that gets results.

You can advance to the more complex (but adaptable) and difficult fashion figure by working through how to draw foreshortening in a pose. Foreshortening is a term used to explain the visual displacement of a bend in the body as it moves forward or back from the rest of the pose. This bend, or foreshortening, moves a portion of the body away from or closer to your eye level in the sketch.

For example, in a pose, the lower portion of the leg, the calf, moves away, backward from the thigh. Now the leg is bent and there will be foreshortening from the knee down into the ankle. In another example, the upper portion of the leg, the thigh, moves forward, bending at the knee. This type of figure work is important if you want to draw the ever-favorite walking runway pose.

In this chapter you get to study all of the little nuances in figure drawing that serve to accentuate all of the fashion posing work you did in Chapter 1.

Torso Definition

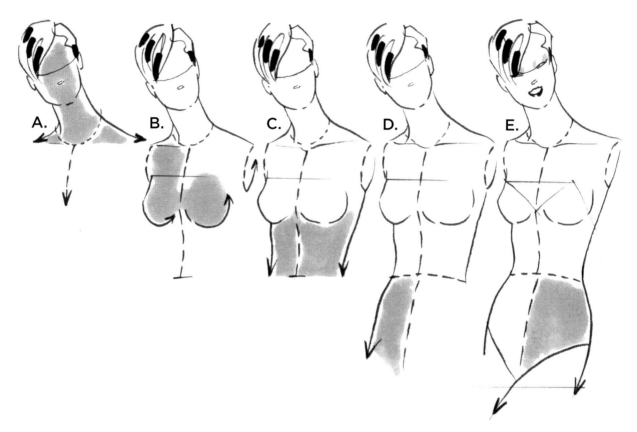

A. The neck slopes into the shoulders. On this turned pose, the neck breaks into the far shoulderline.

B. The shoulderline curls into the fashion armhole. The bustline curves start just below the armpit.

C. Complete the rest of the chest, the rib cage, from beneath the bustline curves, down to the waist.

D. The concave, horizontal line of the waist swings into the convex, vertical hipline contours.

E. With the finished hipline, start the slanted edges of fashion's panty line, at the end of the torso.

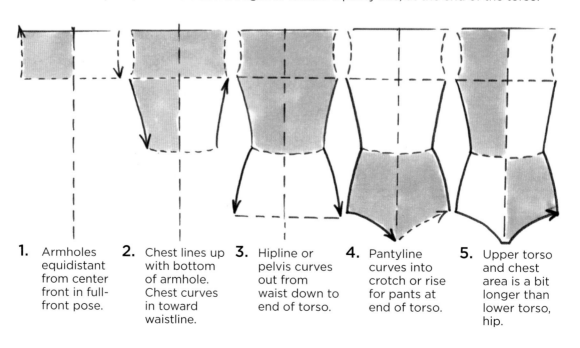

1. Armholes equidistant from center front in full-front pose.

2. Chest lines up with bottom of armhole. Chest curves in toward waistline.

3. Hipline or pelvis curves out from waist down to end of torso.

4. Pantyline curves into crotch or rise for pants at end of torso.

5. Upper torso and chest area is a bit longer than lower torso, hip.

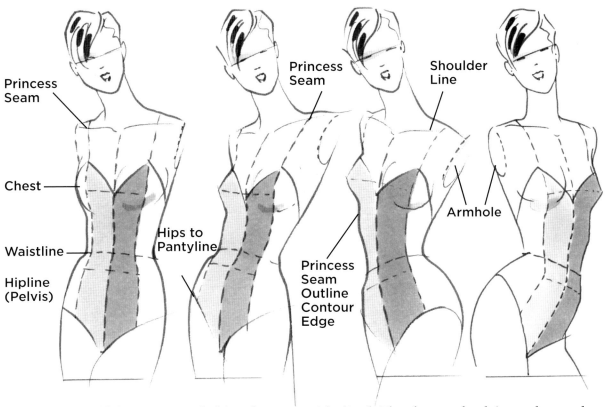

Princess Seam

Chest

Waistline

Hipline (Pelvis)

Hips to Pantyline

Princess Seam

Princess Seam Outline Contour Edge

Shoulder Line

Armhole

Remind yourself that torsos in fashion figures are idealized. The chest and pelvis are drawn elongated, subject to the trends in the definition of figure beauty that can change in a season. Stylistically, the torso gets elongated to boost the visual content or impact of a fashion statement in "looks." Whatever your style objectives, you will still need a strong sketching foundation in believable contours and proportions within your fashion figure's torso. Part of this fashion focus is the use of the sewing lines within the torso as guidelines for posing dynamics.

The Interior Sewing Lines Work with the Torso's Posing Angles

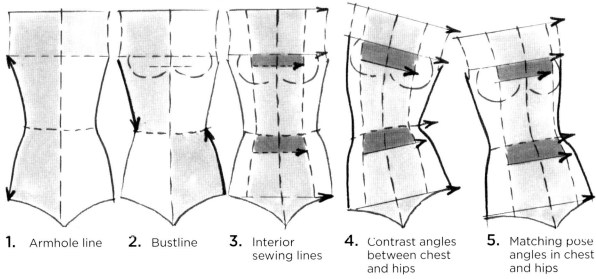

1. Armhole line

2. Bustline

3. Interior sewing lines

4. Contrast angles between chest and hips

5. Matching pose angles in chest and hips

Drawing Legs: Form and Shape

In regard to bones and muscles, the fashion leg is an abbreviation of a real human form.

1. The leg's shape tapers all the way down to its ankle. The knee is in the middle of the leg.
2. The two widest curves in the leg come from the thigh and the calf, followed by the knee.
3. The thigh (the part of the leg above the knee) is drawn wider than the calf.
4. The calf (the part of the leg below the knee) is drawn narrower than the thigh.
5. The knee has its own subtle curviture, drawn as a bend in the leg's contouring.
6. The leg can be divided by its proportions, drawing the thigh's length equal to the calf's length.
7. The curves in the leg are drawn in even longer stretches for fashion design figures.

Heads Tall Grid

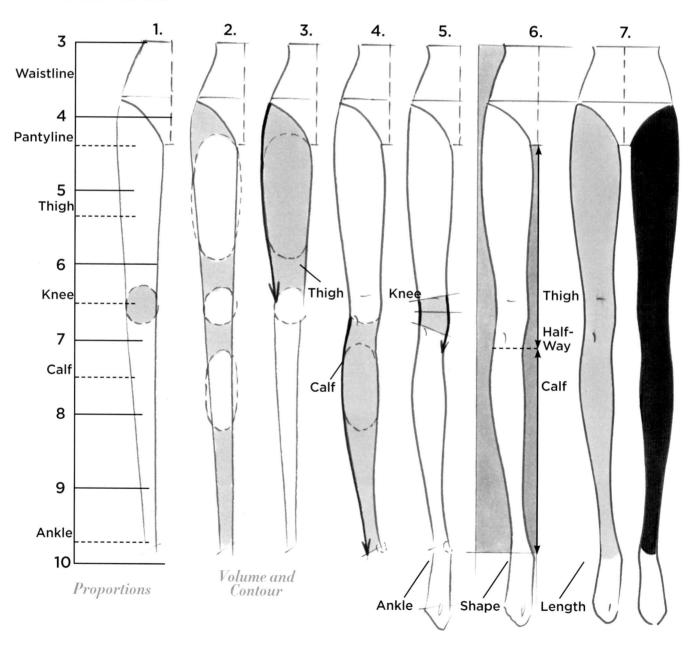

Proportions

Volume and Contour

Methods to Elongate Legs

A. The leg can have its own center front, running from the pantyline down to the toes.

B. The leg's fashion curves are roughly equal in place with anatomy's muscle mass.

C. Those leg curves each have their own set of contoured angles imitating real form.

D. The leg's center front can curve with the leg's contours as it gets into posing.

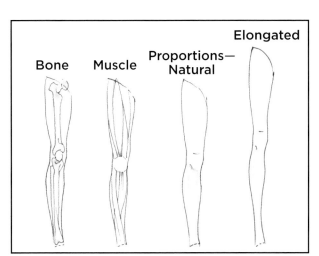

Bone   Muscle   Proportions—Natural   Elongated

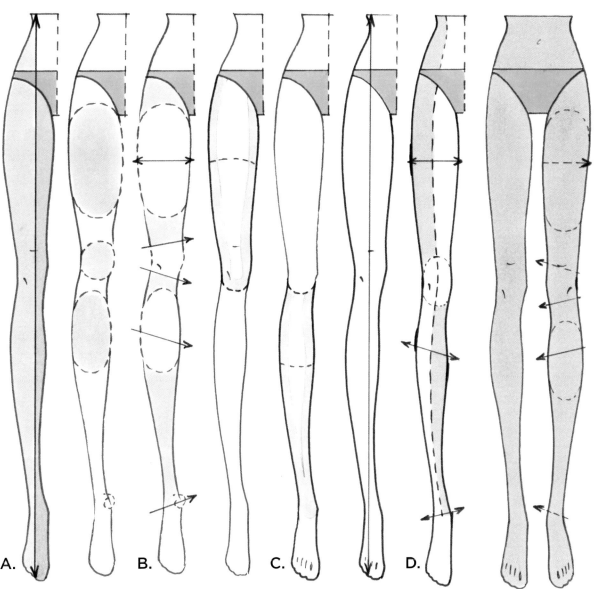

A.   B.   C.   D.

Posing Legs

The knee is drawn in the middle or upper middle of the leg. Following the knee position on the leg, as it turns with different poses, makes it easier to map out the leg's length and contours.

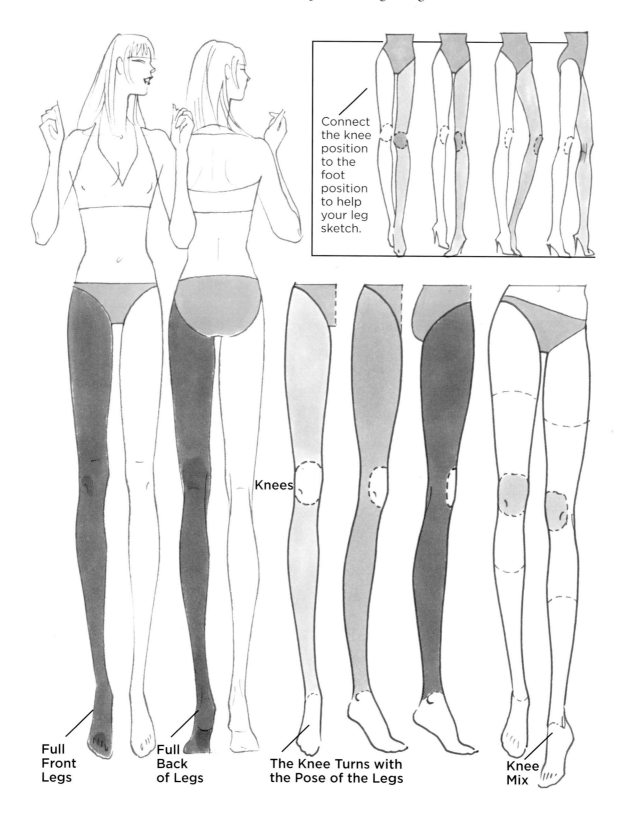

Connect the knee position to the foot position to help your leg sketch.

Knees

Full Front Legs

Full Back of Legs

The Knee Turns with the Pose of the Legs

Knee Mix

The weight-bearing leg that anchors a pose is called the supporting leg. The other, non-weight-bearing leg that is free to move in a pose is called the extended leg.

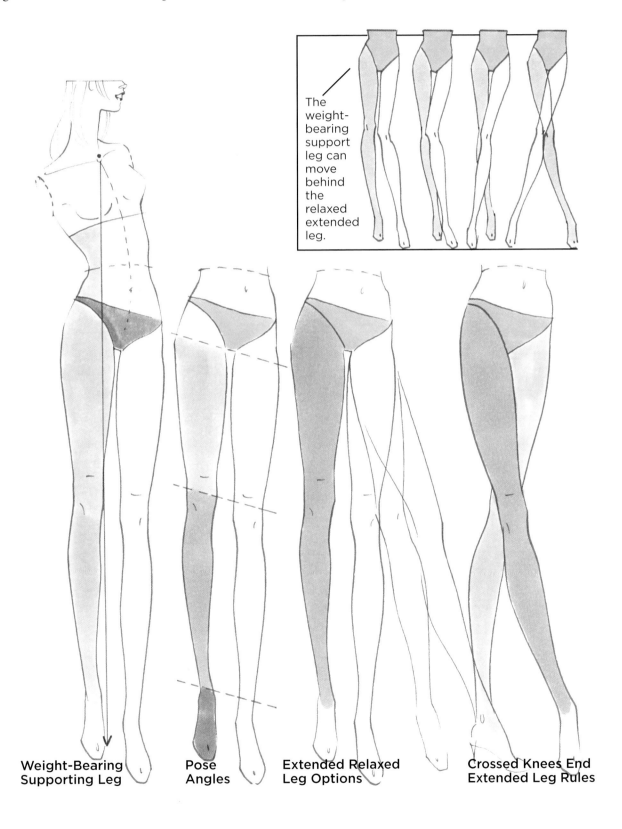

The weight-bearing support leg can move behind the relaxed extended leg.

Weight-Bearing Supporting Leg

Pose Angles

Extended Relaxed Leg Options

Crossed Knees End Extended Leg Rules

Foreshortening: Legs

Foreshortening is an optical illusion of sorts. It is a visual change in form that appears in a drawing when there is a particular angle or bend in a pose. You might notice that one part of the arm or leg looks shorter than its counterpart. This usually means that part of the body is closer or further away from the viewer's eye level. To draw a foreshortened area in a pose, it is best to practice on a live model or a photographic reference. In the beginning it is too difficult to draw this kind of pose from memory.

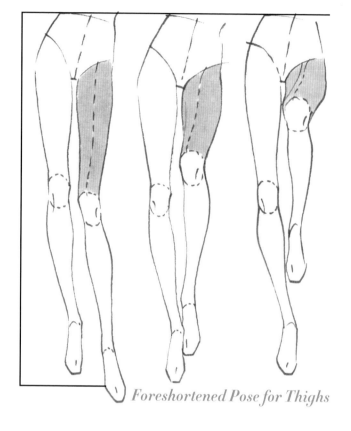

Foreshortened Pose for Thighs

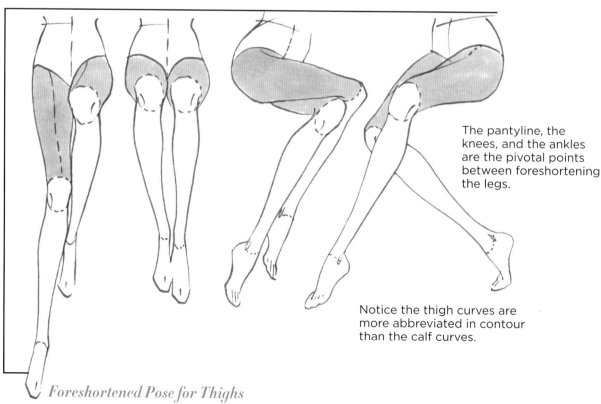

The pantyline, the knees, and the ankles are the pivotal points between foreshortening the legs.

Notice the thigh curves are more abbreviated in contour than the calf curves.

Foreshortened Pose for Thighs

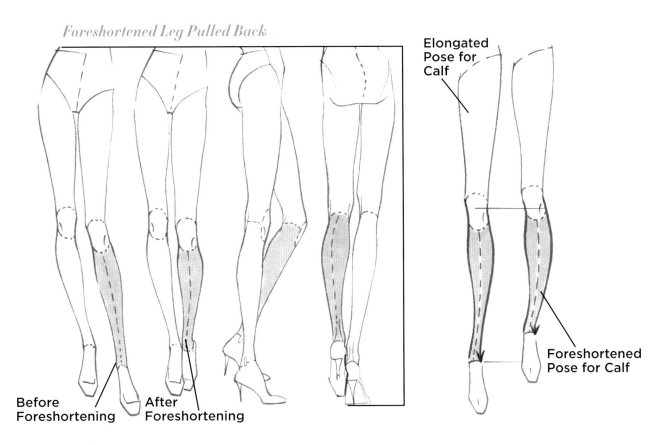

Foreshortened Leg Pulled Back

Elongated
Pose for
Calf

Foreshortened
Pose for Calf

Before
Foreshortening

After
Foreshortening

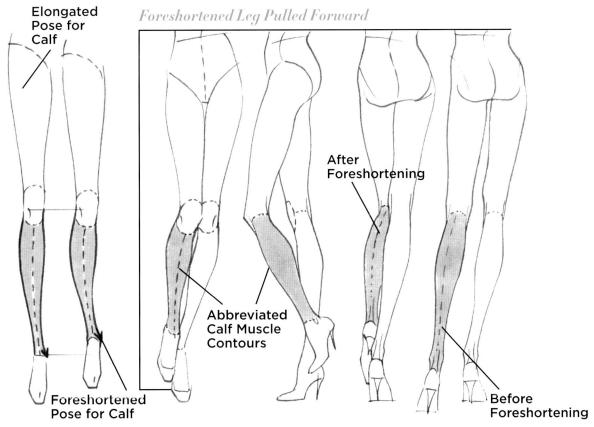

Elongated
Pose for
Calf

Foreshortened Leg Pulled Forward

After
Foreshortening

Abbreviated
Calf Muscle
Contours

Before
Foreshortening

Foreshortened
Pose for Calf

Drawing Feet

The profile view of the foot puts the posing foot sideways from the tip of the toes to the curve of the heel. The toes are barely visible. The heel is in full view and so is the ankle. The fashion elongation is most pronounced between the arch and the instep of the foot.

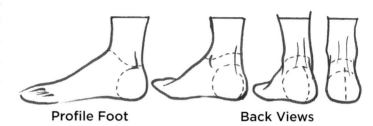

Profile Foot   **Back Views**

Features

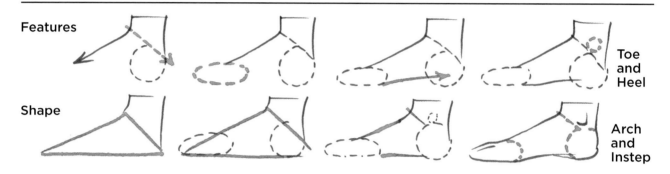

Toe and Heel

Shape

Arch and Instep

Sketching formulas can provide the framework for definition, helping you to study the shapes and forms of fashion feet.

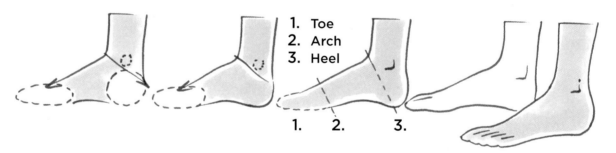

1. Toe
2. Arch
3. Heel

1.   2.   3.

Proportions are part of the simplification of drawing feet. Toes can equal the heel, which can equal the arch of a foot.

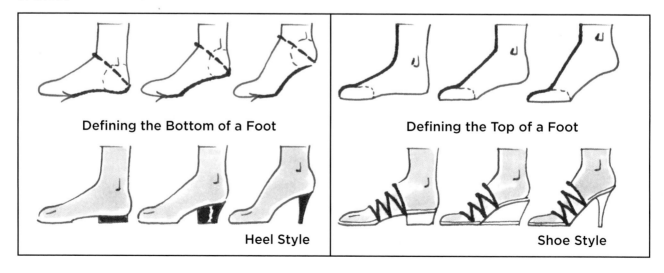

Defining the Bottom of a Foot   **Defining the Top of a Foot**

Heel Style   **Shoe Style**

Three-Quarter Turned Foot

The three-quarter turned foot is the middle pose between the full-front and profile views. In this view there are more toes than a profile but less than in full front. Conversely, there is less heel in this view than in profile but more than in full front. Study the floor angles to help with heel height.

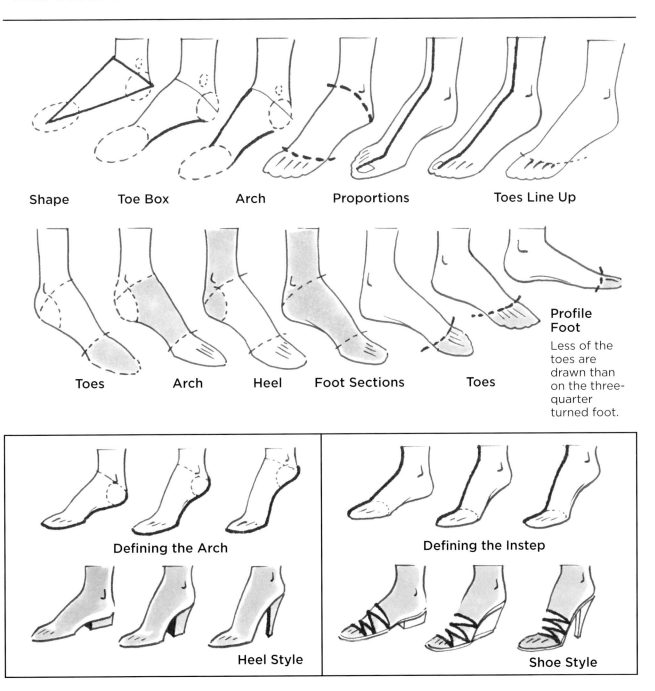

Shape Toe Box Arch Proportions Toes Line Up

Toes Arch Heel Foot Sections Toes

Profile Foot

Less of the toes are drawn than on the three-quarter turned foot.

Defining the Arch

Defining the Instep

Heel Style

Shoe Style

Drawing Feet (continued)

The full-front foot pose puts the toes in full view. The ankle is less pronounced. It's drawn at a slight angle at the top of the foot where it meets the leg. The heel is nonexistent in this pose. A realistic front view foot rests the heel on the floor, looking foreshortened. The stylized foot is abbreviated in shape and detail. The fashion foot is elongated, standing on the toes.

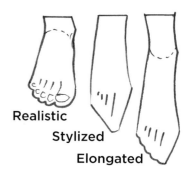

Realistic

Stylized

Elongated

Full-Front Feet

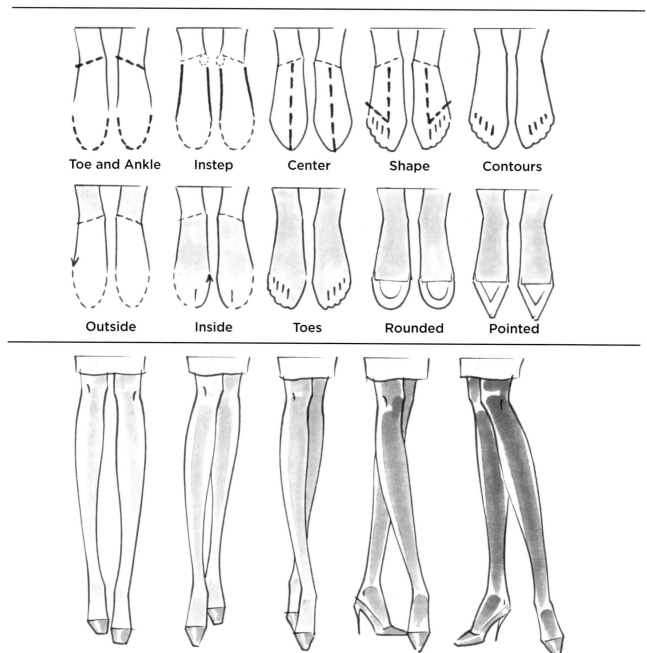

Toe and Ankle	Instep	Center	Shape	Contours

Outside	Inside	Toes	Rounded	Pointed

Focus on Dressing the Foot

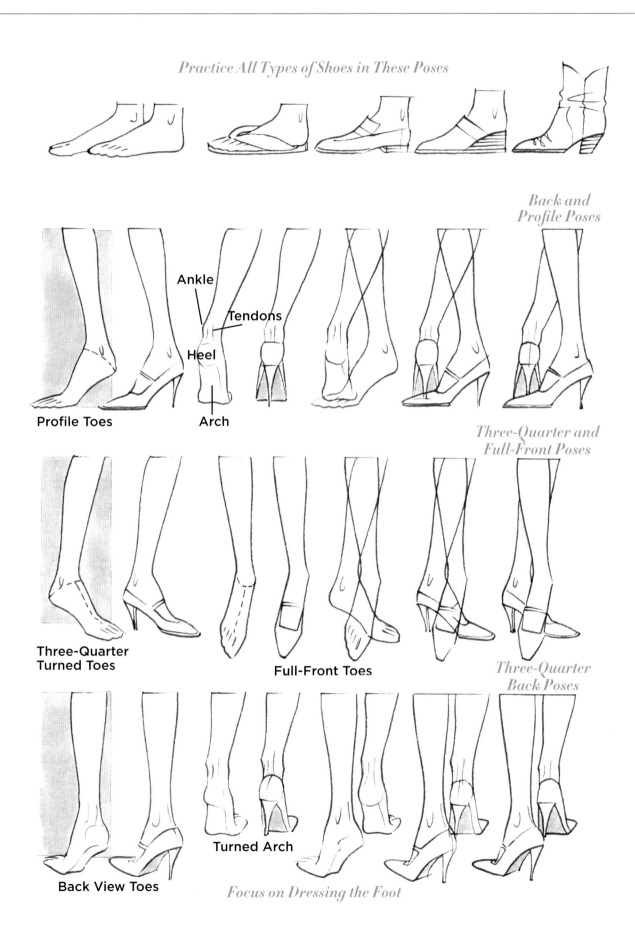

Practice All Types of Shoes in These Poses

*Back and
Profile Poses*

Ankle

Tendons

Heel

Arch

Profile Toes

*Three-Quarter and
Full-Front Poses*

**Three-Quarter
Turned Toes**

Full-Front Toes

*Three-Quarter
Back Poses*

Turned Arch

Back View Toes

Focus on Dressing the Foot

Drawing Arms: Form and Shape

As with the fashion body and leg, the fashion arm is yet another idealized form. It, too, is elongated and simplified beyond bone and muscle.

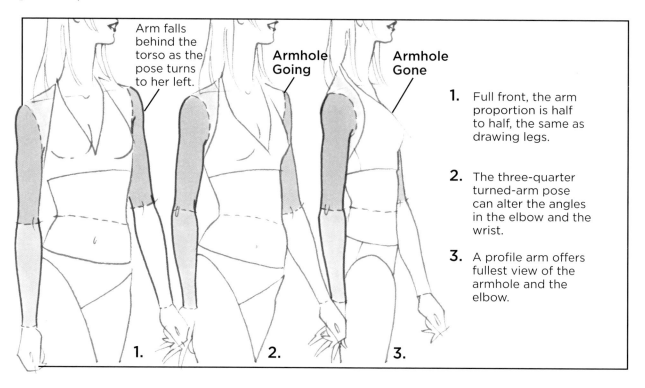

Arm falls behind the torso as the pose turns to her left.

Armhole Going

Armhole Gone

1. Full front, the arm proportion is half to half, the same as drawing legs.

2. The three-quarter turned-arm pose can alter the angles in the elbow and the wrist.

3. A profile arm offers fullest view of the armhole and the elbow.

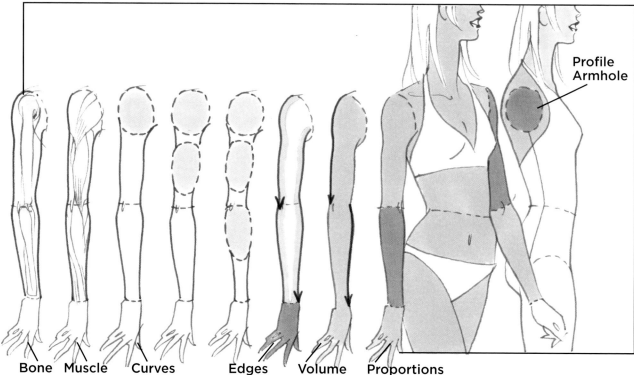

Profile Armhole

Bone   Muscle   Curves   Edges   Volume   Proportions

4. Practice the very subtle curves of the arm by adding in simplified contouring in place of natural muscle curves. Use the elbow as a guide for the middle of the fashion arm.

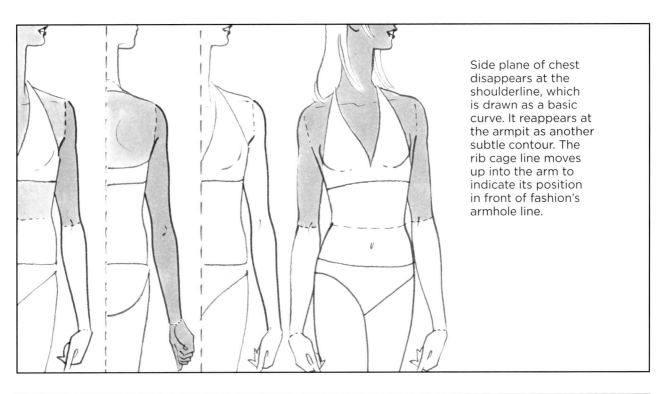

Side plane of chest disappears at the shoulderline, which is drawn as a basic curve. It reappears at the armpit as another subtle contour. The rib cage line moves up into the arm to indicate its position in front of fashion's armhole line.

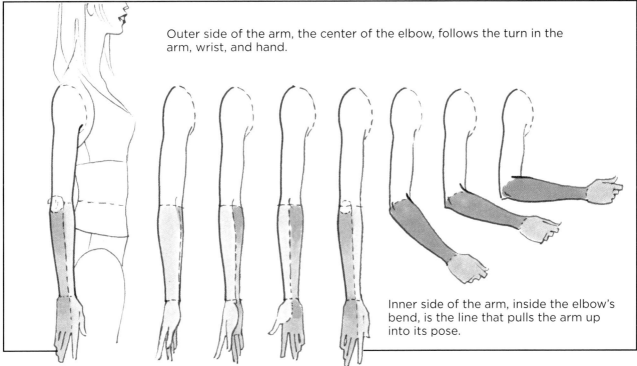

Outer side of the arm, the center of the elbow, follows the turn in the arm, wrist, and hand.

Inner side of the arm, inside the elbow's bend, is the line that pulls the arm up into its pose.

Foreshortening: Arms

As stated earlier, foreshortening is the illusion that one part of the body is pushed closer or further away than its other parts. This illusion alters the form and, while it is an important part of understanding and drawing the fashion figure, it can be a nuisance in fashion design detailing because of the forced angles in form.

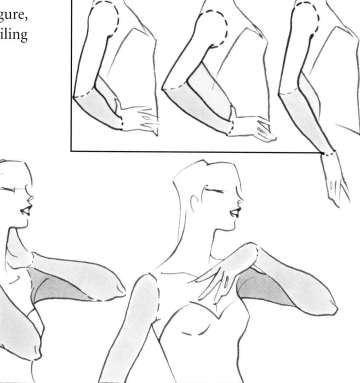

Note that the shoulders lift up with the arms in a pose.

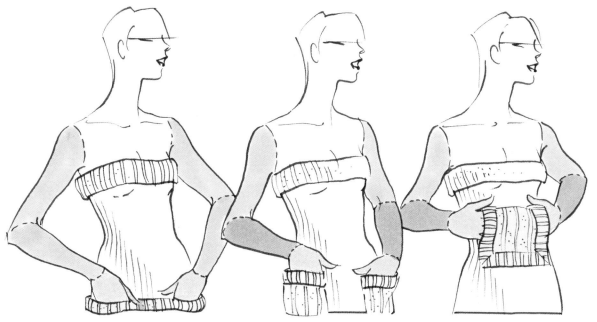

Arms can be foreshortened to accent garment detail in a pose.

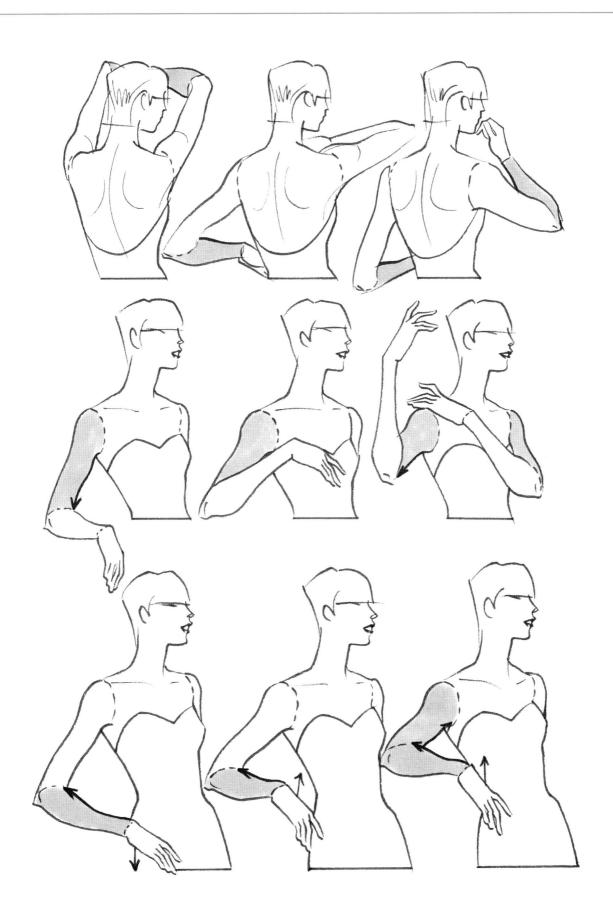

Drawing Hands

Hands in fashion art can be modified to make them easier to draw. Keep them long and tapered. Practice both the left and the right hand in all poses. Use the knuckle area and center front of the hand to help you draw foreshortened poses.

From Fist to Full Hand

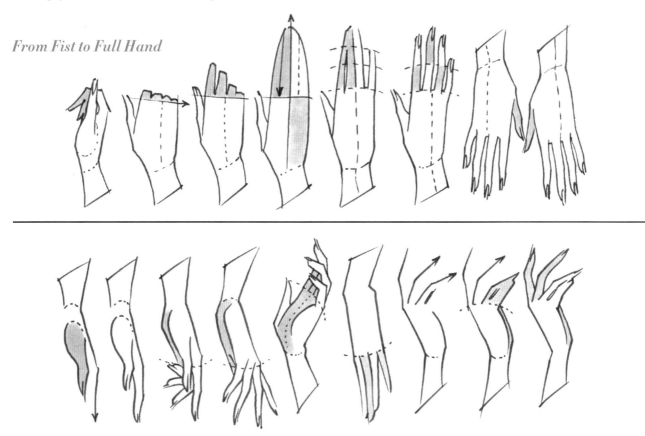

Long Tapered Fingers with Only a Hint of Knuckle Curve

Stylized—Less Knuckle Curve

Realistic—More Knuckle Curve

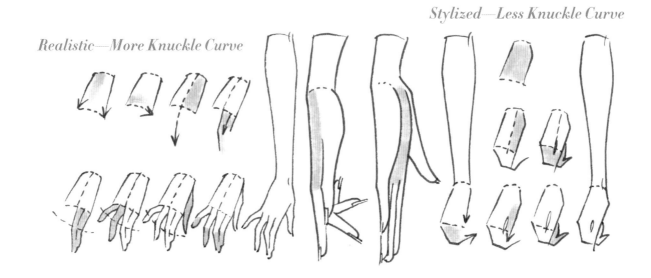

The following examples illustrate a few of the positions for hands that you may find challenging as you work on the fashion figure.

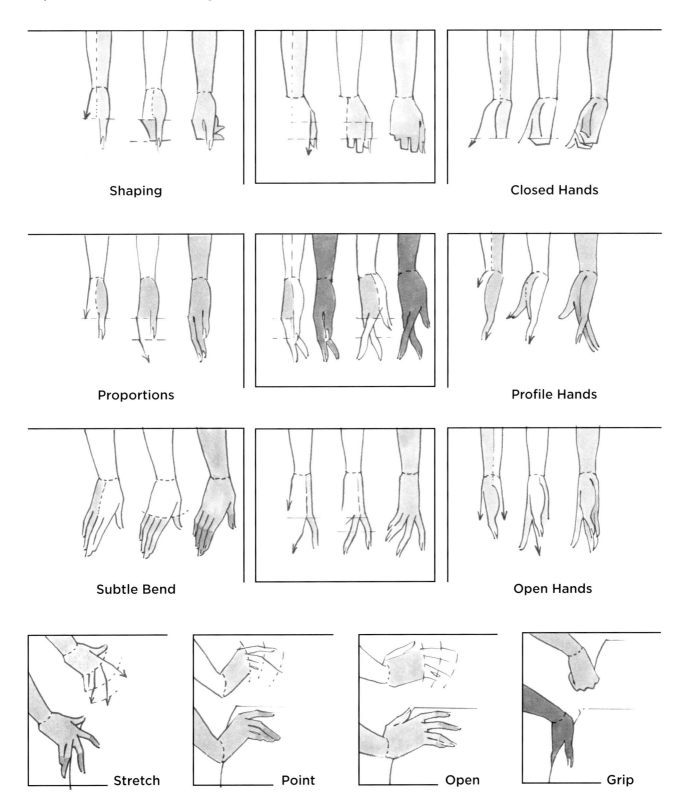

Shaping

Closed Hands

Proportions

Profile Hands

Subtle Bend

Open Hands

Stretch

Point

Open

Grip

Figure Tips

There are subtle nuances to drawing specific areas of the fashion figure. These nuances can make or break the design detail when you dress the figure. They are subtle because these areas either complement what you see or interfere with what you were hoping to see. The areas most affected by subtle nuances in drawing are the guidelines (sewing lines) or the areas where one part of the body meets another part of the body. The examples on these pages offer tips on those areas.

A. In a front view, the armpit moves onto the chest. In the back view, the upper torso moves over the back of the arm.

B. In the front view, the elbow curves into the upper arm. In the back view, the upper arm curves into or over the elbow.

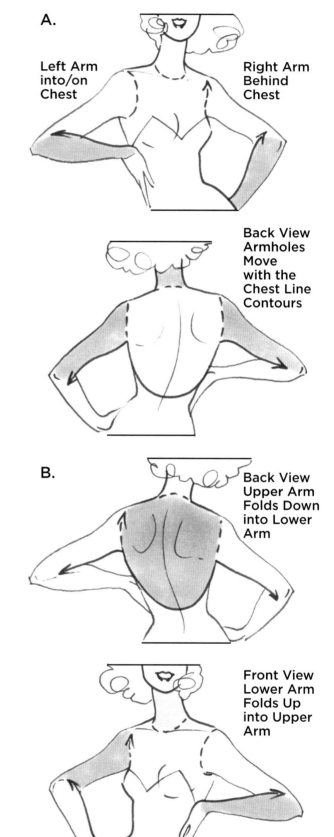

A.

Left Arm into/on Chest

Right Arm Behind Chest

Back View Armholes Move with the Chest Line Contours

B.

Back View Upper Arm Folds Down into Lower Arm

Front View Lower Arm Folds Up into Upper Arm

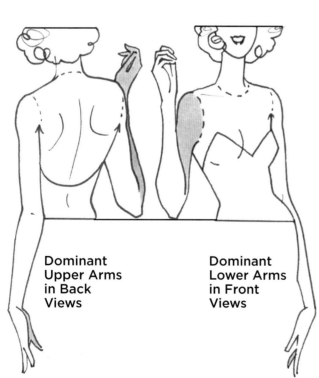

Dominant Upper Arms in Back Views

Dominant Lower Arms in Front Views

C. The easiest way to remember how to position the neck is to draw the neck to move in the same direction as center front. Recognize the direction that center front is facing, and no matter what position the head is in, draw the neck in the same direction as center front.

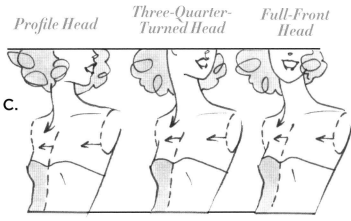

C.

Neck Curve Follows Center Front's Direction

D. In most poses, center front—from the waistline to the crotch—will curve in the same direction as the hip that turns away. The hip that is turned away is the one you see the least of in the pose.

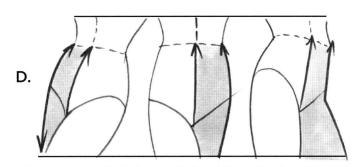

D.

The Turned Side Is the Side of the Hip You See Least

E. When the figure is turned, more of the facing armhole shows and less of the armhole is shown on the side that is turned. On the turned side, it helps to draw the side plane of the chest to separate it from the armhole.

E.

Armhole and Bustline Curves Divide the Chest

F. The armhole curve starts at the top of the shoulder and ends at the bottom of the armpit. This curve takes on the shape of an ellipse. The armholes are drawn on the right and left sides of the body in matching curves. They also match the curve direction of center front when the figure turns and are parallel to each other.

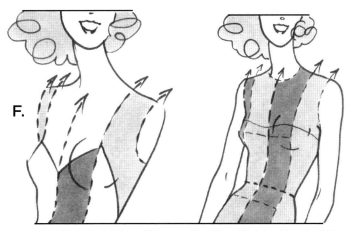

F.

Let the Sewing Line Curves Be Parallel to Each Other

Figure Tips (continued)

Bare knees, calves, and ankles

Draw a slight indent for the inside curve of the knees. Stretch out the calf curves so they are super subtle, down into another indent, for the ankle.

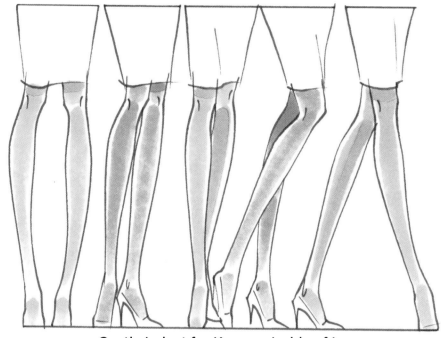

**Gentle Indent for Knee on Inside of Leg;
Subtle Curve for Calf on Outside of Leg**

Dressed knees, calves, and ankles

As you design and detail fabric shapes over the legs, draw the garment as if it were rolling over, draping around the leg's contours.

**Fabric Bends by Front or Back of Knee;
Fabric Rolls Over Thigh, Calf, or Ankle as It Drapes**

Shoulders

A line from the neck gently breaks into the shoulder cap's curve, on the turned side of a pose.

Nuances of Clavicle/Shoulderline

Armpits

There is a tiny hook in your line as you get the underarm to meet with the plane of the chest.

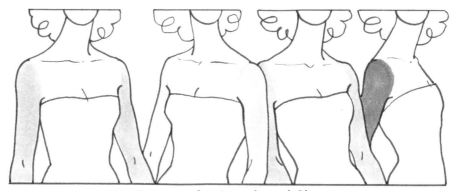

Demi Curves for Armpit and Cleavage

Bustline

For the form of the bustline's curves try rendering some soft shading beneath those curves.

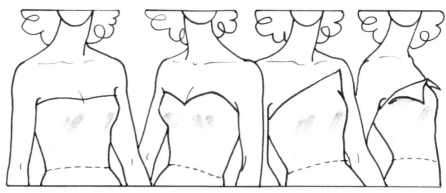

Hint of Bustline Shaping with Shading

Hand

Easier to draw posing the hands with most of the fingers close together, rolled up, or closed in a fist,

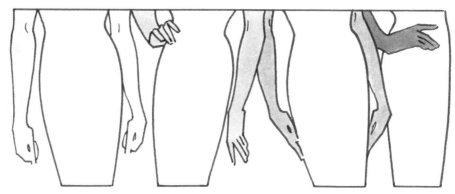

Simplifying Hands in Any Pose

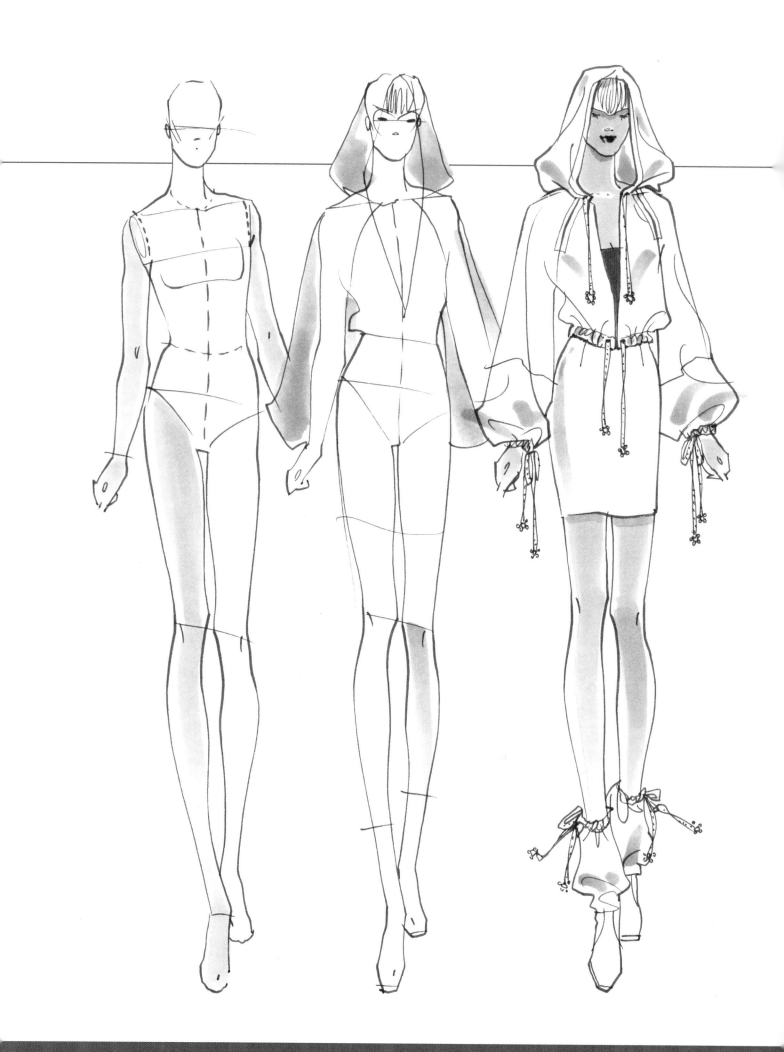

3

Model Drawing

Model drawing is the next step in polishing your fashion figure drawing skills. In the two previous chapters, you learned about the body's proportions and elongation. This chapter introduces photographic model references for fashion designer poses. What you learned in the previous chapters about the torso, arms, legs, hands, and feet will be combined with this chapter's lessons on sketching from real models. This can be easier than drawing a pose from your imagination, inventing the figure in your mind's eye, breaking the figure down into practice parts. Here, you'll be drawing the figure—the whole pose—from a visual reference.

Model drawing is not about tracing from a photograph: It is about creating your own sketch based on its image. In this chapter, you will use photographs of models to decode and reinvent the posing models, and turn reality back into fashion fantasy in your drawing. Model drawing increases your figure drawing skills and encourages you to develop your own drawing style, making your visual expression of the figure more personal and unique.

Model Drawing, a separate book devoted to a complete course of study in model drawing, is published by Fairchild Books. It is based on this chapter's premise of learning to draw by studying photographic poses. *Model Drawing* includes a CD-ROM and combines photographic reference and illustrated lessons on women's, men's, and children's poses.

Model Drawing Poses

These are full-front poses, also described as high hip/low shoulder poses due to the model's stance. Each of the four poses presents another form of figure analysis to help you apply these drawing techniques to your sketching process.

Balance Line

Angles

Torso

Gesture Components

Balance Line

This is the same type of balance line/figure posing support introduced in Chapter 1. A balance line drops from the pit of the neck, down through the pose, stopping at the feet, on the floor of your page. It keeps the pose standing up, not tipping over (off balance).

Balance Line

Angles in a Pose

In a gesture sketch, three lines are drawn across the torso, thus creating the shoulderline, the waistline, and the hipline (also called the end of the torso or the pantyline). These three lines are the action lines and set a pose into motion as you draw them.

The action lines perform the dynamics in the pose and help to establish the rules of balance for the body. For example, it's the low shoulder and high hip connect with the supporting leg that keeps the figure standing on your page.

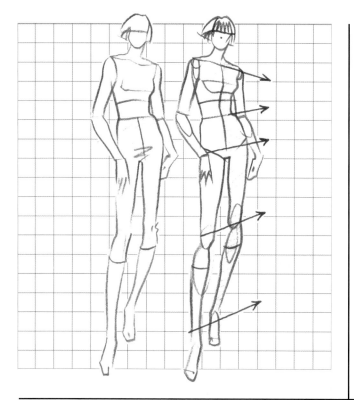

Angles in a Pose

This is a sample gesture sketch of the model drawing pose at center right on this page. Notice how the shoulderline, waistline, and hipline angles have been exaggerated.

The model in this photo reference (above right) has dropped her left shoulder at a specific angle to her left hip. These are the angles along with the waistline that you want to emphasize in your sketch.

Notice how the rib cage and pelvis create the low shoulder and high hip angles in a pose.

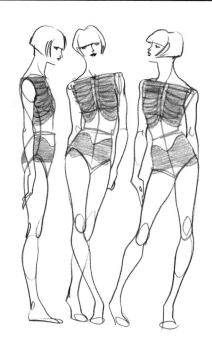

The angles in this pose can be used as guidelines, structure to pin your figure sketching on, or visual points of reference to work with as you build the figure.

The Fashion Elongated Gesture Sketch

A Full-Front Pose

The Fashion Proportions Finished Sketch

Torso in a Pose

A good way to start drawing your figure is by sketching the main segment of the body, the torso, which has two units, the chest and the hips. Anatomically, these two units would be called the rib cage and the pelvis. The connective middle of your gesture sketch of the torso would be the center front, running from the shoulderline down to the crotchline. This center front mimics the line of the center back, or the spine.

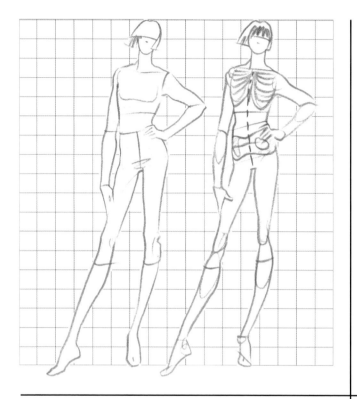

Torso
Definition

Here is one example of how to use the grid/graph paper portion of this chapter. Use the photo (above right) as a visual reference while you draw that pose in a gesture sketch. This is your model drawing photo reference for this exercise. It is the pose you are going to draw for yourself, using the grid/graph paper as a guide.

The two figures at the right help you to focus in on the torso. The torso's rib cage and pelvis have been accented to illustrate their roles in posing the body.

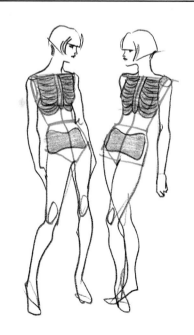

This pose has a low shoulder and high hip on the model's right side. This side of the torso has more bend at the waist, and the left side has more stretch. If you include the invisible center front line on your sketch, it will help you to define the volume as well as the bend and stretch of this model's torso.

Gesture Components

Pose analysis, sketching technique broken into separate steps

Head to define height of your figure.

1. Balance line to fix pose in upright stance.

2. Angles in torso set up proportions.

3. Torso definition from left to right side of body.

4. Completed exterior torso curves.

5. Adding the torso's interior curves.

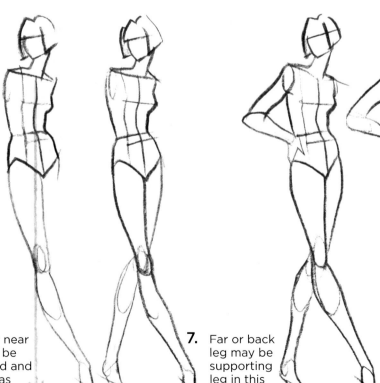

6. Front or near leg may be extended and relaxed as shown here.

7. Far or back leg may be supporting leg in this pose.

8. The arms create their own angles in this pose.

In a gesture sketch, you can start by drawing a head. The size of the head that you draw will establish the size of the body onto which it will fit. By drawing the head first you have automatically begun to break the body into its natural segments. Segments are parts of the gesture body where there is a natural bend in the form. For example, the head at the chinline bends into the neck. The neck slopes into the shoulders and the chest blends into the waist. Use the grid portion of this page to sketch your version of this pose.

Gesture
Pose

Interpreting Anatomy

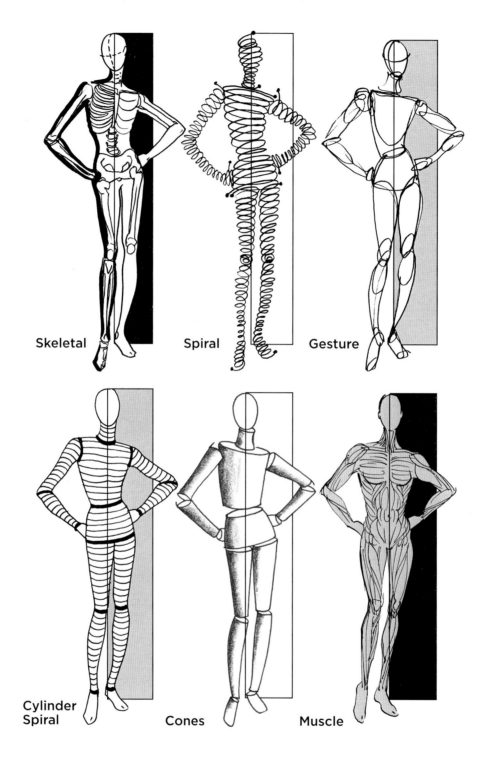

Skeletal   Spiral   Gesture

Cylinder
Spiral   Cones   Muscle

Fashion anatomy combines sketching methods, figure study, and contour development. Sketching methods help you divide the body into drawing segments. Figure study gets you to explore the bones and muscles for the interior structure of the human form. Contour development gives you some crucial insights on the outside edges of figure illustration. This page gives you six drawing techniques to interpret in any pose. Practice each to find the one that works for you.

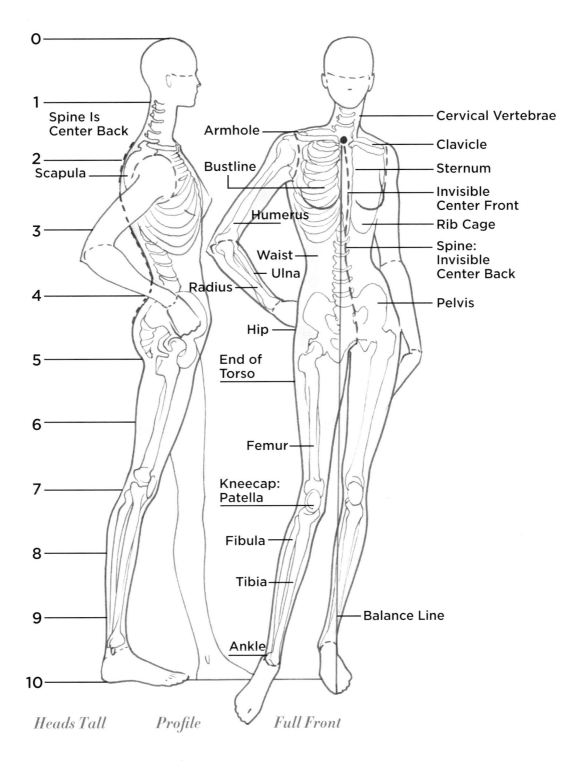

0

1 — Spine Is Center Back

2 — Scapula

3

4

5

6

7

8

9

10

Heads Tall　　*Profile*　　*Full Front*

Armhole

Bustline

Humerus

Waist — Ulna

Radius

Hip

End of Torso

Femur

Kneecap: Patella

Fibula

Tibia

Ankle

Cervical Vertebrae

Clavicle

Sternum

Invisible Center Front

Rib Cage

Spine: Invisible Center Back

Pelvis

Balance Line

Combining a simplified skeleton with a basic form is an effective and useful drawing exercise. By using both of these elements—structure and contour—you will be able to suggest a pose from the inside to the outside, which will give your figure both volume and weight. To give your figure height, you must create "heads tall" (see pages 8 and 9 for the figure road map to help you accomplish this). For normal anatomy, the figure can be 7 to 8 heads tall. Fashion elongation often extends the figure to 9 or 10 heads tall.

Fashion Runway and Showroom Poses

The figures in these photos represent a runway, walking pose. Based on the figure work you have studied in this chapter, use these poses as your model drawing reference. Sketch the fashion poses on the grid.

Caffe
Swimwear

Nicolita

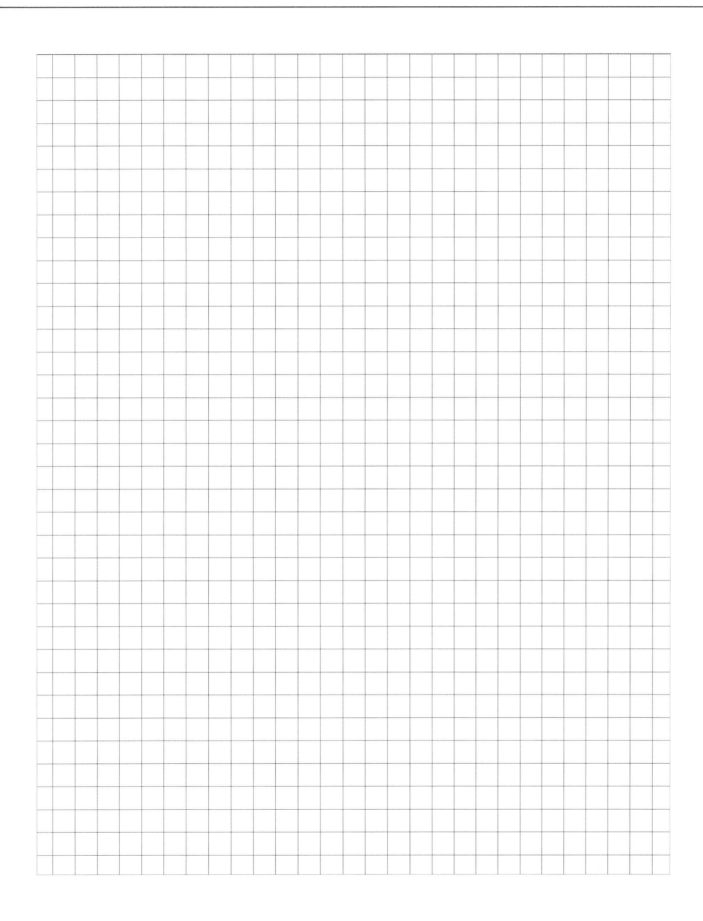

Fashion Runway and Showroom Poses (continued)

These figures offer the unique opportunity to study a pose front to back. They also present a chance to practice the back view runway, walking pose. Sketch one or both fashion poses on the grid.

Ed Hardy

Fashion Runway and Showroom Poses (continued)

The figures in these photos represent runway walking poses. Based on the figure work you have studied in this chapter, use these poses as your model drawing reference. Sketch these fashion poses on the grid.

Jeremy Scott

Tavik Swimwear

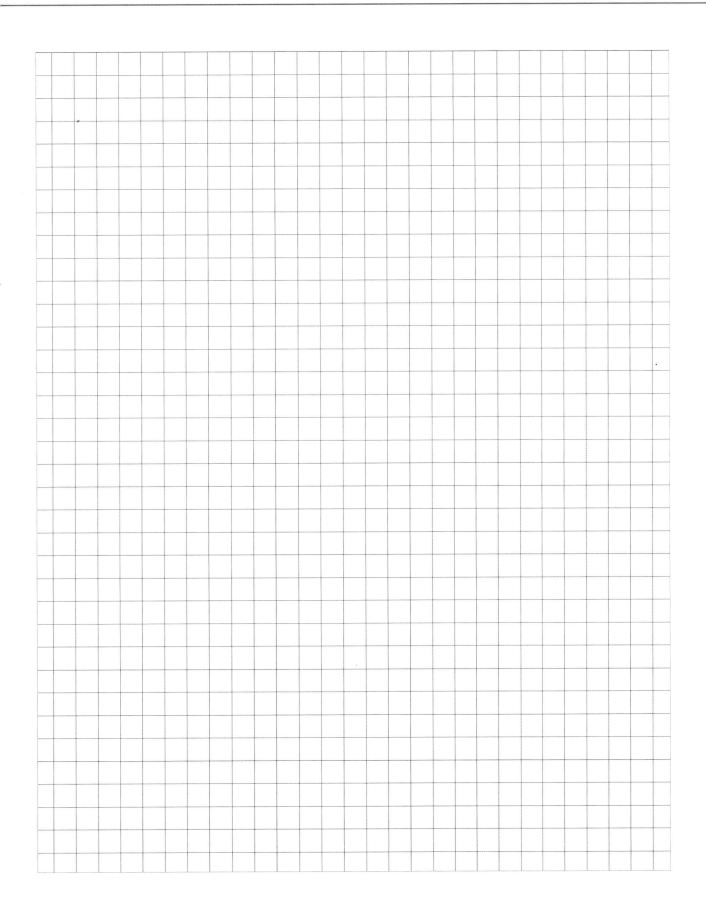

Fashion Runway and Showroom Poses (continued)

The figure in this photo represents a showroom pose. Based on the figure work you have studied in this chapter, use this pose as your model drawing reference. Sketch this fashion pose on the grid.

Ralph
Lauren

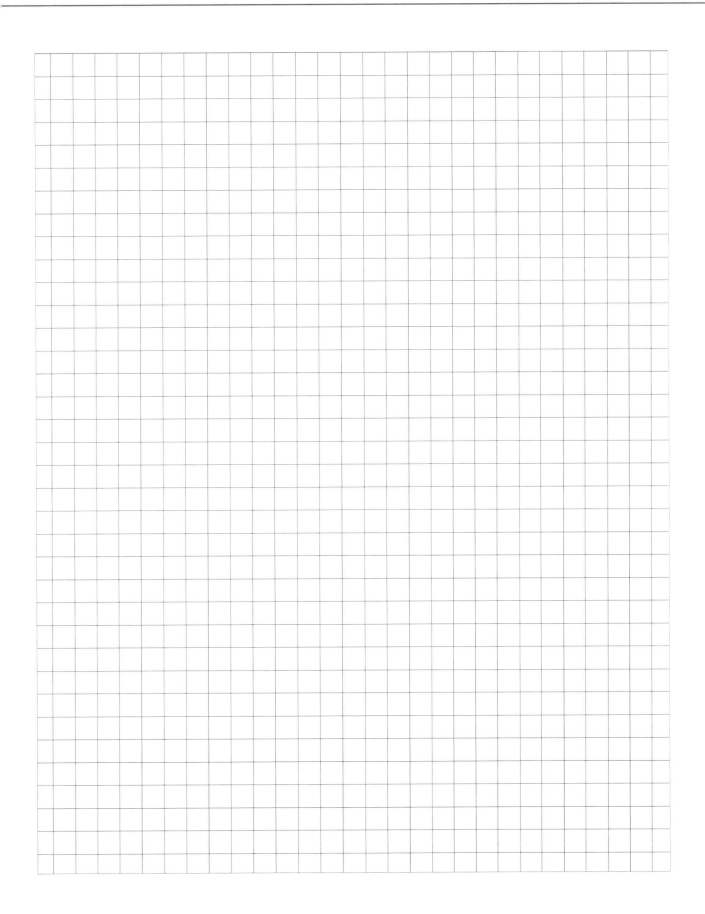

4

Fashion Heads

Faces are very personal and unique. Each artist's interpretation of a face has something new to offer in its stylistic nuances. The sheer variety is cause for visual appreciation. With regard for all of the exquisite possibilities in features, race, and age, you, as an artist, must come to terms with and decide what type of face you want to draw for your fashion muse. How to approach that complex, three-dimensional face in the simplified line and shape of fashion art is the focus of this chapter.

In this chapter, we will explore the basic structure of the head in the same way that we explored the body in Chapter 1. The head will be modified and all of the nuances in the face—based on fashion's point of view—will be illustrated as a type of signature style and designer client. Abbreviating the features in a drawing of the head will follow the same basic principles of full-front, three-quarter-turned, and profile positions that were explained earlier. After you have learned what to draw in shape, features, and hairstyle, you will be ready to create your own type of face. This is called a "signature head," because it will be as individual and as natural for you to draw as it is for you to write your name.

There are many methods for creating the fashion face. This chapter explores the gridding system, setting up some simple sketching formulas. The goal here is to expose you to new ways of observing facial features. There are many ways in which to treat the eyes, nose, and mouth, and any method will work as long as you place the features evenly, blocking them on the face. After that, you can move onto the planes and angles in posing the head. All of what you practice in this chapter should help you create your own version of a signature fashion head.

Drawing Heads and Fashion Faces

As you learn to draw faces, you explore the range of applications for a fashion head. Four such applications are: (1) a portrait, characteristic of fine arts realism—sketches of a real person's actual features; (2) a fictitious personality—defining a repeat character, as in a graphic novel; (3) the commercial advertising face—a face that a consumer could identify with or imagine being like; and (4) the fashion designer's signature face—an abbreviation, the most minimal head that serves to complement a fashion category such as casual, career, or dressy looks.

At least two different artistic and fashion styles can be used: (1) fine arts versus fashion illustration for faces, and (2) historical references versus stylistic retro looks. The heads in this chapter are open to all interpretations and drawing applications, cultural or personal. Idealized beauty is never constant, changing according to trends and fashion whimsy. True beauty includes all races and all nationalities.

Historic Heads

Fashion Faces

Drawing Heads

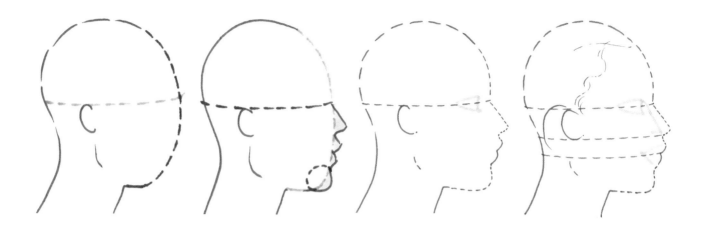

Profile Head

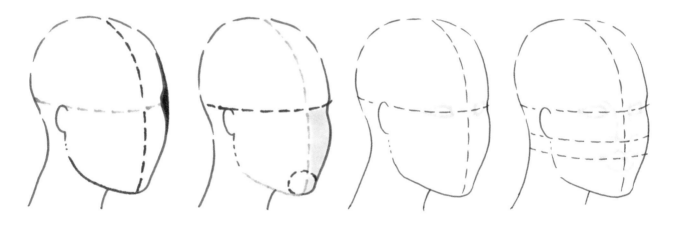

Three-Quarter-Turned Head

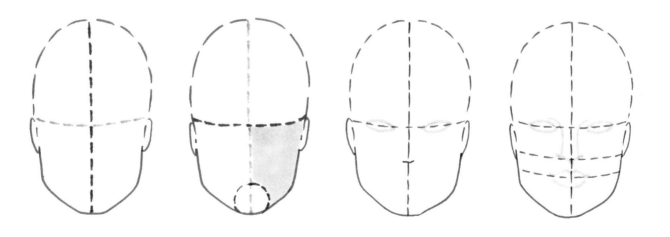

Full-Front Head

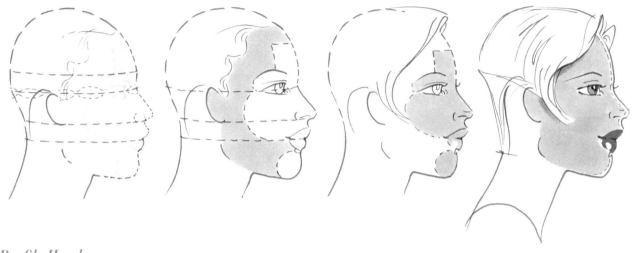

Profile Head

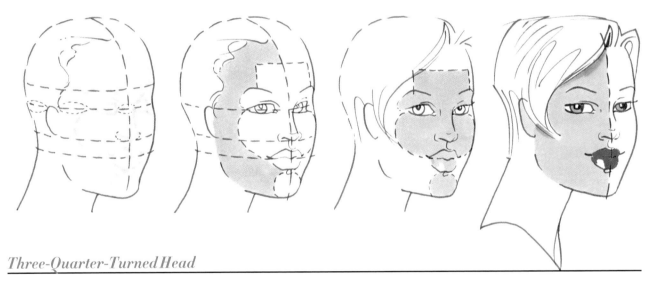

Three-Quarter-Turned Head

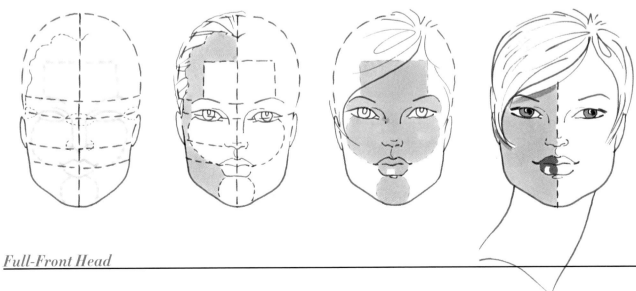

Full-Front Head

The Diamond Technique

The diamond technique for dividing the face is an alternative to the lessons on facial grids and mapping the features on upcoming pages. This teaching tool helps you to focus your attention on the central portion of the head. The diamond technique places the features in a cluster, leaving the corners to be filled and presenting the eyes, nose, and mouth from a different perspective.

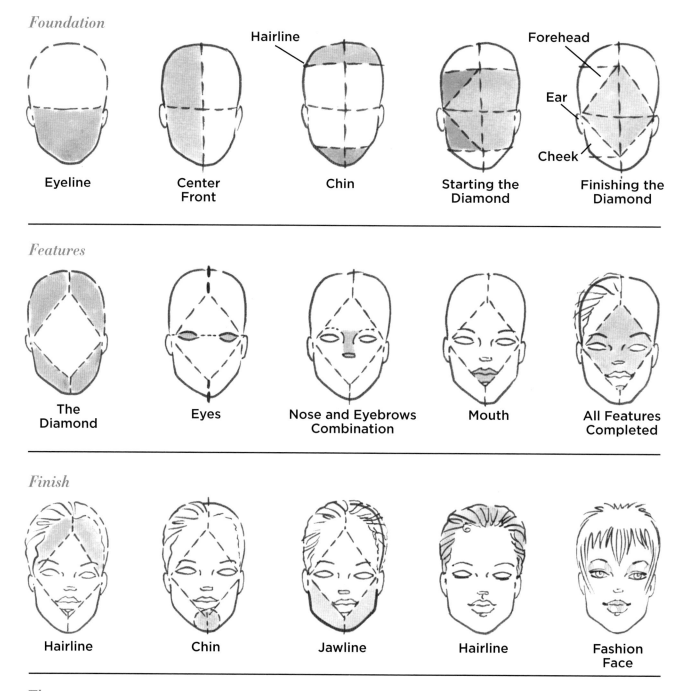

Foundation

Eyeline

Center Front

Chin

Hairline

Starting the Diamond

Forehead

Ear

Cheek

Finishing the Diamond

Features

The Diamond

Eyes

Nose and Eyebrows Combination

Mouth

All Features Completed

Finish

Hairline

Chin

Jawline

Hairline

Fashion Face

Tips:

Use the outside of the diamond to help you control the shape of the head. For example, the space between the point by the ear and the point by the chin can help you control the shape of the jawline on both sides of the head.

Drawing a Full-Front Head

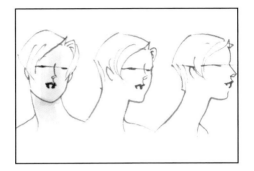

The fashion head and face are subject to interpretation. In addition to changing with fashion trends, there are certain parameters, for example, the placement of features. No matter how realistic or stylistic the drawing, the location of eyes, nose, and mouth does not change. In this chapter, these formulas for building the head and face (like the figure) are presented and explored for structure, not style. Structure always precedes style. Practice the basics and then develop your own fashion faces.

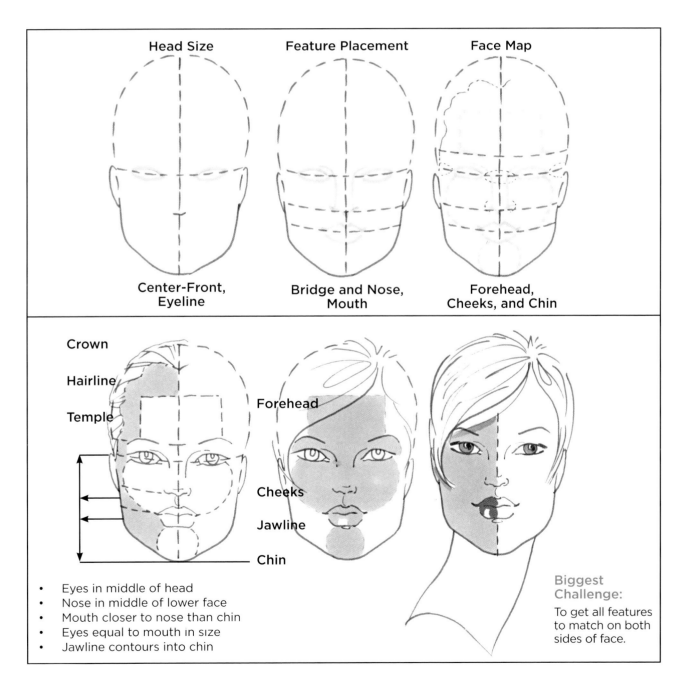

Head Size
Center-Front, Eyeline

Feature Placement
Bridge and Nose, Mouth

Face Map
Forehead, Cheeks, and Chin

Crown

Hairline

Temple

Forehead

Cheeks

Jawline

Chin

- Eyes in middle of head
- Nose in middle of lower face
- Mouth closer to nose than chin
- Eyes equal to mouth in size
- Jawline contours into chin

Biggest Challenge:

To get all features to match on both sides of face.

Drawing a Three-Quarter-Turned Head

Divide the full-front view of the head into four quarters. Turn the head slightly to the left or slightly to the right, subtracting about one quarter from the total. This is how the three-quarter-turned head position was named. This turn of the head shifts the contours of the face and the features enough to redefine their shapes, presenting new sketching challenges.

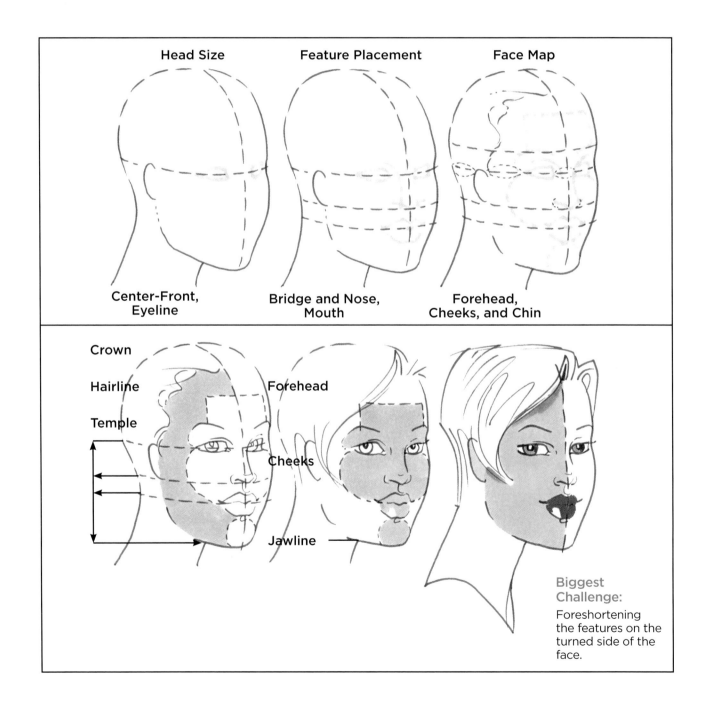

Head Size

Feature Placement

Face Map

Center-Front, Eyeline

Bridge and Nose, Mouth

Forehead, Cheeks, and Chin

Crown

Hairline

Temple

Forehead

Cheeks

Jawline

Biggest Challenge: Foreshortening the features on the turned side of the face.

Drawing a Profile Head

In the profile view, the head is turned completely sideways. Suddenly all of the subtle contours of the face become pronounced. The soft edges of the features are sharply defined. The eyes, nose, and mouth are now one half of their usual forms. This reduction also makes a profile easy to draw because there is less to sketch.

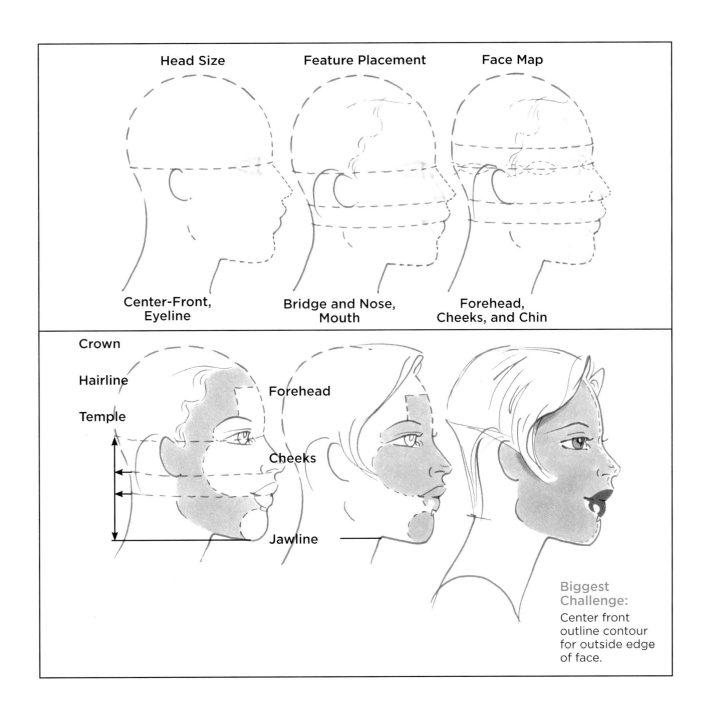

Head Size

Feature Placement

Face Map

Center-Front, Eyeline

Bridge and Nose, Mouth

Forehead, Cheeks, and Chin

Crown

Hairline

Temple

Forehead

Cheeks

Jawline

Biggest Challenge:
Center front outline contour for outside edge of face.

Fashion Faces, Sketching Features

Signature faces and maintaining consistency in drawing your fashion client's head are an integral part of your skills. Here is where sketching formula meets stylistic options. When the head turns, its center front turns and previous facial features are no longer equal and will become foreshortened. The more the face turns, the more you have to explore drawing the eyes, cheeks, nose, and jawline areas of the face in your interpretation for the fashion head.

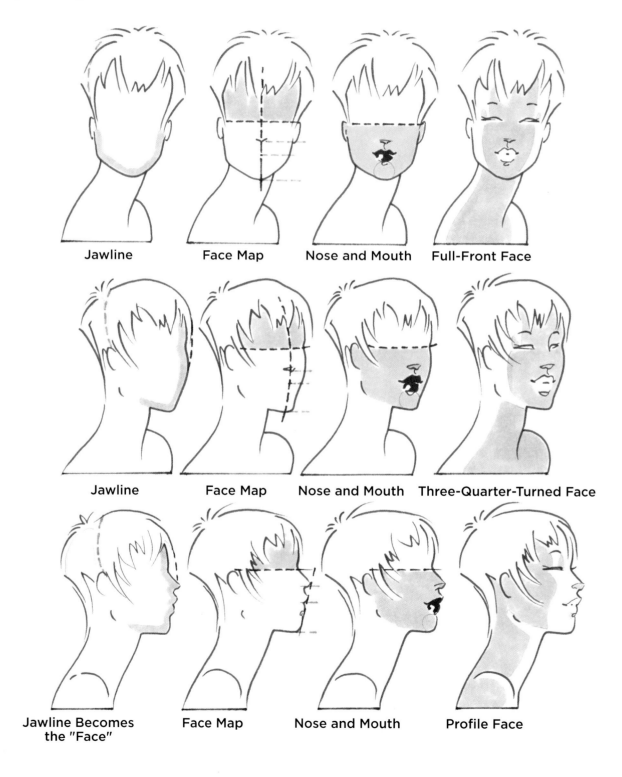

Jawline   Face Map   Nose and Mouth   Full-Front Face

Jawline   Face Map   Nose and Mouth   Three-Quarter-Turned Face

Jawline Becomes the "Face"   Face Map   Nose and Mouth   Profile Face

Different styles of fashion heads should be used to accentuate your design aesthetic and complement your collections. For example, if your garment or collection has a playful look, then the head of your figure should reflect that as well.

Playful

This face signals fun, casual, young.

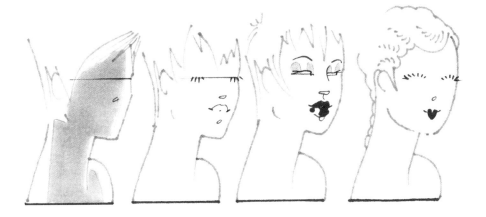

Retro

This face signals a period look or influence.

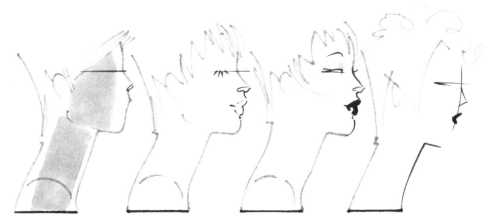

Stylized

This face can become a signature look and client.

Simplify: Quick croquis heads   **Intensify:** Image-focused faces

Posing the Head

Having practiced the three basic views—full front, turned, and profile—for the fashion face, the next step is learning to pose the head. Try to pick simple poses in which the model looks slightly up or down or tilts the head a bit to one side—nothing overly challenging or difficult. Too much emphasis on elaborate posing of the head subtracts interest from the fashion statement of your entire figure. As you pose the head, consider it as an integral part, another facet of the fashion styling for your sketch. Here are some of the facets to incorporate into your drawing practice.

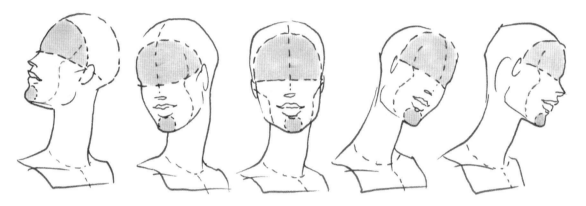

Facial Contouring

Contouring the face is a process of rounding out the cube or the form of the head. For fashion—just as with the figure—the three-dimensional construction of form is reduced to a flat surface of one dimension on the page. Within these limits you can practice with the planes and angles in a pose for the head by creating areas for shadow on the face. When you delete the shadows, you will be left with lines to use as contours on the face.

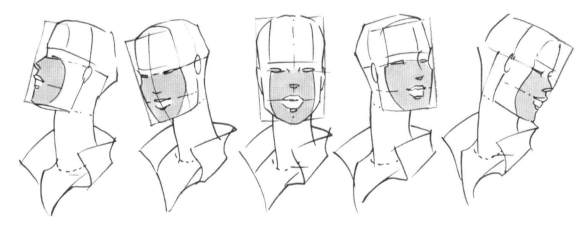

Facial Blocking

Sketch the head as a square, a box, or a trapezoid. Turn and tilt this box or trapezoid. It moves up, down, and sideways when you sketch a face on the side of the box you see as the "front." This simple form makes it easier to see the planes in the head. Try these preliminary sketches for yourself.

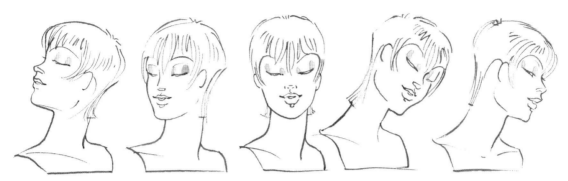

Facial Expressions

The fashion face presents a customer attitude appropriate to the category of look being represented (usually casual, career, or dressy). Fashion attitude should convey one basic expression—happy to be wearing "the" outfit. Other possible expressions are sultry, shy, or confident. Anything that complements the style of the clothing on your figure is appropriate.

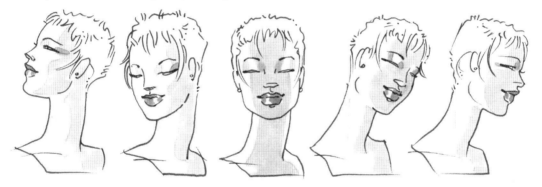

Facial Planes

The planes of the face become more pronounced when the head is tilted. You do not have to sketch those planes but it is important to study them. The interior planes of the face work with the exterior structure of the head. This extra bit of shaping will give you a basis for posing the head. The planes of the face suggest how far the turn or the tilt of the head will go.

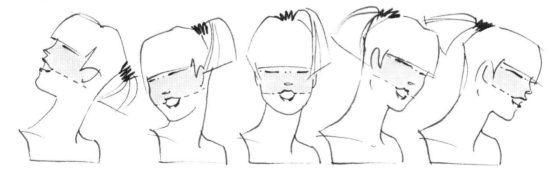

Facial Angles

Tilt the head and the angles for the features on the face will follow the direction of the tilt. When the head is tilted, either draw under the chin or over the chin as the chin meets the neckline. Sketch the eyeline with the edge of the eyes following the direction of the curve in the angle. The shape of the face will need more structuring at the jawline.

Sketching Features

Combine the proportions for the features with their placement in location to each other, and practice drawing the face in segments. Mastering these facial segments will provide a strong foundation on which to conceptualize the fashion head that most relates to your style of drawing.

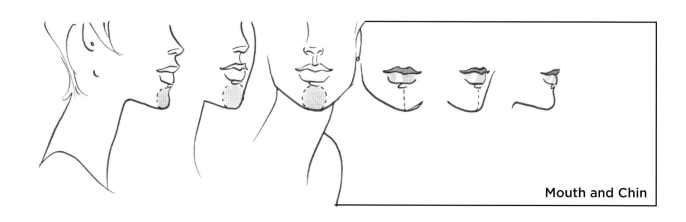

Mouth and Chin

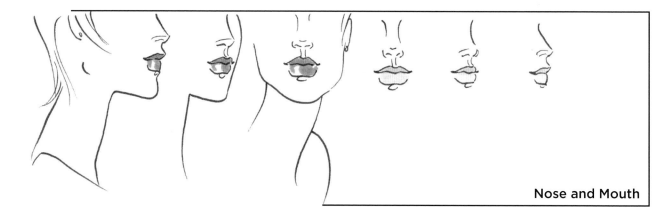

Nose and Mouth

Bridge of Nose and Eyes

Isolate the features and practice drawing them, one by one, in each of the three views from the previous pages. Begin with the full-front shape, because it will be the fullest and easiest to sketch. Then work on the other two views, and tackle the foreshortened or turned views of these shapes.

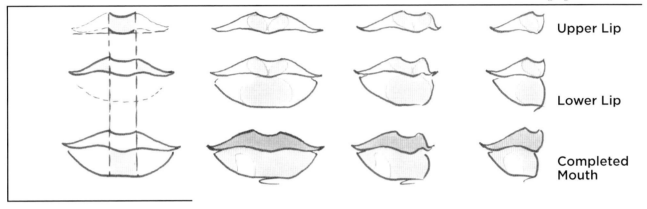

Upper Lip

Lower Lip

Completed Mouth

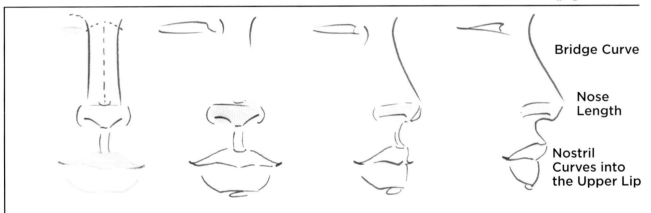

Bridge Curve

Nose Length

Nostril Curves into the Upper Lip

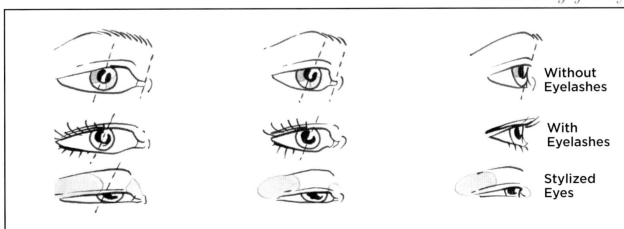

Without Eyelashes

With Eyelashes

Stylized Eyes

Stylizing the Face

Minimalistic fashion faces on designer sketches often have little to no actual features. Instead they are drawn with a quick head shape, hairstyle, and only a hint of features.

Hairstyling, in conjunction with the minimalistic fashion face, adds to a look by virtue of its cut, length, and trend factors. Keeping the hair cut similar, between a group of figures, adds to variety.

Fashion faces can set a mood or set the pace for a collection. Faces that are drawn specifically, for example, in an anime, playful, or retro look will help to communicate your design style directives.

To accentuate customer attitude, from classic to trendy to whimsy, play around with your set of facial features. The eyes, nose, and mouth are the key, switching from realistic to impressionistic.

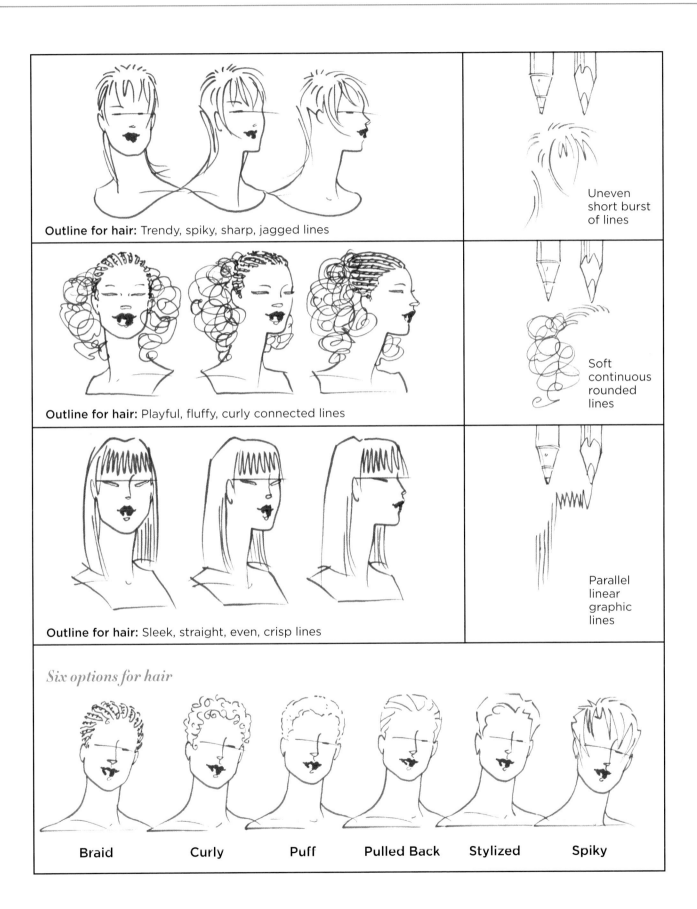

Outline for hair: Trendy, spiky, sharp, jagged lines

Uneven short burst of lines

Outline for hair: Playful, fluffy, curly connected lines

Soft continuous rounded lines

Outline for hair: Sleek, straight, even, crisp lines

Parallel linear graphic lines

Six options for hair

Braid   Curly   Puff   Pulled Back   Stylized   Spiky

Rendering Hair Color

Hair can be drawn and rendered in reference to any race or color, and in all lengths and types of hairstyle (or coloring) trends. Outline shaping can imitate any haircut or hair type. The examples on this page give you a start on how to color the interior of that hairstyle shape. As a designer, you simplify hair so it does not overpower your designs.

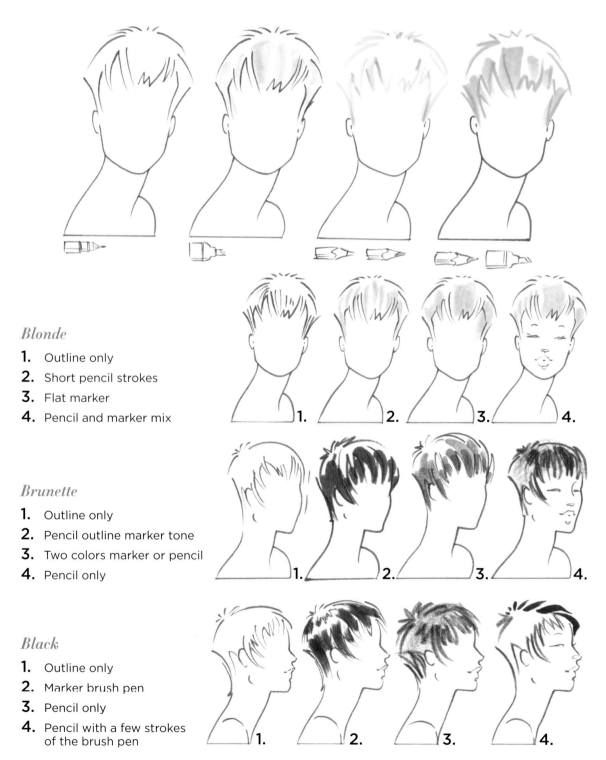

Blonde
1. Outline only
2. Short pencil strokes
3. Flat marker
4. Pencil and marker mix

Brunette
1. Outline only
2. Pencil outline marker tone
3. Two colors marker or pencil
4. Pencil only

Black
1. Outline only
2. Marker brush pen
3. Pencil only
4. Pencil with a few strokes of the brush pen

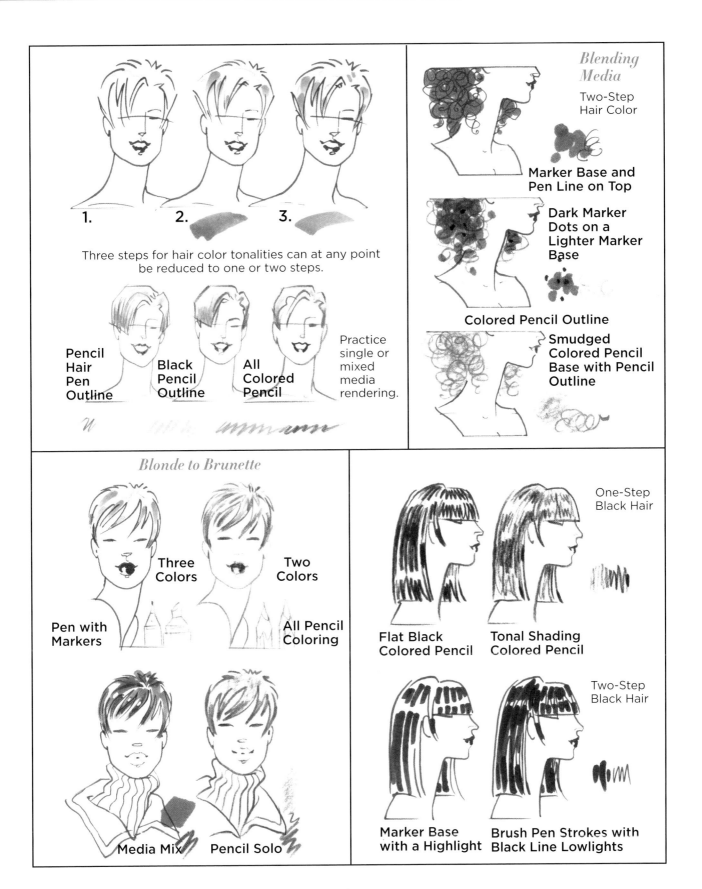

Three steps for hair color tonalities can at any point be reduced to one or two steps.

1. 2. 3.

Pencil Hair Pen Outline

Black Pencil Outline

All Colored Pencil

Practice single or mixed media rendering.

Blending Media

Two-Step Hair Color

Marker Base and Pen Line on Top

Dark Marker Dots on a Lighter Marker Base

Colored Pencil Outline

Smudged Colored Pencil Base with Pencil Outline

Blonde to Brunette

Three Colors

Two Colors

Pen with Markers

All Pencil Coloring

Media Mix

Pencil Solo

One-Step Black Hair

Flat Black Colored Pencil

Tonal Shading Colored Pencil

Two-Step Black Hair

Marker Base with a Highlight

Brush Pen Strokes with Black Line Lowlights

Fleshtone and Pencil

This page includes tips on how to combine pencil with paint or marker. Either can smear pencil unless the pencil outlining is drawn on last.

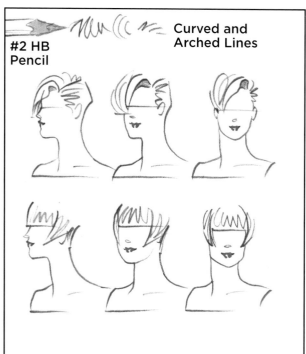

#2 HB Pencil

Curved and Arched Lines

Step 1. Marker flesh tone
Step 2. Pencil outline
Step 3. Pencil hair color

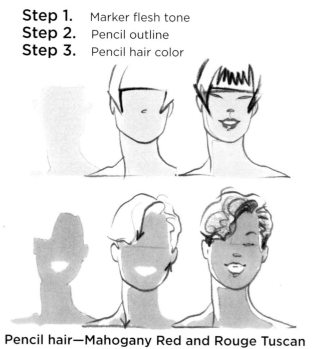

Pencil hair—Mahogany Red and Rouge Tuscan

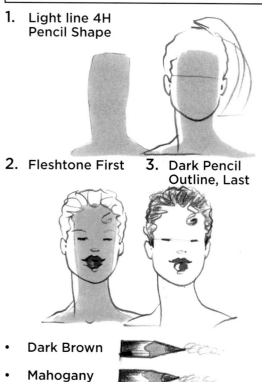

1. Light line 4H Pencil Shape

2. Fleshtone First   3. Dark Pencil Outline, Last

- Dark Brown
- Mahogany Red

Jagged Lines and Dots

#2 HB Pencil

Fleshtone Color Options

1. Powder Pink   2. Sand   3. Light Walnut

Period Looks

1900s
"Gibson Girl"

1940s
"The Pompadour"

1950s
"Page Boy"

1920s
"Louise Brooks"

1960s
"Beehive"

1930s
"Marcel (Finger) Waves"

1970s
"Afro"

Hairstyles, like everything else in the fashion world, are also subject to trends. This page is proof that a fashion decade can be identified through a given hairstyle. It could be a look that was born in that space of time, or possibly a look that has since been repeated or refined but was not necessarily seen before that defining time period.

Fashion Heads, Runway Looks

The heads in the photos on this spread represent the three views of the head that you have been studying in the chapter—the full-front, three-quarter-turned, and profile views. Like in the previous chapter, use these photos as drawing reference. Sketch each head on the grids on this spread and the next.

Diane von Furstenberg

The head in this photo offers the opportunity to draw the head with sunglasses, creating a look that is synonymous with fashion styling.

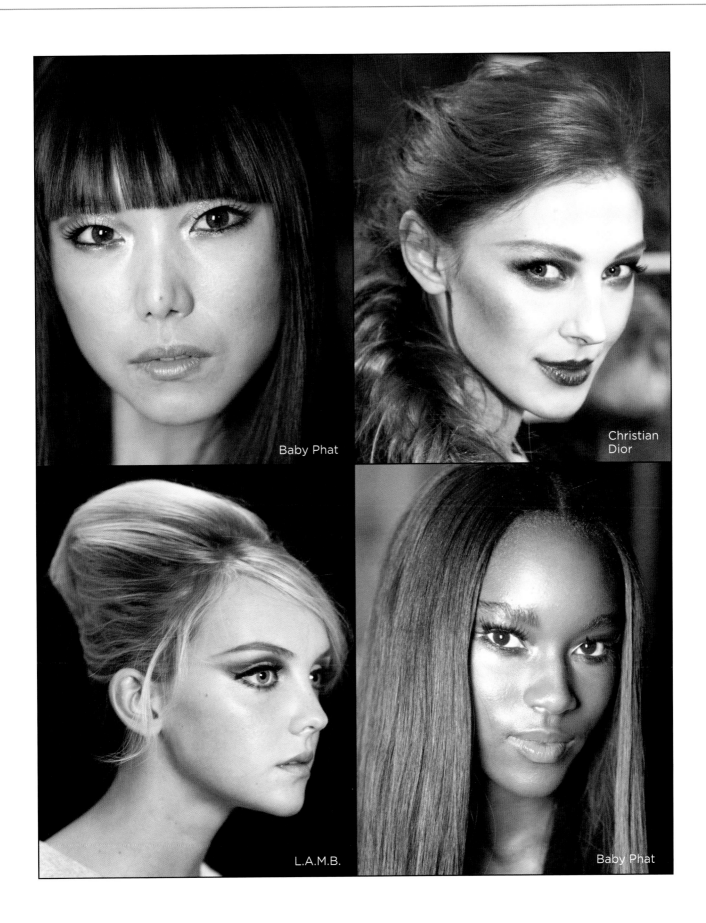

Baby Phat

Christian
Dior

L.A.M.B.

Baby Phat

Fashion Heads, Runway Looks (continued)

Baby Phat

L.A.M.B.

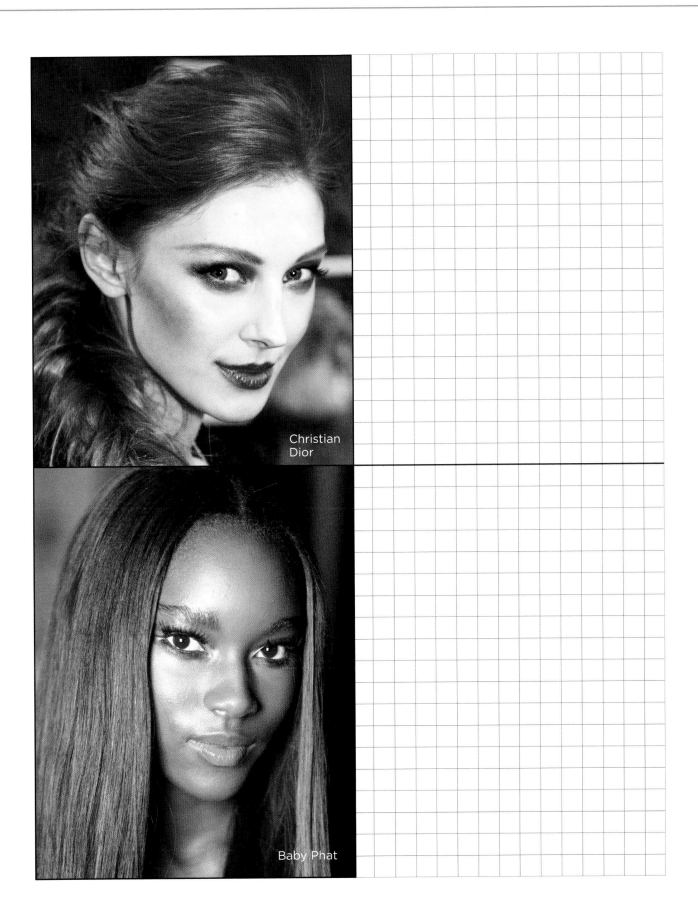

Christian
Dior

Baby Phat

5

Garments and Garment Details

In this chapter, after all of the figure work of the earlier chapters, the focus moves to clothing, dressing the figure in some of the staple fashion design details that show up every season. Basic sketching methods are used to help you design on the figure and to create some simple silhouettes. Garment detailing of necklines, collars, and cuffs will be incorporated into easy tops, pants, and skirts for faster drawing exercises. While dressing the figure from top to bottom typically is defined as a silhouette, this chapter will explore how to shift your focus from exterior shape to interior drape, making dressing the figure a more informative yet imaginative process.

In this chapter, there is more fashion clothing in both studio muslins and *WWD* runway and studio photos to study and draw. You will learn how to sketch fabric in loose folds, precise pleats, or other basic garment details so that they fit contours of the body while presenting your design visions.

Research into almost any period of fashion or art history will turn up wonderful references that you can apply to your own illustration and design techniques for fashion. Almost any book on fashion decades will have plenty of archival illustration for you to find stylistic inspiration or to observe how other artists handled drawing or rendering clothing.

Sketching Necklines and Collars

Necklines move above or below the base of the neck. They often follow the basic sewing lines on the torso. Collars are connected to the neckline, draped above or below the neck, set down on the shoulders or spread across the chest. To dress the neck, to draw and design necklines and collars, utilize the sewing lines on the torso as a guide. Collars sewn above the base of the neck usually follow the cylindrical form of the neck, reflecting the base of the neck's contour. Collars below the base of the neck usually follow the shoulderline angles.

Notched collars are full of design variety in their widths, cuts, and closure details. Most are based on a V-neckline, with a single- or double-breasted closure, as shown here.

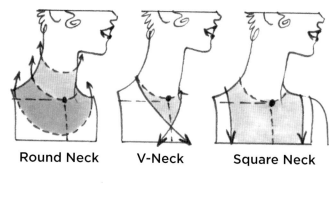

Round Neck   **V-Neck**   **Square Neck**

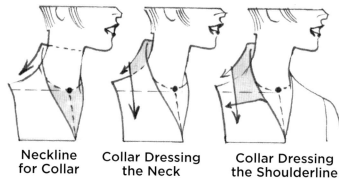

Neckline for Collar   **Collar Dressing the Neck**   **Collar Dressing the Shoulderline**

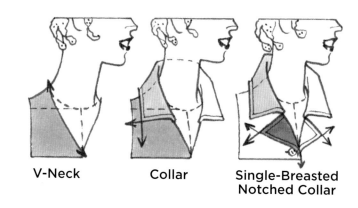

V-Neck   **Collar**   **Single-Breasted Notched Collar**

Band Collar

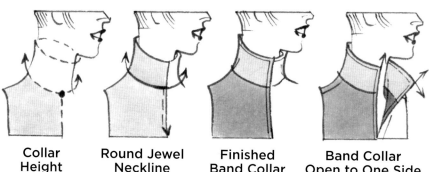

Collar Height   **Round Jewel Neckline**   **Finished Band Collar**   **Band Collar Open to One Side**

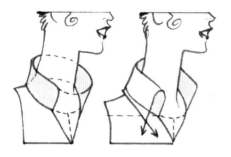

Band Collar

This is the inside structure or base for the spread or shirt collar.

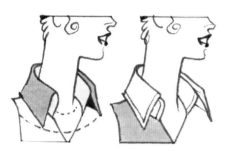

Spread or Shirt Collar

This collar has "wings" sewn on the band that help the collar stand up, away from the neck, to rest on the shoulderline.

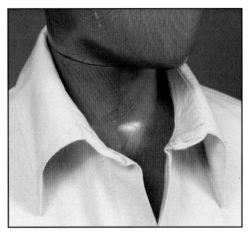

Spread or Shirt Collar

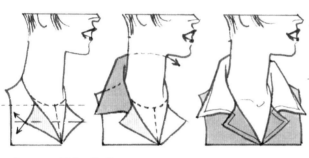

Convertible Collar Closed

Convertible Collar

Here part of the bodice, when open, appears to be part of the collar, folding over, until the bodice is closed.

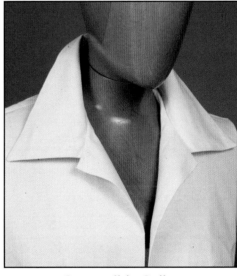

Convertible Collar

Lapels

This is the name given to the bottom portion of this type of collar when it is on a suit jacket or coat.

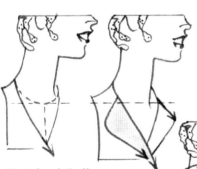

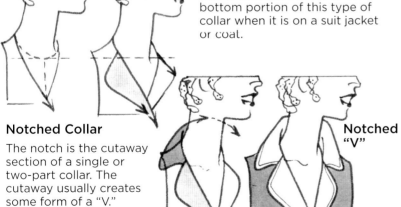

Notched "V"

Notched Collar

The notch is the cutaway section of a single or two-part collar. The cutaway usually creates some form of a "V."

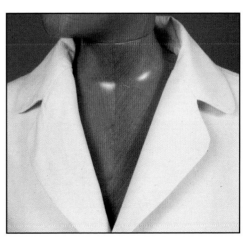

Notched Collar

Sketching Sleeves

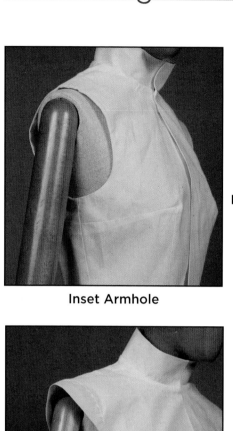

Inset Armhole

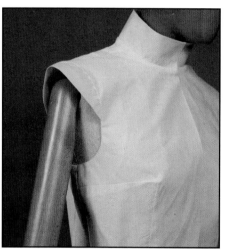

Cap Sleeve

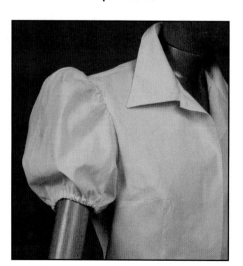

Puff Sleeve

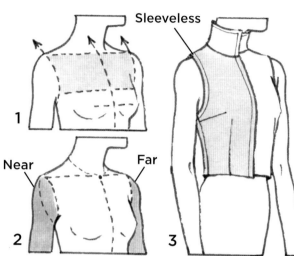

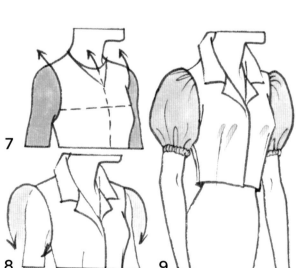

Without Sleeves

1. The armhole lines follow the curve of the center front.

2. Arm on the fur side is behind the chest. Arm on the near side is in front of the chest.

3. Matching armhole curves.

Cap Sleeve

4. Lines across the chest will help you even out the sleeve details.

5. Measure the depth of a cap sleeve, matching up the sleeves on both sides.

6. The angle on a cap sleeve is open. You can see up into it.

Puff Sleeve

7. The contour of the armhole follows the contour direction of center front.

8. A puff sleeve has volume. Get the outline to stand up, away from the arm.

9. The puff sleeve has gathers emanating from the armhole, the elastic casing, or both.

Bishop Sleeve on a Blouse

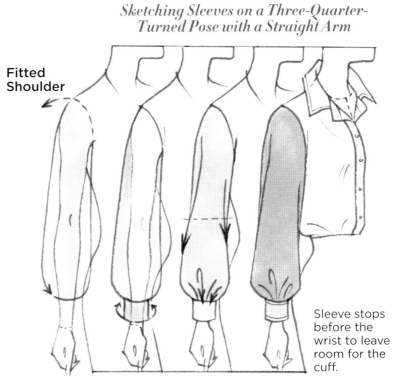

Fitted Shoulder

Sleeve stops before the wrist to leave room for the cuff.

1. The fit of the sleeve from its top to bottom.
2. The shape of the sleeve as it fits the arm.
3. The drape of the sleeve near the elbow.
4. Example of the finished illustration of this sleeve.

Full-Length Sleeve on a Blazer

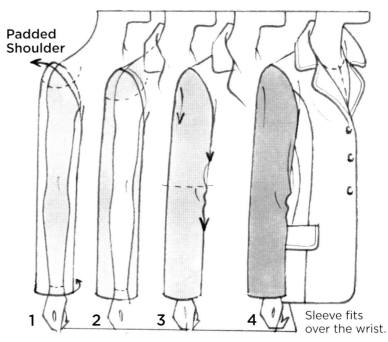

Padded Shoulder

Sleeve fits over the wrist.

Sketching Blouses and Dresses

Illustrated on this spread is one of many approaches to dressing the figure in a blouse or a dress. It begins at the base of the neck, includes the waist, moving down to the hemline. It doesn't matter which side you start first (left or right) as long as you complete one area of definition before going on to the next. You can use the natural contours of the chest to get the blouse or dress to drape over the form if the fabric has any cling factors.

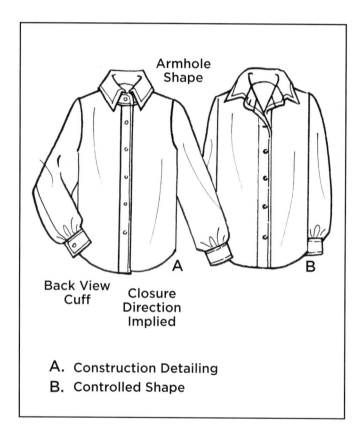

Armhole Shape

Back View Cuff

Closure Direction Implied

A. Construction Detailing
B. Controlled Shape

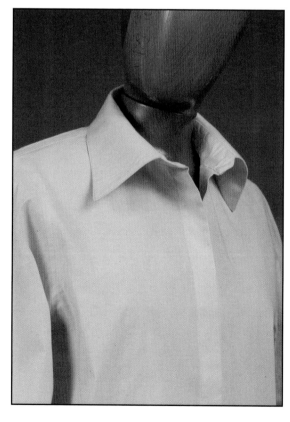

The sketching setups on the facing page illustrate how some of the sewing lines can help support the development of garment details on the figure. They also serve to define the areas of focus, like completing the bodice details before drawing the sleeves.

Collar and Button Packet · *Bodice Shape* · *Sleeve and Cuff* · *Completed Sketch*

Begin with the neckline or collar shapes.

Follow sewing line construction panel details.

Define the bodice— how wide or long the shape will be.

Finish sleeves— use drape lines to soften shapes.

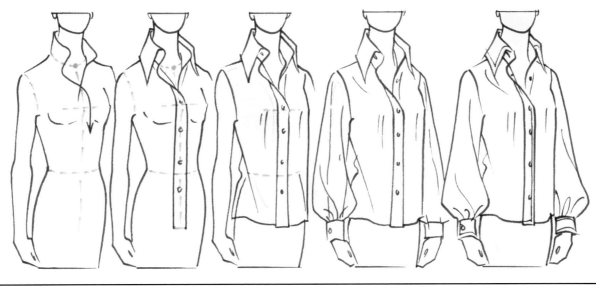

Working with center front on a pose.

Planning details using construction sewing lines.

Defining shape for bodice and skirt of dress.

Completed sketch.

Sketching Skirts

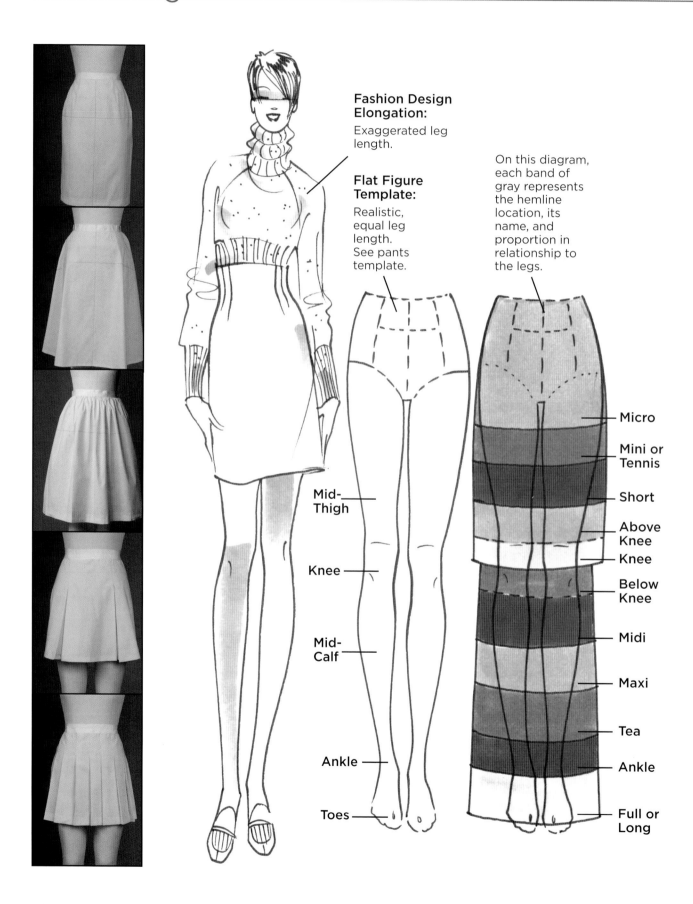

Fashion Design Elongation: Exaggerated leg length.

Flat Figure Template: Realistic, equal leg length. See pants template.

On this diagram, each band of gray represents the hemline location, its name, and proportion in relationship to the legs.

Mid-Thigh

Knee

Mid-Calf

Ankle

Toes

Micro

Mini or Tennis

Short

Above Knee

Knee

Below Knee

Midi

Maxi

Tea

Ankle

Full or Long

Some drape or construction details are taken for granted and are too fine or tiny to illustrate on the dressed figure or in a flat. Here are a few things that can be done on your sketch.

Fine-point pen

.005 extra-fine-point pen

Line quality makes the difference in a seam; use completed lines for seams; use broken lines for stitching. Practice drawing all types of lines with your extra-fine and ultra-thin pens.

Line Qualities

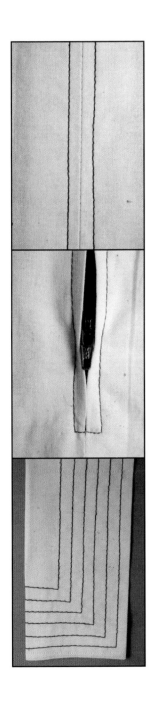

Flat Feld Seam:
Jeans' Stitch

Kissing Zipper:
with Crossover Stitch

Trapunto Stitching:
Sometimes Padded
Channels

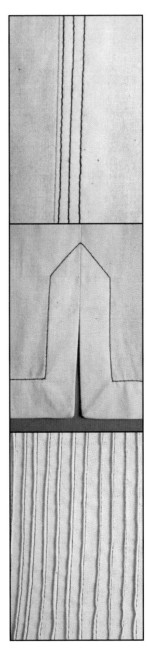

Top Stitching:
Seam to One Side

Vent:
Also Called a Slit

Pintucks:
Close Together,
Stitched Down

Sketching Flares and Gathers

The flared or gathered skirt folds and moves on the body in a random, free-form way in direct opposition to a pleated skirt, which has an organized, exact style. To emphasize the movement of a flared skirt, draw each fold a different size from the next one. The folds of a skirt on the figure should follow the flow of the pose. Notice the widest fold comes off the high hip. The smallest fold comes from the center, and a third midsize fold rests on the low hip side.

Flared Skirt

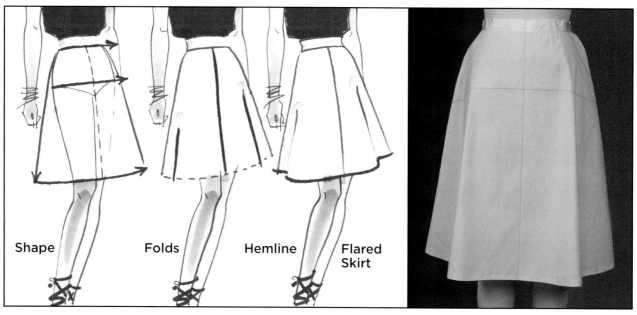

Shape   Folds   Hemline   Flared Skirt

Notice that the fabric on the flared skirt lies flat against the hipline, while the fabric on the gathered skirt puffs up away from the hipline at the waistband.

Gathered Skirt

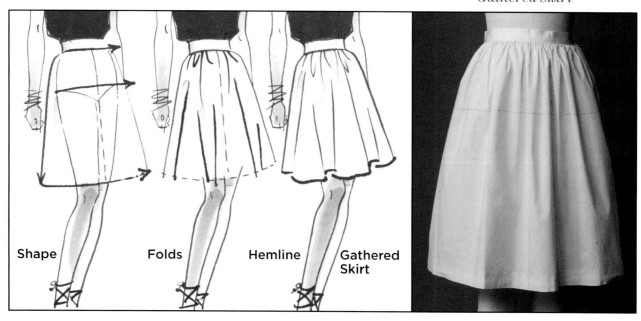

Shape   Folds   Hemline   Gathered Skirt

A flounce has a straight seam, with a few folds. A ruffle has a gathered seam, with lots of folds.

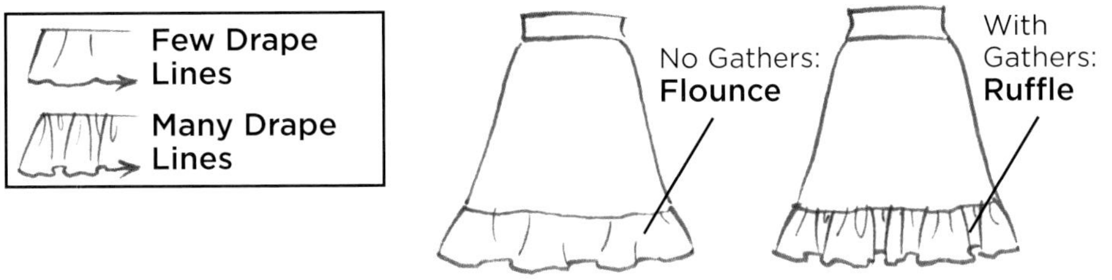

	Few Drape Lines
	Many Drape Lines

No Gathers: **Flounce**

With Gathers: **Ruffle**

Shape	Folds	Hemline	Finish

Flared Skirt

Gathers

Gathered Skirt

Seams

Tiered Skirt

Layers

Layered Skirt

Notice that the rows on the tiered skirt are connected, while the rows on the layered skirts are separated.

Sketching Pleats

These pages demonstrate how to plan for drawing pleats. Each line on a pleated skirt usually has to match, unlike the folds in flares and gathers. Pleating is more regimented, organized, and systematic, regardless of fabric choice. This does not include engineered pleating in, for example, broomstick, mushroom, or crystal pleats.

Box Pleats

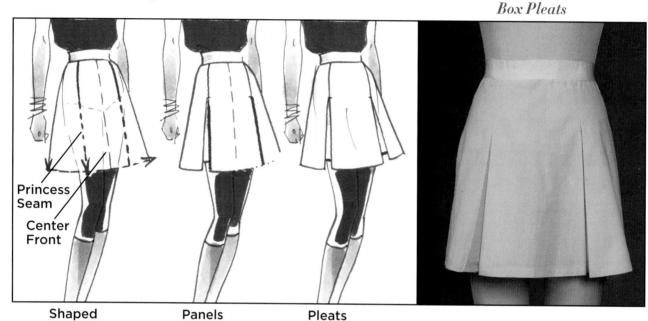

Shaped   Panels   Pleats

Follow the body center and princess seam lines illustrated here. Start building the pleats, using these lines as guides. It is easier to start in the middle and move out.

Side Pleats

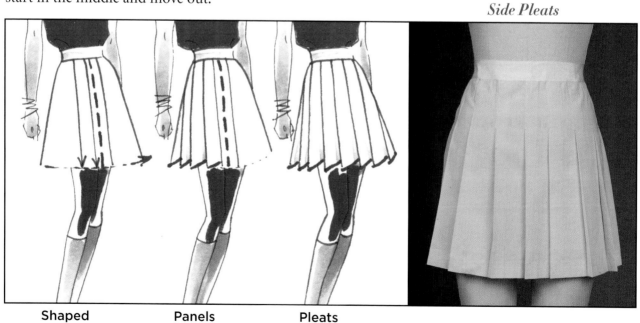

Shaped   Panels   Pleats

Notice how the panels—the narrow rectangular shapes—appear to be a bit closer together at the waist. They widen toward the bottom of the hem, opening up to show the back or inside of the pleat.

These three pleats break the rules, are drawn less regimented, and, like all pleats, can be done any size, anywhere on a garment.

Pleating

1. Mushroom
2. Broomstick
3. Accordian or Crystal

1.   **2.**   **3.**

Hemlines

Lettuce Edge

Broken Edge

Zigzag Edge

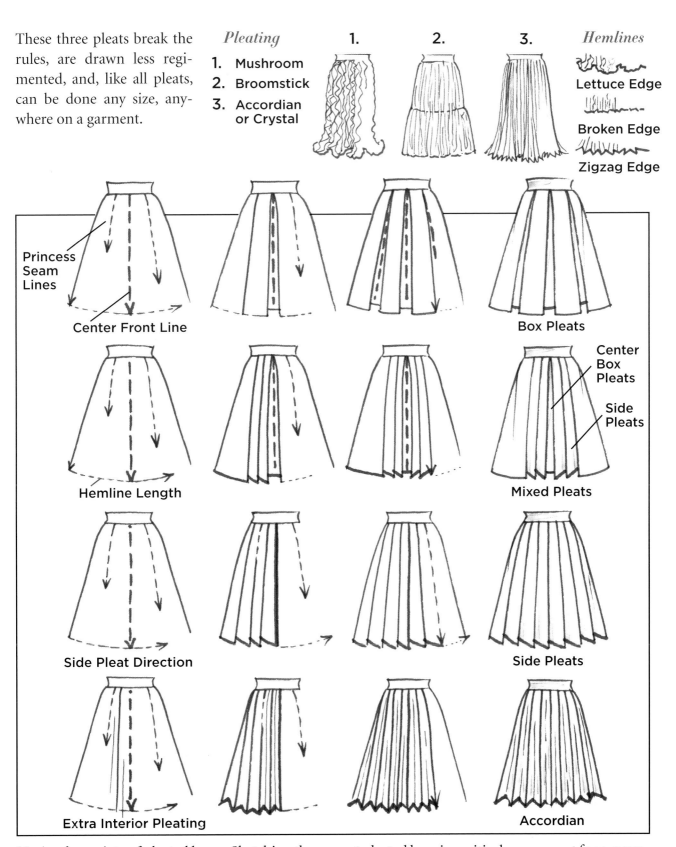

Princess Seam Lines

Center Front Line

Hemline Length

Side Pleat Direction

Extra Interior Pleating

Box Pleats

Center Box Pleats

Side Pleats

Mixed Pleats

Side Pleats

Accordian

Notice the variety of pleated hems. Sketching the correct pleated hem is a critical component for expressing your design.

Blouses, Skirts, and Dresses

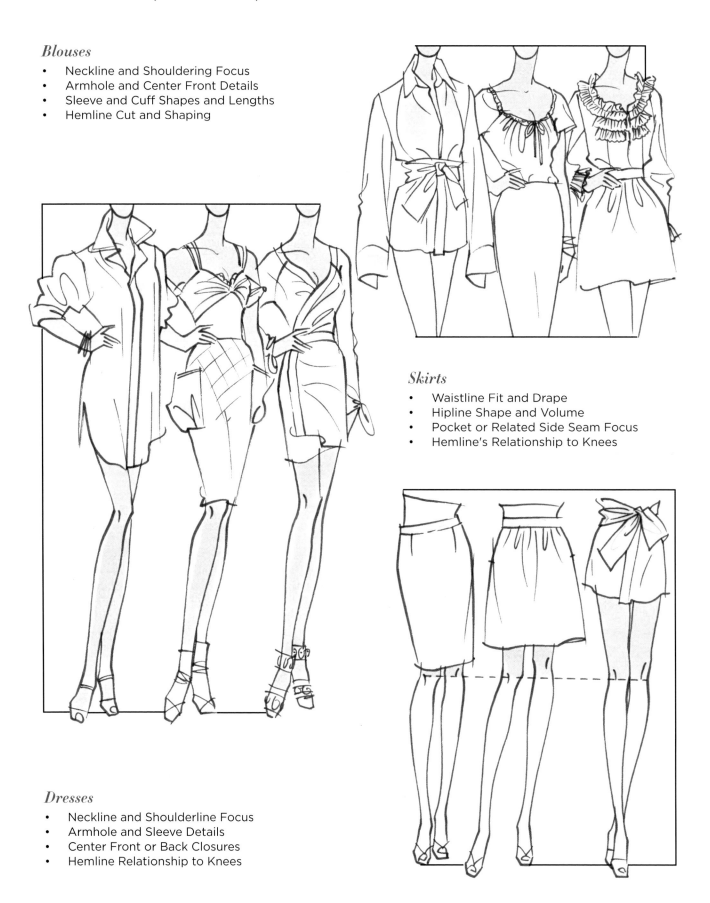

Blouses

- Neckline and Shouldering Focus
- Armhole and Center Front Details
- Sleeve and Cuff Shapes and Lengths
- Hemline Cut and Shaping

Skirts

- Waistline Fit and Drape
- Hipline Shape and Volume
- Pocket or Related Side Seam Focus
- Hemline's Relationship to Knees

Dresses

- Neckline and Shoulderline Focus
- Armhole and Sleeve Details
- Center Front or Back Closures
- Hemline Relationship to Knees

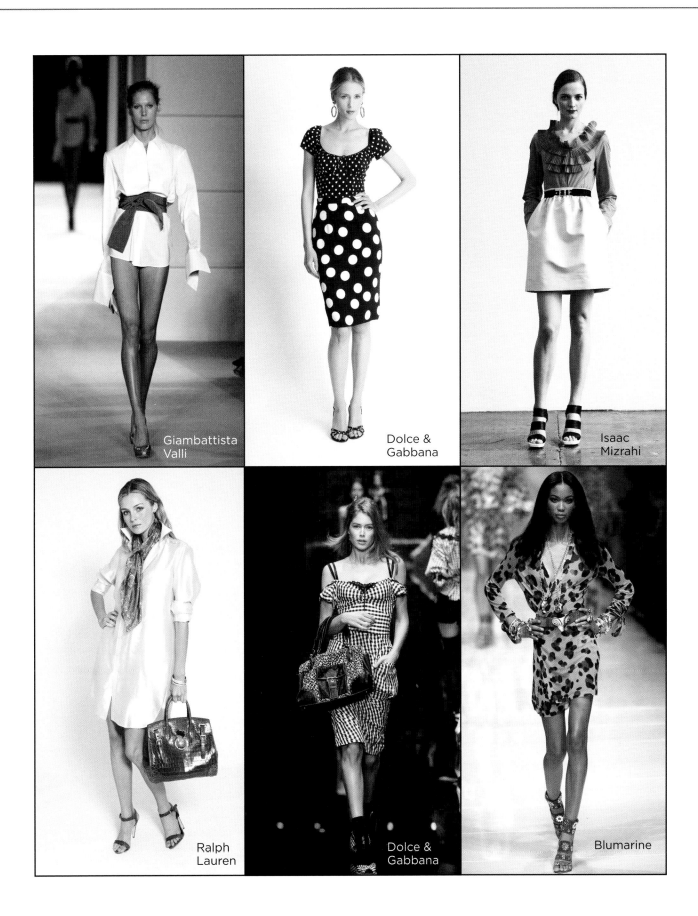

Giambattista
Valli

Dolce &
Gabbana

Isaac
Mizrahi

Ralph
Lauren

Dolce &
Gabbana

Blumarine

Sketching Pants

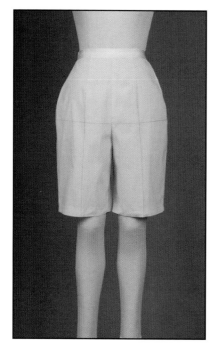 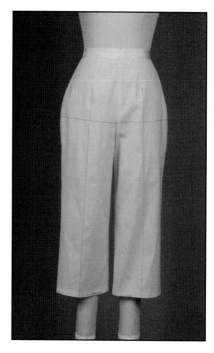 

The examples here, shown from the waist to the ankle, focus on hemlines for the legs.

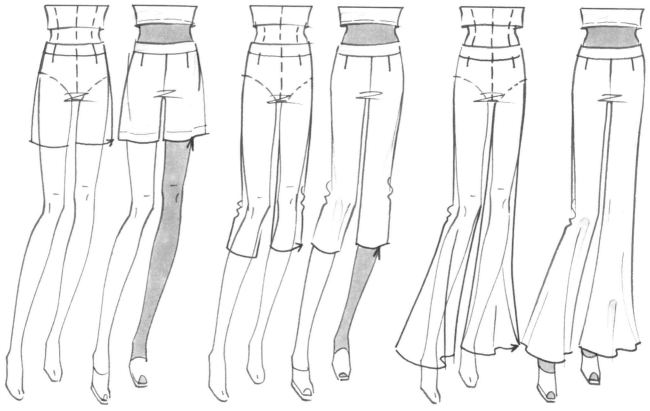

Shorts

For this garment the hemline length, from the thigh to the knee, will be important.

Capris

Here the hemline length has to show the spacing between calf to the ankle.

Bell-Bottom Pants

This hemline length has its own specific lengths from ankles to the toes (or shoe height).

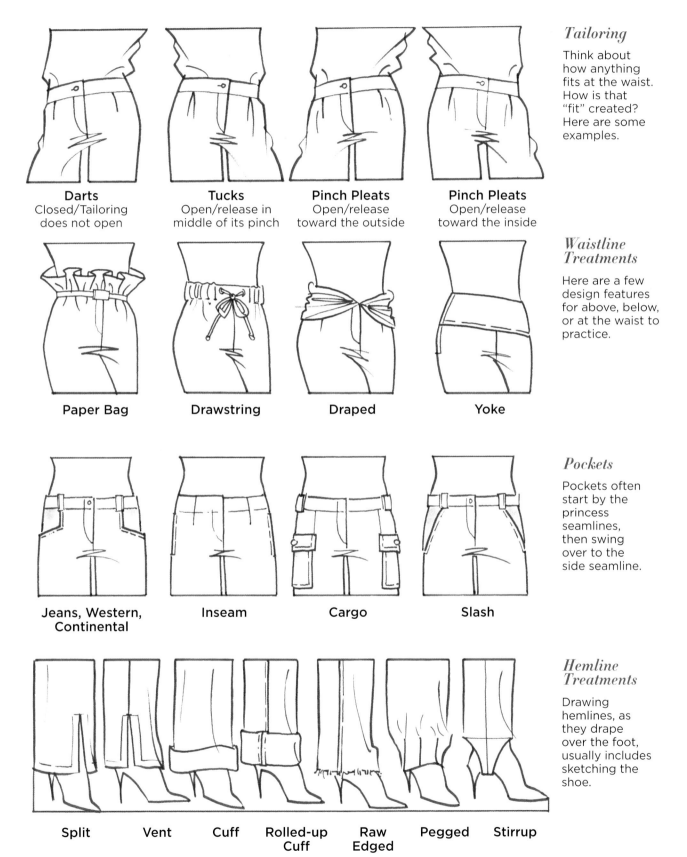

Darts
Closed/Tailoring
does not open

Tucks
Open/release in
middle of its pinch

Pinch Pleats
Open/release
toward the outside

Pinch Pleats
Open/release
toward the inside

Paper Bag

Drawstring

Draped

Yoke

**Jeans, Western,
Continental**

Inseam

Cargo

Slash

Split

Vent

Cuff

**Rolled-up
Cuff**

**Raw
Edged**

Pegged

Stirrup

Tailoring

Think about
how anything
fits at the waist.
How is that
"fit" created?
Here are some
examples.

*Waistline
Treatments*

Here are a few
design features
for above, below,
or at the waist to
practice.

Pockets

Pockets often
start by the
princess
seamlines,
then swing
over to the
side seamline.

*Hemline
Treatments*

Drawing
hemlines, as
they drape
over the foot,
usually includes
sketching the
shoe.

Drawing Pants

Here are some drawing issues that distract from your design silhouette focus:

1. Drawing knees too high up on the thigh can interfere with pocket shapes.
2. Drawing knees too low on the leg can throw off your figure proportions.
3. Knees drawn centered on the leg are never a problem with garment detailing.

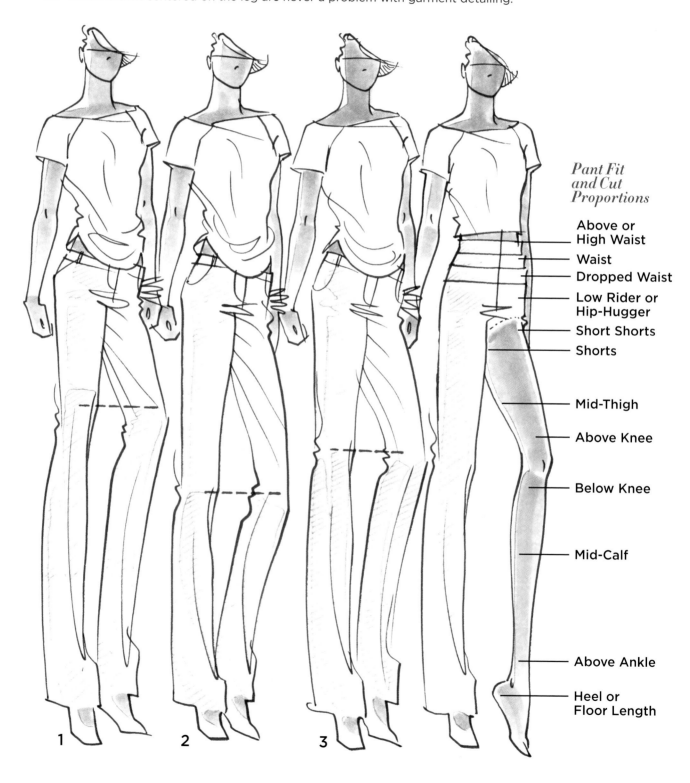

Pant Fit and Cut Proportions

— Above or High Waist
— Waist
— Dropped Waist
— Low Rider or Hip-Hugger
— Short Shorts
— Shorts
— Mid-Thigh
— Above Knee
— Below Knee
— Mid-Calf
— Above Ankle
— Heel or Floor Length

1   2   3

Knee Level

Keeping the crotch, knees, and leg lengths in your figure groupings matching makes it easier to read your garments' design proportions.

Posing Options

Below are some of the poses that can maximize the potential for your pants shapes and keep them from looking like long skirts.

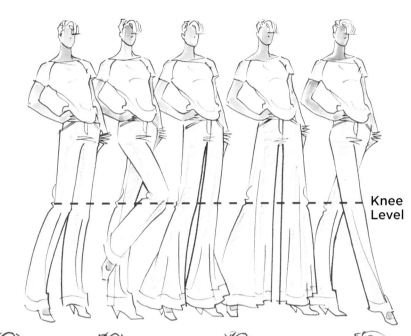

Knee Level

Poses that maximize pants design and emphasize pant legs shape

Shorts and Pants

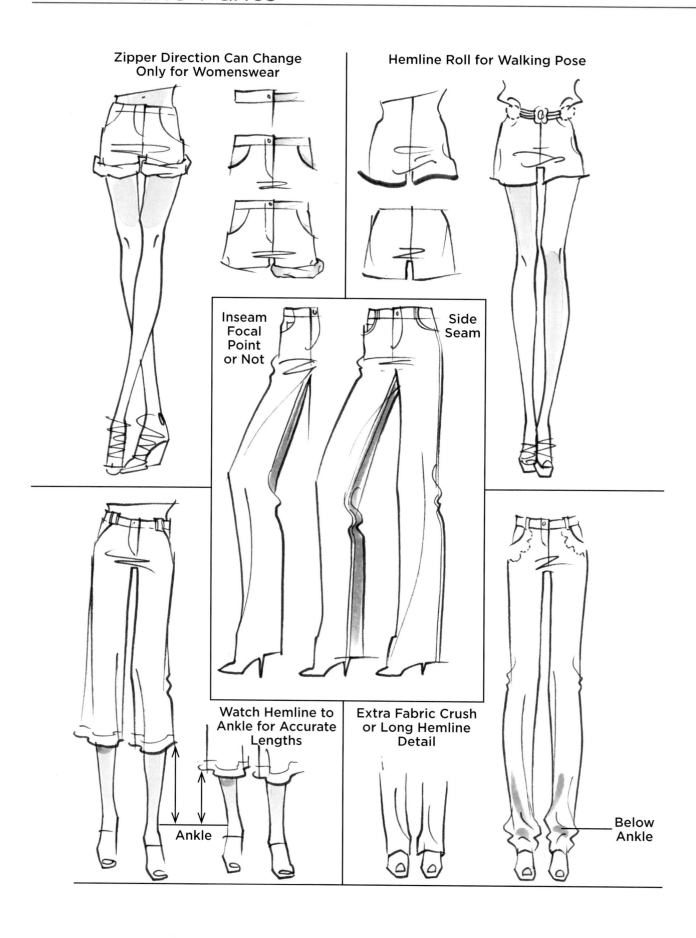

Zipper Direction Can Change Only for Womenswear

Hemline Roll for Walking Pose

Inseam Focal Point or Not

Side Seam

Watch Hemline to Ankle for Accurate Lengths

Ankle

Extra Fabric Crush or Long Hemline Detail

Below Ankle

J. Crew

Ralph
Lauren

Ralph
Lauren

J. Crew

Dolce &
Gabbana

Sketching a Blazer

A blazer often fits closer to the form of a figure than a jacket or a coat does. To suggest this closer fit you need to choose an appropriate pose to dress the figure in that blazer. In your sketch, follow and utilize the angles in the torso to plan the tailored details in the design of the garment. There is a direct relationship between the shoulderline and drawing the points in your collar, which is also true for the hipline and the pocket points. The fit or shape of a blazer may depend on the fabric weight or volume.

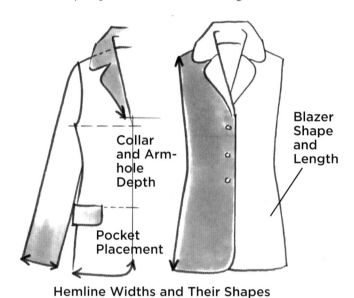

Collar and Arm-hole Depth

Pocket Placement

Blazer Shape and Length

Hemline Widths and Their Shapes

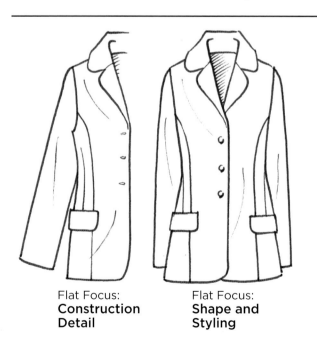

Flat Focus:
Construction Detail

Flat Focus:
Shape and Styling

Most blazers have a lining inside their sleeves, so the sleeve fits the arm like a crisp cylindrical shape, without too much cling. Blazers often have specific tailoring, darts, or seaming that usually falls between the side and princess seams.

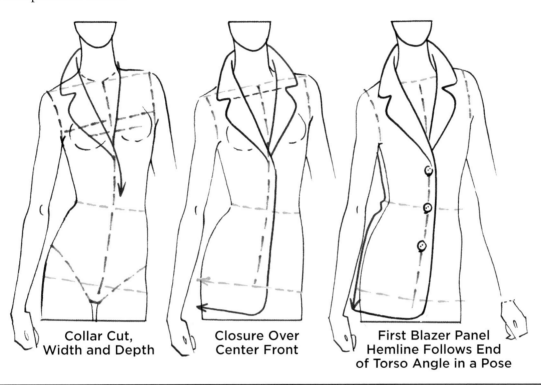

Collar Cut,
Width and Depth

Closure Over
Center Front

First Blazer Panel
Hemline Follows End
of Torso Angle in a Pose

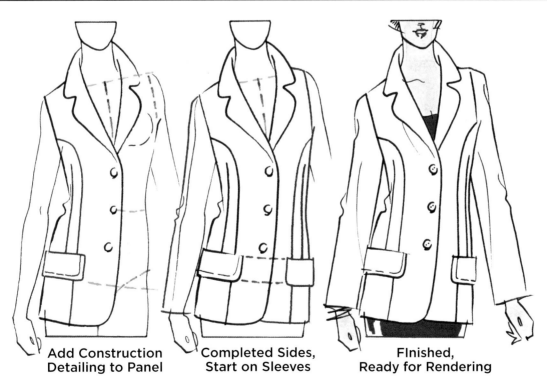

Add Construction
Detailing to Panel

Completed Sides,
Start on Sleeves

Finished,
Ready for Rendering

Drawing Jackets

Below is an example of a short, cropped jacket with a boxy shape and a quilted surface. It fits the figure in a different way compared to the tailored shape of a blazer with a smooth surface that you saw on the previous pages. The tailored blazer was more fitted; this cropped jacket is less fitted.

1. Compare the left and right sides to determine the fuller side, which you will dress first.

2. Sketch the jacket shape over the chest on the fullest side of the figure.

3. Add volume to the collar so that it appears to roll around the back of the neck.

4. To sketch the jacket open or closed, follow center front line. Note in this view the far, turned side armhole is not seen. The sleeves are drawn in the same width on both arms.

Working on the Neck and Shoulders

Working on the Center-Front Closure

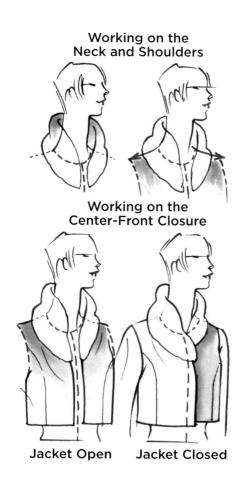

Jacket Open   Jacket Closed

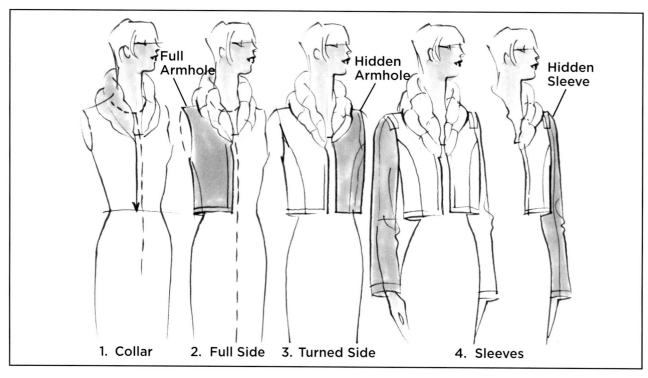

1. Collar   2. Full Side   3. Turned Side   4. Sleeves

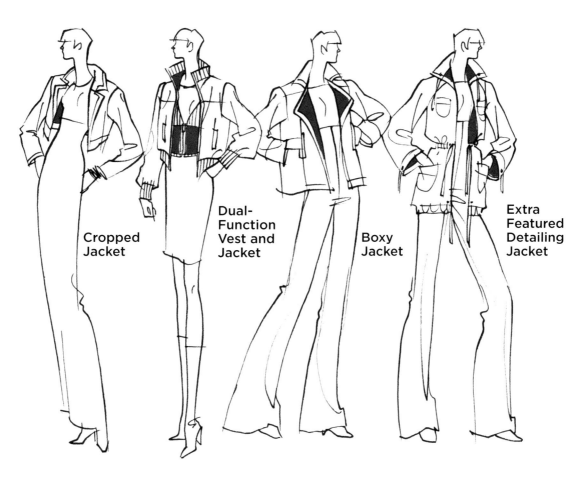

Cropped
Jacket

Dual-
Function
Vest and
Jacket

Boxy
Jacket

Extra
Featured
Detailing
Jacket

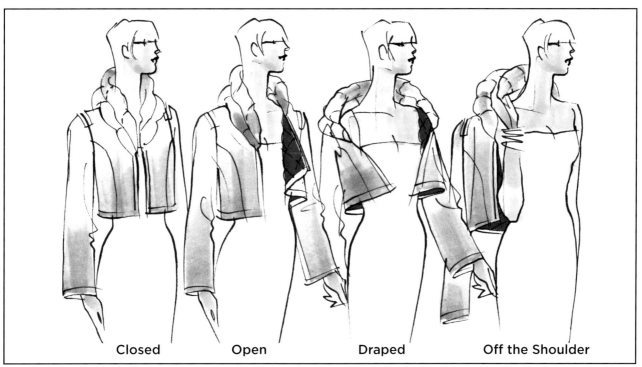

Closed   Open   Draped   Off the Shoulder

Drawing Coats

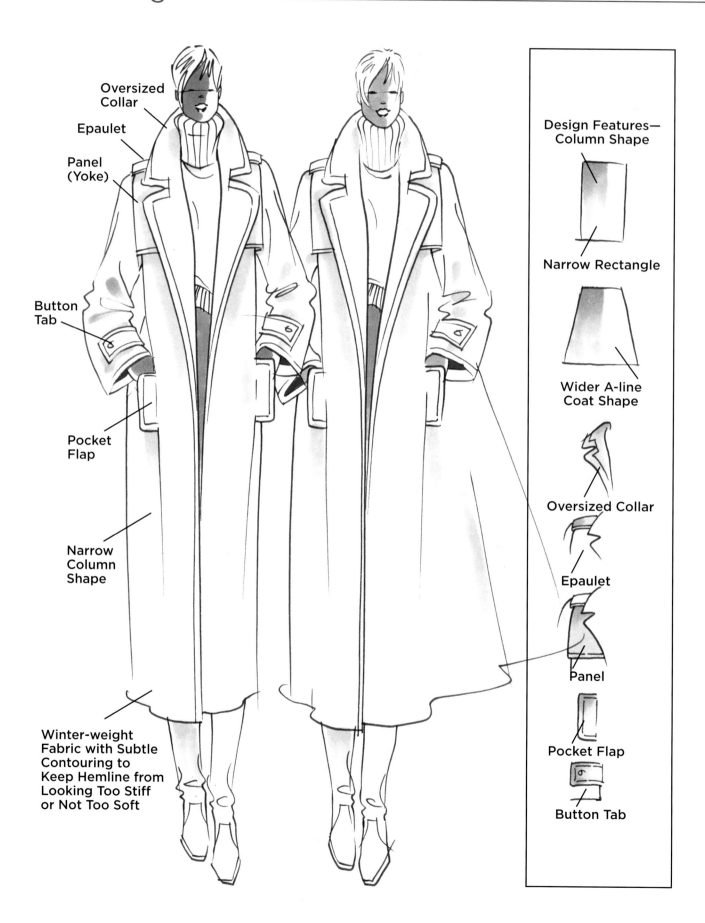

Oversized Collar

Epaulet

Panel (Yoke)

Button Tab

Pocket Flap

Narrow Column Shape

Winter-weight Fabric with Subtle Contouring to Keep Hemline from Looking Too Stiff or Not Too Soft

Design Features— Column Shape

Narrow Rectangle

Wider A-line Coat Shape

Oversized Collar

Epaulet

Panel

Pocket Flap

Button Tab

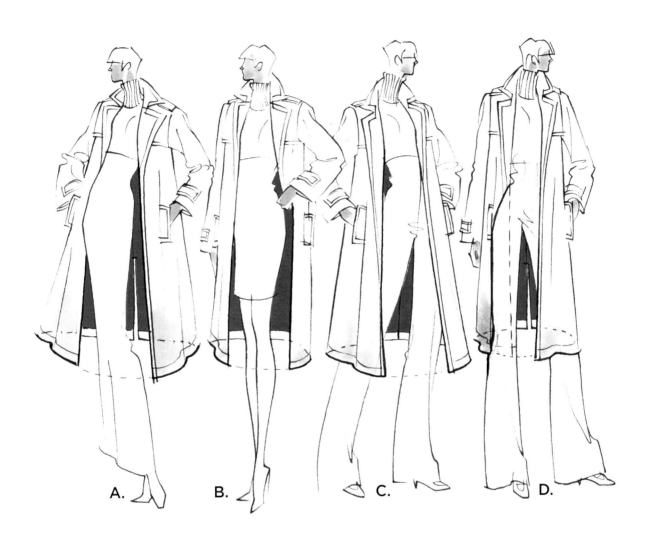

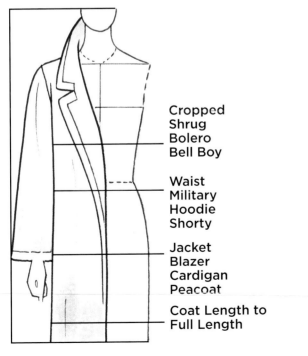

Cropped
Shrug
Bolero
Bell Boy

Waist
Military
Hoodie
Shorty

Jacket
Blazer
Cardigan
Peacoat

Coat Length to
Full Length

To emphasize the design and shape of the garment, a coat can be sketched closed or open to reveal the outfit beneath the coat.

A. This coat has been sketched closed on a subtle pose with just enough slouch in the hip to swing the coat open.

B. Here the hip is used to pull the coat open but only on one side, keeping the coat's shape narrow.

C. This wide leg pose flips the coat open. Notice the hemline has an elliptical curve as it circles the form, front to back.

D. To keep the coat's shape, draw the coat in two separate units. One side draped over the body, the other side falling behind the body.

Jackets and Coats

Jackets

Fabric Weight

Collar Volume

Sleeve Width and Length

- Thicker collar and cuffs
- Deeper, wider armholes
- Center front details
- Hemline in relationship to waistline or kneeline

Coats

- Chunkier collars

- Thicker fabrics

- Wider sleeves

- Deeper armholes

- Closure details

- Sleeve length and cuffs

- Pockets

- Buttons and trims

- Hemline relative to ankles

Ralph
Lauren

M Missoni

Narciso
Rodriguez

TSE

Chloé

Michael
Kors

The media mix for this design is gouache and pencil for both of the capsule collections, two different fabric stories, and the colorways. The posed figures play up the layered silhouettes, construction details, and color coordinations. Static figures complement the more contemporary linear shaping and neutral color palette in the alternative collection.

The bolero pocket flaps are fake; the bolero has no pockets; the flaps are tabs to hold pens & scarves.

Scarf starts out from the side of the sweater, wraps around her neck and travels through the bolero pocket flap tab.

CONCEALING & REVEALING

The media mix for this design is gouache, pencil, and acrylic or Pro-White (brighter than gouache whites) on a single sheet of faux woodgrain paper (parchment paper is an alternative choice). Her inventive figure art emphasizes design silhouette and construction detail. Flats of her tops are drawn on vellum paper and pinned to pivot on their page.

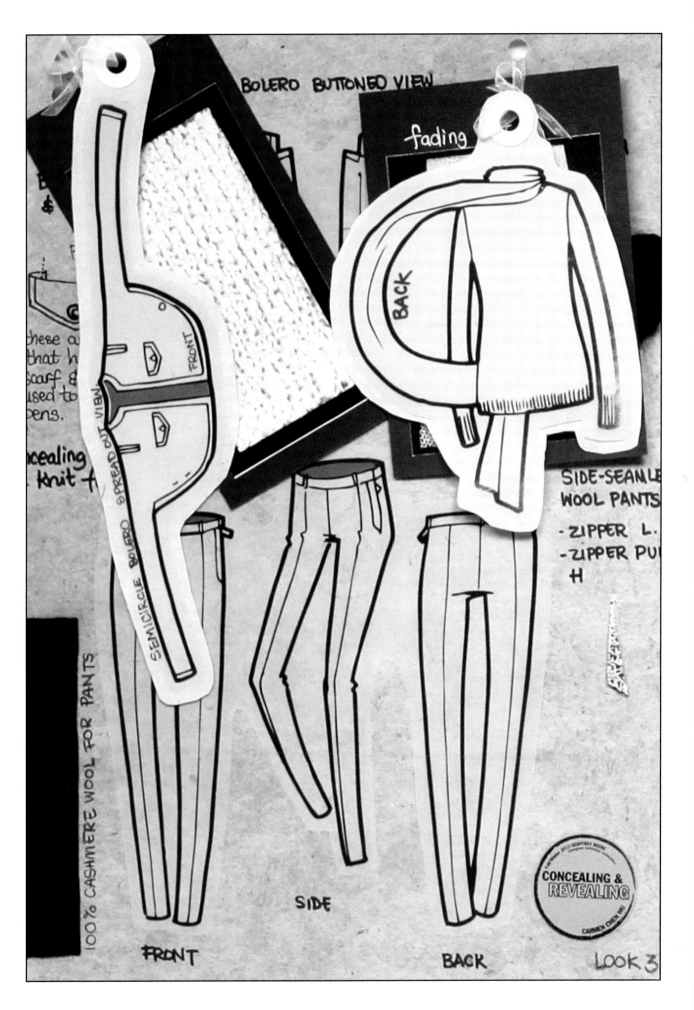

BOLERO BUTTONED VIEW

fading

these a
that h
Scarf &
used to
pens.

ncealing
knit f

SEMICIRCLE BOLERO SPREAD OUT VIEW

FRONT

BACK

SIDE-SEAM LE
WOOL PANTS

- ZIPPER L.
- ZIPPER PU
H

100% CASHMERE WOOL FOR PANTS

FRONT

SIDE

BACK

LOOK 3

CONCEALING &
REVEALING

CARMEN CHEN WU

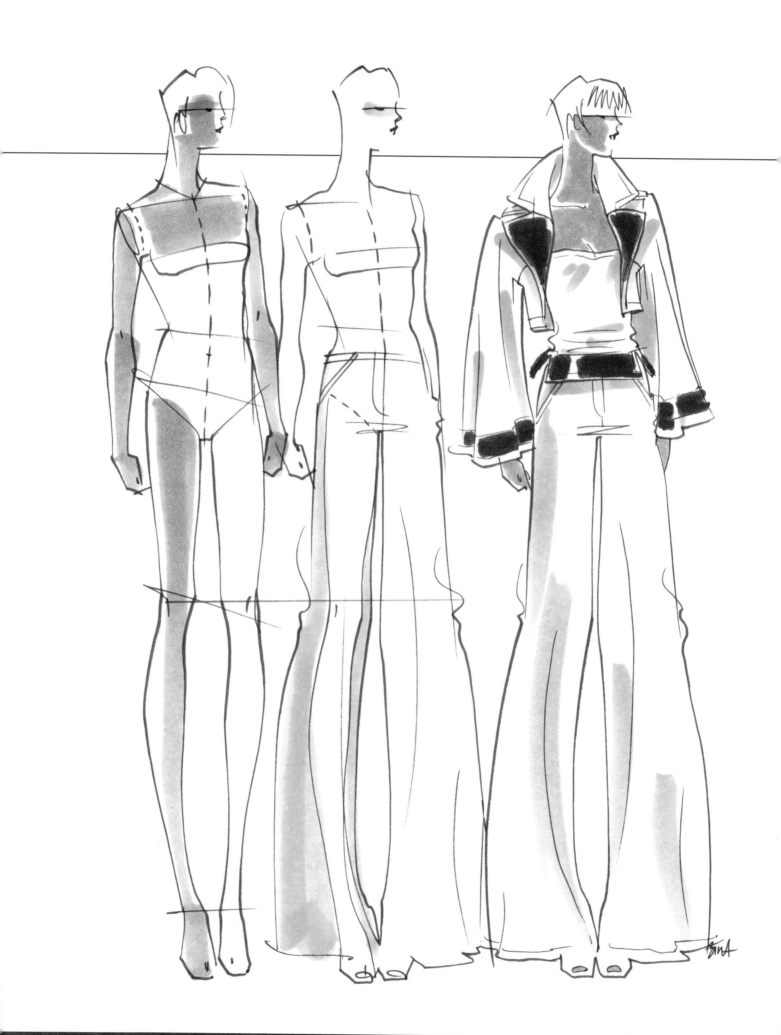

6

Drawing Flats and Specs

This chapter covers an area that often is overlooked by both the novice and the professional, but is one that is integral to the design process. Throughout the fashion design industry, flats and specs are used in conjunction with illustrations in a portfolio and on the job.

Garments worn, posed on the figure, as illustrations, are informative but not as precise as that same garment as a flat or as a spec. Take the garment off the figure, laying the garment out flat. That flat will communicate more of the garment's shape and construction detail. To make the garment's flat into a spec, including its shape and construction, you add measurements of all its details for garment production.

All of those measurements are used for pattern grading and sizing. That kind of spec drawing and construction is beyond the scope of this book. The purpose of this chapter is to give you insight into this process, teaching you how to draw flats and specs.

There are two main approaches to drawing flats and specs. One approach is to use the computer; the other is to draw flats freehand (or with the aid of a ruler). Either method is fine, but learning both is recommended. Computer versions of flats can be quicker and more precise than those drawn by hand; however, drawing flats by hand is an industry-based skill and has a more authentic look in a portfolio. Any understanding of how to draw flats, as demonstrated in this chapter, is essential, even when these flats are scanned and then copied by a computer program.

Flat Figure Templates

This static, non-posed realistic body is a reference for drawing flats.

1A. This figure represents the elongated form and is used, as reference, for stylized flats.

1B. These figures have more average proportions and are better reference for the real fit in a flat.

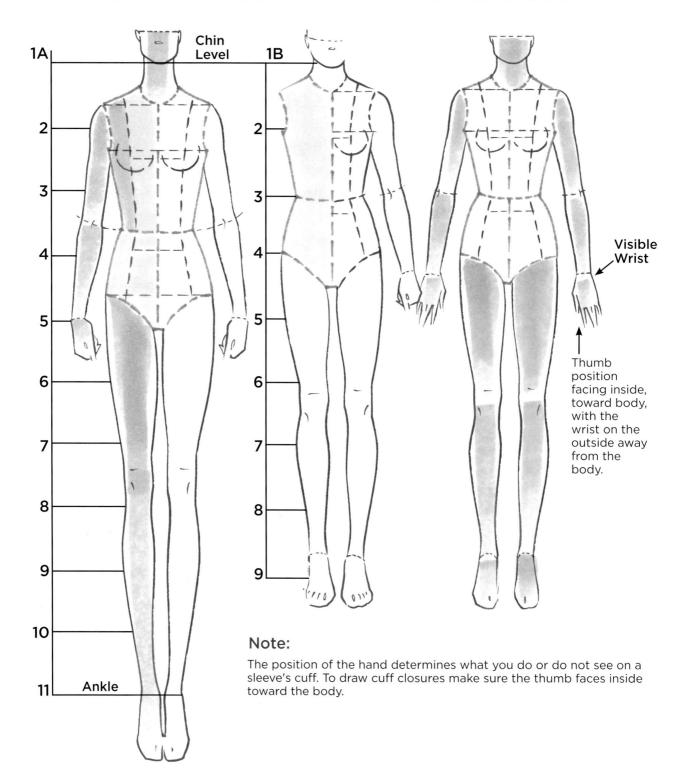

1A

1B

Chin Level

Visible Wrist

Thumb position facing inside, toward body, with the wrist on the outside away from the body.

Ankle

Note:

The position of the hand determines what you do or do not see on a sleeve's cuff. To draw cuff closures make sure the thumb faces inside toward the body.

The flat figure template is an essential form of design reference in both front, back, and profile views. Together, these three body views are a valuable flat drawing resource. You can customize your own flat figure sketch, like with arm positions—options critical for creative armhole, sleeve, or cuff detailing.

Drawing Flats by Hand

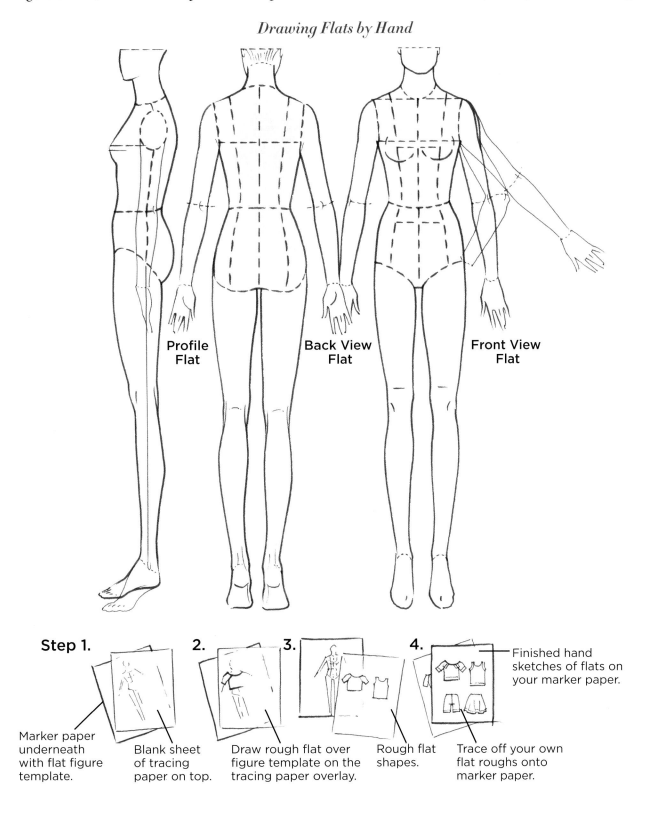

Profile
Flat

Back View
Flat

Front View
Flat

Step 1.

2.

3.

4.

Finished hand
sketches of flats on
your marker paper.

Marker paper
underneath
with flat figure
template.

Blank sheet
of tracing
paper on top.

Draw rough flat over
figure template on the
tracing paper overlay.

Rough flat
shapes.

Trace off your own
flat roughs onto
marker paper.

Figure Formulas for Flats

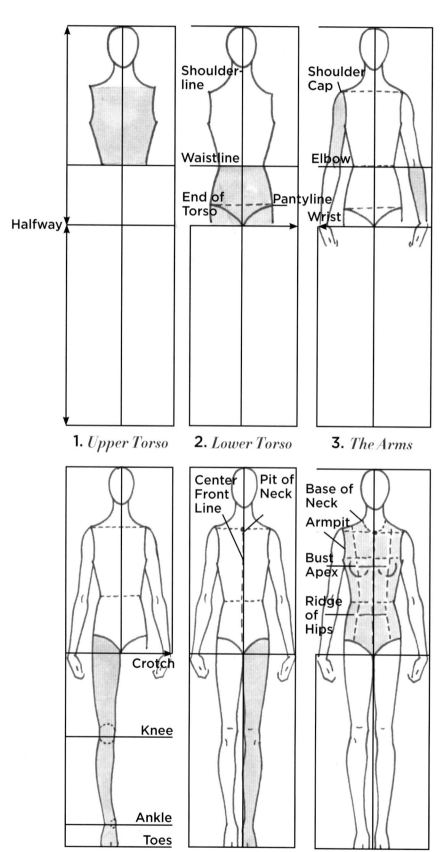

1. *Upper Torso* **2.** *Lower Torso* **3.** *The Arms*

4. *The Legs* **5.** *Center Front* **6.** *Sewing Lines*

This is an example of how to draw the flat figure in segments. These segments work in any size, for any height. This method of drawing is adaptable to your needs.

1. Work on completing the upper torso, to build out the proportions for this figure.

2. Then complete the lower torso.

3. The arms are as long as the torso. Draw them next.

4. The length of the legs is equal to that of the torso (see Chapter 1 measurements). They start at the pantyline and finish at the toes.

5. Center front is an invisible sewing line that you draw from the pit of the neck, down through the middle of the figure into the crotch at the end of the torso.

6. Add in all of the sewing lines on the torso (from Chapter 1). These lines are critical to creating accurate, precise flats or specs for all garments.

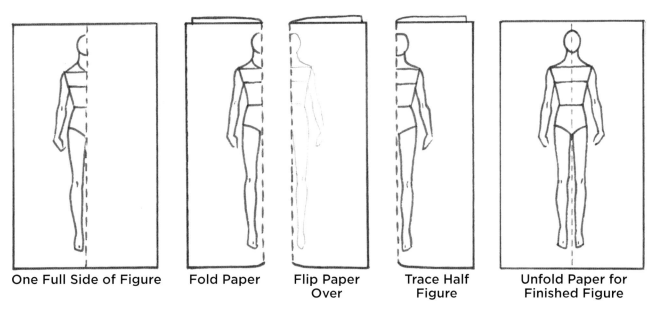

One Full Side of Figure   **Fold Paper**   **Flip Paper Over**   **Trace Half Figure**   **Unfold Paper for Finished Figure**

A flat or croquis figure is one used exclusively for drawing flats (a garment laid out "flat," off the posed fashion figure) or for specs (a garment laid out with all of its measurements or "specifications" for production). These flat or croquis figures have realistic proportions with all the sewing lines on the torso to aid in drawing accurate detail and construction on a flat or a spec. One of the quickest methods for sketching a flat figure is to draw one full half of the figure, fold over the paper, trace off that existing half to create a mirror image, and unfold the paper to reveal a figure with matching sides.

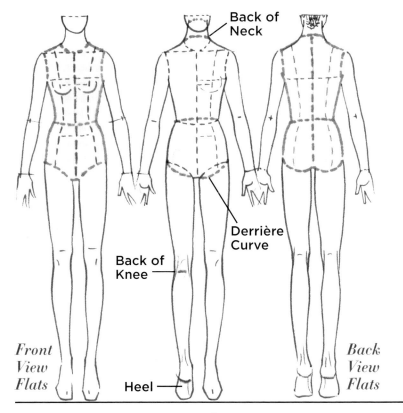

Back of Neck

Derrière Curve

Back of Knee

Heel

Front View Flats

Back View Flats

Reversing the Image

Another shortcut in drawing figures for flats or specs is to trace over your front view and turn it into a matching, reverse image—a back view flat figure. First, very little of the actual outline has to change except for the head, hands, and feet. Second, in the interior, or the torso, the prominent changes are at the back of the neck, the elimination of the bustline, and the convex curves of the derrière muscles at the end of the torso.

Tops: Templates for Shirts, Blouses, and Dresses

The upper torso has a unique blend of stylistic focal points that are complex enough to warrant its own template dedicated to just tops—blouses, shirts, blazers, and dresses—anything that starts at the shoulders. There are so many areas of intersecting sewing lines cutting across the neck, the chest, and the arms that it makes sense to have a specific figure half (or whole) just for tops. The figure template devoted to bottoms, starting at the waist, is on the next spread. On this page are the types of flat figure templates that you need for tops, with enough sewing lines to help you with the accuracy and tailoring that make or break your flats.

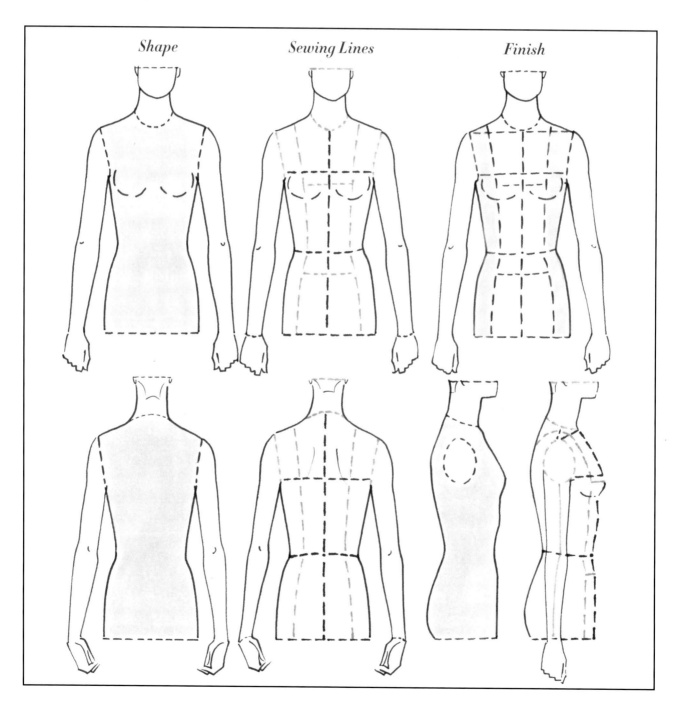

Shape   *Sewing Lines*   *Finish*

A. This example illustrates the arms being manipulated to show how fit, construction details, and proportions are explored on a figure template and are used to emphasize shape and fit in your sketching process.

B. and C. These two templates address the form lines that better serve the tailoring on a dress bodice or blouse, making it easier to match left and right sides of construction details in a flat sketch.

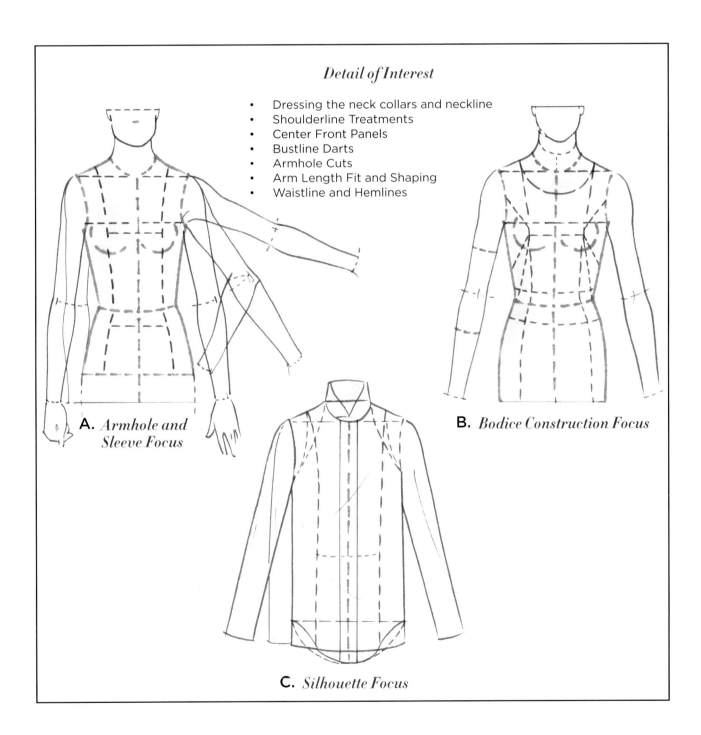

Detail of Interest

- Dressing the neck collars and neckline
- Shoulderline Treatments
- Center Front Panels
- Bustline Darts
- Armhole Cuts
- Arm Length Fit and Shaping
- Waistline and Hemlines

A. *Armhole and Sleeve Focus*

B. *Bodice Construction Focus*

C. *Silhouette Focus*

Bottoms: Templates for Shorts, Pants, and Skirts

The lower torso has its own set of design criteria. The waistline, hips, and legs are areas of design definition, like pockets or the rise and inseam, in bottom flats. Shorts deal with leg length issues. Pants have that thin margin of space all the way down the legs. Skirts often rely on shape as well as length.

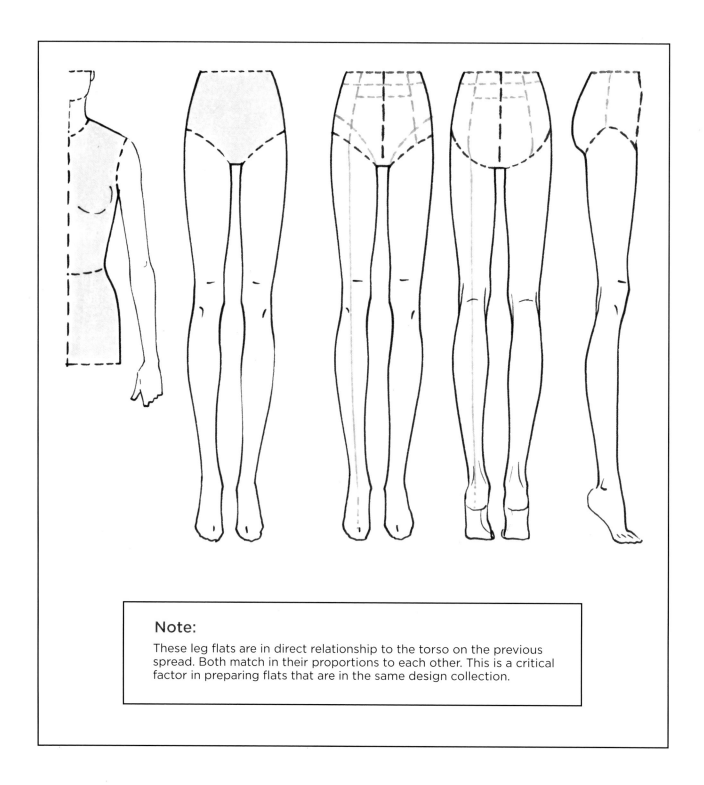

Note:
These leg flats are in direct relationship to the torso on the previous spread. Both match in their proportions to each other. This is a critical factor in preparing flats that are in the same design collection.

The realistic contours of the leg are not as crucial to your flat as the actual length of the leg from crotch to knee and knee to ankle, the knee being approximately halfway between the crotch and the ankle. Another area of interest, especially for a trouser-cut pant, is the middle of the hips and leg where the pinch pleat or pressed crease runs down, perpendicular to the hem.

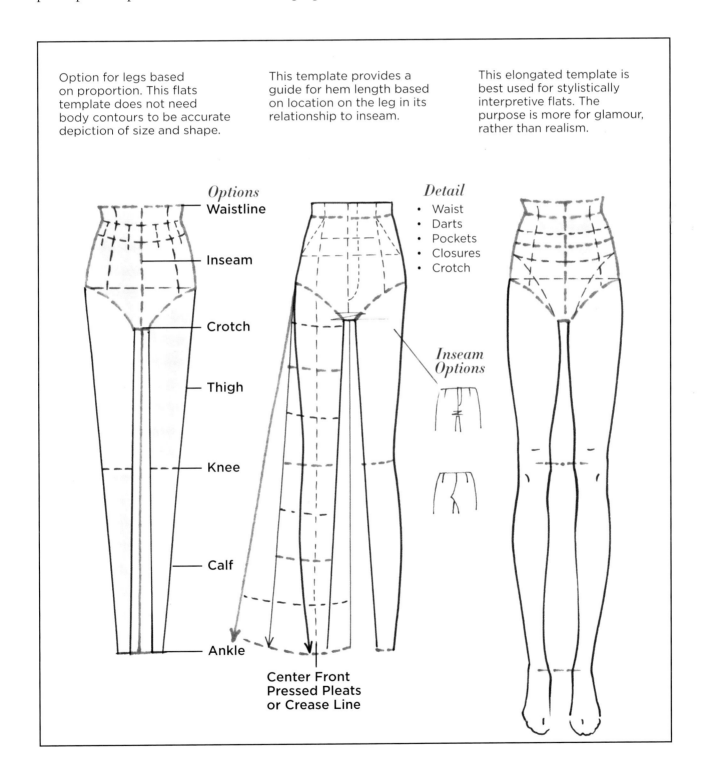

Option for legs based on proportion. This flats template does not need body contours to be accurate depiction of size and shape.

This template provides a guide for hem length based on location on the leg in its relationship to inseam.

This elongated template is best used for stylistically interpretive flats. The purpose is more for glamour, rather than realism.

Options
Waistline
Inseam
Crotch
Thigh
Knee
Calf
Ankle

Center Front
Pressed Pleats
or Crease Line

Detail
• Waist
• Darts
• Pockets
• Closures
• Crotch

Inseam Options

Structure for Flats

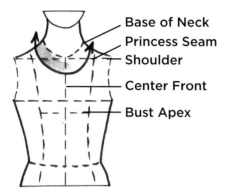

- Base of Neck
- Princess Seam
- Shoulder
- Center Front
- Bust Apex

Precision
Try to be specific, consistent, and precise about every cut and shape in your design.

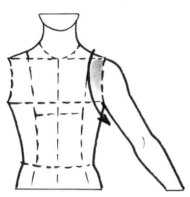

  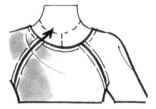

Construction
Make your details fit exactly where they are supposed to fall on the body.

Shaping
Remember all of the tailoring details that you put into the fit of your garment.

Note:
Figure demo inside/under these flats does not exist on a finished on-the-job flat.

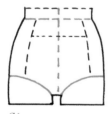    

Size
Practice drawing flats in all different types of fit and styling to build your skills.

Too Small
You know your flats are too small when you cannot draw in critical detailing.

Information structured into a flat is a balance between too much information (confusing) and too little information (no construction focus). The flat you draw has one primary job: to report on fit, shape, and construction, down to the last line of topstitching. This spread points out some of the information and structure you want to perform on your flats, reasons to opt for one method or another, and the benefits or consequences in these choices. For instance, the examples on the right demonstrate how one shape can be sewn in a variety of techniques and still have the same fit. Notice that the use of three thick to thin types of pen lines can help you to achieve these sketching nuances for flats.

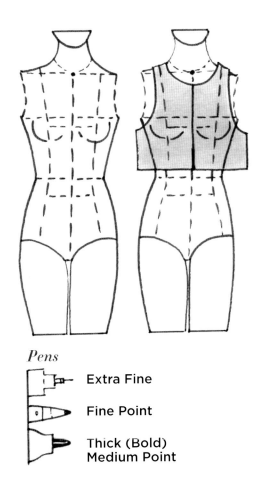

Pens

▭ Extra Fine

▭ Fine Point

▭ Thick (Bold) Medium Point

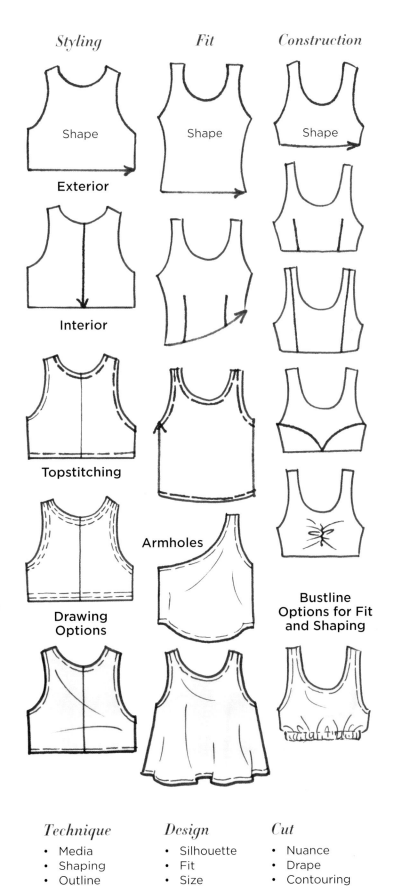

Styling	*Fit*	*Construction*
Shape	Shape	Shape
Exterior		
Interior		
Topstitching		
	Armholes	
Drawing Options		Bustline Options for Fit and Shaping

Technique	*Design*	*Cut*
• Media	• Silhouette	• Nuance
• Shaping	• Fit	• Drape
• Outline	• Size	• Contouring

Swimwear and Lingerie Flats

Swimwear and lingerie share a lot of interchangeable fashion shapes, but lingerie is usually given the more structured, complex construction treatments. This design detailing goes beyond the molded and stretch fabrics for function and variety. Still, with the similarities, the same croquis or flats figure template can be used for both swimwear and lingerie garments.

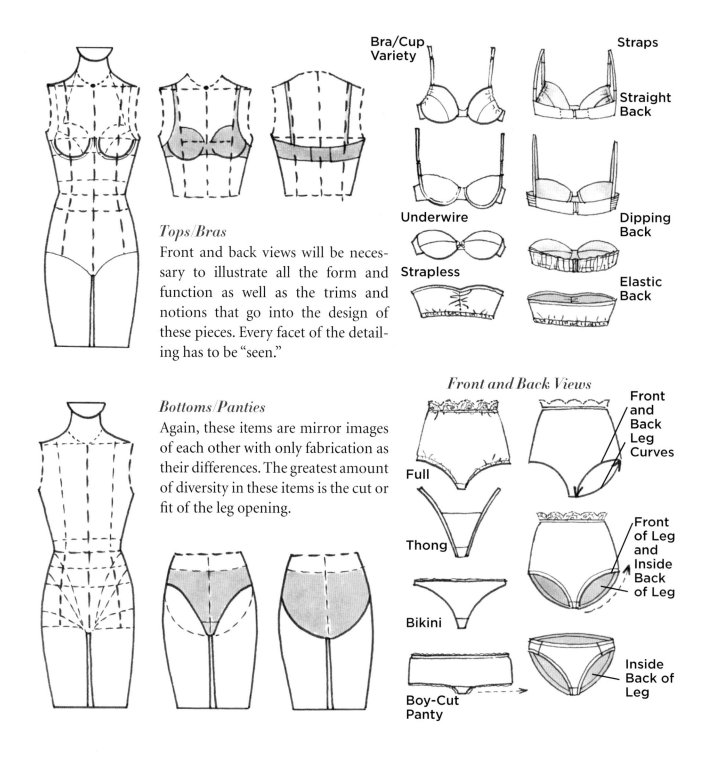

Tops/Bras

Front and back views will be necessary to illustrate all the form and function as well as the trims and notions that go into the design of these pieces. Every facet of the detailing has to be "seen."

Bra/Cup Variety

Straps

Straight Back

Underwire

Dipping Back

Strapless

Elastic Back

Bottoms/Panties

Again, these items are mirror images of each other with only fabrication as their differences. The greatest amount of diversity in these items is the cut or fit of the leg opening.

Front and Back Views

Full

Thong

Bikini

Boy-Cut Panty

Front and Back Leg Curves

Front of Leg and Inside Back of Leg

Inside Back of Leg

Swimwear and lingerie flats can be a challenge to draw when you attempt to sketch all the delicate detailing in the straps, the seaming, the tiny little closures, or exquisitely fine edging that is integral to the garment—details that can't possibly fit on the average-size figure croquis or template. The solution is this larger, torso-only, flat figure. A template this size can accommodate more information, yet still leave you with the agility to fit a bunch of flats (your collection) on a page.

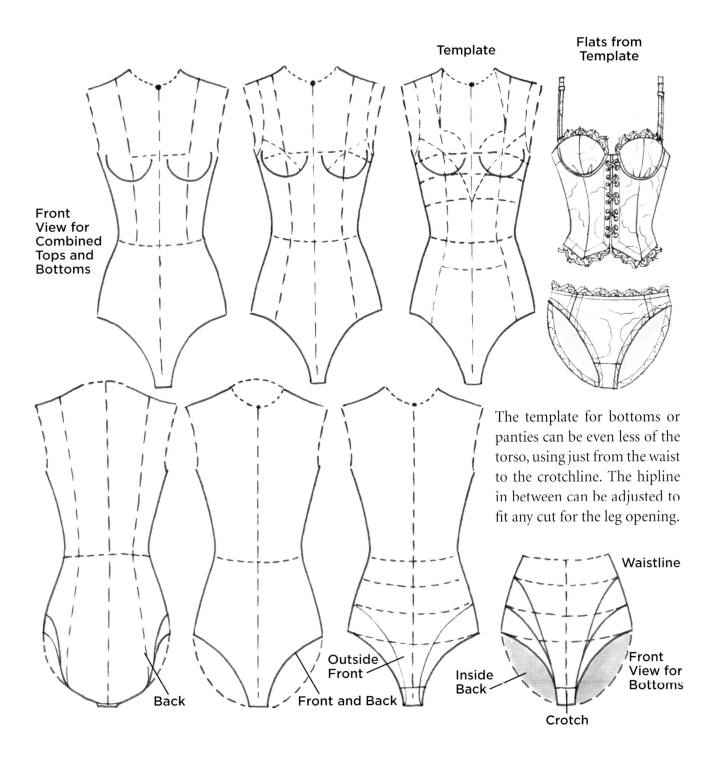

Template

Flats from Template

Front View for Combined Tops and Bottoms

The template for bottoms or panties can be even less of the torso, using just from the waist to the crotchline. The hipline in between can be adjusted to fit any cut for the leg opening.

Back

Outside Front

Front and Back

Inside Back

Waistline

Front View for Bottoms

Crotch

Comprehensive Flats

Flats point to the production value of a garment. They are the precursor to the spec (see end of chapter) and to your pattern drafting of a garment. Flats are drawn to define shape, fit, construction, and sometimes fabrication—its mix, drape, or volume.

Flats by definition are more factual, more precise than the same garment drawn on the figure, posed for dramatic looks and styling. Flats show how a garment is to be made versus how it will be worn. Here is a sampling of what you want your flat to say, and how to say it.

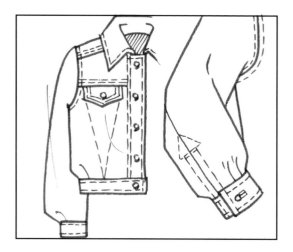

Shape

Cuff Detail

A flat drawn on or over a grid (or graph) can reinforce its symmetry. Left to right side detailing can get more exacting. It also helps to emphasize the back of arm construction by folding over the sleeve.

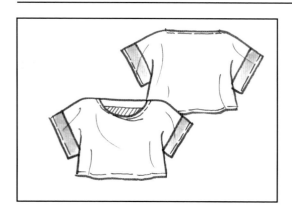

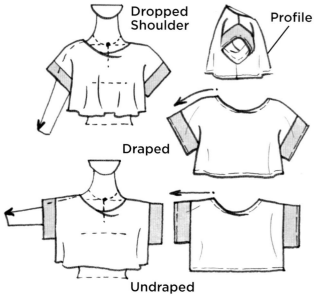

Dropped Shoulder

Profile

Draped

Undraped

What a garment looks like on and off the body can be different and may need to be drawn with two types of flats to convey how those looks (flat shapes) change.

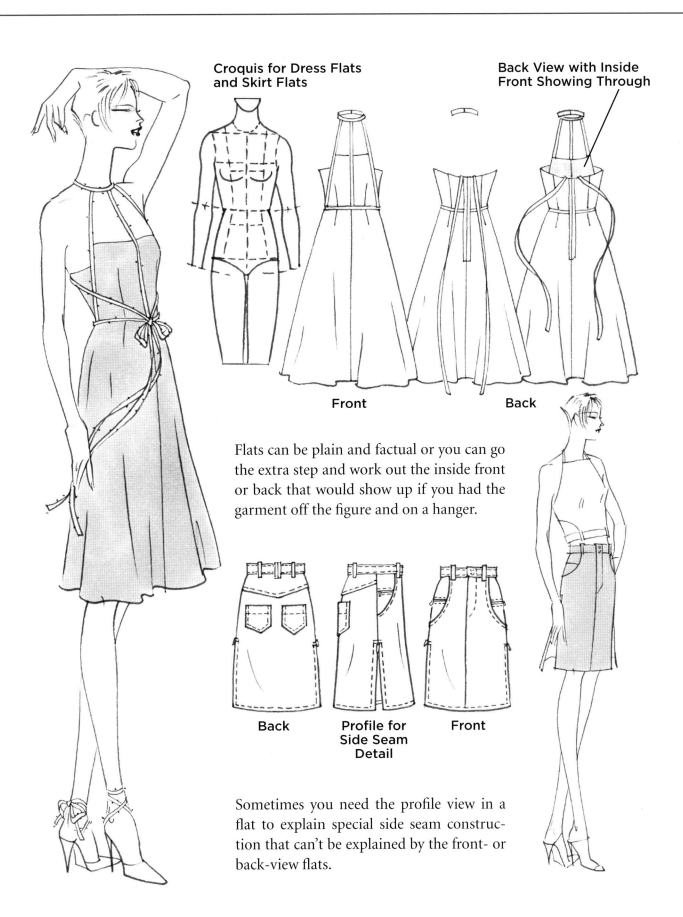

Croquis for Dress Flats and Skirt Flats

Back View with Inside Front Showing Through

Front   Back

Flats can be plain and factual or you can go the extra step and work out the inside front or back that would show up if you had the garment off the figure and on a hanger.

Back   Profile for Side Seam Detail   Front

Sometimes you need the profile view in a flat to explain special side seam construction that can't be explained by the front- or back-view flats.

Women's Outerwear Flats

Outerwear flats introduce fabric weights, heavier materials, wider silhouettes, volume, and an emphasis on closures—buttoning (or lack of it). These garments are worn over other clothes, which adds volume to your shape, while sleeves often get wider with deeper armholes to accommodate the layering of garments plus a lining (if there is one). With closures and button placement you need to get very specific, as illustrated on this page.

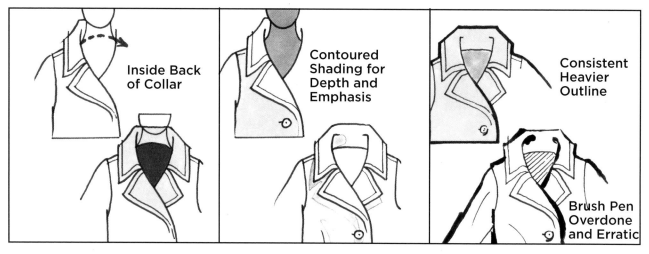

Working on Construction Details for Buttons

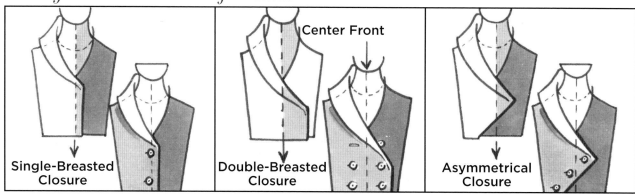

Options in a Trench Coat Flat

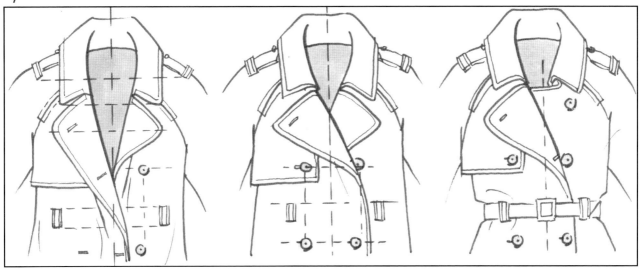

Match Up the Detailing
Left to Right; Coat Open

Planning for the
Double-Breasted Coat

Coat Closed, Belted
Buckle on Center Front

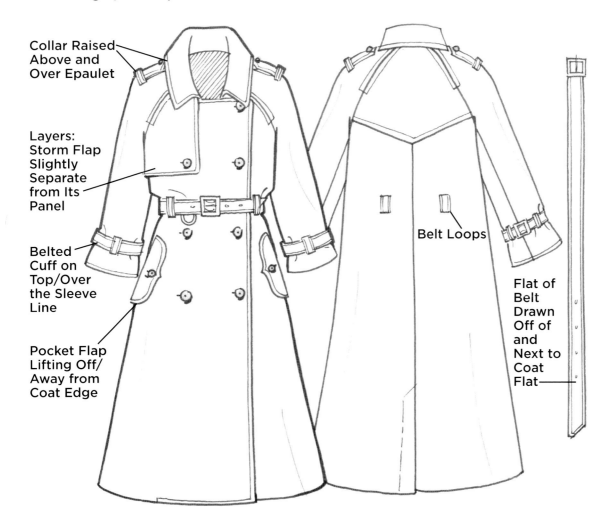

Collar Raised
Above and
Over Epaulet

Layers:
Storm Flap
Slightly
Separate
from Its
Panel

Belted
Cuff on
Top/Over
the Sleeve
Line

Pocket Flap
Lifting Off/
Away from
Coat Edge

Belt Loops

Flat of
Belt
Drawn
Off of
and
Next to
Coat
Flat

Presentation or Portfolio Flats

1. *Arranged by Outfit*

2. *Coordinated by Fabric*

3. *Collected into Categories*

Presentation or portfolio flats are drawn to emphasize the number, options, and style in a collection of garments. Illustrated here are six different layouts that fit into the business needs of the fashion industry. The layouts shown here can be adapted to use in any designer category, season, or price point, and could include accessories.

1. Flats can be drawn in a column, suspended over each other, implying layers or a "look" to an outfit. Each set of garments gets its own invisible center front that connects its "look."

2. Design collections have featured fabrications. This layout shows which garments come in which fabrics. Do one row of garments per fabric, combining tops and bottoms by running an invisible ruler-line through their collars or waistbands.

3. This layout divides the flats into two groups, tops and bottoms. Invisible lines run through the shoulderline for the tops and through the waistband for the bottoms. These rows are independent of each other (not in columns as in #1).

4. Compositions are based on pleasing forms of balanced volume, shapes, and fabrics. These flats are drawn in proportion to each other, without crowding on the page or uneven slanting, and can include or exclude back views.

5. This mirror image of one garment, front to back, maximizes design information by doubling the level of construction detail. To conserve space on the page, step all the back views (up) above or down (below) the fronts. Be consistent with this layout for the whole page or grouping.

6. This composition, unlike #2, emphasizes the repeats in fabrics (or color choices) per one garment for all the silhouettes in the collection, which is a marketing mix for coordinating outfits.

4. *Arranged into Layout*

5. *Arranged Front and Back Views*

6. *Arranged in Colorways*

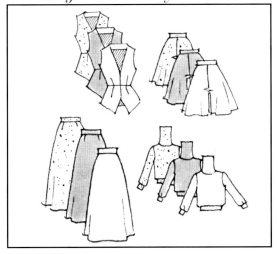

All front views stepped up in three different fabrics for each garment

7. *Explaining a Garment*

- How It Works
- What Fabrics
- Proportions between Garments

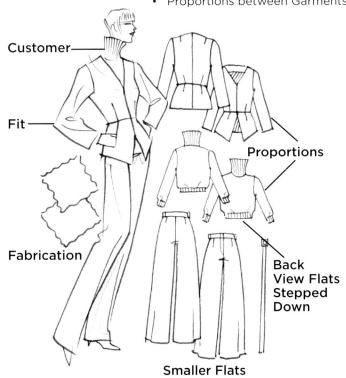

Customer

Fit

Fabrication

Proportions

Back View Flats Stepped Down

Smaller Flats

Smaller-Sized Figure with Larger-Sized Flats to Emphasize Garment Construction

Larger Flats

Croquis Mixed with Flats

Croquis, a group of figures for fashion design, can also be teamed up with flats. The flats can be of the garments worn by the figures or they can be the other coordinating pieces that go with the group. The flats can be drawn in proportion to the size of the clothing on the figures or they can be drawn to a different scale. Swatches can also be added for rendering purposes. You can add information to flats in any area in your sketch. (Flats with captions or callouts are referred to as "talking" flats.) This kind of drawing represents a working fashion journal or a diary of ideas.

Notice that when these croquis line up they have the same proportions and the same ceiling and floor to stand on even though the poses are different. Their matching proportions make it easy to read the fashion message at a quick glance.

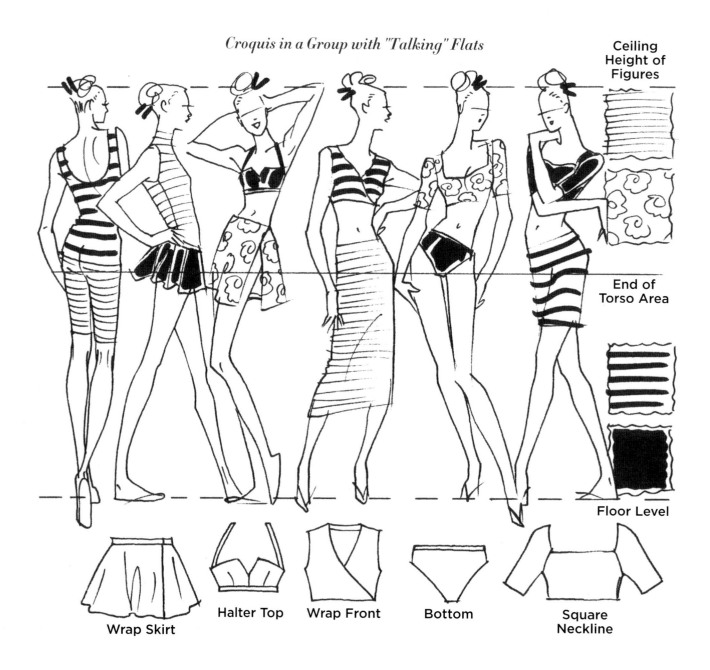

Croquis in a Group with "Talking" Flats

Ceiling Height of Figures

End of Torso Area

Floor Level

Wrap Skirt

Halter Top

Wrap Front

Bottom

Square Neckline

Flats and Figures Mixed

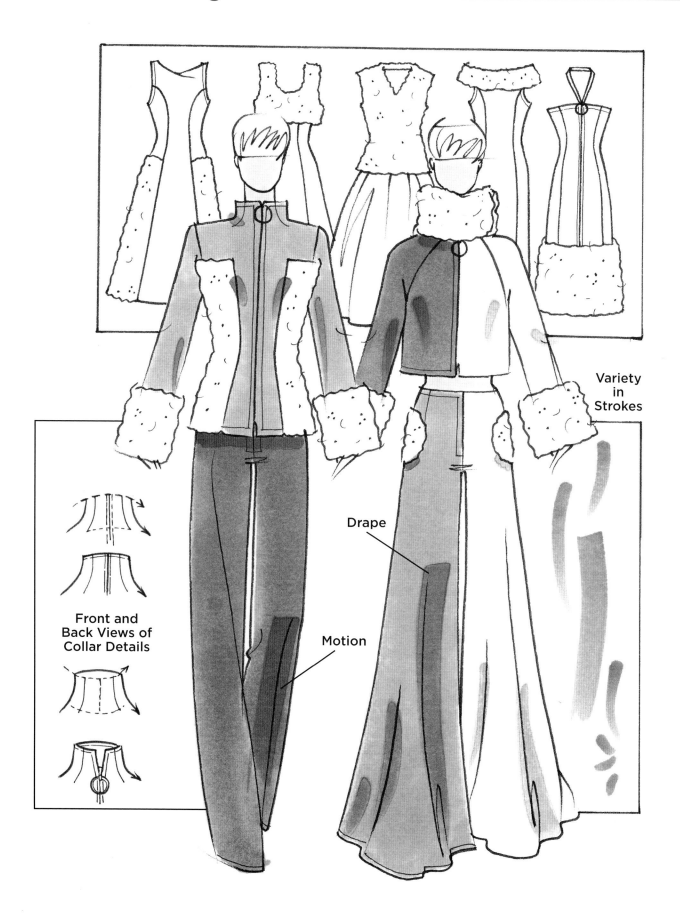

Front and
Back Views of
Collar Details

Motion

Drape

Variety
in
Strokes

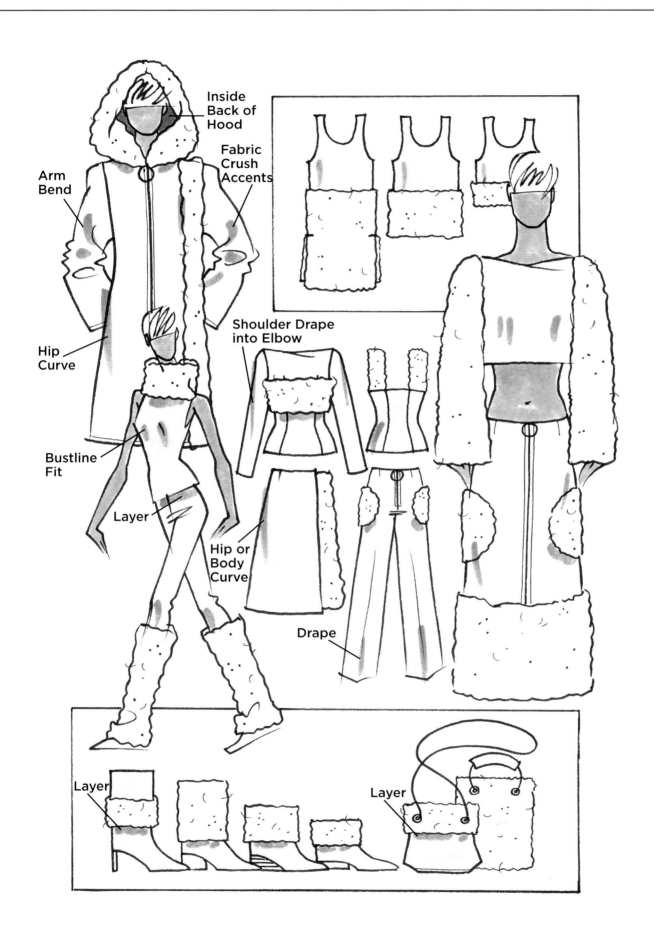

Inside
Back of
Hood

Fabric
Crush
Accents

Arm
Bend

Hip
Curve

Bustline
Fit

Shoulder Drape
into Elbow

Layer

Hip or
Body
Curve

Drape

Layer

Layer

Flats and Figures Mixed (continued)

Contrast in Textures

Accent on Swing of Folds

Layer

Inside Back

Elbow to Wrist Drape

Knee to Ankle Drape

Sending the Accurate Visual Message with Your Flats

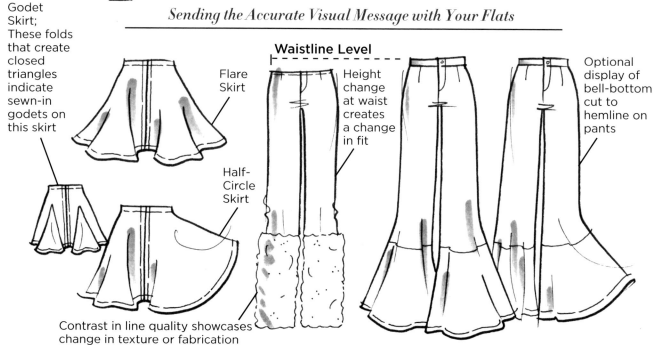

Godet Skirt; These folds that create closed triangles indicate sewn-in godets on this skirt

Flare Skirt

Half-Circle Skirt

Waistline Level

Height change at waist creates a change in fit

Optional display of bell-bottom cut to hemline on pants

Contrast in line quality showcases change in texture or fabrication

There Are Many Different Methods to Lay Out Your Flats with Your Croquis

Note:

No darts in a shaped or fitted top indicates stretch fabric.

A. Croquis-sized flats can be larger than figure.

B. Flats can be layered as to which goes over what.

C. Hoods on a flat can be shown up or down.

Note:

Use of a variety of knit rows helps to define type of knit treatments.

D. Flats can be lined up at the shoulder to display proportions.

E. In a space crunch, pants have been lined up with the waistline level of the turtleneck (top) flat.

Specs

Specs, short for specifications, are the last drawing step for a garment before it goes into pattern drafting, a sample is made, and put into production. To this end, the spec must be precise in shape, fit, and construction detail. Meticulous measurements are drawn across both the exterior and the interior of this flat. Accuracy on every level is your goal when drawing specs.

Almost every design specialization or fashion category will have its own set of criteria for spec measurements on a garment. What is measured for (innerwear) lingerie may be different from what is measured for outerwear (coats). Here are some generalized areas of spec measurements to explain their fit analysis and context for the lines that you will be drawing around and through the forms. All are important to practice. On the job, each of the dotted lines or measurements would get a number for its distance between arrows.

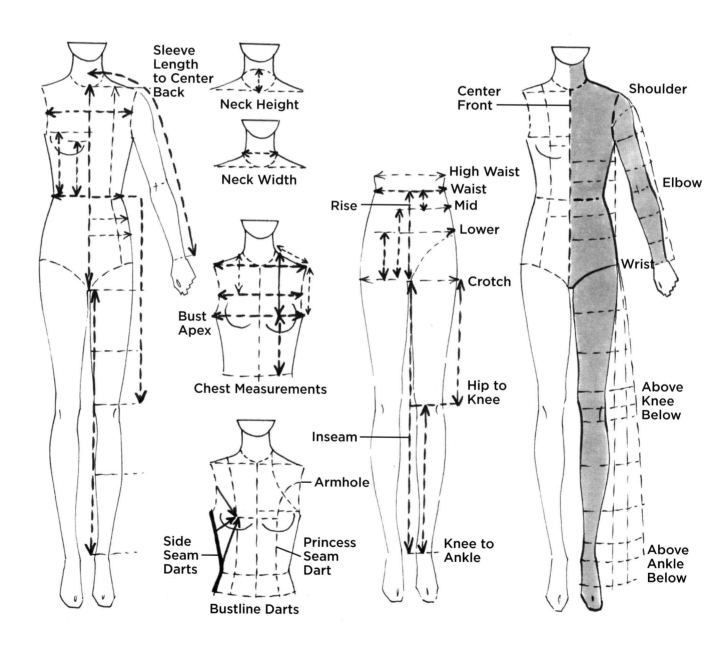

To understand a spec, why it is drawn, and how it is used, examine these two pages. There are specific figure measurements that directly correspond with garment measurements. This is one factor in the fit or sizing of clothes. Mass-produced clothing that uses general measurements is different from made-to-order clothing that is cut and sewn with one person's exact measurements. Using size 10 as an example, the measurement of all of the details in a garment must be executed in relationship to the garment being a size 10. Within the garment, these measurements are both figure and nonfigure references. Reference to the figure in a spec could mean the measuring of the distance from center back all the way to the wrist, for example. An example of a nonfigure reference to a measurement in a spec could be for the placket, pocket, or lapel.

Note: A sloper is a basic pattern for a garment section, without style lines or seam allowances developed from model form, live model specific measurements, or manufacturer's specifications. It is used to develop original patterns and create new designs. A sloper also is called a standard pattern, foundation pattern, block pattern, and master pattern.

Women's Chart

Sizes	XS	Small		Medium		Large		XL
	4	6	8	10	12	14	16	18
Bust	32½"	33½"	34½"	35½"	37"	38½"	40"	41½"
Waist	24"	25"	26"	27"	28"	29"	30"	31"
Hip	35"	36"	37"	38"	39"	41"	43"	45"
Sleeve	28½"	29"	29½"	30"	30½"	31"	31½"	32"

Match body measurement to corresponding size.

Men's Chart

Sizes	XS	Small		Medium		Large		XL	
	26	28	30	32	34	36	38	40	42
Neck	13½"	14"	14½"	15"	15½"	16"	16½"	17"	17½"
Chest	32"	34"	36"	38"	40"	42"	44"	46"	48"
Waist	26"	28"	30"	32"	34"	36"	38"	40"	42"
Sleeve	32"	32½"	33"	33½"	34"	34½"	35"	35½"	36"

Match body measurement to corresponding size.

Unisex Chart

Unisex Size	XS	Small	Medium	Large
Women's Size	6-8	10-12	14-16	18

Women can wear many men's items. This chart shows women's equivalent sizes for these items. Unisex sizing is based on the men's size chart.

Belts

XS	Small	Medium	Large	XL
25"-27"	27"-29"	30"-32"	33"-35"	36"-38"

Match waist measurement to corresponding size.

Hats

	Small	Medium	Large	XL
Head Size	21½"-22"	22"-22¾"	22¾"-23½"	23½"-24¼"
Hat Size	6⅞"-7"	7"-7¼"	7½"-7⅝"	8"-8¼"

Socks

	Small	Large
Shoe Size	5-9	9-12
Sock Size	9-11	11-13

Measuring and Detailing for Specs

Specs must be drawn with accuracy for all the measurements and details to make visual sense because specs are used for production and pattern drafting to begin construction of a garment. Because of the exact nature of a spec, you must practice precision sketching for details on a flat sketch. On these two pages are some of the measurement lines that you will draw as well as some of the detailing that you may need to do in a blowup or enlarged-size spec. Remember that every line and edge is vital in these drawings. You have to regard all of the construction on a garment as information that you must draw.

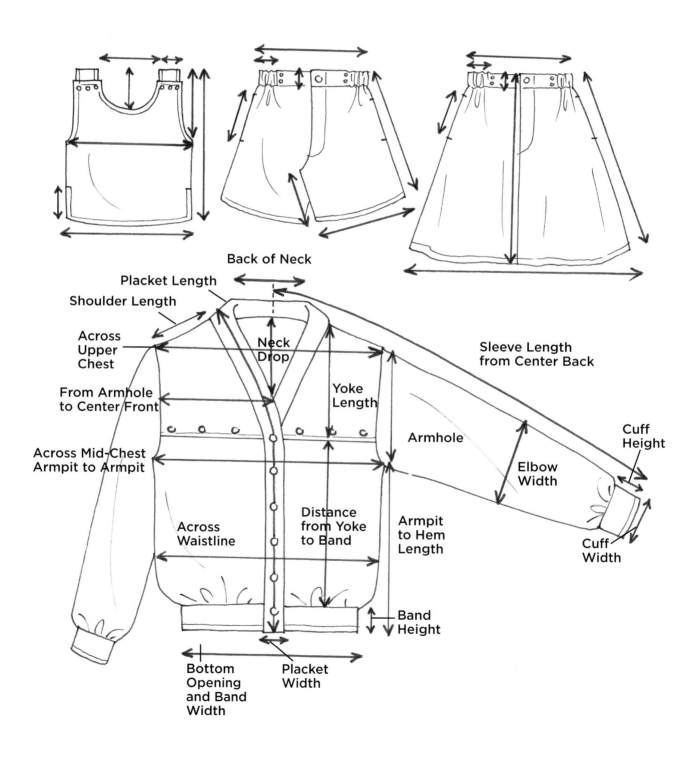

Nuances in Detailing for Flats and Specs

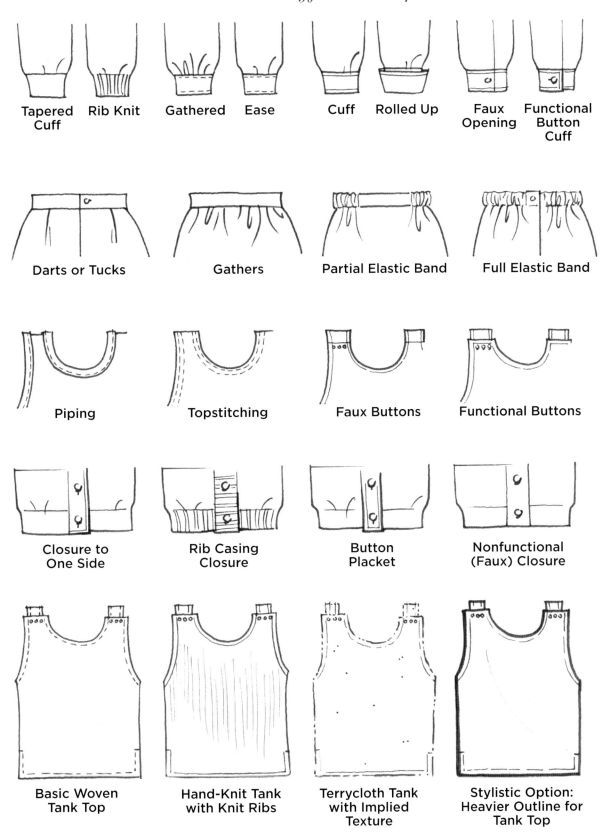

Tapered Cuff   Rib Knit   Gathered   Ease   Cuff   Rolled Up   Faux Opening   Functional Button Cuff

Darts or Tucks   Gathers   Partial Elastic Band   Full Elastic Band

Piping   Topstitching   Faux Buttons   Functional Buttons

Closure to One Side   Rib Casing Closure   Button Placket   Nonfunctional (Faux) Closure

Basic Woven Tank Top   Hand-Knit Tank with Knit Ribs   Terrycloth Tank with Implied Texture   Stylistic Option: Heavier Outline for Tank Top

Analyzing a Garment for Flats and Specs

This spread and the following one illustrate methods of garment analysis that can help you create a stronger, more accurate fashion sketch. The study of one garment, in these examples an oversized cardigan-style jacket, can be critical to communicating specific design information. Keep in mind that the garment you want to draw, especially if it exists only in your imagination, has to convince someone else of its fashion potential and its form on and off the figure, as a flat or as a spec. It is the job of your sketch of a garment to inspire as well as inform someone about how to make that item or why to buy it. If your sketch is clear and precise, it will stand out, and it will be successful in its mission.

Precision in Hand Drawing

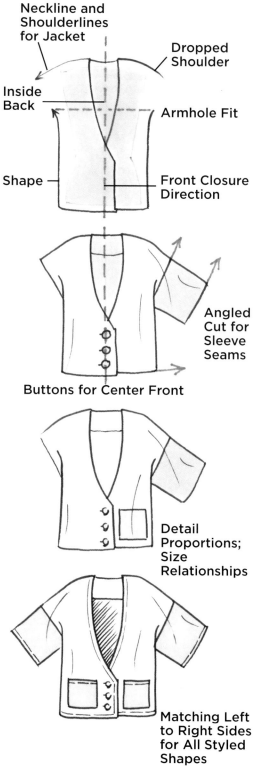

Neckline and Shoulderlines for Jacket

Dropped Shoulder

Inside Back

Armhole Fit

Shape

Front Closure Direction

Buttons for Center Front

Angled Cut for Sleeve Seams

Detail Proportions; Size Relationships

Matching Left to Right Sides for All Styled Shapes

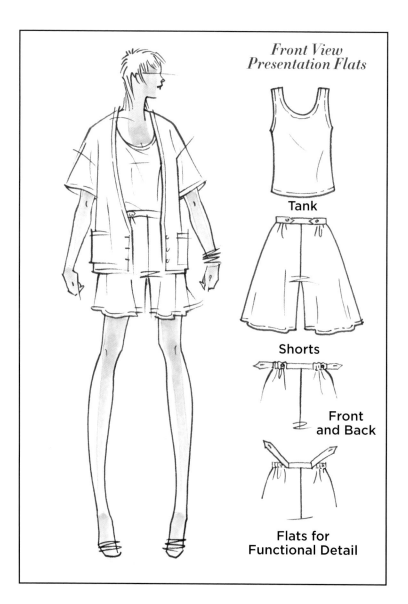

Front View Presentation Flats

Tank

Shorts

Front and Back

Flats for Functional Detail

Breaking down a sketch into its separate components is another method of study, of processing information about your garment. On the one hand you are learning to draw more meticulously; on the other you are creating, finalizing your concept for this design down to the last detail (short of the measurements for production spec of your creation). This page also shows you how to draw a flat freehand, in steps, without using a grid or a croquis figure as reference. Of course, in your sketch, you would not use the dotted lines or gray tone and all eight steps would be condensed into a single sketch of a garment.

Pencil or Pen

A free-hand sketch means drawing without the support of the flats figure template as your base of reference.

Media Options for Sketching Your Flats by Hand

Drawing Steps

1. Neckline over the center front line on chest

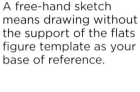

2. Completing neckline and closure direction over center front

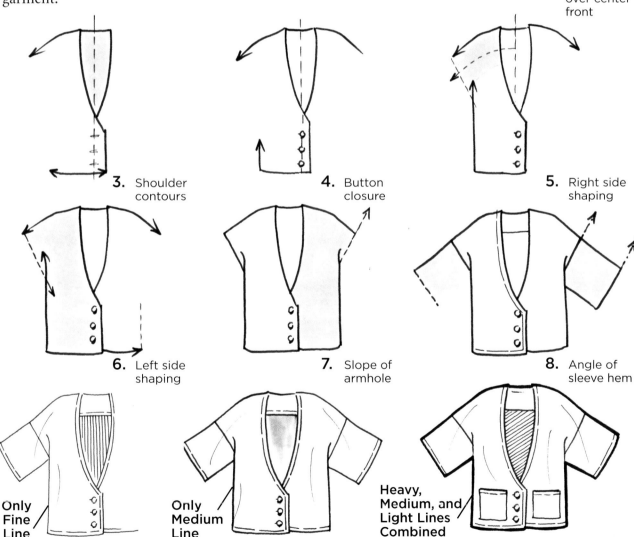

3. Shoulder contours

4. Button closure

5. Right side shaping

6. Left side shaping

7. Slope of armhole

8. Angle of sleeve hem

Only Fine Line

Only Medium Line

Heavy, Medium, and Light Lines Combined

Flats and Specs

The examples on this page demonstrate how and why to compare one garment to another. You need to understand the relationship between the pieces of a collection or in an outfit. Without comparisons, how could you decide if the jacket was longer, shorter, wider, or bigger than the other units in the collection or in an outfit? Proportion is everything in fashion. It is the driving force in trends. One season is oversized, the next is not; tight is in, loose is out. You draw to interpret these style nuances. Your flats reflect these trends. Proportions affect everything from sewing, to fabric, to all other production concerns.

It is critical to draw the inside, outside, front, and back proportions of this jacket shown on the facing page accurately. The measurements for producing this jacket make sense visually as well as numerically.

Proportion Ratios

Size, volume, cut. How to gauge the relationship of fit from one piece to another.

Tank to Shorts

Tank to Jacket

Shorts to Jacket

Line Up for Lengths between Garments

Overlap for Proportions of Widths between Garments

Sample Spec	
Body length from H.S.P. to tail	A
Body width from shoulder seam to shoulder seam	B
Body width 1″ below armhole	C
Body width 16″ below from H.S.P.	D
Sleeve length from C.B. to end of sleeve	E
Sleeve length from shoulder seam	F
Armhole straight measure at seam	G
Sleeve width 4″ below shoulder to underseam	H
Mid-armhole to mid-armhole width	I
Inside neck with measurement	J
Front neck drop from imaginary line to top of front neck	K
Back neck drop from imaginary line	L
Cuff length	M
Cuff width	N
Cuff placket length	O
Cuff placket width	P

COLLAR (width)	(length)
PLACKET (width)	(length)
BUTTON (amount)	(type)
POCKET (width)	(height)
POCKET (from H.S.P.)	(from side seam)

Spec Sheets

Development Sheet for Prototype Sample			
Style #:	319F4	**Sample Needed:**	1/5x
Style Name:	Pieced Rugby	**Delivery Date:**	6/1x
Factory:			
Fabric:	100% Cotton Jersey		

Sketch:

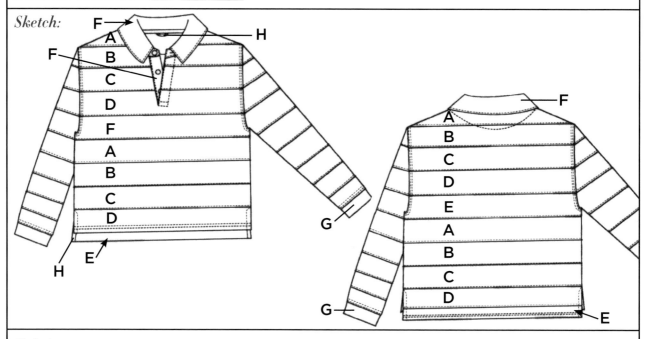

Fabric:

Colorway	Combo Body	Combo: Collar/Placket/CB "U" Facing		Combo: Flat Knit Rib
1	A) Apple Red	F) White		G) Apple Red
1	B) New Navy			
1	C) Gold			
1	D) Emerald			
1	E) Steel Blue			

Trim/Accessories:

Type	Quantity	Size	Placement
Buttons	3	20 ligne (4H Rubber)	CF Placket
H) Twill Tape		3/8"	Side seam hem vents, Neckline, CB loop
(White)			

Construction Details: *** Follow issued label guidelines

* Edge stitch placket
* Cover stitch armholes, sleeve at cuff and hem
* Pieced seams are edge stitched with D.T.M. thread
* Sending sample for construction reference

Initial Spec Sheet

Style #:	319F4
Style Name:	Pieced Rugby
Factory:	
Fabric:	100% Cotton Jersey
Sample Needed:	1/5x
Delivery Date:	6/1x

Sketch:

	POINT OF MEASUREMENT	SPEC
	SHIRT	**3 YR**
1	FRONT LENGTH FROM HPS	17 1/2
2	BACK LENGTH FROM HPS	18 1/2
3	CHEST @ UNDERARM	27
4	BOTTOM WIDTH	28 1/2
5	ACROSS SHOULDER	14
6	SHOULDER SLOPE	3/4
7	ACROSS FRONT	13 1/2
8	ACROSS BACK	13 3/4
9	ARMHOLE CIRCUMFERENCE	13 1/2
10	SLEEVE LENGTH FROM SHOULDER SEAM	12 1/2
11	CUFF HEIGHT	1 1/2
12	CUFF OPENING - RELAXED	6 1/2
13	CUFF OPENING - STRETCHED	10
14	NECK WIDTH @ HPS	5 3/4
15	FRONT NECK DROP FROM HPS TO SEAM	1 7/8
16	BACK NECK DROP FROM HPS TO SEAM	1/2
17	COLLAR HEIGHT @ CB	1 1/2
18	COLLARSTAND HEIGHT @ CB	7/8
19	COLLAR POINT	1 7/8
20	CF PLACKET HEIGHT	4 3/4
21	CF PLACKET WIDTH	1
22	BOTTOM HEM HEIGHT	1
23	SIDE SLIT (FRONT BOTTOM EDGE)	2
24	TOTAL # OF BUTTONS	3
25	STRIPE PIECE WIDTH	2

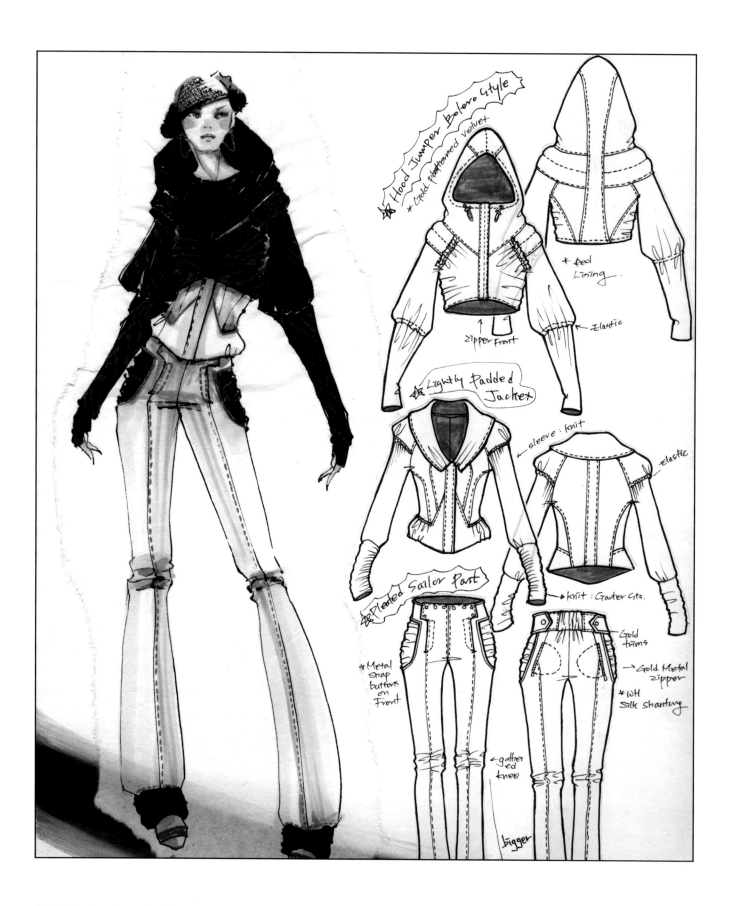

This designer's skiwear designs are whimsical and quirky. These sketches prove that when you
match the spirit of the clothes with your drawing style and layout composition, your presentation's point of view complements your design character. Playful drawing translates into a playful
quality to the skiwear. This symmetry in mood adds to the visual momentum in this layout and the
powerful drawing style of this designer. The flats look just as playful as the design story.

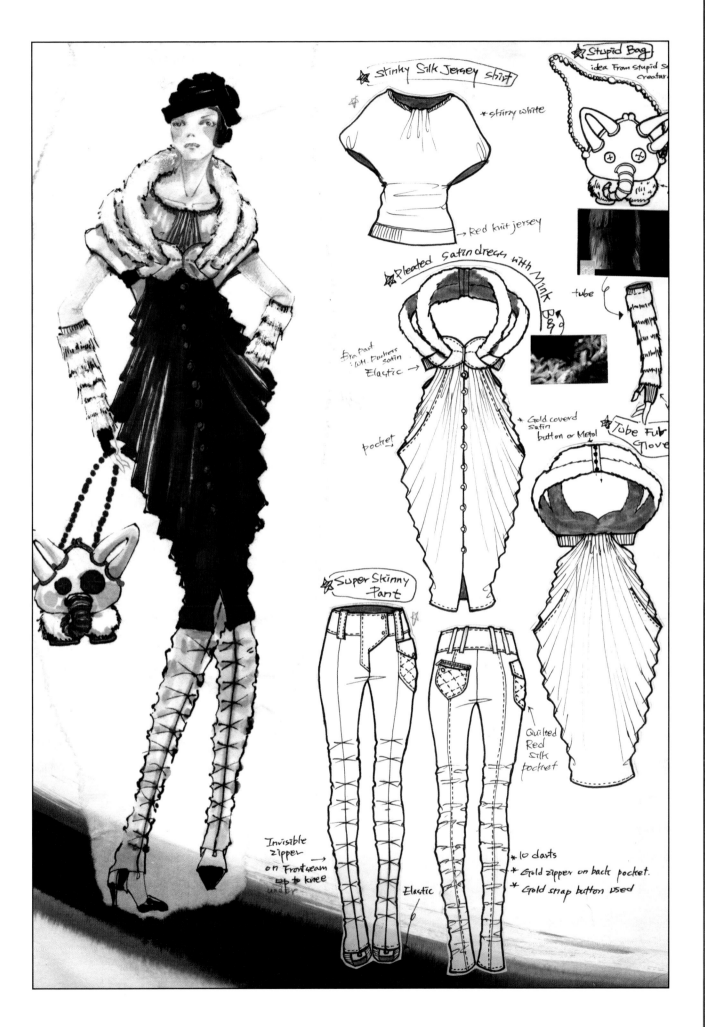

✰ Stinky Silk Jersey shirt
*shinny white
→ Red knit jersey

✰ Stupid Bag,
idea from stupid creatur

tube

✰ Pleated satin dress with Mink
Bra Part
: Wh. Duchess satin
Elastic →
pocket
* Gold covered satin button or Metal

✰ Tube Fur Glove

✰ Super Skinny Pant

Quilted Red Silk pocket

Invisible zipper on front seam up to knee under

Elastic

* 10 darts
* Gold zipper on back pocket.
* Gold snap button used

KIDSWEAR

Jodie's style of rendering is relaxed, combining fun with martial arts poses for her children's sketches. Cultural referencing combines with contemporary looks that keep the style smart and playful. Her style includes fully rendered flats. She used gouache washes, sizes #4 and #8 pointed-tip brushes, markers, and Prismacolor pencils on bond (croquis book) paper.

7

Basic Rendering Techniques

When you use media to color in your sketch, like for fleshtones or fabrics, the process is called rendering. Fleshtones are a personal choice, and there are lots of tints and shades to explore. Fabric in your drawing (in a fashion design illustration) is not just about fiber or weave; it is about the surface interest of a particular fabric—a stripe or a plaid or a floral print, for example. It could be about the other properties of fabrics, such as transparency, textures, or elements of appearance, like matte versus shiny. This chapter provides practice exercises in a single color, using mixed media for that color and exploring the range and possibilities in fashion design fabric rendering.

This chapter has been expanded to include more in-depth color rendering for a wide variety of easy solid color fabrics to more complex surfaces such as jacquards or sheer fabrics. Runway and showroom photographs from *WWD*, the fashion industry's trade paper, and archival designer clothing images are provided as visual references to accentuate some of fashion's staple fabrics. These fabric rendering techniques should serve as a baseline guide to help you invent new coloring solutions for garment illustration. There is always more than one way to render any specific fabric. You will develop your own methods or sets of coloring shortcuts after practicing the preliminary media techniques shown in this chapter. Problem-solving for drawing fabric becomes easier after you become more familiar with the materials and media options. The main goal of this chapter is to create time-saving, simplified rendering techniques to help you work more efficiently to meet your fashion design project deadlines.

Rendering Fleshtones

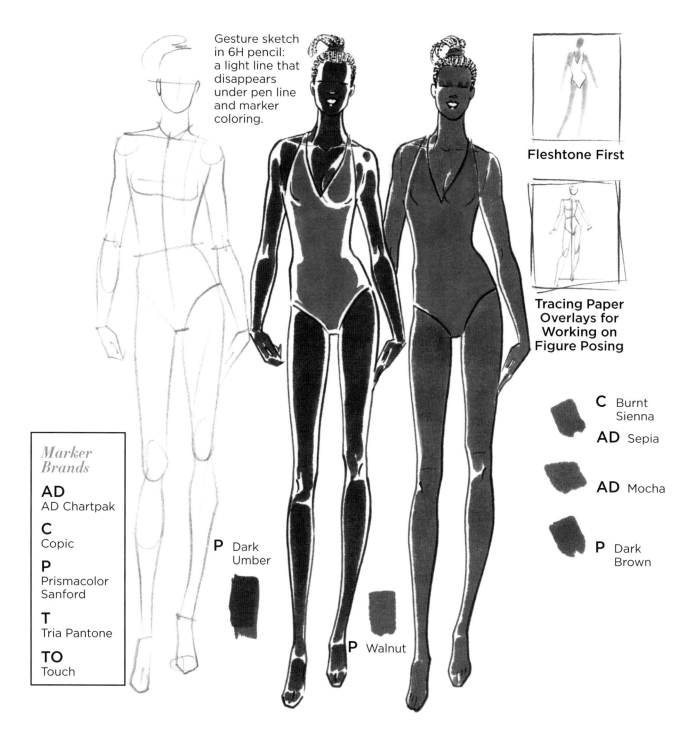

Gesture sketch in 6H pencil: a light line that disappears under pen line and marker coloring.

Fleshtone First

Tracing Paper Overlays for Working on Figure Posing

Marker Brands

AD
AD Chartpak

C
Copic

P
Prismacolor Sanford

T
Tria Pantone

TO
Touch

P Dark Umber

P Walnut

C Burnt Sienna

AD Sepia

AD Mocha

P Dark Brown

You learned to draw a gesture sketch in Chapter 3. A gesture sketch is the beginning pose premise for either a croquis or a finished drawing. It can be done in line on tracing paper or started by applying fleshtone directly onto marker paper. It won't matter if there is a pen or pencil outline on the croquis sketch. Rough or more smooth-looking, it is still a loose drawing for content. As you work on your rendering for fleshtone, remind yourself of all of our nationalities and races, and let your skin tones range through all the various possibilities.

You have many choices when rendering in color. Your choices, as shown here, should look like test strips. Remember to label all your fleshtones (mixes) by brand and by color name so that you will not forget how to replicate those results. Test and label your paper choices as well.

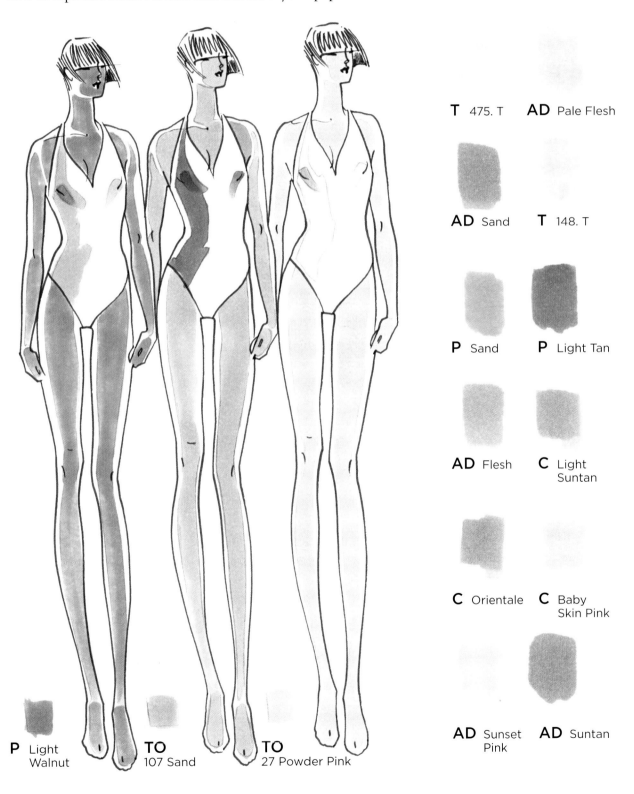

T 475. T   **AD** Pale Flesh

AD Sand   **T** 148. T

P Sand   **P** Light Tan

AD Flesh   **C** Light Suntan

C Orientale   **C** Baby Skin Pink

AD Sunset Pink   **AD** Suntan

P Light Walnut

TO 107 Sand

TO 27 Powder Pink

Gouache

#7 Brush

Start at the top of the figure.

Watercolor Cold Press Paper

Palette

Dab Excess Paint

Work on a Slant

Finish at the toes.

6H Pencil

2B Pencil

Ebony Pencil

Fleshtone watercolor is a wet mix—only a dab of paint to a large volume of water in a palette. The wetter the wash of color, the smoother it will dry.

For a light line under the paint, try a 6H pencil. You can always add a darker line when the paint is dry. To use a heavier line with paint, test it first to see if it smears under brush and water.

Work on a slant so that gravity pulls the paint down. Start at the top of your figure and paint down toward the toes to finish the fleshtone coloring.

Mixing Colors for Watercolor

Before you render the garments or fabrics, make sure the fleshtones are dry. If the color has no sheen to it, then it is probably dry.

To begin painting the fabrics, start at the top of the garment. Again, let gravity work for you. Pull the color down through the shape, gently out from the center to the outline edges.

For smaller areas, a #3 pointed brush is best. It doesn't hold too much paint, and it won't flood the area with too much color.

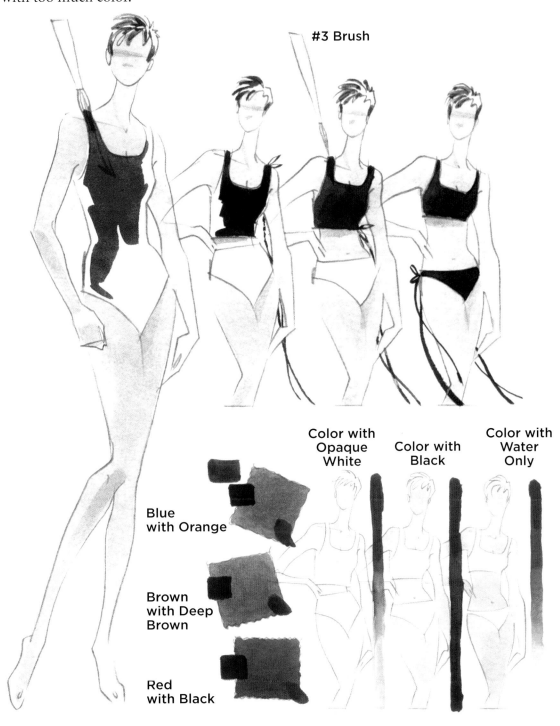

#3 Brush

Blue
with Orange

Brown
with Deep
Brown

Red
with Black

Color with
Opaque
White

Color with
Black

Color with
Water
Only

Rendering Fabrics in Watercolor

2B Pencil
Outline

Think "Shape"

Control the Edges

Paint by
Section

Contoured or
Rounded

Two Layers

Up and Down
Strokes to
Avoid Puddle
at Bottom

Shading

Flat Deep
Solid Color

One Single
Layer

One Brush
Full: Working
It Back, Up,
and Down

Tonal:
Not
Flat

Double:
Layer of
Shading

Work in Sections

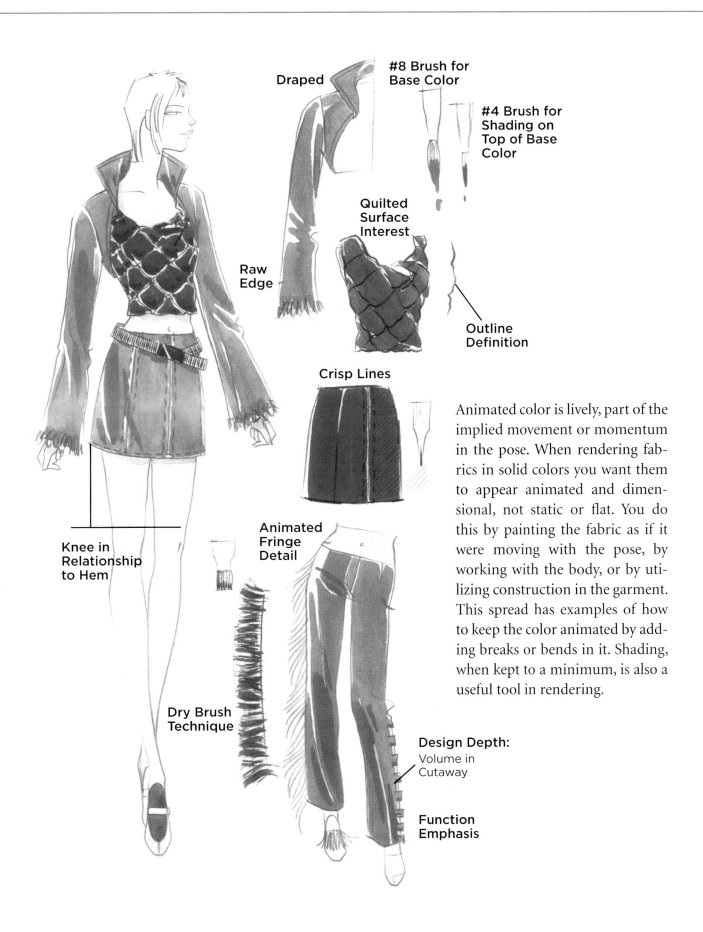

Draped

#8 Brush for
Base Color

#4 Brush for
Shading on
Top of Base
Color

Quilted
Surface
Interest

Raw
Edge

Outline
Definition

Crisp Lines

Knee in
Relationship
to Hem

Animated
Fringe
Detail

Dry Brush
Technique

Design Depth:
Volume in
Cutaway

Function
Emphasis

Animated color is lively, part of the implied movement or momentum in the pose. When rendering fabrics in solid colors you want them to appear animated and dimensional, not static or flat. You do this by painting the fabric as if it were moving with the pose, by working with the body, or by utilizing construction in the garment. This spread has examples of how to keep the color animated by adding breaks or bends in it. Shading, when kept to a minimum, is also a useful tool in rendering.

Reducing a Print

Each print has its own unique size, from a giant motif to a tiny repeat. Your task is to convey the essence of this size. This is done in direct relationship from actual size, reduced to fit to the size of your figure drawing's proportions.

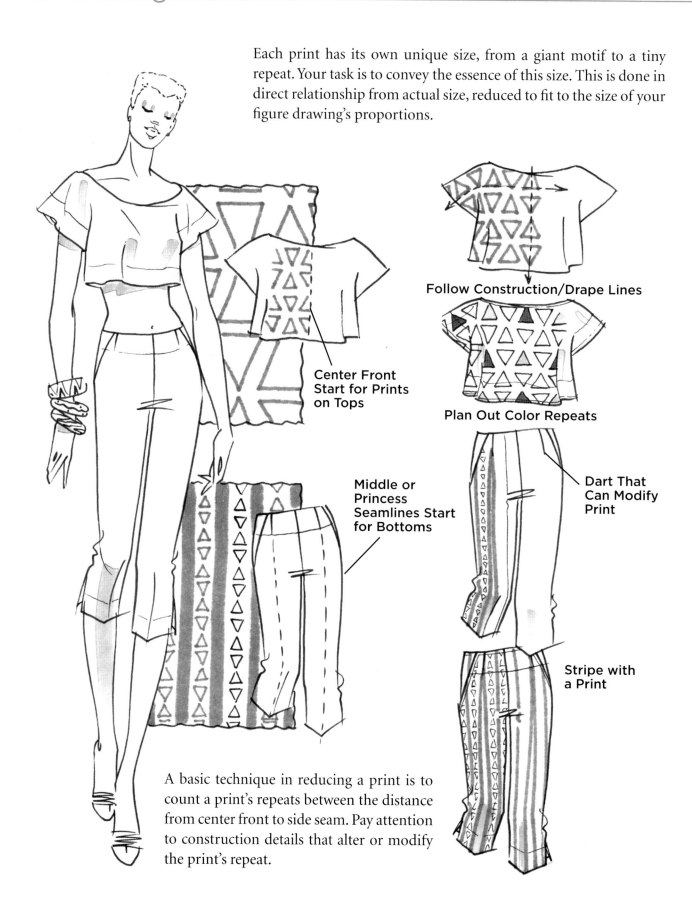

Follow Construction/Drape Lines

Plan Out Color Repeats

Center Front Start for Prints on Tops

Dart That Can Modify Print

Middle or Princess Seamlines Start for Bottoms

Stripe with a Print

A basic technique in reducing a print is to count a print's repeats between the distance from center front to side seam. Pay attention to construction details that alter or modify the print's repeat.

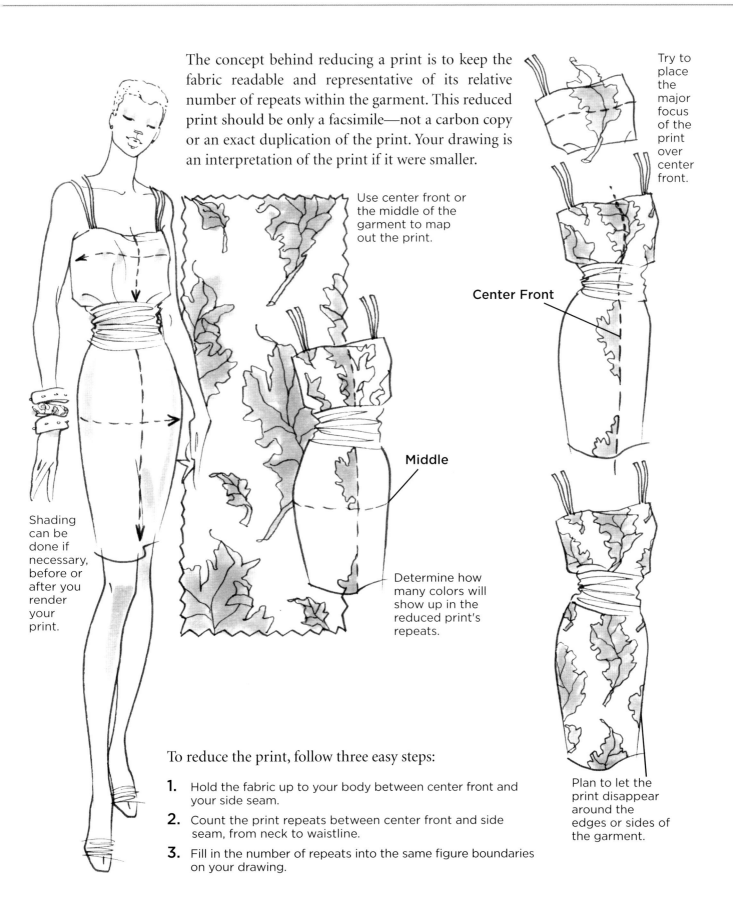

The concept behind reducing a print is to keep the fabric readable and representative of its relative number of repeats within the garment. This reduced print should be only a facsimile—not a carbon copy or an exact duplication of the print. Your drawing is an interpretation of the print if it were smaller.

Try to place the major focus of the print over center front.

Use center front or the middle of the garment to map out the print.

Center Front

Middle

Determine how many colors will show up in the reduced print's repeats.

Shading can be done if necessary, before or after you render your print.

Plan to let the print disappear around the edges or sides of the garment.

To reduce the print, follow three easy steps:

1. Hold the fabric up to your body between center front and your side seam.

2. Count the print repeats between center front and side seam, from neck to waistline.

3. Fill in the number of repeats into the same figure boundaries on your drawing.

Finished versus Partial Rendering

The goals of rendering are to express fashion's shape, construction, and the fabric. The fantasy for rendering is art—to focus on the drama and styling.

Partial Rendering Options

Light Source Direction Side

Color slides away from one side of the garment.

Mimic the Drape

Color into the folds but not up to their edges.

Coloring Accents

Add on a deeper color to accent top of drape instead of using gray as shading underneath it.

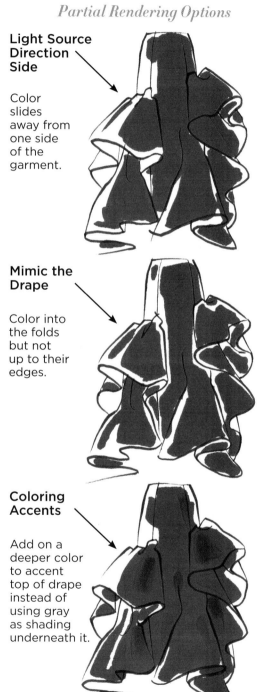

Carolina Herrera

The main purpose of partial rendering is to speed up the process of coloring—in a group or collection—to save time when there is a lot of work to do.

Paint Prep-
4H Pencil
to start.
Ebony
Pencil
finish after
color dries.

Finished
rendering is
tight, edge to
edge coloring
with or without
the same careful
shading.

Partial or loose
rendering
is interior
splashes of
coloring that
is incomplete,
impressionistic.

Finished
rendering looks
polished. Partial
rendering looks
fresh. Both are
techniques to
practice.

Media Options

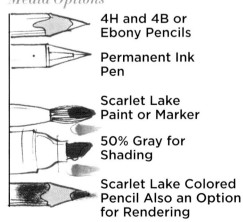

4H and 4B or
Ebony Pencils

Permanent Ink
Pen

Scarlet Lake
Paint or Marker

50% Gray for
Shading

Scarlet Lake Colored
Pencil Also an Option
for Rendering

Rendering Style—Finished versus Partial

Neat:
Pull color
down

Loose:
Splash color in
fold directions

Fabric Practice Templates

A. Repeat fashion silhouette to isolate and practice rendering steps.

B. Use multiples as options in exploring colorways or alternative fabrications.

C. Work on tight, filled-in rendering versus loose, partial-color rendering.

Practicing Fabric Rendering Steps

1. Start with base or dominant (background) color.

2. Add on the shading lines that accentuate fit or detail.

3. Next, work on creating the print focus or pattern elements.

4. Last step: completing secondary print motifs and their colors.

Tight versus Loose Rendering

- Top row—tight color, partial print.
- Bottom row—loose color, full print.

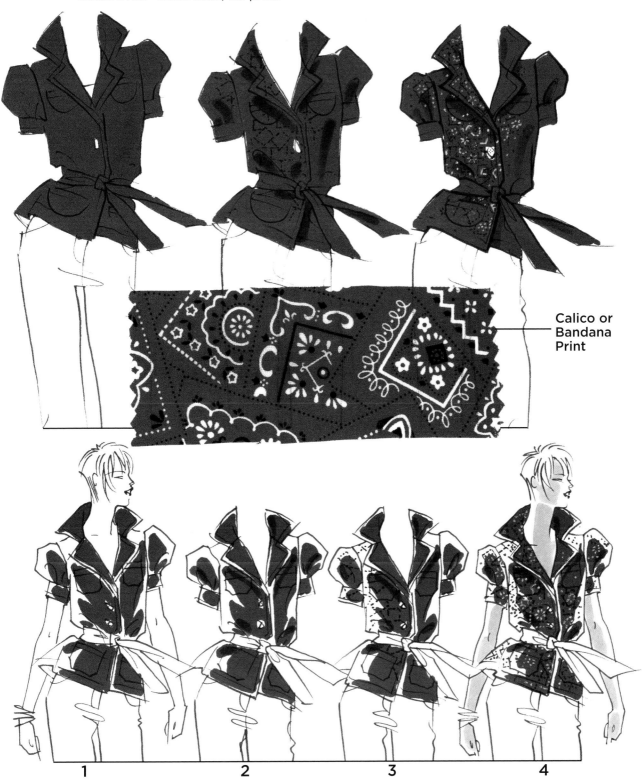

Calico or
Bandana
Print

Color Testing

Become familiar with your media. Test what it is capable of, to practice handling it. Start with choices in watercolor or marker paper. Many have a specific top side for media use. Explore the range and options in media. Speed up your rendering skills in mixed media by sample testing through a single color; push the limits of how many ways in which you can alter your rendering results. Work on achieving the results as shown on this spread.

Mixed media rendering steps done in layers.

Analogous or monochromatic hues used to represent surface interest.

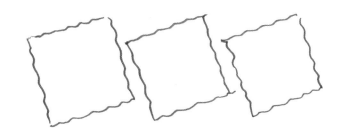

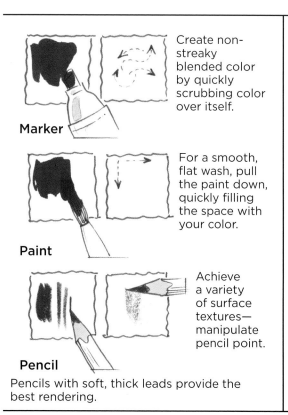

Marker
Create non-streaky blended color by quickly scrubbing color over itself.

Paint
For a smooth, flat wash, pull the paint down, quickly filling the space with your color.

Pencil
Achieve a variety of surface textures—manipulate pencil point.

Pencils with soft, thick leads provide the best rendering.

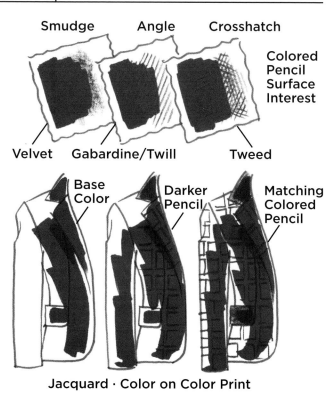

Smudge Angle Crosshatch

Colored Pencil Surface Interest

Velvet Gabardine/Twill Tweed

Base Color Darker Pencil Matching Colored Pencil

Jacquard · Color on Color Print

Base Color

Matte versus Sheen

Accent
Coloring

Two Steps,
Two Layers

Three Steps,
Three Layers

Two Layers
of Colors
Same Media

Three Layers
of Colors
Mixed Media

Base

Mixed Media

Surface
Interest

Light—
Silk

Heavy—
Corduroy

Start to Finish
Chiffon Layering on
Top of Solid Skirt Fabric

Flat, Solid Color

Slub, or
Crinkle Weave

Knit, or
Corduroy

Open Weave,
or Thick Mesh

Squiggle,
Shimmer,
Line

Highlight
or Partial
Rendering
Light Source

Inside
Highlight
(Satins)

Full
Rendering

Outside
Highlight
(Velvets)

Simple
Sheen

Tonal
Sheen

Ombré
Tonal coloring, three
analogous colors

Dupioni Silk
Wavy lines, dark color,
accents

Corduroy
Series of controlled
strokes, mixed media

Tweed
Four crosshatch layers,
four mixed media

Color Nuances

Dolce & Gabbana

Dolce & Gabbana

Dolce & Gabbana

Matte Fabric

Shiny Fabric

Velvety Fabric

Crimson Red

Gray 50%

Flat, solid color is a basic two step, two layers of #1 base color and #2 shading over the base.

Carmine Red

Crimson Red

Gray 70%

Tonal color with lighter interior shimmer or highlights in the fabric.

Three-step rendering with a last hit of gel pen shimmer line.

Centered Shimmer

Exterior Sheen

Centered Shadow

Tonal color with two or three layers of base color, then shading. Here the sheen is on the exterior edging.

Carmine Red

Raspberry

Gray 70%

Marc by
Marc Jacobs

Milly by
Michelle
Smith

Jean Paul
Gaultier

Corduroy	*Fabric Mix*	*Plaid*

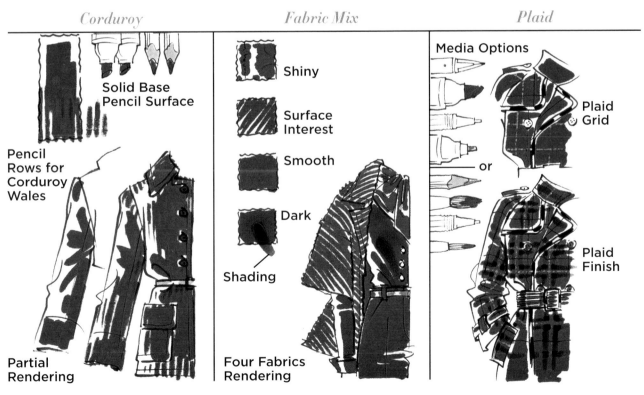

Corduroy

Solid Base
Pencil Surface

Pencil
Rows for
Corduroy
Wales

Partial
Rendering

Fabric Mix

Shiny

Surface
Interest

Smooth

Dark

Shading

Four Fabrics
Rendering

Plaid

Media Options

Plaid
Grid

or

Plaid
Finish

Stripes

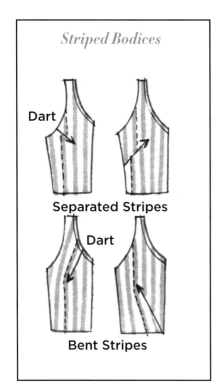

Striped Bodices

Dart

Separated Stripes

Dart

Bent Stripes

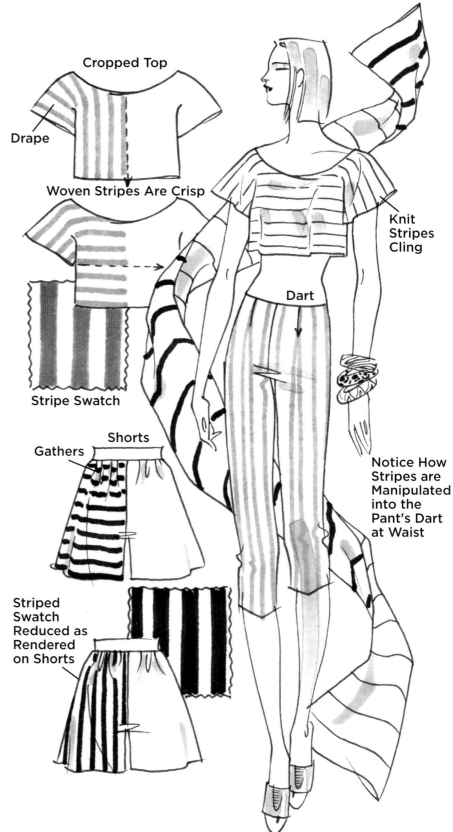

Cropped Top

Drape

Woven Stripes Are Crisp

Stripe Swatch

Knit Stripes Cling

Dart

Shorts

Gathers

Striped Swatch Reduced as Rendered on Shorts

Notice How Stripes are Manipulated into the Pant's Dart at Waist

Stripes are affected by a production cut—the direction for the stripe. They are also affected by construction—manipulation of the stripe—and by fabrication—a woven versus a knit stripe. The cut of a stripe, as shown on the cropped shirt flats, can drape enough to alter the stripe's direction. Construction can separate or bend a stripe, as in the darts on the bodices, or gather up the stripes, as on the flats for the shorts. A woven stripe is usually crisper and less drapey than a knit stripe. A knit stripe often has more cling factor than a woven stripe fabric.

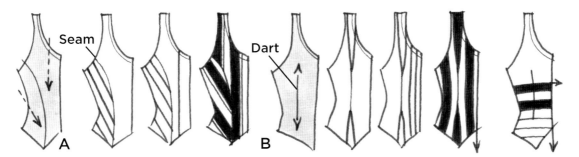

A. Engineered stripes can change fabric grain lines between seams.

B. Vertical darted stripes get altered. Horizontal stripes do not.

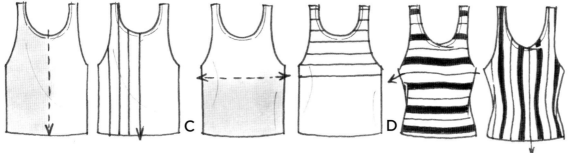

C. Use center front as a guideline to map in vertical stripes.

D. Find the middle of the garment to map in horizontal stripes. Notice the cling factor in the knit stripe.

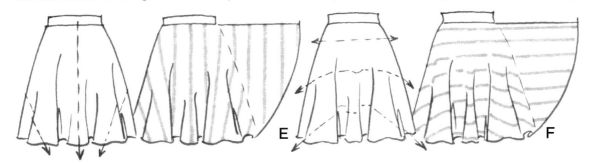

E. Vertical stripes on a full circle skirt appear to gradually fall to the side.

F. The same optical illusion happens to horizontal stripes on a full circle skirt.

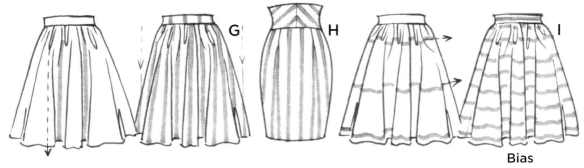

G. Gathered vertical stripes get lost in the folds.

H. Fitted skirt with mitered waistband manipulates the stripes in darts and seaming.

I. Gathered horizontal stripes roll with the shapes of the folds in the skirt.

Checks, Gingham, and Plaids

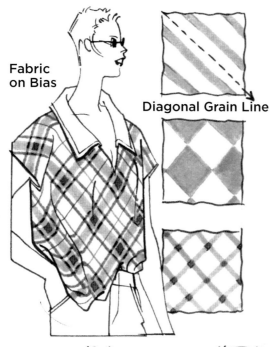

Fabric on Bias

Diagonal Grain Line

Checks, gingham, and plaids are drawn in a similar way as stripes. They travel vertically and horizontally at the same time. All of these patterns are based on straight lines and will begin to curve on a posed figure—even the crisscross of a pattern on the bias. When you are planning to render these fabrics, start with one direction first. Draw either the top-to-bottom stripe or the left-to-right stripe. When you have completed all the stripes in one direction, then draw them in the opposite direction. For a top-to-bottom or shoulder-to-waistline stripe, use the sewing lines of princess seams to guide you. Working left to right across the chest, extend the bustline apex to move the stripe in a curve around the chest contours. Make sure to plan each line of the checks, gingham, or plaids to be equidistant from one another as the lines curve on the body, so the pattern appears to still be geometric in form.

| *Fabric Looks* | Stripes/ Casual | Plaid/ Weekend | Checks/ Day | Gingham/ Evening |

All these geometric patterns are made in a variety of fibers and weaves. You find them in any design category. Regardless, if they are done in sequins or terrycloth, their basic rendering structure remains the same.

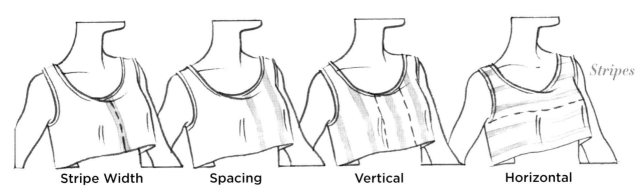

Stripes

Stripe Width   **Spacing**   **Vertical**   **Horizontal**

Carefully plan out stripes before you render them. Planning will guarantee even, equal spacing between your stripes. Practice will help you to establish the width of your stripes, keeping them similar with each stroke of color.

Gingham

Center Front

Windowpane

Buffalo Checks

Ginghams, windowpane, and buffalo checks are all similar in structure. All three patterns use the same basic grid setup. Only ginghams go one step further as they cross over each other, creating their trademark darker centers.

Plaid

Plaids look difficult but can be simplified with this trick: Try to see your plaid as a mix of gingham and windowpane grids crossing over each other. Use the thin lines of the windowpane next to the wider lines of the gingham as you create the color repeats in both the horizontal and vertical lines of a plaid.

Geometric Patterns

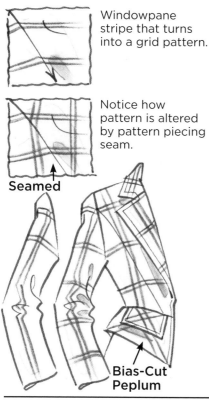

Windowpane stripe that turns into a grid pattern.

Notice how pattern is altered by pattern piecing seam.

Seamed

Bias-Cut Peplum

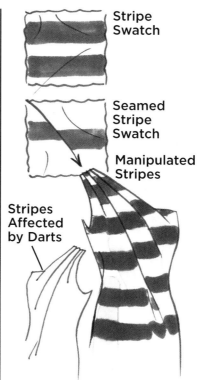

Stripe Swatch

Seamed Stripe Swatch

Manipulated Stripes

Stripes Affected by Darts

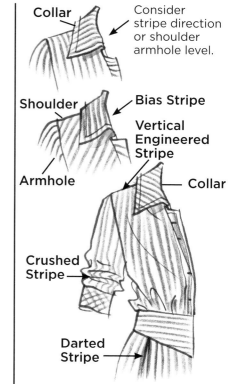

Collar

Consider stripe direction or shoulder armhole level.

Shoulder

Bias Stripe

Vertical Engineered Stripe

Armhole

Collar

Crushed Stripe

Darted Stripe

Christian Dior

Escada

Diane von Furstenberg

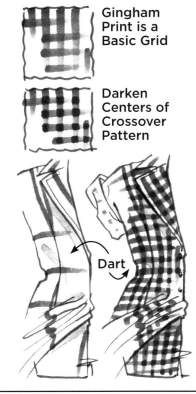

Gingham Print is a Basic Grid

Darken Centers of Crossover Pattern

Dart

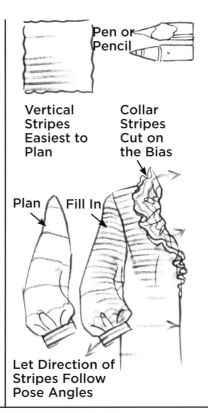

Pen or Pencil

Vertical Stripes Easiest to Plan

Collar Stripes Cut on the Bias

Plan   Fill In

Let Direction of Stripes Follow Pose Angles

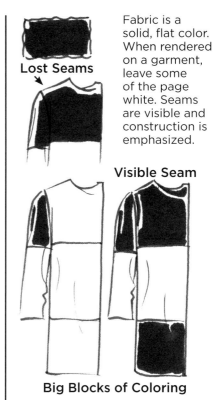

Lost Seams

Fabric is a solid, flat color. When rendered on a garment, leave some of the page white. Seams are visible and construction is emphasized.

Visible Seam

Big Blocks of Coloring

Roberto Cavalli

Kate Spade

M Missoni

Fall Fabrics

Fall fabrics will hone your rendering skills and sharpen your eyes for deciphering the texture mixes of rough, ribbed, embossed, fuzzy, furry, or just plain woolly materials that come together in fall fashion collections. This spread pushes your marker coloring and pencil work into heavier, thicker, and more bulky surface interest looks. Use the marker coloring color range and the texture range for colored pencils (shown below) as a guide to practice preparing your media test strips. Match your colors up to the value range example and your pencil to the texture range example. Pen line was used here as part of the furriest edges, but these can just as easily be done with colored pencil lines.

Color Value and Marker Color Range

These rendering techniques work in any medium.

Color Pencil and Texture Range

Watercolor

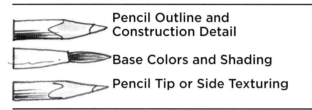

Pencil Outline and Construction Detail

Base Colors and Shading

Pencil Tip or Side Texturing

Marker Color

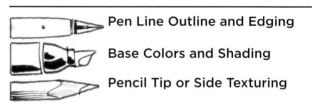

Pen Line Outline and Edging

Base Colors and Shading

Pencil Tip or Side Texturing

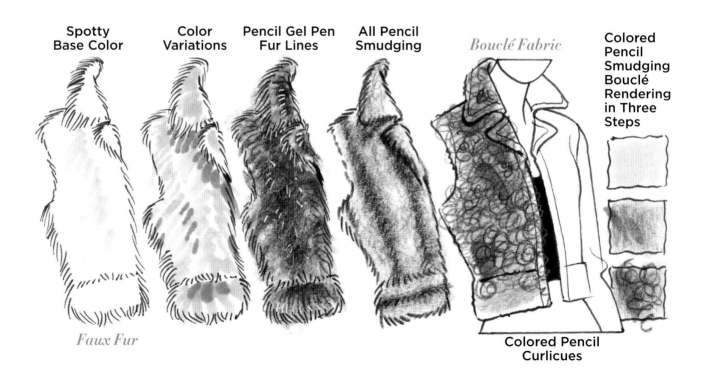

Spotty Base Color　　Color Variations　　Pencil Gel Pen Fur Lines　　All Pencil Smudging　　*Bouclé Fabric*　　Colored Pencil Smudging Bouclé Rendering in Three Steps

Faux Fur

Colored Pencil Curlicues

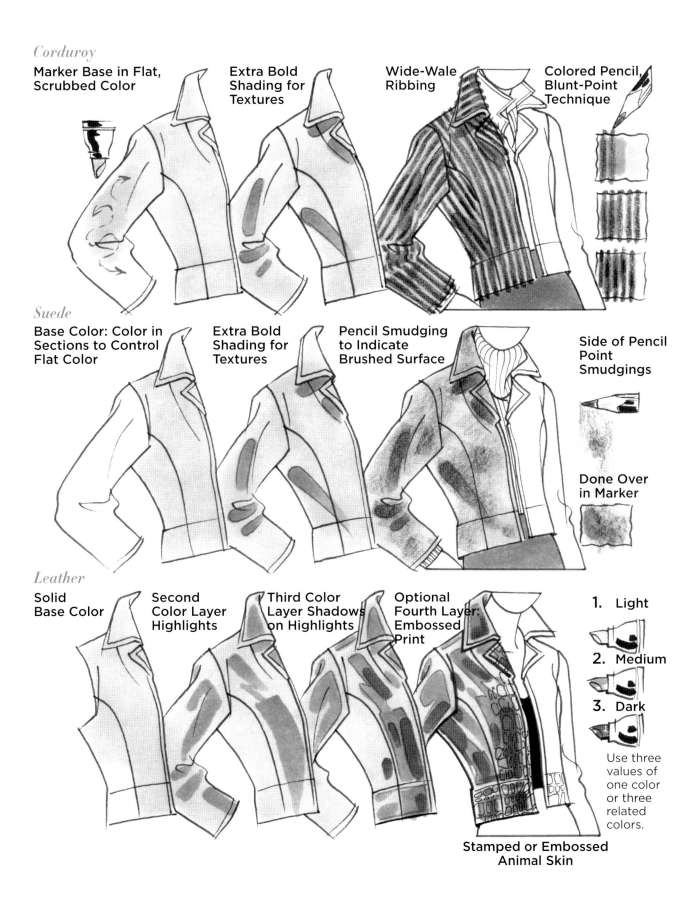

Corduroy

Marker Base in Flat, Scrubbed Color

Extra Bold Shading for Textures

Wide-Wale Ribbing

Colored Pencil, Blunt-Point Technique

Suede

Base Color: Color in Sections to Control Flat Color

Extra Bold Shading for Textures

Pencil Smudging to Indicate Brushed Surface

Side of Pencil Point Smudgings

Done Over in Marker

Leather

Solid Base Color

Second Color Layer Highlights

Third Color Layer Shadows on Highlights

Optional Fourth Layer: Embossed Print

1. Light

2. Medium

3. Dark

Use three values of one color or three related colors.

Stamped or Embossed Animal Skin

Fall Fabrics (continued)

Suede

1. **Base Color**

2. **Uneven Mix of Deeper Tones**

3. **Rough Smudges of Uneven Colored Pencil**

Donna Karan

Chloé

Leather

Base for Leather with a Shine to It	Second Layer with Related, Darker Color	Two Layers of Same Color as Base Color	Matte Leather, No Shine
One Step	*Two Steps*	*Two Steps*	*Three Steps*

Pinstripe

Glen Plaid

Pencil Lines

Pen Lines

Herringbone

Houndstooth

Salvatore
Ferragamo

Express

Salvatore
Ferragamo

Douglas
Hannant

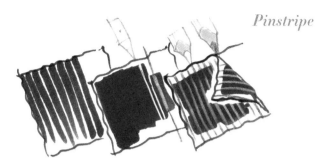

Pinstripe

1. One color in tight stripes.
2. Solid base with gel pen stripes.
3. Base color with colored pencil stripes.

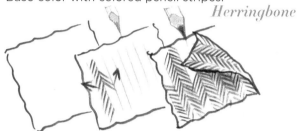

Herringbone

1. Solid base color, one layer.
2. HB Pencil lines evenly spaced.
3. Alternating rows of colored-pencil chevrons.

Glen Plaid

1. Crosshatch or solid base color.
2. Alternating rows of broken lines, large pen.
3. Alternating crosshatch rows, small pen like a micron pen 005, also in broken lines.

Houndstooth

1. Base color with HB Pencil grid on top.
2. Broken lines in a larger crosshatch weave.
3. In alternating rows, fill in every other square, making little black boxes. Connect each box with a tail up, off the side and down the bottom. These tails will create a star motif between the boxes.

Animal Prints

Christian
Dior

Louis
Vuitton

Roberto
Cavalli

Louis
Vuitton

Dolce &
Gabbana

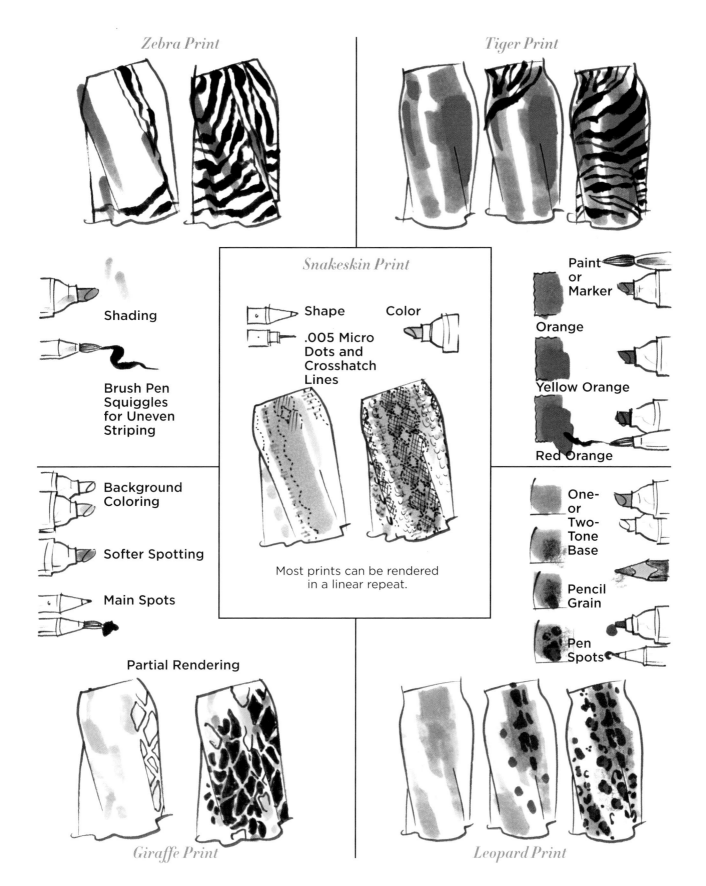

Zebra Print

Shading

Brush Pen
Squiggles
for Uneven
Striping

Background
Coloring

Softer Spotting

Main Spots

Partial Rendering

Giraffe Print

Snakeskin Print

Shape   Color

.005 Micro
Dots and
Crosshatch
Lines

Most prints can be rendered
in a linear repeat.

Tiger Print

Paint
or
Marker

Orange

Yellow Orange

Red Orange

One-
or
Two-
Tone
Base

Pencil
Grain

Pen
Spots

Leopard Print

Fashion Designer Color Challenges

André Courrèges Emilio Pucci Carolina Herrera Rudi Gernreich Geoffrey Beene James Galanos Arnold Scaasi

Archival fashion, even the more recent 20th-century historical garments in educational collections, can be valuable sources of both design inspiration and information. Casual observations at a fashion gallery show, or a museum's designer or costume exhibit, can still teach about the craft beyond the glamour and function of style. Add fashion history to your list of studies, and combine observation with illustration, as these next few pages do.

Here are a few designer garments: simple silhouettes in basic fabrics that can serve as an interesting source of rendering goals. After working on these examples, you'll note how challenging it is to work from photographs. However, it is preferable to learn from something that already exists when creating something that doesn't . . . something at the edge of your imagination and on the tip of your pen.

André Courrèges: 1960s Wool Serge Pantsuit

Another form of rendering for solid-colored fabrics gives the coloring process more depth and uses two or more tints or shades of a color to convey dimension or nuances in the fabric. The rendering examples here show you the differences between flat color rendering and dimensional color rendering for the same fabric. Flat coloring is quicker. Dimensional coloring takes longer and requires more art supplies.

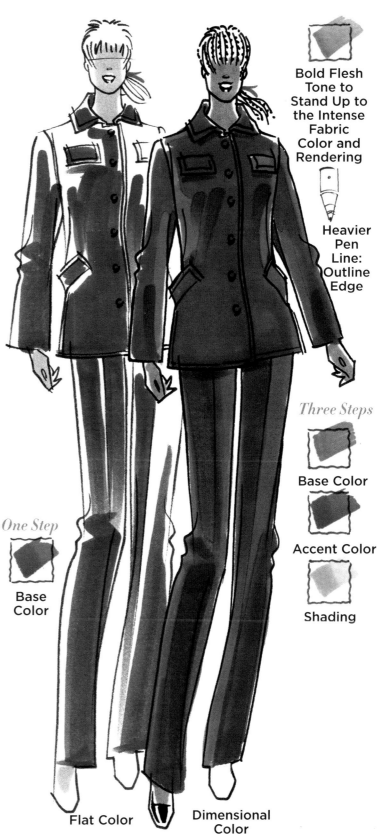

Bold Flesh Tone to Stand Up to the Intense Fabric Color and Rendering

Heavier Pen Line: Outline Edge

Three Steps

Base Color

Accent Color

Shading

One Step

Base Color

Flat Color

Dimensional Color

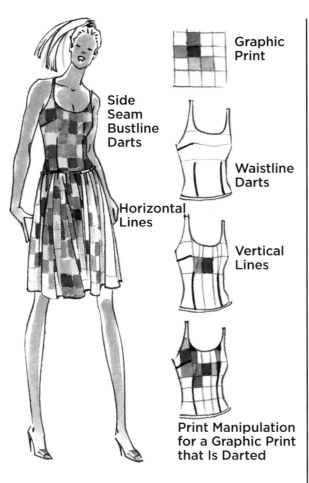

Graphic Print

Side Seam Bustline Darts

Waistline Darts

Horizontal Lines

Vertical Lines

Print Manipulation for a Graphic Print that Is Darted

Herrera

Another type of loose rendering, active coloring, is used to emphasize both the bias seaming and the drape of the cascading flounces across the skirt of this dress. For solid, tight rendering, use shading to emphasize the drape and layers of fabrics.

Pucci

Darting can affect some types of prints. Notice how the vertical lines in this print are altered by the dart construction for fit across the bustline. Map out the grid of a print like this in 4H pencil to make it easier to render a manipulated fabric.

Partial Rendering Active Coloring

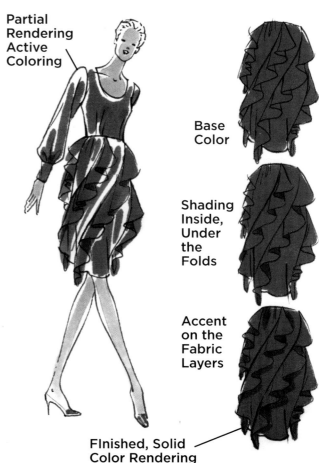

Base Color

Shading Inside, Under the Folds

Accent on the Fabric Layers

Finished, Solid Color Rendering

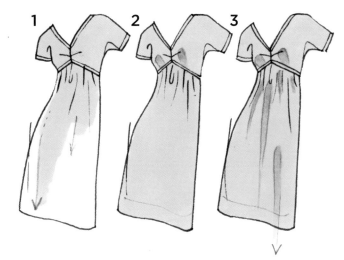

1. Start to color by working in sections. This controls marker streaking. Start at the top, pulling the color down into the hemline.

2. Let the base color dry or cure for a minute. Start the shading with the bustline contours. This establishes fit.

3. Drop some shading into the gathers to emphasize construction and fabric volume for this wool jersey fabric.

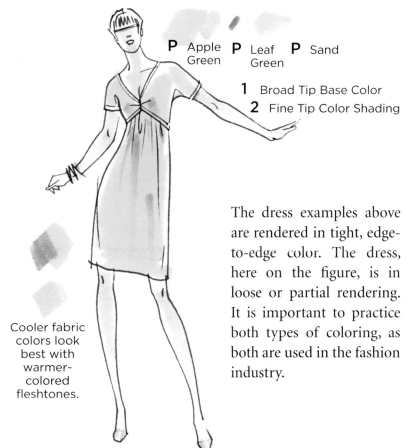

P Apple Green **P** Leaf Green **P** Sand

1 Broad Tip Base Color
2 Fine Tip Color Shading

Cooler fabric colors look best with warmer-colored fleshtones.

The dress examples above are rendered in tight, edge-to-edge color. The dress, here on the figure, is in loose or partial rendering. It is important to practice both types of coloring, as both are used in the fashion industry.

Geoffrey Beene: 1970s Silk Jacquard Dress
James Galanos: 1970s Silk Crêpe de Chine Dinner Dress

Partial Rendering
Fabric done in three steps—one color per step for this color-on-color print.

Geoffrey Beene

Retro Broad Shoulders

Partial Rendering
Fabric done in two steps—one step per color.

James Galanos

1. Short, thin directional strokes for pleating on bodice. Long strokes for sleeves.

2. Broad strokes of color for skirt.

1. Background base color.
2. Pattern.
3. Surface crinkle.

Notice that the volume or weight of rendering is done on the supporting leg side of poses.

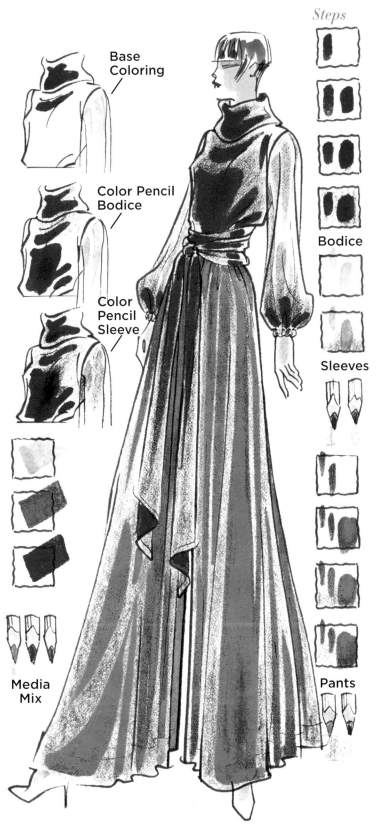

Steps

Base Coloring

Color Pencil Bodice

Color Pencil Sleeve

Bodice

Sleeves

Media Mix

Pants

Use a pose that focuses attention on design features, like this pose, which accentuates the pants leg on what looks like a skirt. The dress turns into the jumpsuit that it is.

Mixing media is another form of dimensional rendering for solid-colored fabrics. Pencil over marker conveys transparency and graininess in a silk organza fabric.

The media mix for this design is gouache, colored pencils, and pencil outline. Inspired by bar-codes and kente cloth, runway poses help convey the sense of motion that adds to the sculpted draping. The designer created a focal point for her construction, fabrication, and coloring for these intensely rendered, multipaneled silhouettes.

The media mix for this design is gouache, gel pens, and pencil outline. For this collection the designer used the duel design inspiration of radio activity and the blue-ringed octopus to influence detail, using selective figure poses to emphasize specific design details. Figures overlap to work as a group, displaying fit, shape, and coloring without sacrificing critical rendering on her expressive sketching style.

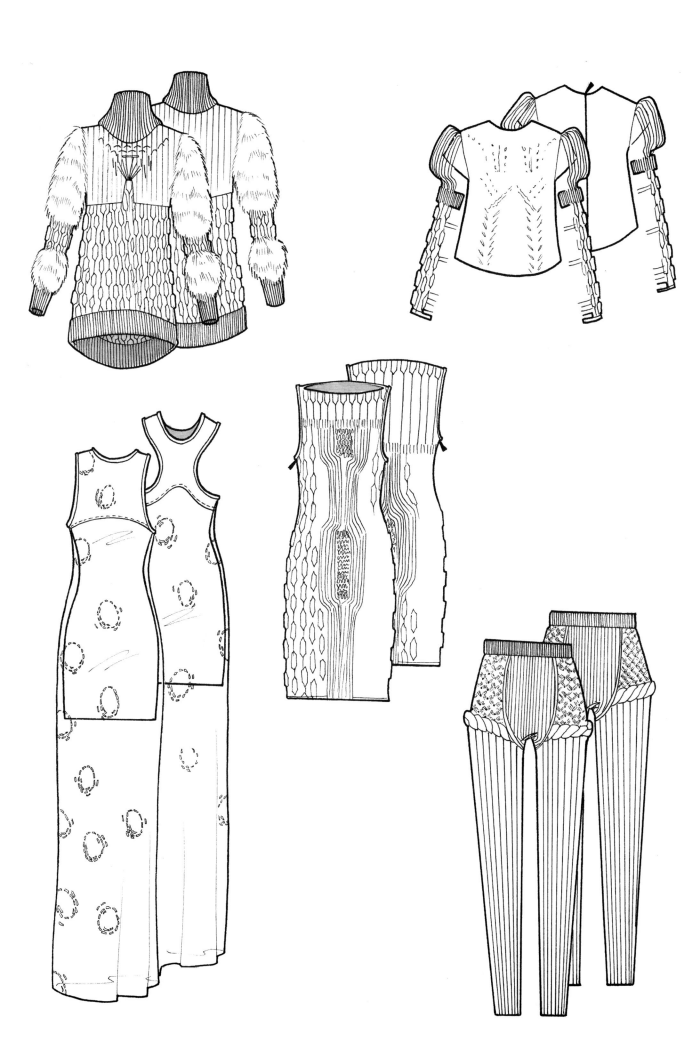

8

High-End Rendering Techniques

This chapter breaks down both the drawing instructions and the rendering process into layered steps. The drawing instructions focus on delicate and ornate fabrications featuring new layered steps for more advanced fashion design sketches using mixed media. Each spread offers another draped element for study and inspiration, with detailed illustrations, studio muslins, and *WWD* runway photographs as reference examples. These give you a stronger background in research to help develop your potential and push your rendering skills, for all types of fabrics, to the next level. That next level is the blend of confidence and expertise in how quickly you can work on and complete your design sketches in color. Design sketches that clearly represent and convey your ideas will earn instant recognition and approval.

To accomplish this new level in drawing and rendering you have to combine what you learned in Chapter Five, Garments and Garment Details, and Chapter Seven, Basic Rendering Techniques. This chapter is draping intensive. It includes more challenging, but also glamorous, elements of drape and types of luxurious fabrics with which to design. The challenges include how to incorporate fancier embellishments like beading or lace edges and intangibles like transparency in a gown's fabrication into your sketching. These are elements of visual nuances that can make or break a sketch.

Sketching Ruffles

Ruffles are sewn in a strip or band of fabric gathered into a bunch of folds that are held in place by a seam. The opposite side is the hemline of the ruffle. It rolls, curls, and pops with the drape of the ruffle depending on its direction—up, down, or sideways. The difference between a ruffle and a flounce is that a flounce does not have gathers.

Ruffles come in so many fabrics, widths, lengths, and volume of gathers that it is hard to pinpoint exactly what every style of ruffle is going to look like in any of these three positions—up, down, or sideways—on a garment. Here are a few basic types of ruffles to practice.

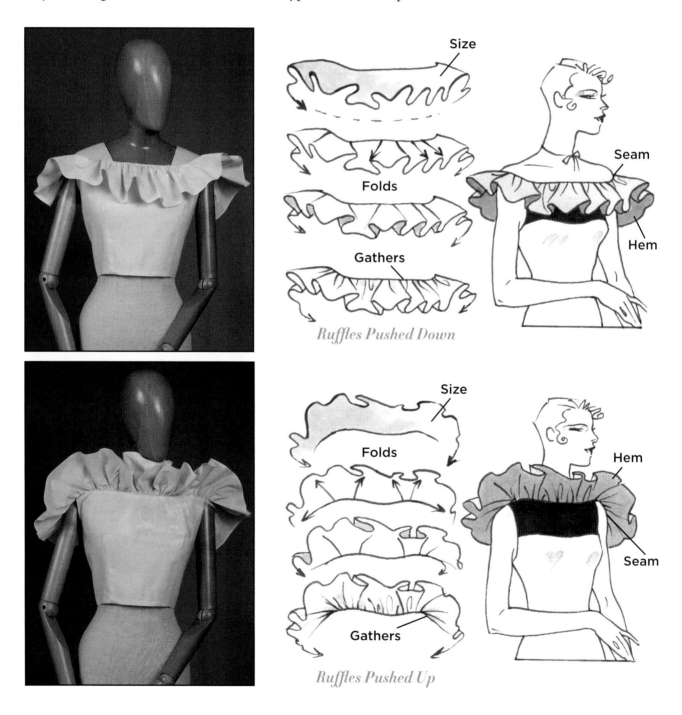

Ruffles Pushed Down

Ruffles Pushed Up

Ruffle Size	Folds	Gathers	

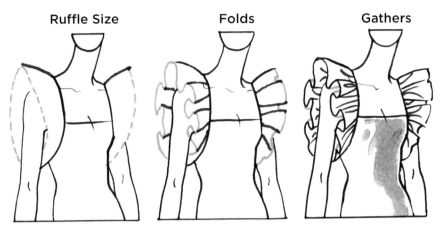

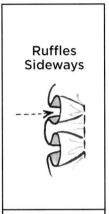

Ruffles That Turn Toward and Away from View

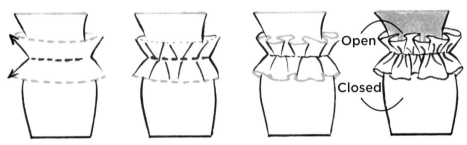

Open

Closed

Up and Down Ruffles

Ruffles Opened and Closed by Positioning

Falling Down Ruffles

Ruffles That Are Soft and Drapey

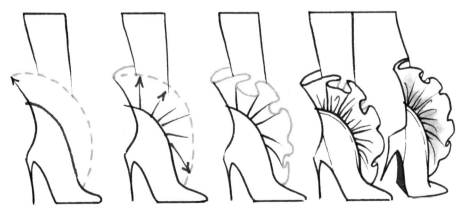

Sticking Out or Standing Up Ruffles

Ruffles That Are Crisp and Stiff Even as They Roll Over

Sketching Cascades

A cascade creates wide, rolling folds that flip back and over each other. The folds in a draped cascade look random but are always sewn to a specific seam placement. Cascades, unlike ruffles, do not have gathers. They have more drape—pronounced folds that roll over to reveal both the inside and the outside of the material. Cascades are often cut from fabric on the bias to maximize their ability to drape. These panels of cascading fabric come in lots of widths, lengths, and types of fabric (crisp or soft) that can either add to or restrict the number of folds that will be created when the cascade is sewn on the garment.

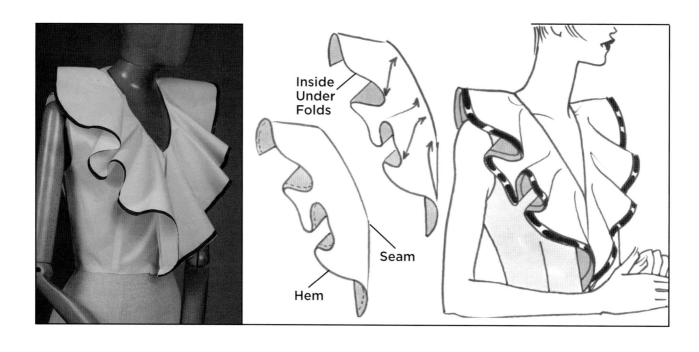

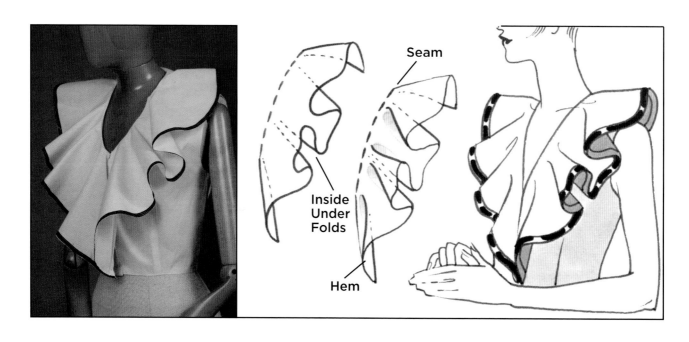

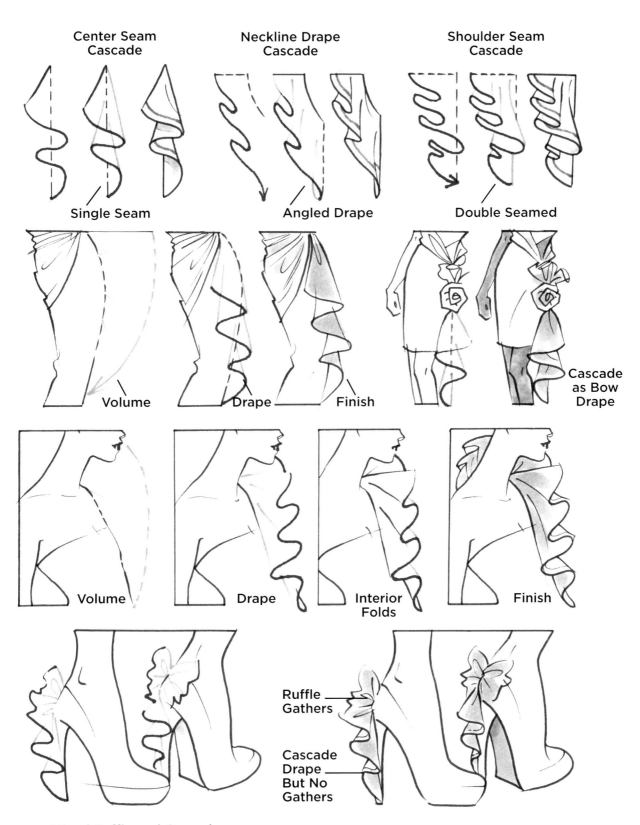

Center Seam Cascade

Single Seam

Volume — Drape — Finish

Neckline Drape Cascade

Angled Drape

Shoulder Seam Cascade

Double Seamed

Cascade as Bow Drape

Volume — Drape — Interior Folds — Finish

Ruffle Gathers

Cascade Drape But No Gathers

Mixed Ruffle and Cascade
Difference: Ruffles have gathers; cascades do not have gathers.

Sketching Cowls

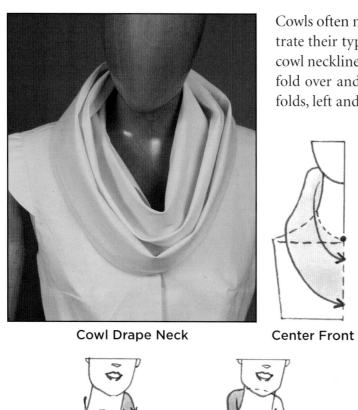

Cowls often need tonal values of light and shadows to illustrate their type of nuanced folding inside each other. For a cowl neckline, use center front as your guide to collapse the fold over and under each other, increasing the dips in the folds, left and right of your center front.

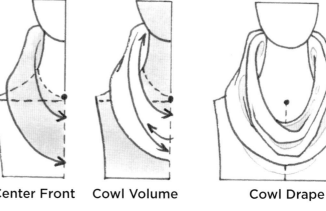

Cowl Drape Neck

Center Front   **Cowl Volume**   **Cowl Drape**

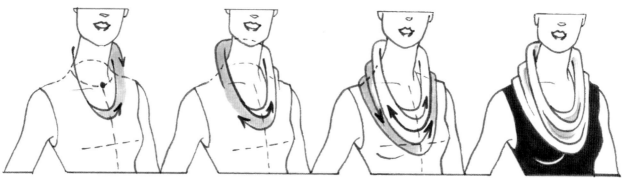

As the pose turns, let your cowl-drape neckline fold in the direction of center front as the cowl drape follows the figure. Profile and side views of the cowl drape look like descending folds, slipping into and underneath each other on the garment.

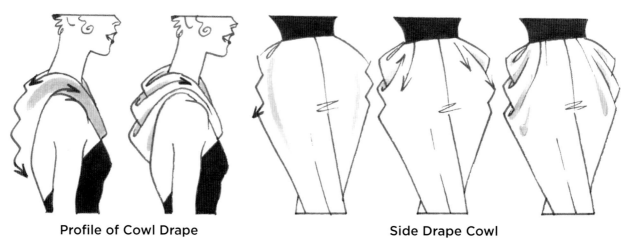

Profile of Cowl Drape   **Side Drape Cowl**

Sketching Smocking and Shirring

Smocking Treatment

Smocking and shirring are forms of gathers that emanate from seams done in stretch fabric or elastic threads. Both are drawn similar to a ruffle except that smocking is drawn in horizontal rows or bands and shirring is drawn in vertical panels. Smocking has puffed sides, and shirring can get quite drapey. Ruffles have folds.

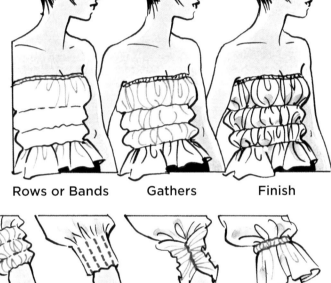

| Rows or Bands | Gathers | Finish |

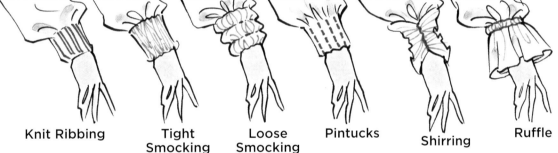

Knit Ribbing   **Tight Smocking**   **Loose Smocking**   **Pintucks**   **Shirring**   **Ruffle**

Six cuff treatments, each with their own specific construction, have to be drawn with a different form of line quality to express those design variables.

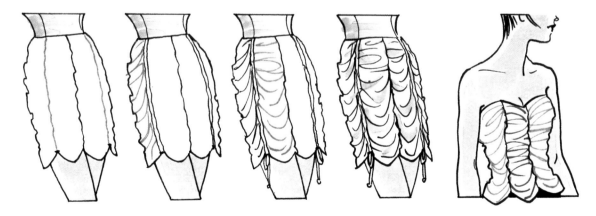

Shirring treatments shape channel's drape. Also called "parachute drape."

Gathers, Gores, Cowl Drape, and Pintucks

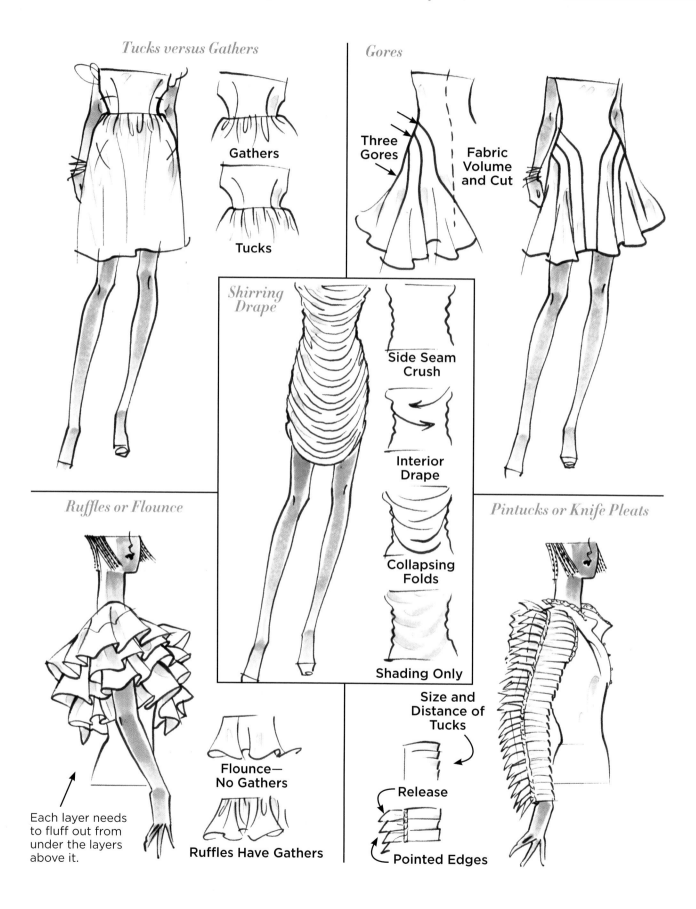

Tucks versus Gathers

Gathers

Tucks

Gores

Three Gores

Fabric Volume and Cut

Shirring Drape

Side Seam Crush

Interior Drape

Collapsing Folds

Shading Only

Ruffles or Flounce

Each layer needs to fluff out from under the layers above it.

Flounce— No Gathers

Ruffles Have Gathers

Pintucks or Knife Pleats

Size and Distance of Tucks

Release

Pointed Edges

Alexandre
Herchcovitch

Gathers versus Tucks

Betsey
Johnson

Gores

Michael
Kors

Stella
McCartney

Jean Paul
Gaultier

Ruffles   *Shirring*   *Pintuck Pleating*

Changing Proportions

Fashion elongation pulls the figure to its greatest lengths for most formal, special-occasion looks. Bridal can also get dramatic exaggeration. This drawing technique, emphasizing the length and volume of fabric, accentuates the fantasy and glamour.

Illustrated here are the changes you can make between your sportswear figure and your eveningwear figure. While the upper torso remains the same, notice how the legs elongate.

> **Note:**
> Broadway and costume design figures are drawn with much more realistic or average-body proportions to better reflect their actors' forms.

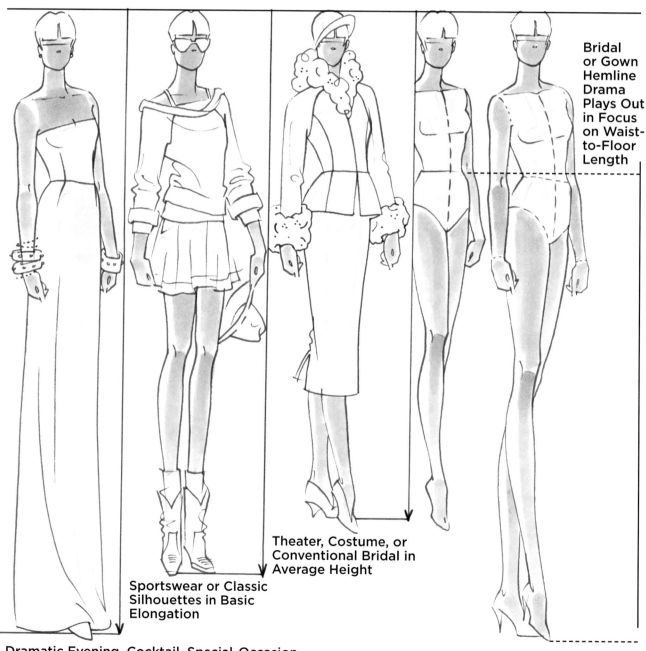

Bridal or Gown Hemline Drama Plays Out in Focus on Waist-to-Floor Length

Theater, Costume, or Conventional Bridal in Average Height

Sportswear or Classic Silhouettes in Basic Elongation

Dramatic Evening, Cocktail, Special-Occasion, or Bridal, in Exaggerated Elongation

Another version of fashion elongation for gowns or bridalwear is to use the ratio of the bodice's length to the length of the skirt. This means that for any gown there are up to five bodice lengths from the waistline to the hemline versus the single length of the bodice from the waistline to the shoulderline, as seen in the example below. Elongating the legs or elongating the skirt of a gown gives you the same results—a place to display design, fabrication, and coloring. Note that while the fashion figure elongates, theater or costume designers use the more realistic figure, because they are dressing specific "characters" versus fashion's elusive "customer."

Note:

Ratio of 1 to 5— the length of the skirt in a gown or wedding dress— can be drawn five times as long as the bodice of that garment.

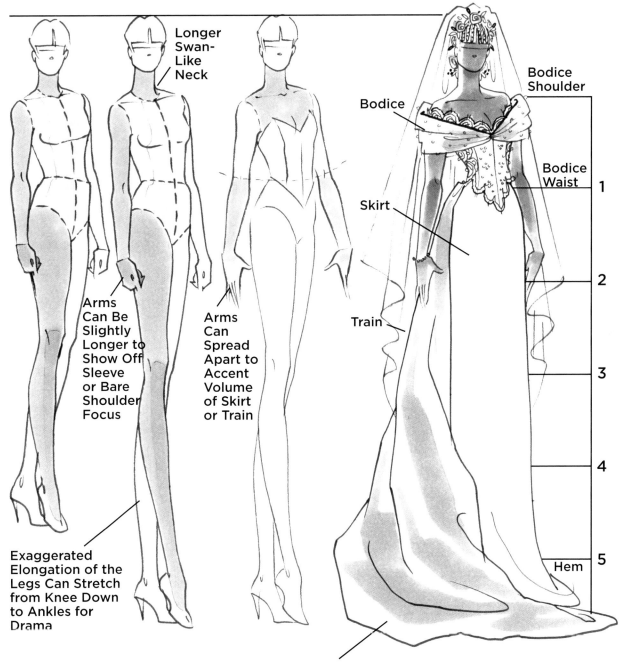

Longer Swan-Like Neck

Bodice

Skirt

Train

Arms Can Be Slightly Longer to Show Off Sleeve or Bare Shoulder Focus

Arms Can Spread Apart to Accent Volume of Skirt or Train

Exaggerated Elongation of the Legs Can Stretch from Knee Down to Ankles for Drama

Bodice Shoulder

Bodice Waist

1

2

3

4

5

Hem

Warm-Tone Pastel Colors Work Best with Cool-Tone Fleshtones

Bridal Looks

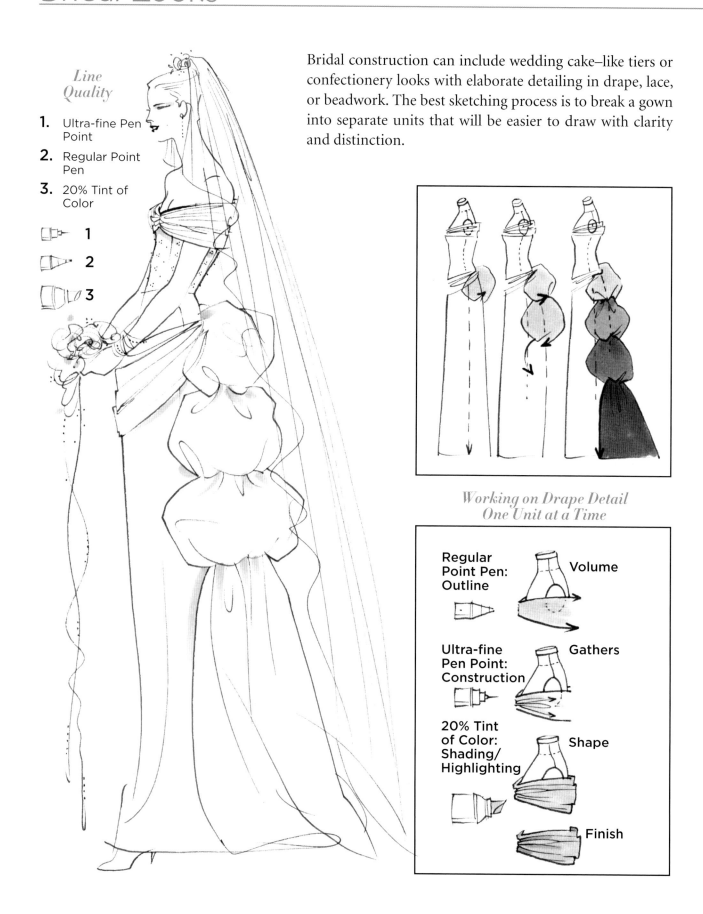

Bridal construction can include wedding cake–like tiers or confectionery looks with elaborate detailing in drape, lace, or beadwork. The best sketching process is to break a gown into separate units that will be easier to draw with clarity and distinction.

Line Quality

1. Ultra-fine Pen Point
2. Regular Point Pen
3. 20% Tint of Color

1

2

3

Working on Drape Detail One Unit at a Time

Regular Point Pen: Outline — Volume

Ultra-fine Pen Point: Construction — Gathers

20% Tint of Color: Shading/Highlighting — Shape

Finish

The bridal veil (or headpiece) often presents two main challenges: tranparency and paleness.

- Transparency: Sketching the veil's length and volume.
- Coloring: Hinting at both under and over the veil.

The tulle, or netting, in the veil is often gathered into the headpiece or tiara.

A. The traditional-style veil.

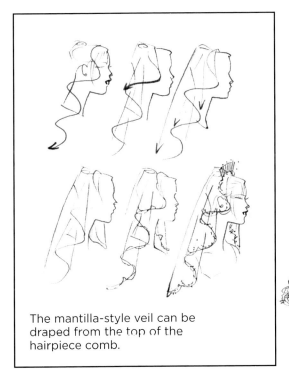

The mantilla-style veil can be draped from the top of the hairpiece comb.

B. The mantilla lace–style veil.

Line Quality in Bridal Gown Rendering:

Subtleties are one part control and one part pen-point selections.

1. Extra Fine for Veil

2. Fine for Beading

3. Regular for Gown

Bridal Trains

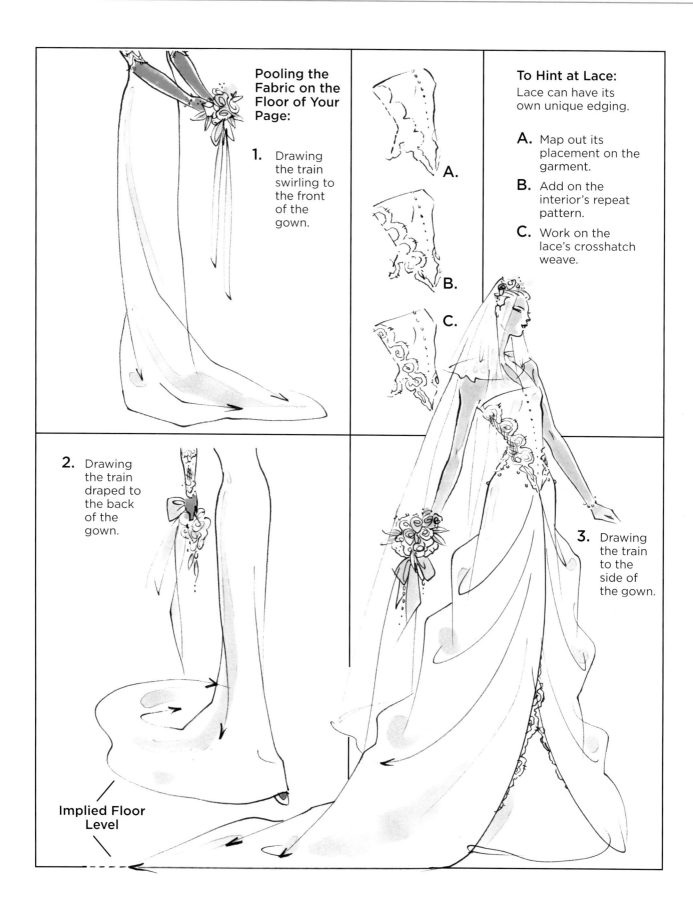

Pooling the Fabric on the Floor of Your Page:

1. Drawing the train swirling to the front of the gown.

A.

B.

C.

To Hint at Lace:
Lace can have its own unique edging.

A. Map out its placement on the garment.

B. Add on the interior's repeat pattern.

C. Work on the lace's crosshatch weave.

2. Drawing the train draped to the back of the gown.

Implied Floor Level

3. Drawing the train to the side of the gown.

The back view pose for a wedding gown is often used to put the focus on the train itself. You can fan out the train to both sides of the pose or to just one side in a specific direction.

Shading Underneath the Pouf Drape

Shading Across the Drape

Notice that the best way to illustrate this train is to start at its seam, at the waistline. Work your lines from the start of the train, down toward its hemline, and across the floor of your page.

Center Back

Shading emphasis down the length and direction of the train as it trails to find the floor of your page.

Floor Level

Dress and Gown Flats

Dresses and gowns, whether casual or formal, come with their own sets of requirements in flats. Design details often present overlapping special features and competing points of interest or reference in one flat. The bodice has neckline, collar, and sleeve styles and a myriad of seaming and dart lines across the chest. The skirt has, from the waistline to the hemline, all kinds of unique treatments in pockets, gores, vents, and layers. Lots of information is squeezed into one flat, front or back. One solution is to undo, detach, or deconstruct some of the more complex silhouettes if it does not interfere with comprehension of the overall garment. All steps should be taken to maximize content. Whatever drawing device you choose to broadcast the details, make sure it is accurate as well as beautiful.

Front View

Back View

Back View Train (Detached)

Back view hemlines can change in length from front view.

A. Undefined, misleading lines

B. Precise, defined, informed lines

C. Follow design curves and construction

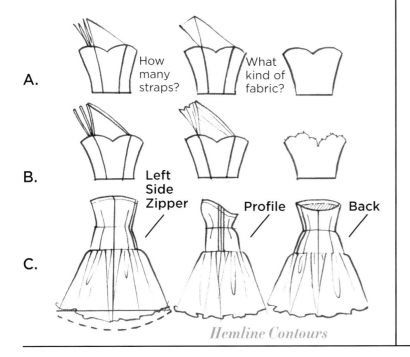

A. How many straps?

What kind of fabric?

B. Left Side Zipper

C. Profile   Back

Hemline Contours

A. Every line you draw is design information; be specific about construction.

B. Details: when drawing straps, clearly show their volume, shape, or fabrication.

C. Use straight and curved lines with precision to express the nuances in fit.

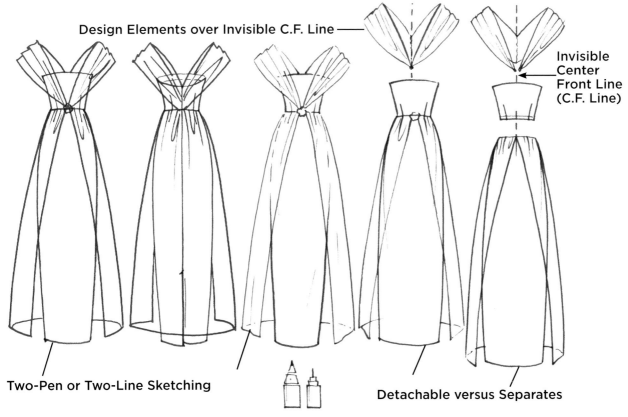

Design Elements over Invisible C.F. Line ——

Invisible Center Front Line (C.F. Line)

Two-Pen or Two-Line Sketching

Detachable versus Separates

Drape and Volume

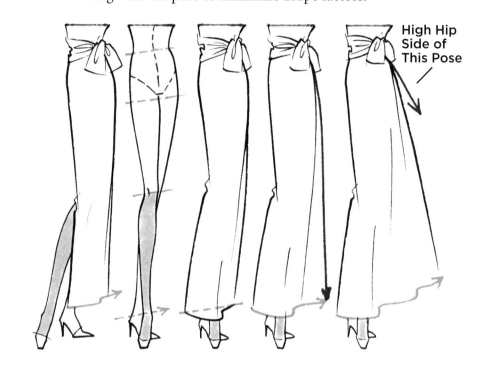

Volume influences shape. Increasing the shape's volume means working with the pose to maximize drape factors.

High Hip Side of This Pose

Avoid Cardboard Cutouts

Windowblown Interior Effect

Wet or Wrinkled

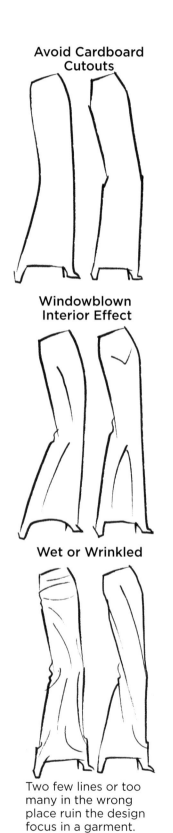

Two few lines or too many in the wrong place ruin the design focus in a garment.

Drape Lines   **Hemlines Follow Drape Lines**

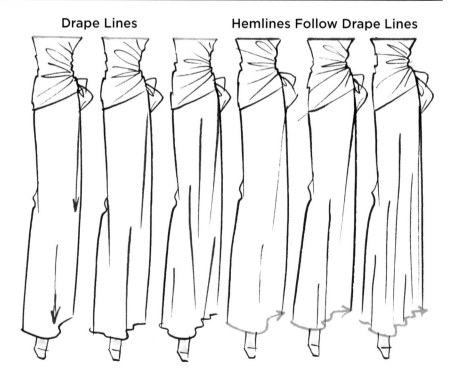

Fabric type and drape also influence shape. The lighter fabrics have more folds, while the heavier fabrics have less.

Control over line
content; shape
and drape

Pencil

Soft, darker
line for shape

Hard, lighter
line for drape

Pen

Medium,
heavier line for
shape

Fine, thinner
line for drape

Shape:

Design
silhouette

Drape:

Fabric
type and
construction

1. Descending
    angled
    godets

2. Folds tucked
    into and
    under each
    other

3. Crisp yet
    lightweight
    fabric in a
    cascade
    spray

4. Fabric pulled
    and draped
    from a single
    point

5. Tight ruching
    with side
    cowl drape

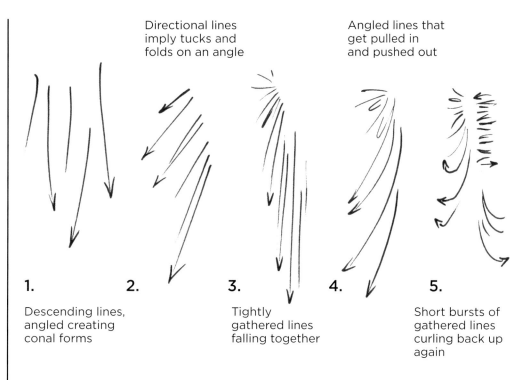

Directional lines
imply tucks and
folds on an angle

Angled lines that
get pulled in
and pushed out

1.
Descending lines,
angled creating
conal forms

2.

3.
Tightly
gathered lines
falling together

4.

5.
Short bursts of
gathered lines
curling back up
again

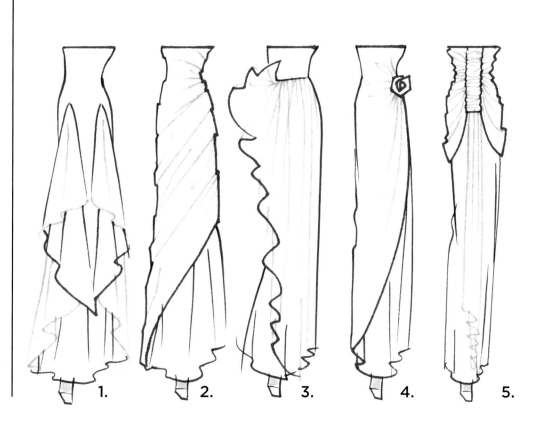

Drape and Volume (continued)

For all of the variety in shape and styling, your drawing line has to distinguish beween drape and construction in every garment.

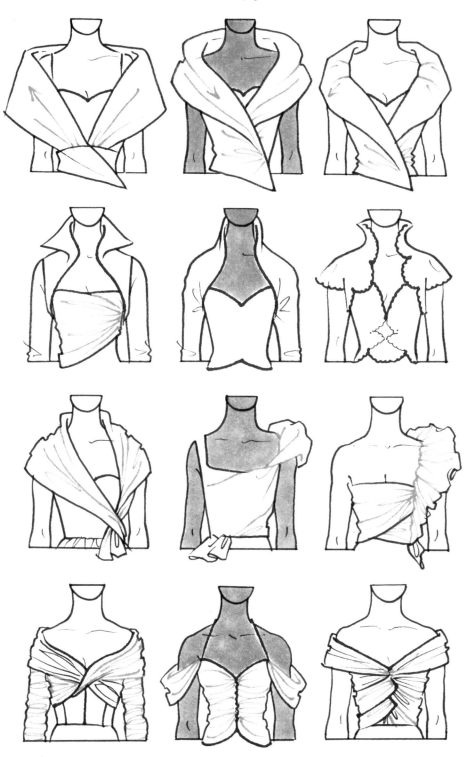

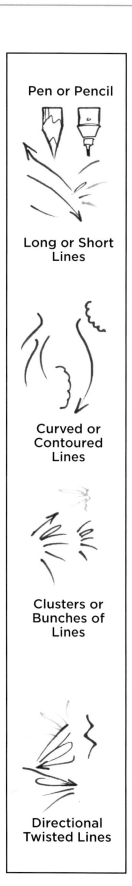

Pen or Pencil

Long or Short Lines

Curved or Contoured Lines

Clusters or Bunches of Lines

Directional Twisted Lines

Drape lines can also be done with rendering color or shading, but a definitive line, edge, or contour still conveys the sharpest style.

Hemline Treatments

- Fabric bunching under and over itself

- Multiple layers that fan out on top of each other

- Gores that fishtail into rolling folds

Drape Treatments

- Descending poufs tucked under each other

- Mutiple columns of tight, little pin-tucks

- Rosettes or ruched fabric in ruffled twists

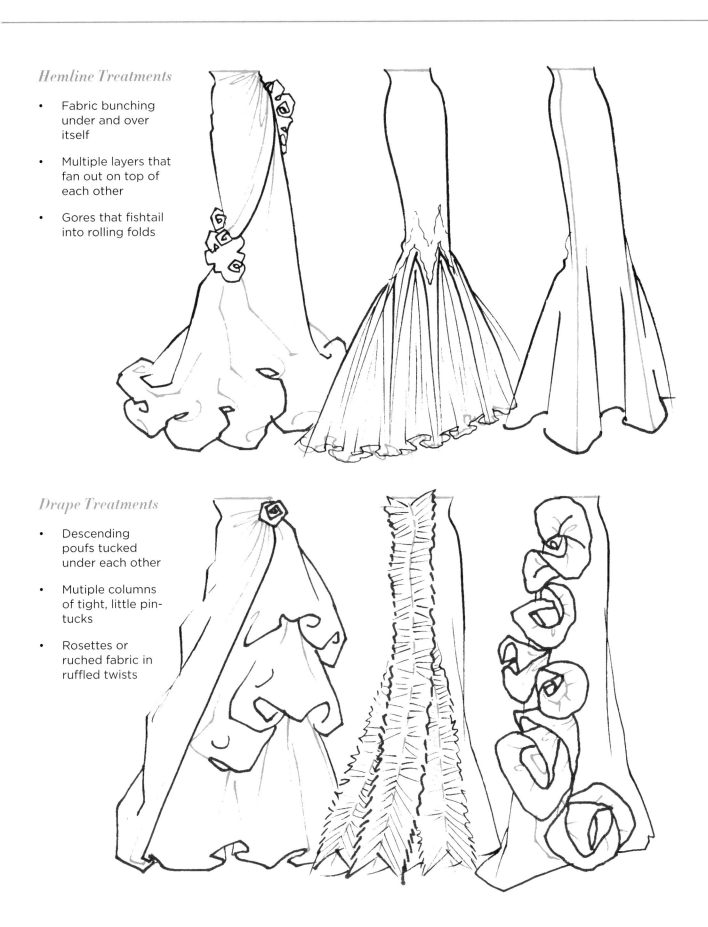

Luxe Fabric Rendering

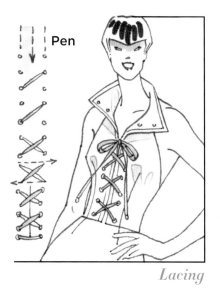

Pen

Lacing

Pen

Lacing

Create matching, cross-over angles. Establish width and length of lacing's "X" repeat.

Fringe

Map in the width and height of fringe. Use undulating same-length lines to fill in fringe strands.

Fringe

Pen

Tulle

Pen

Tulle

Draw tight crosshatching lines. Create fine net-like weave. Bunch up weave lines if tulle is gathered.

Lace

Roll edges if lace is scalloped. Fill in repeat motif. Add in delicate, light, and airy weaving over motifs.

Lace

Marker
Dabs

Pencil
Smudges

Pencil
Dots

.005 Fine
Point
Pen

Maribou Feather Boa

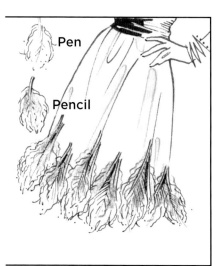

Pen

Pencil

Maribou Feathers

Dab on flecks of marker color. Add in soft, uneven pencil peaks and smudges. Use ultra-thin lines for downy bits.

Ostrich Feathers

Lightly indicate feather size and shape. Use pencil or pen in the shafts or quill lines. Cluster up the Flue and fluff of the plumes with pencil.

Ostrich Feathers

Velvet

Start with a marker base with highlights. Use pencil smudges for a textured surface.

Chiffon Layers

Use only pencil coloring. This gives it a grainier look than velvet.

Velvet Needs Plush Texture and Dense Coloring

Chiffon Needs a Grainy Look

Soft Pressure in Scrubbing Method for Pencil

Moiré Taffeta

Start with marker for the base coloring. Use pencil for the moiré pattern and gel pen accents for sheen.

Satin

Use layers of marker coloring for this fabric.

Moiré Print Looks Like Wood Grain Lines

Use Nib First, Then Small, Fine Tip

Use Lots of Broken, Fractured Color for Shine

Brocade

Use a marker base with pencil weave lines. Add pen or pencil for print.

Sequins

Start with larger dots that get increasingly smaller with each color change. Add highlights.

Use Pencil Lines to Imply Weave Direction

Sequins Can Get Up to Three Color Values to Convey One

Black Fabric Rendering

Ralph
Lauren

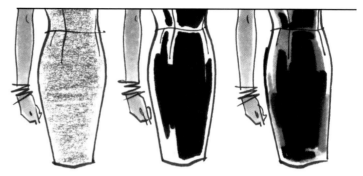

- Pencil rendering also resembles crepe fabric.
- Flat marker also looks like leather.
- Tonal black also reads as a glossy fabric.

The biggest challenge here is to add color without losing all of your essential garment detailing. Rendering for any type of black fabrics is a delicate balance of coloring versus construction information on any sketch.

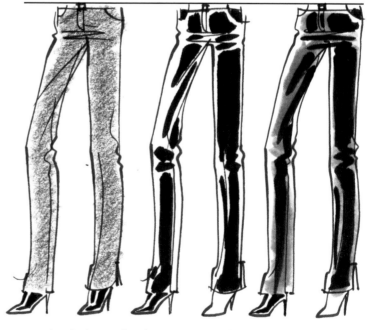

- Angled pencil coloring can read as a twill.
- Partial black rendering can read as shiny.
- Tonal gray and black can read as glossy.

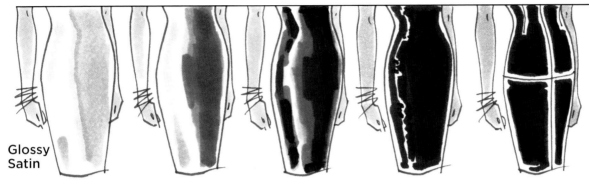

Glossy Satin

- Gray 40%
- Gray 70%
- Pure Black

- Three steps layered color sheen for satins
- One step black with a shimmer line for taffetas
- One step matte black for leather seaming

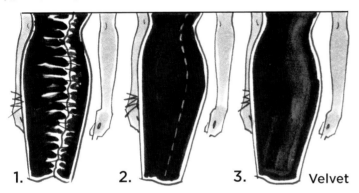

1.   **2.**   **3.**   **Velvet**

Silver or White Pencil Smudging

Note:

To render black fabric, there are only a few methods that can be done with the same steps in any media.

1. Use construction detail/drape to direct coloring.
2. Make princess seam a guide line for highlighting.
3. Mix media to create different effects over black.

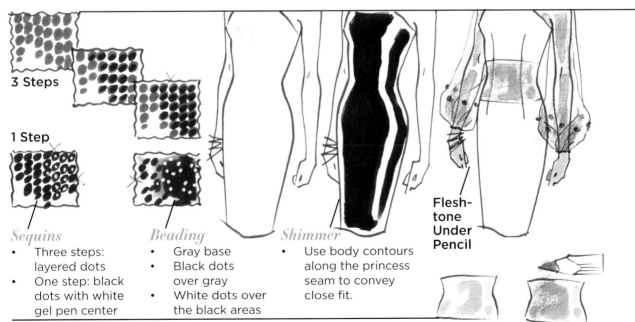

3 Steps

1 Step

Sequins
- Three steps: layered dots
- One step: black dots with white gel pen center

Beading
- Gray base
- Black dots over gray
- White dots over the black areas

Shimmer
- Use body contours along the princess seam to convey close fit.

Flesh-tone Under Pencil

Transparent, See-Through Fabrics Like Organza
- Step 1: Partial Fleshtone   •   Step 2: Pencil Smudging

Black Fabric Rendering (continued)

Marco de Vincenzo

Krizia

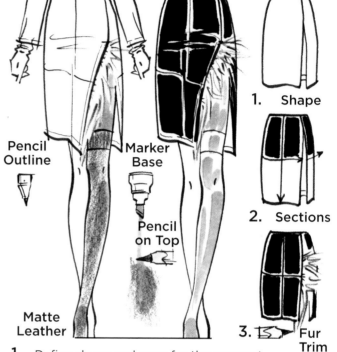

Pencil Outline

Marker Base

Pencil on Top

Matte Leather

1. Shape

2. Sections

3. Fur Trim

1. Define shape and pose for the garment.
2. Color in, up to, but not over all seamlines.
3. Work on contrast trims/media changes last.

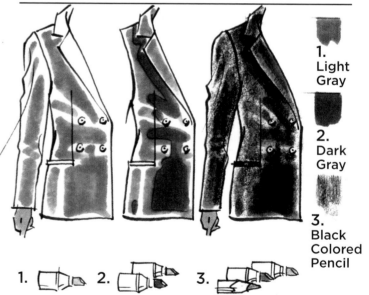

1. Light Gray

2. Dark Gray

3. Black Colored Pencil

1. Partially render in lightest value gray.
2. Add darker gray shading over base gray.
3. Use colored pencil over layered grays to create silvery black shimmer.

Giles

Elie
Tahari

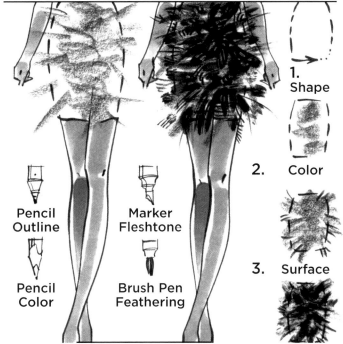

Pencil
Outline

Marker
Fleshtone

Pencil
Color

Brush Pen
Feathering

1. Shape

2. Color

3. Surface

1. Establish garment shape and outline edges.

2. Fill in fleshtone and baseline pencil.

3. Finish surface interest with brush pen mini strokes in all different directions. Add gel pen white lines on top of darkest feathering.

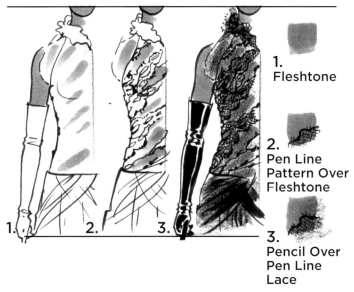

1. Fleshtone

2. Pen Line Pattern Over Fleshtone

3. Pencil Over Pen Line Lace

1. Break up fleshtone areas.

2. Work on lace repeats and fill in pattern.

3. Use colored pencil over pen line to create fabric transparencies.

Beading, Satin, Chiffon, Crystal Pleating, and Tulle

Elie Saab

Stephane Rolland

Vera Wang

Christophe Josse

Christian Dior

Delicate Beading

1. Fleshtone
2. Colors
3. Color dots
4. Pencil smudge

Strokes
of a
Flesh-
tone
Before
Fabric
Coloring

Hint of
Fleshtone
Done First
Before
All Color
Layers

Pencil
Strokes
Down
Toward
Hem

Crystal Pleating

Layers
of Pencil
Smudges
Over a
Gray Base

Time-saving rendering tips are to cut
back on the extra color tonalities that
are not neccessary in rough sketches.

*Sharp Jagged
Coloring*

Color with
Grain of
Fabric
Direction

Base
Paint or
Marker

Duchess Satin

Steps
for
Paint

1 2 3 4 5

1.
2.
3.
4.
5.

Steps for
Marker

Chiffon Layers

Feathers, Fringe, and Lace

- Soft pencil smudges
- Sharp pencil squiggle lines

- Soft pencil rows
- Fine pencil frayed edges

- Sharp pencil feathers
- Delicate pencil fringes

Naeem
Khan

Alexander
McQueen

Jean Paul
Gaultier

Dolce & Gabbana

Brood

- Two separate fleshtones done before lace-like print

- One fleshtone two ways: solid and broken, done first before print

- Gel pen white rendered over fleshtone

Pencil Print

- Transparent fabrics can display their see-through characteristics with clever coloring manipulation for what lies beneath—other fabrics or fleshtones.

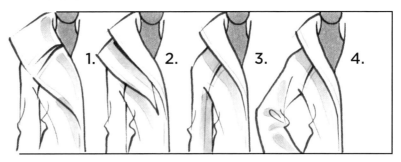

Add shading emphasis to:

1. Accentuate volume or function.
2. Convey and demonstrate layers.
3. Separate body planes in a pose.
4. Indicate a fold or bend in a pose.

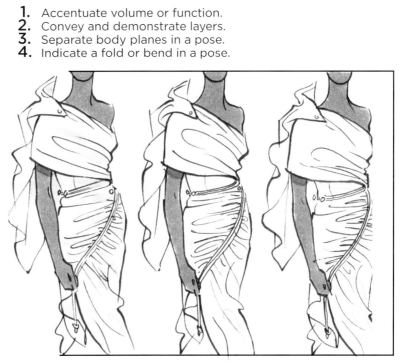

- Shading or highlighting on white fabric can involve more pale tints than gray coloring.

This evening gown layout can be used to demonstrate the interplay among specific elements that make a layout dynamic. These three elements are figure posing, garment shapes, and fabric colors. Use poses that complement, rather than contradict, the garment shapes. Play up the contrast between the garment silhouettes so that the shapes are exaggerated, not subdued. Divide the fabric colors so they carry the eye across the page instead of too much to one side. Balancing all three of these elements will maximize visual interest, like with this designer's work. Her layout is in balance, so the glamour quotient is high instead of hidden.

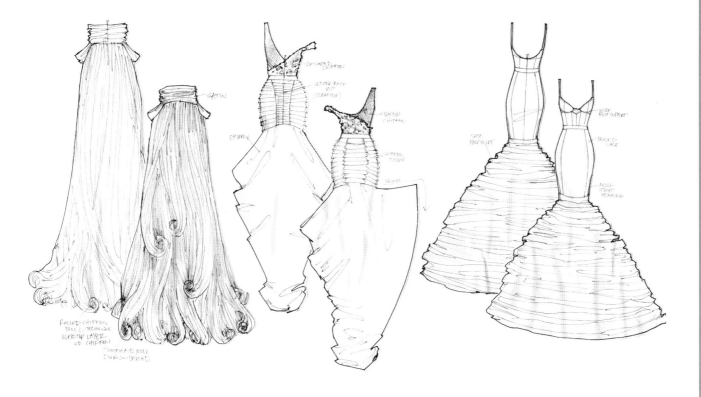

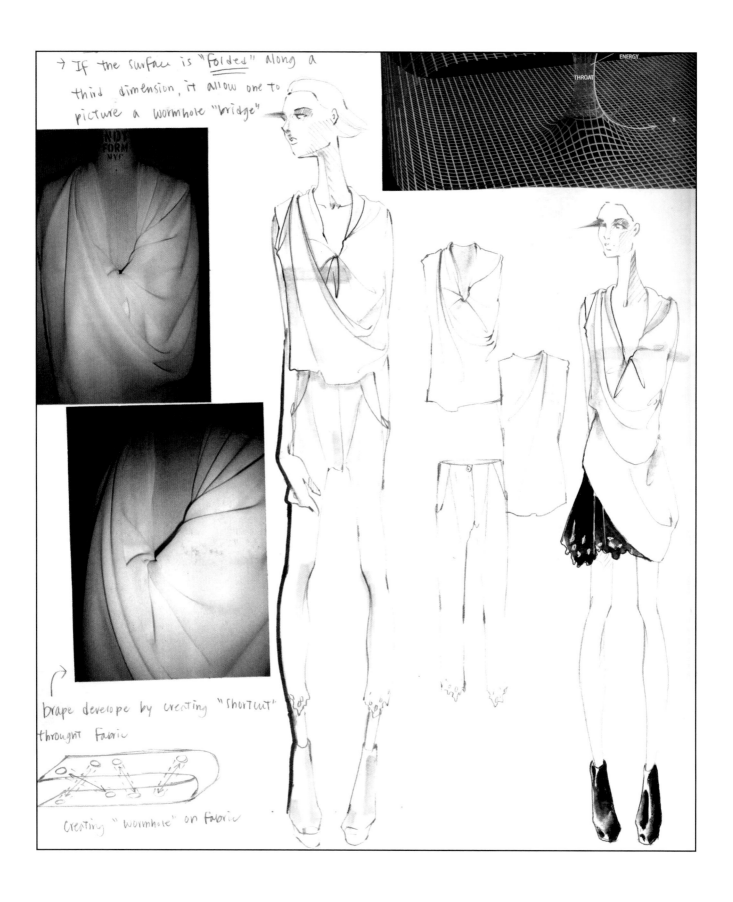

→ If the surface is "Folded" along a third dimension, it allow one to picture a wormhole "bridge"

ENERGY

THROAT

IND FORM NYC

Drape develope by creating "shortcut" throught fabric

Creating "wormhole" on fabric

The media mix for this design is gouache and colored-pencil outline on a spiral binder pad in book form. The first spread (of two on this designer's work) is her sketching stage. Exploring her creative options, she combines draping directly on the mannequin, flats, and figure work. This provides a sense of knowing the customer as well as style, driven by choices in color, texture, and laser cuts.

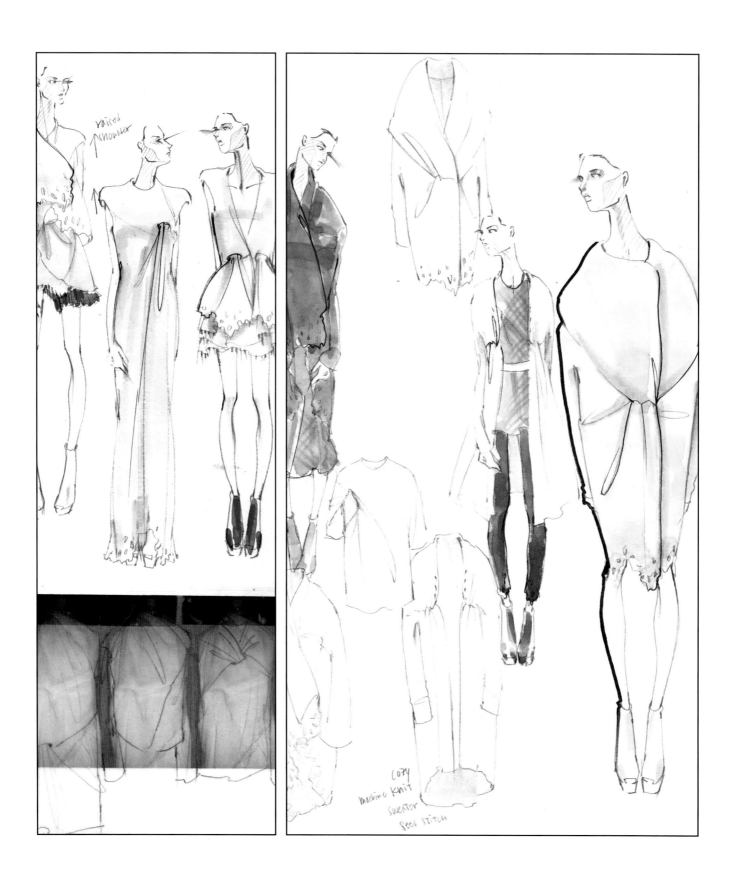

The media mix for this design is gouache and colored-pencil outline. Careful study of her sketching pages provides insight on how a designer edits rough sketches. She selects her strongest design silhouettes, picks the best poses for those garments, and illustrates these featured designs on a group of figures to maximize her collection's potential.

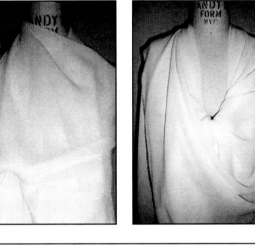

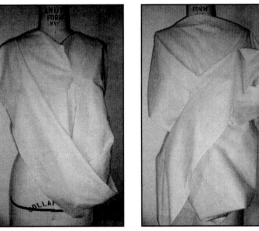

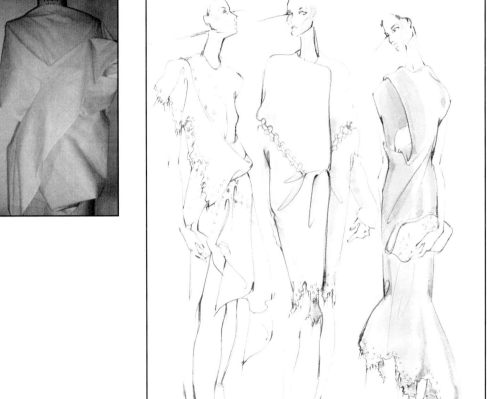

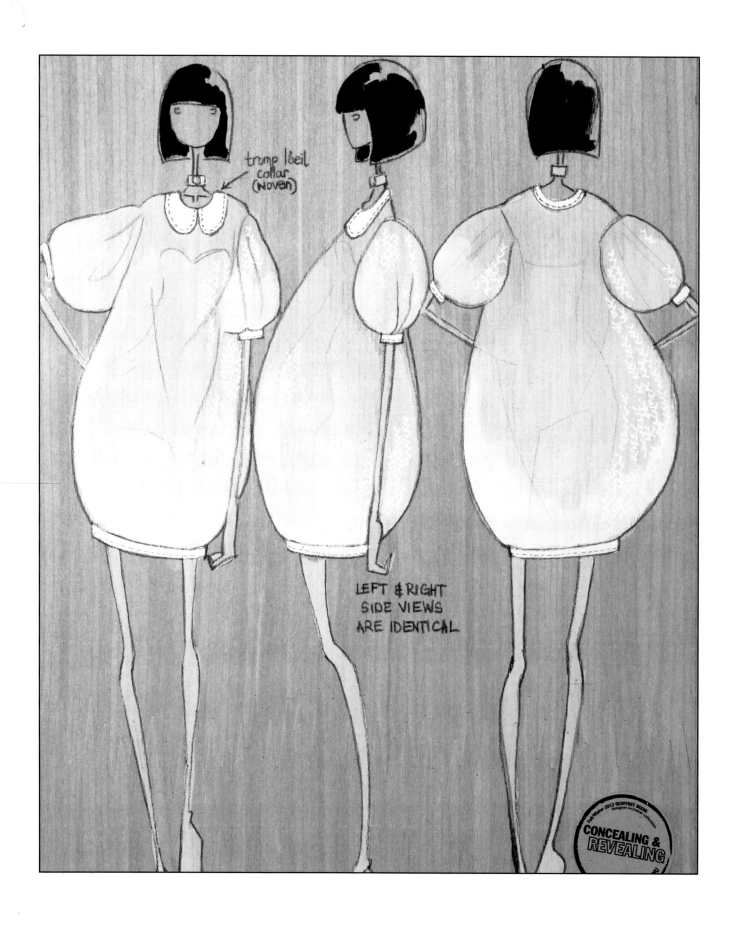

The media mix, left page: wood-grain paper, gouache, Pro-White, and pencil. On the right page: Canson paper, gouache, markers, and burn marks on the paper. These two spreads convey design direction and illustrate the value of developing a broader base of drawing styles to reshape a fashion identity.

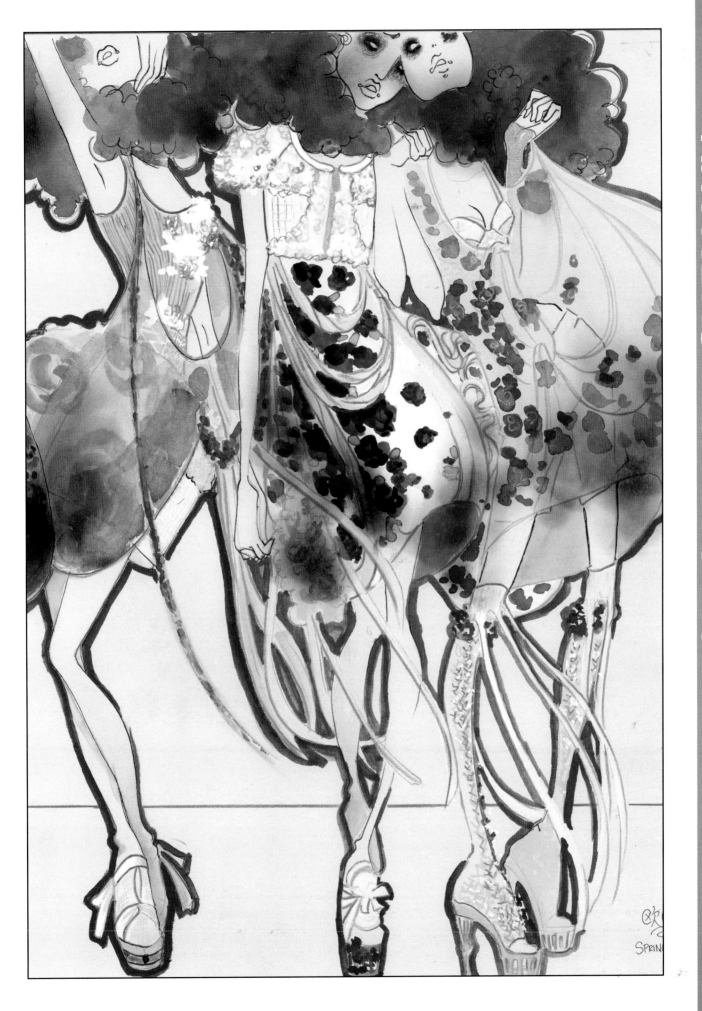

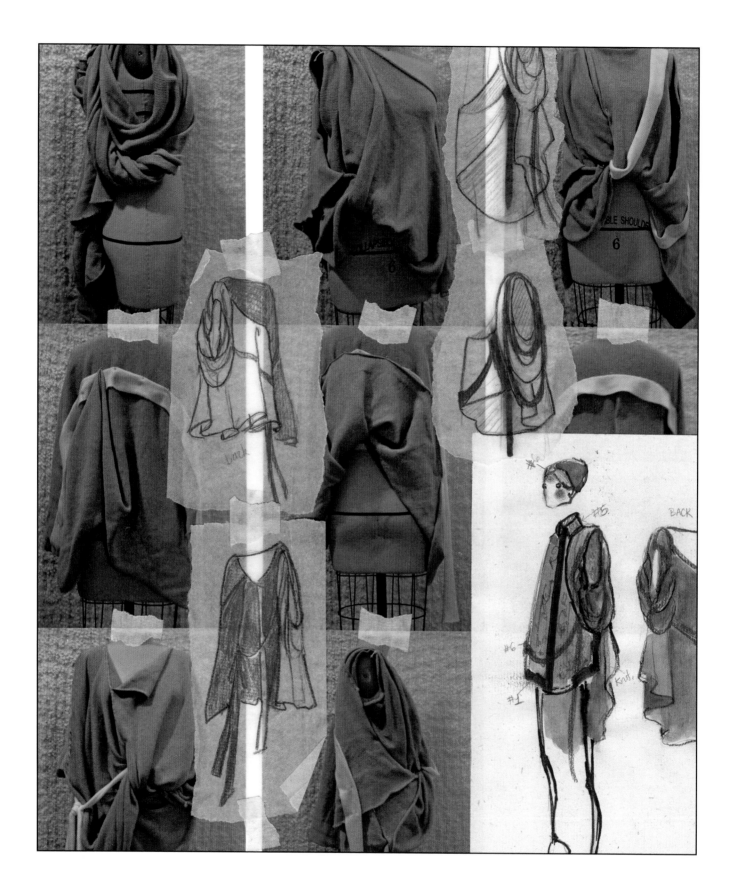

The media mix of this design is gouache, pen, and pencil (figure sketches on tracing paper). This designer's creative diversity is extensive. One of her approaches, shown here, is to explore a concept that integrates imagination with construction; she uses muslin on the dress form as design inspiration, and she approaches her draping as an art form, letting that process influence her design direction.

9

Drawing Knits

This chapter is an introduction to the nuances of drawing, styling, and rendering fashion knitwear for women's, men's, and children's garments. Knits created by hand or machine are a constant in the fashion industry regardless of fibers, yarns, or seasons. Knits will always be "in" somewhere and should be a part of your drawing vocabulary.

This chapter covers the basics of developing the intricate surface interest and creating complex dimensional prints for knitwear designs. These basic drawing techniques start with ribbing and continue with sketching textures and print motifs. A few of the most common terms for knits are included. This chapter is not a technical "how to" on knit fabrics; instead you will learn how to draw them.

Some stitching, weaving, and embroidery rendering techniques are also introduced. The more you practice knitwear styling the more you'll want to know. By the end of this chapter you may be curious enough about knits to do research on their mechanics. There are some beautiful instructional manuals on how to knit. It's a craft and an art of its own. Combining your drawing skills with your research on knits and knitting will help you to develop your own visual images to demonstrate the incredible variety in today's knitwear market.

Knit Essentials

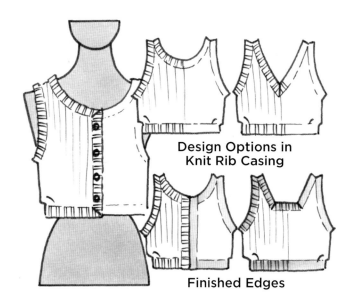

Design Options in Knit Rib Casing

Finished Edges

Line quality and context are essential in knitwear illustration. Line quality for the interior and exterior defines variety and variations in knit stitch types and patterning. Context, in line, will mean yarn type for knit stitches and patterning. Imagine in your mind's eye how you would draw the same sweater in a thin, fine yarn type versus a thick fuzzy yarn. One sweater style, but two distinct sketching and rendering techniques; one smooth and one textured. Resolving these drawing distinctions begins here.

Exterior and Interior Definition

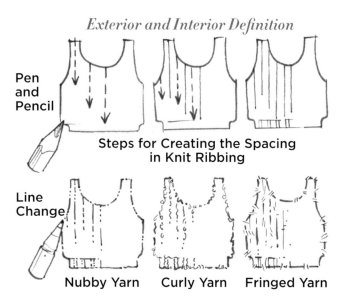

Pen and Pencil

Steps for Creating the Spacing in Knit Ribbing

Line Change

Nubby Yarn   **Curly Yarn**   **Fringed Yarn**

Exterior Outline Variety Affected by Yarn Type

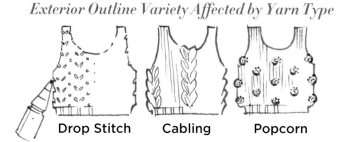

Drop Stitch   **Cabling**   **Popcorn**

Knit stitch illustration conveys dimensionality as well as texture in yarn type or knit stitches.

Tight **Loose**

Open Weaves

A weave can be done as a knit or a woven. Either method has the same visual appearance. This look is very linear, more grid-like than the usual ribbed rows. This rendering technique relies on the weight of your line and the spacing between those lines.

Embroidery **Lacing** **Fringe** **Crochet**

Extra Fine Point Pen or Pencil:
All four sketches

Micron .005:
Crochet, embroider, intarsia

Fine Point Pen or Pencil:
Ribs and outline edges

Treatments

Lots of treatments can be added to embellish the knit design shapes. The four types shown here each use a different kind of line to achieve a look.

Options

This is an example of how to communicate, in your sketch, the differences among three treatments that can create one look. It is your job to know how to illustrate these options—to be able to define these changes so that the image and technique in creating that pattern are clear.

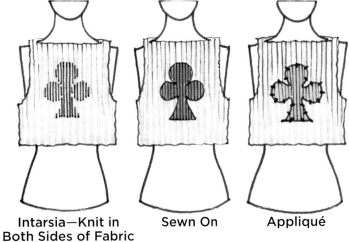

Intarsia—Knit in Both Sides of Fabric **Sewn On** **Appliqué**

Knitwear Flats

As you learned in Chapter 6, flats are an integral part of your fashion drawing repertoire. A flat is a way of displaying a garment off the figure in a factual manner that expresses size, fit, and proportion. To draw flats so they provide all the construction detail, it helps to use a croquis figure template or a grid. The croquis supplies body sewing lines for reference. The grid offers parameters for shaping a flat. Both are valuable support structures, especially for knits that often get more detailed than woven fabric flats. This is because knits often have more specific interior or exterior information, starting with ribs or finished edges. Based on the premise that all the flats on this page are in one size, the drawing narrative is about the comparison of these design shapes to each other.

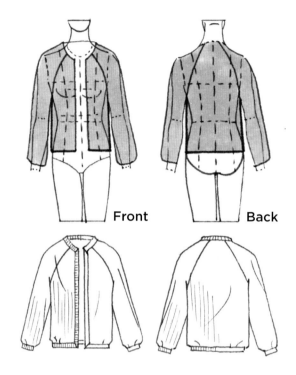

Front   Back

Templates for Flats

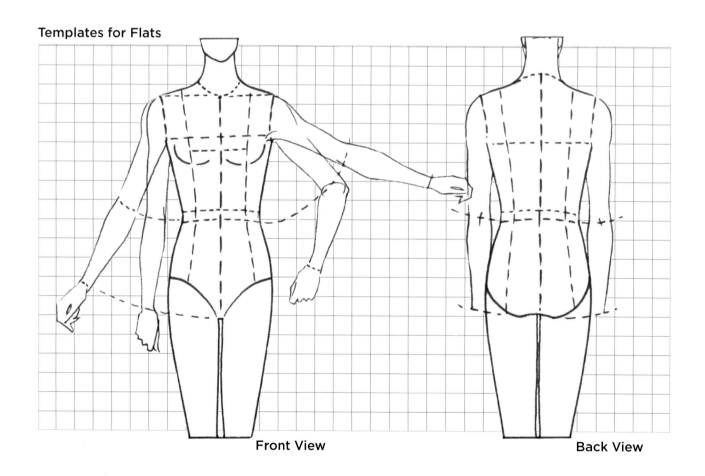

Front View   Back View

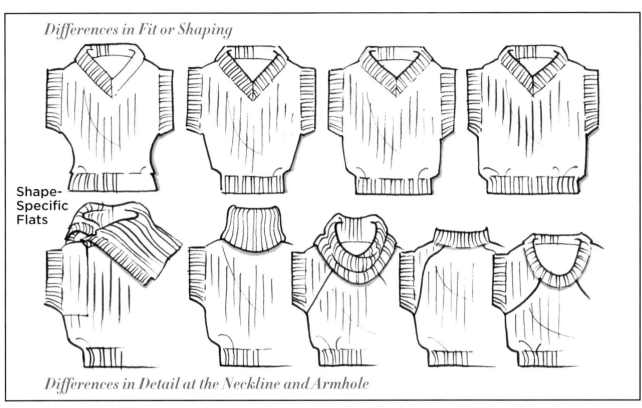

Differences in Fit or Shaping

Shape-Specific Flats

Differences in Detail at the Neckline and Armhole

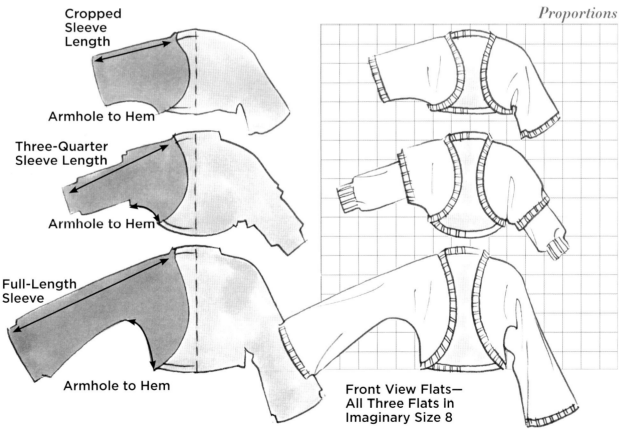

Cropped Sleeve Length

Armhole to Hem

Three-Quarter Sleeve Length

Armhole to Hem

Full-Length Sleeve

Armhole to Hem

Proportions

Front View Flats—
All Three Flats In
Imaginary Size 8

Basic Knit Stitches

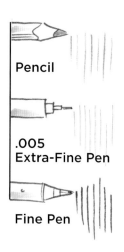

Pencil

.005 Extra-Fine Pen

Fine Pen

The basic rendering technique for knits is universal, drawn using rows of partial, broken, light lines. Changes in stitch, as seen below, can be shown through different techniques that demonstrate the variety of inherent knit qualities. Despite these variations, the basic rendering of knits remains constant. The sketch on this page lets you know that this is a knit fabric regardless of yarn type or specific knit stitch. It takes practice with your line to keep knits from looking like stripes.

Shaping

Alternating Rows

"V" or Chevron Pattern

Broad knitting needles, thick yarn, and chunky knit stitches make wider knit rows of ribbing to render. To imitate the appearance of this stockinette stitch, draw in alternating lines of plump seed-like "V" or chevron patterns.

Alternative Flat: Drawn like a sleeve or a tube that, when worn, conforms to body contour.

Shaped Flat: A full-fashioned knit is made preformed to reflect how it will conform to body contour.

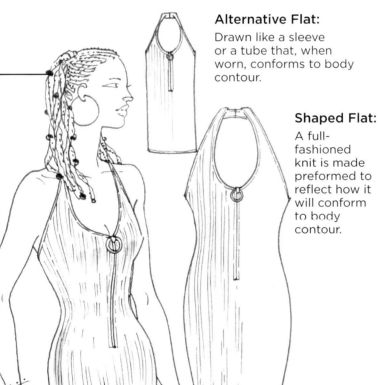

Repeating clusters of bands of ribbing, like this 3×3 rib, are simple to render. Conversely, they are hard to define if the garment is drawn too small, or easy to overstate if the garment is drawn too clingy or tight on the figure. Make sure to practice partial rib rows so that your lines are knits, not stripes.

Repeat Patterns

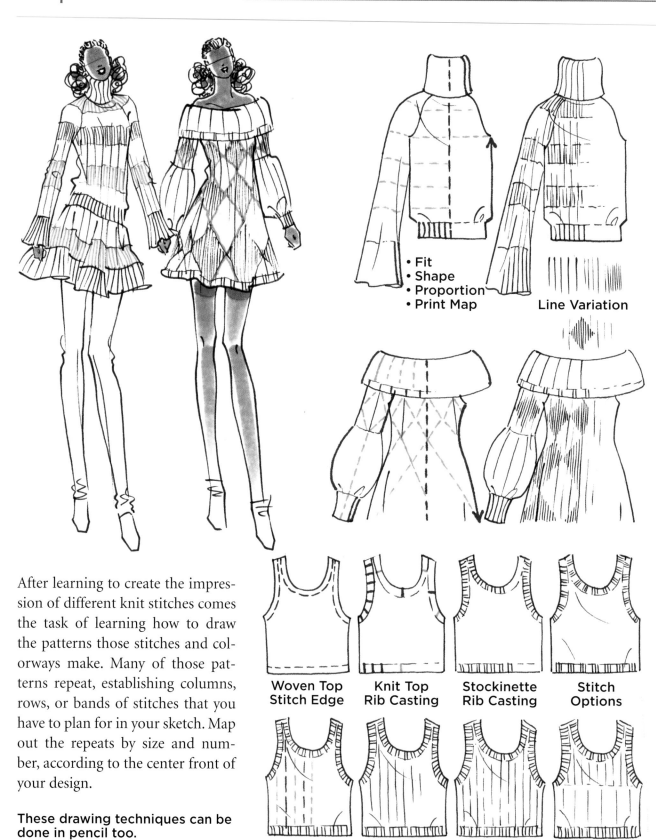

- Fit
- Shape
- Proportion
- Print Map

Line Variation

After learning to create the impression of different knit stitches comes the task of learning how to draw the patterns those stitches and colorways make. Many of those patterns repeat, establishing columns, rows, or bands of stitches that you have to plan for in your sketch. Map out the repeats by size and number, according to the center front of your design.

These drawing techniques can be done in pencil too.

Woven Top Stitch Edge

Knit Top Rib Casting

Stockinette Rib Casting

Stitch Options

Interior Knit Rows

Partial Rendering

Full Rendering

Change in Ribs/Rows

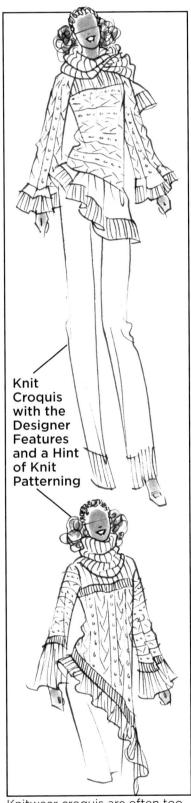

Knit Croquis with the Designer Features and a Hint of Knit Patterning

Knitwear croquis are often too small for pattern definition, so they get impressionistic detail.

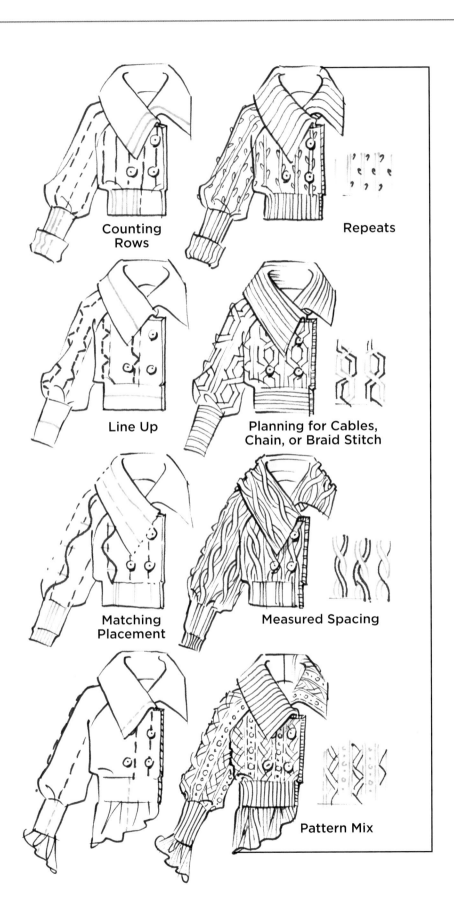

Counting Rows

Repeats

Line Up

Planning for Cables, Chain, or Braid Stitch

Matching Placement

Measured Spacing

Pattern Mix

Repeat Patterns (continued)

	Rib Casing	*Interior*	*Finished Sketch*
	Direction and type	Knit stitch styling	Drawing technique in a flat

Vertical

The basic setup for this type of stitch is to map out the number of rows by their width or distance from each other.

Horizontal

Again, establish your rows by height to each other. If there is a sleeve, you need to work out the direction of its rows in a relationship to your posing of the arms.

Gridded

This time, plan on creating a mix of horizontal and vertical lines to create a baseline, or grid, for your repeat pattern.

Diagonal

Here you need to work out the angle or slant of the repeat as it moves sideways across your knit piece.

Diamond

This is another form of a grid. It may be more critical where you map it out because of its visual impact on either the shoulder or hemline area on your garment.

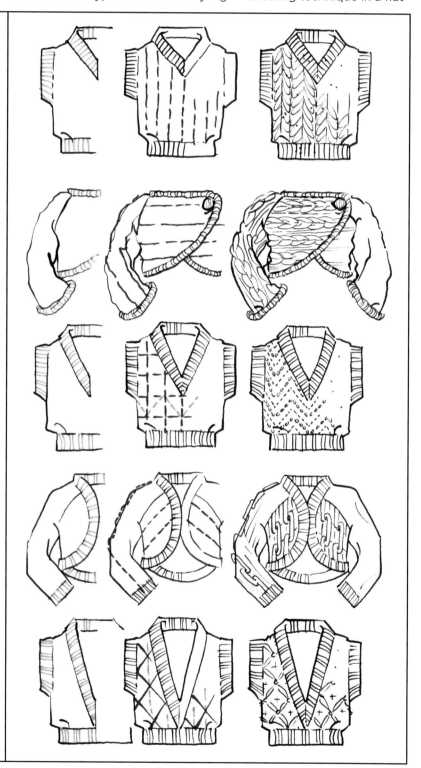

This type of knit rendering can be done in any media, pen or pencil, drawn by hand.

Each boxed set of line variety demonstrates another knit rendering technique to practice. Any combination of these lines can be used to imitate knit's novelty stitches.

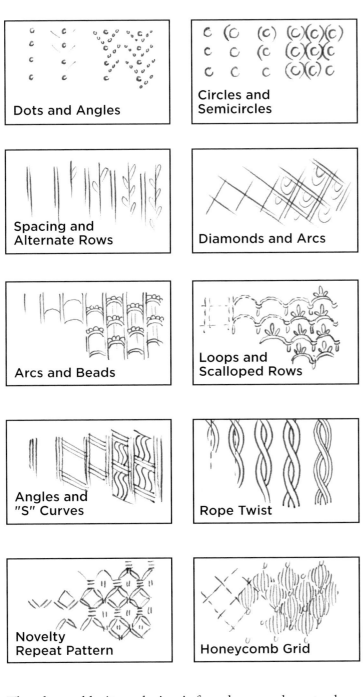

Dots and Angles

Circles and Semicircles

Spacing and Alternate Rows

Diamonds and Arcs

Arcs and Beads

Loops and Scalloped Rows

Angles and "S" Curves

Rope Twist

Novelty Repeat Pattern

Honeycomb Grid

The planned knit rendering is for when you have to draw a specific knit to explain its exact sequencing or illustrate its repeats precisely. This is a "real" knit for production versus an "impression" of a knit for design direction.

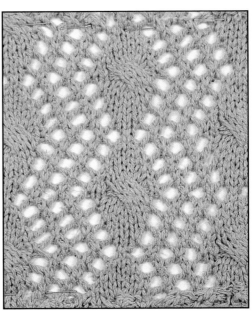

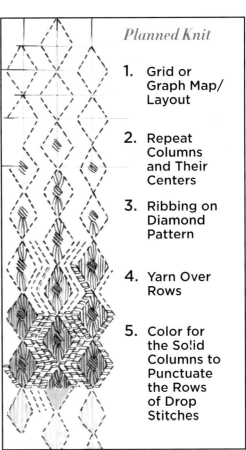

Planned Knit

1. Grid or Graph Map/ Layout

2. Repeat Columns and Their Centers

3. Ribbing on Diamond Pattern

4. Yarn Over Rows

5. Color for the Solid Columns to Punctuate the Rows of Drop Stitches

Cables and Combinations

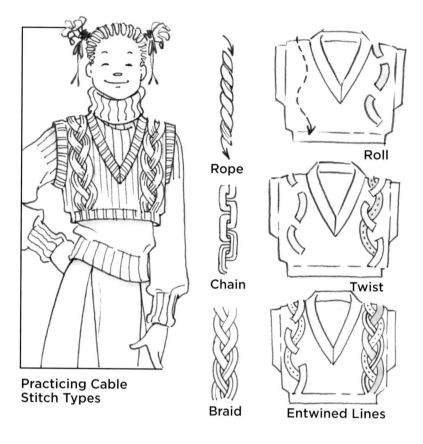

Practicing Cable Stitch Types

Rope

Chain

Braid

Roll

Twist

Entwined Lines

Cables are repeat stitches, combined and coordinated into a column, often in parallel rows. Repeats are the number of times the motif appears. Volume is how much space on the garment is consumed by the cabling or pattern. Placement is the location on the garment, such as center front.

A rope is the simplest form of a cable motif. It resembles a rolling line, curled, angled, and twisted into a column.

A chain looks more like connected links intersecting or locking into each other in a column.

A braided cable appears plaited, entwining three or more rows laced together in a column.

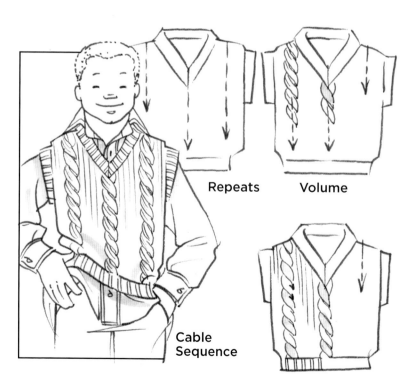

Cable Sequence

Repeats

Volume

Cabling can take three or more stages to completely render its patterns or shapes. Map out the number of repeats and their locations on the garment. Establish the width and count the cables. Add in a few ribs around the cables where possible.

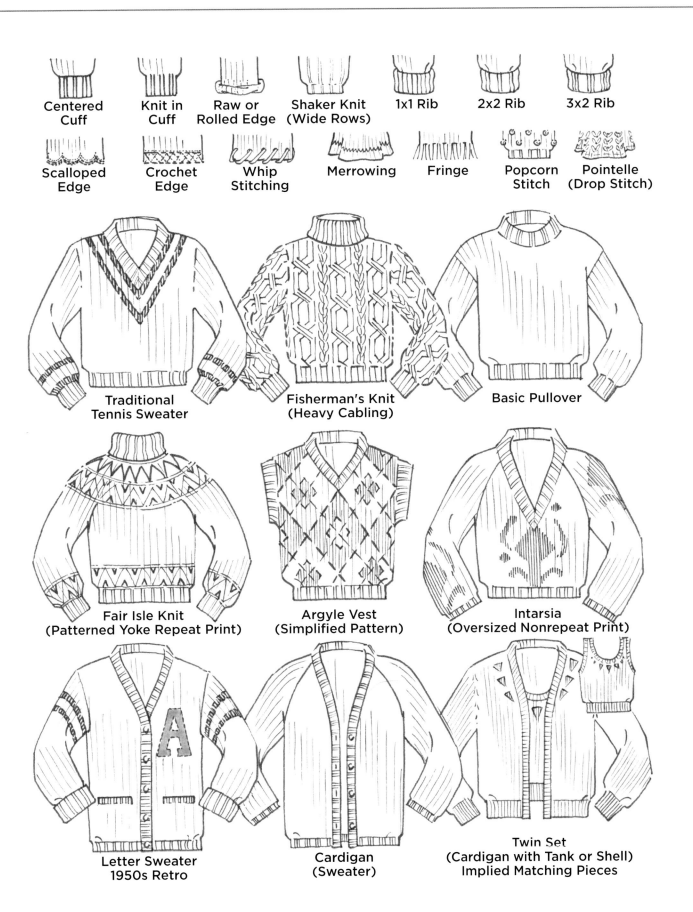

Centered Cuff

Knit in Cuff

Raw or Rolled Edge

Shaker Knit (Wide Rows)

1x1 Rib

2x2 Rib

3x2 Rib

Scalloped Edge

Crochet Edge

Whip Stitching

Merrowing

Fringe

Popcorn Stitch

Pointelle (Drop Stitch)

Traditional Tennis Sweater

Fisherman's Knit (Heavy Cabling)

Basic Pullover

Fair Isle Knit (Patterned Yoke Repeat Print)

Argyle Vest (Simplified Pattern)

Intarsia (Oversized Nonrepeat Print)

Letter Sweater 1950s Retro

Cardigan (Sweater)

Twin Set (Cardigan with Tank or Shell) Implied Matching Pieces

Complex Knits

The examples here serve as a guide on how to plan out a knit sketch with complex sets of mixed stitches on some basic sweater shapes. Like any pattern it helps to map it out first, by counting and planning the knit pattern's repeats across the garment before you start to render it.

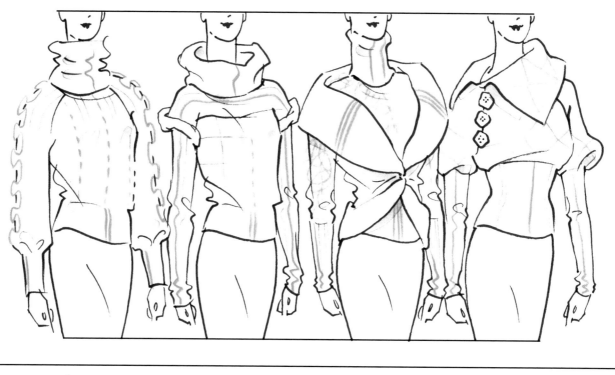

Scrunched Up, Loose Fit   Rolling the Lines   Hugging Waist or Hips

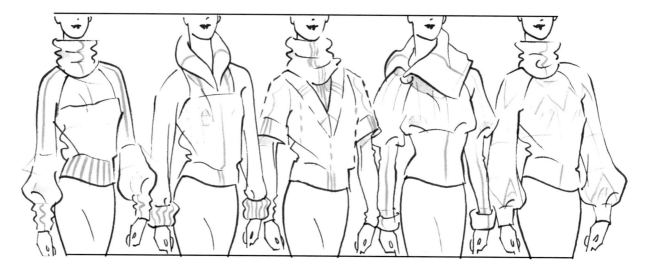

To indicate the stretch factor, knitwear necklines have a soft, rounded edge.

Curl   **Roll Over**   **Stand Up**   **Drape Over**

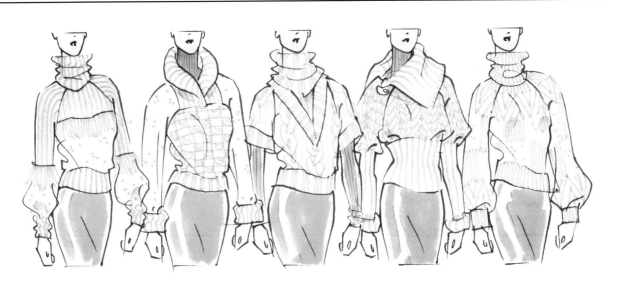

Curls

Braid

Grid

Rows

Links

Loops

Angles

Complex Knits (continued)

Knit Rib Casing
- Plan out height and width.
- Focus on stitch count.
- Work on even spacing for the repeat ribbing.

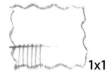
1x1

2x2

3x2

Special Knit Treatments
- Define drawing technique.
- Map out placement.
- Round out over body contouring to emphasize strength and fit.

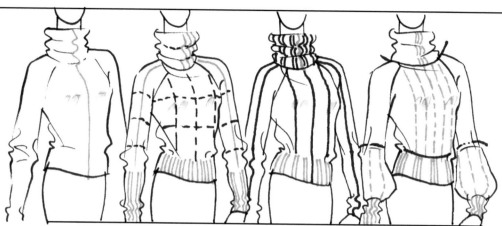

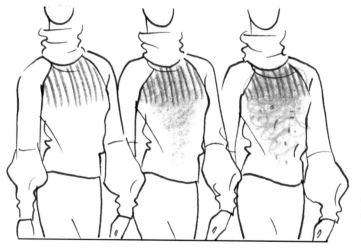

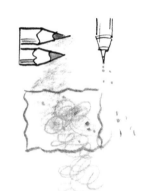

- Pencil Points
- Knit Rows
- Pencil Sides
- Yarn Types

Dressing the Neck
- Up to the chin
- Across the neck
- Down on center front

Dressing the Wrist
- Wrapping around the arm
- Covering the wrist
- Sliding down the hand

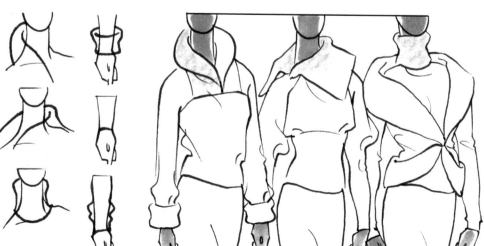

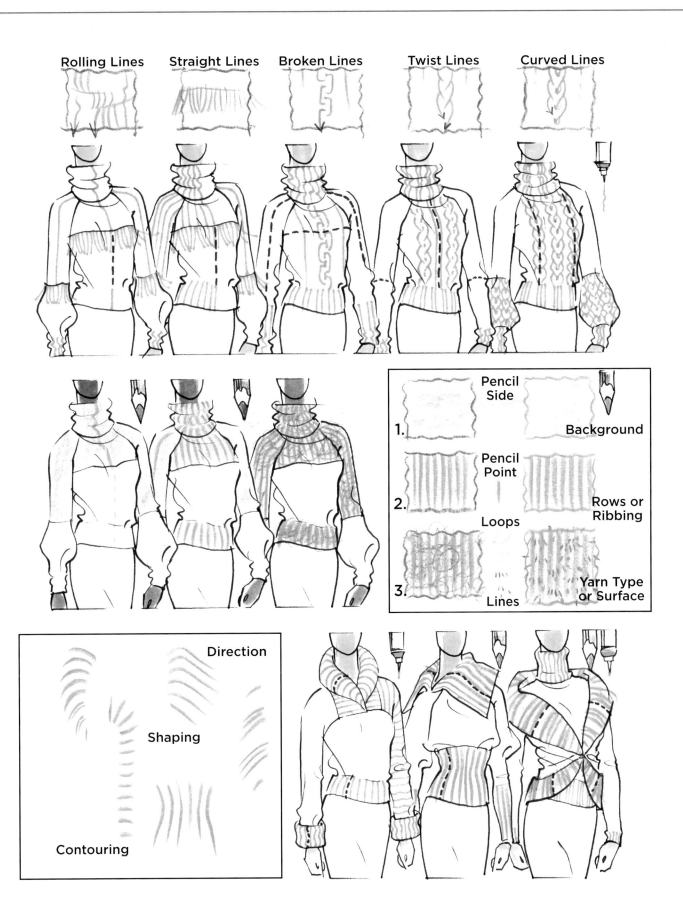

Rolling Lines **Straight Lines** **Broken Lines** **Twist Lines** **Curved Lines**

Pencil
Side

1.   Background

Pencil
Point

2.   Rows or
                                                     Ribbing

Loops

3.   Yarn Type
                                                     or Surface

Lines

Direction

Shaping

Contouring

WWD Photo Reference

Escada

Sacai

Vanessa Bruno

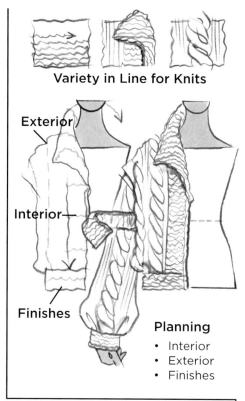

Variety in Line for Knits

Exterior

Interior

Finishes

Planning
- Interior
- Exterior
- Finishes

Line Content and Variety

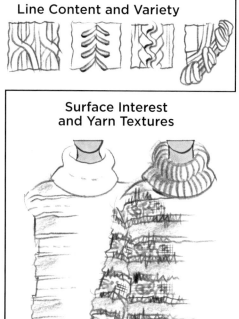

Surface Interest and Yarn Textures

Knit

Accents

- Lace-like inserts
- Arm has same repeat rows or bands as main body

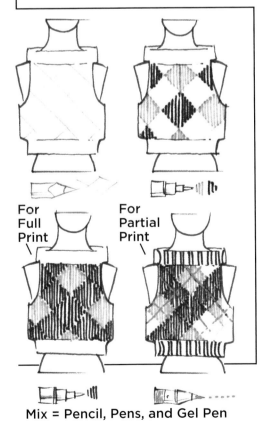

Three Colored Pens

Three Colored Pencils

For
Full
Print

For
Partial
Print

Mix = Pencil, Pens, and Gel Pen

Intarsia Pattern

An intarsia knit creates an image that is a single motif. It usually does not repeat the way a Fair Isle pattern does. Often oversized, the intarsia patterns have "floats"; that is, stop and start yarns versus continuous ones, as the color changes within the motif.

Front

Back

Argyle Pattern

The argyle knit is an all-over pattern in a mix of overlapping, diamond-shaped grids. This includes a single line of color, in alternating angles, over the main grid, to complete its motif.

Fisherman's cable
knits
Feminized.

Cable
forms
Sweater
(super
size)

hand
Knit
fisher
mans
Cable
Skirt

This designer's work presents an air of sophistication and fashion attitude that seems smart, fresh, and young. His sense of style is evident in both his croquis and his finished sketch because this fashion attitude remains consistent between the two drawing methods . . . a styling factor that he takes from minimum to maximum when he is drawing his signature fashion face, as you can see on the facing page. The drawing differences can be defined as rough (for the looser, conceptual croquis) and as finished (for the more polished, studied figure).

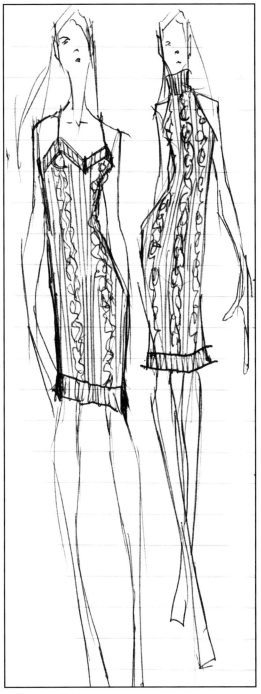

This designer's collection can be studied for its exquisite rendering. Observe her tonal range, the subtle changes in coloring for this navy, monochromatic color palette. This fashion group, based on a specific variety of fabrics, divides the fabric types between the tops and bottoms of the garments, maximizing the fashion styling. The success of the styling for these silhouettes depends largely on the clarity of rendering combined with line drawing precision. The designer faced two challenges—intense coloring and layered sportswear separates. Study her solution. She could have completed one outfit at a time or one fabric at a time across all the garments in the group. Either method works, as this illustration proves so beautifully.

Compare this spread with the previous knitwear design spread. Note that the first layout focused on the designer's figure work, with her flats as backup. On this second layout, the flats are being featured with the figures as backup. Both types of layouts are valid. Which one you choose can be based on its fashion focus or point of view. For example, the first layout's focus could be about who wears the clothes or how to wear them. The focus here could be on construction, shapes, and garment detailing. Always select a focus for your illustration or design presentation to make it as bold and direct as this artist's work.

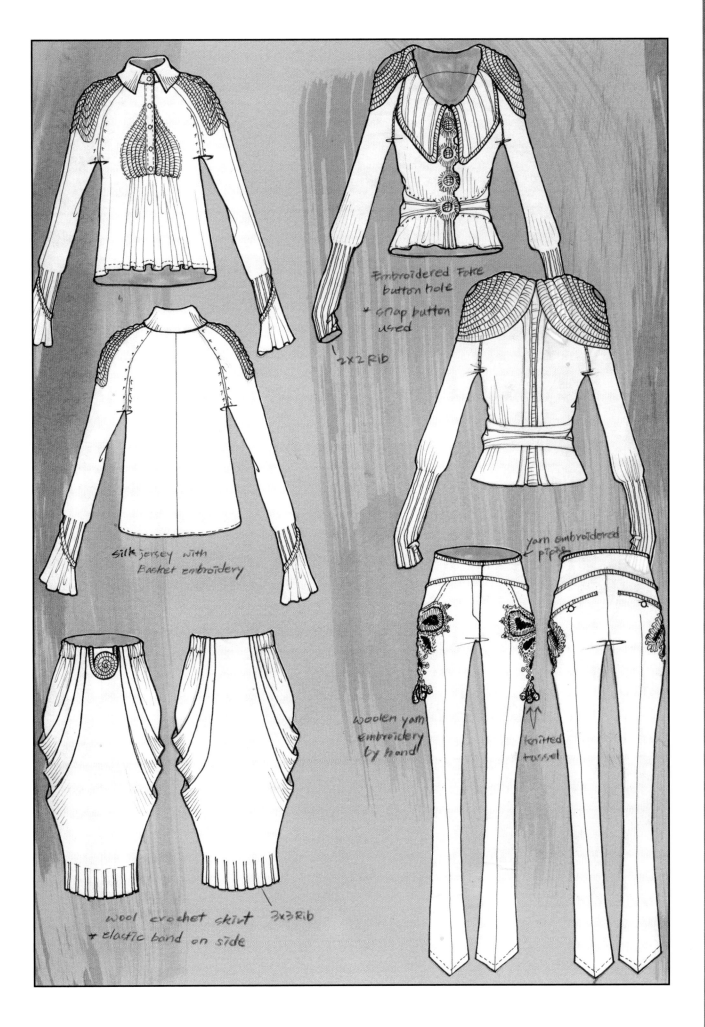

Embroidered Fake
button hole
* snap button
used

2x2 Rib

silk jersey with
Basket embroidery

yarn embroidered
piping

woolen yarn
embroidery
by hand

knitted
tassel

wool crochet skirt   3x3 Rib
+ elastic band on side

The media mix for this design is marker and colored pencils. Inspired by smoke, these complex and sophisticated knit pieces use a wide variety of line quality to illustrate the stitch treatments. Detailed drawings, like these, are critical in visual communication. His sketching process clearly spells out his design intention.

The media mix for this design is gouache, marker, and colored pencils. Inspired by corals and origami, this designer's knitwear collection incorporates the nuances of shape and drape with the combinations of different motifs and textures. His diversity in surface interest comes alive on the page with lush color and his attention to rendering details.

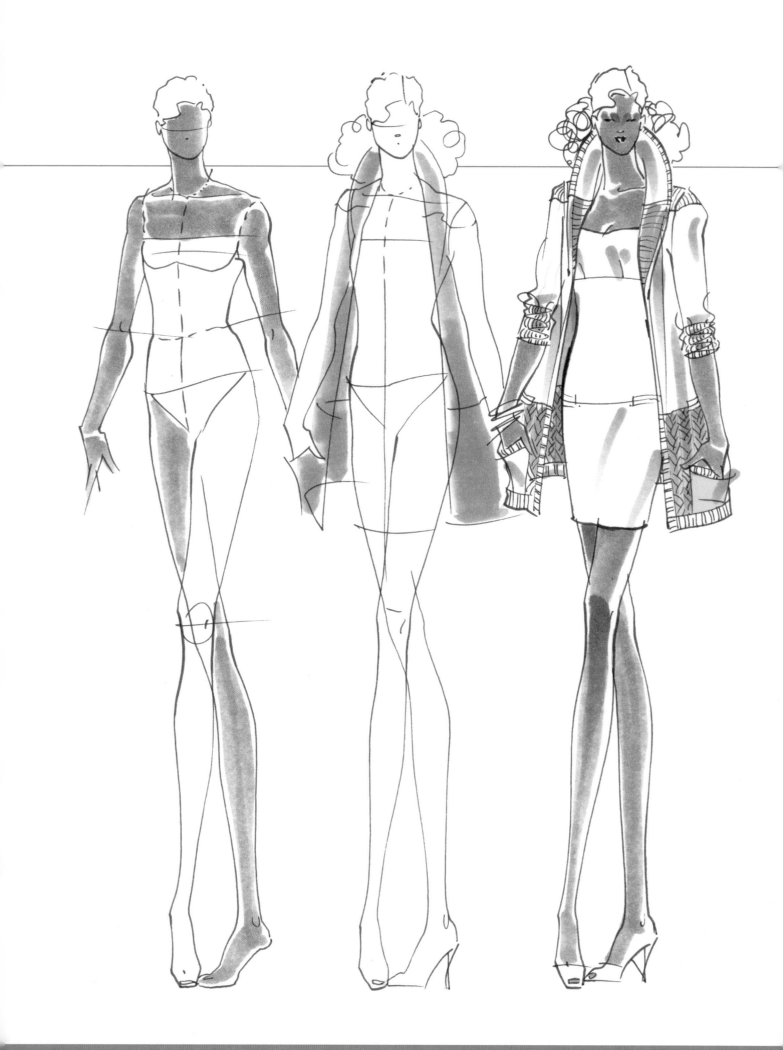

10

Design Focus and Layout

Layout is as synonymous with composition as design focus is with concept. The beauty of the two together is how they build a balance between visual impact and fashion message. Design is a richly creative, diverse project. Layout controls the project based on artistic license as well as personal taste and style. Composition can maximize the potential in a design concept. It can pull multiple images together in a large space or create emphasis in a small space. There are many contributing factors to the success of your fashion design assignments and presentations.

This chapter, through outline details and example illustrations, will explain a few of the simple fashion design presentation formats on a beginner's level. It also brings design focus to basic structures for the mixed images of fashion figures, flats, and accessories, presented as a number of optional templates from which you invent your own layouts. By the end of this chapter, you will have a better grasp of how to coordinate fashion design compositions and layout.

Design Direction

Here are some of the points to make in your fashion illustrations that will apply to all aspects of the fashion industry. The points are visual and verbal. The visual is all about image; the verbal is about the commerce fixed to your image. It's art and language that integrate your fashion design personality (customer) with color, fabric, and style. This combination is called design direction. It takes the visual and verbal to promote your fashion focus on the job or at an interview—words that complete your pictures.

Based on the following outlines, practice putting design direction into a dialogue about style. Study the guest artists on the following spreads. How do you think they would describe the design direction for their illustrations?

A. *Customer Profile:* Describing for whom you design

1. Who wears your clothes....................example....................Executive
2. Why she likes your style....................example....................Independent/Sophisticated
3. Where she wears your clothes.........example....................Boardroom
4. Where she buys your clothes...........example....................High-End/Exclusive Shops/Brand label's own e-trade site (commerce)

1. Personality: "My customer is smart, confident, and elegant."
Who wears your clothes (e.g., executive): List fashion character traits and use words infused with attitude and image as commerce.

2. Rationale: "She wants sophisticated, contemporary looks."
Why she likes (represents) your style (taste level) (e.g., independent, sophisticated): Use words that convey lifestyle, income, and fashion focus.

3. Lifestyle: "She is a high-powered executive who loves city living."
Where she wears your clothes (e.g., in the boardroom): You can also refer to time of day, evening, weekend, etc. Describe occupation, travel, and social activities.

4. Shopping Habits: Where she buys your clothes (e.g., high-end designer or exclusive shops, boutiques or trendy shops, websites).

5. Home: Where she lives (home is an extension of personality):
• Home—big-city loft or suburban home (or both)
• Decor—ultramodern or heirloom antiques
• Locale—fast-paced city or country casual

6. Age Bracket: Age is never specific: "Forever young."
Customer profile is interpreted through style: Contradictions are inherent in design mix.
• Customer/theme—Biker chick meets debutante
• Fabrics/silhouette—Leather jackets and chiffon skirts
• Design category—City weekend separates/fall season
• Color palette—Bold brights and sweet pastels
Note: Price points come in fabric and construction details. How clothing is priced is an optional description.

B. *Design Concepts:* Putting your theme, premise, and inspiration into words

1. Explain the design direction, concept, and focus:
   a. Trend—inspiration and influences on your work
   b. Research—design development and application of ideas
   c. Customer and price points—motivation for concept

2. Describe the color palette or color "story"; its related theme integration color and fabric:
   a. Trends—color forecasting services to make color associations
   b. Research—historical or cultural persuasions for color names
   c. Season—nuances in colorations for climate or region

3. Tell the fabric "story" about the fiber (e.g., cotton) and weave (e.g., brocade):
   a. Types (names) of fabrics, blends, number of mixes of fabrics
   b. Function or technology factor—see design category for fabric typecasting (e.g., high-tech, stretch fabrics for activewear)
   c. Special design features—trims and notions (buttons, zippers, etc.)

4. Describe shape and fit or silhouette "story":
   a. Cut of garments—how they fit or are worn to create a look
   b. Construction or drape factors in this group or collection
   c. Design category influence dictated due to silhouette boundaries

5. Choose the design category:
   a. Lingerie (innerwear): Foundations, sleepwear, loungewear
   b. Coats (outerwear): Jackets, rainwear (seasonal)
   c. Sportswear separates: Career, weekend, activewear
   d. Dresses: Casual, career (one hanger, one price tag)
   e. Bridal: Mother of the bride, bridesmaid, bridal party
   f. Special occasion: Suits, cocktail dresses, gowns, prom wear
   g. Swimwear and cover-ups: Playwear, resort (seasonal)
   h. Specialization: Knitwear, denims, shirts

C. *Design Influence:* Marketing your design; what drives the design concept, inspiration, and theme

1. Trends—always new, based on:
   a. Pop culture influences from music, movies, Hollywood, celebrities, characters
   b. Art, movies, current events, technology
   c. Fashion past and present, vintage or retro updates, street trend websites
   d. Fabric and fiber innovations; color and surface interest trends

2. Customer—who wears what type of clothes, attitudes, and looks (always young):
   a. Classic, sophisticated, career woman
   b. Junior, trendy, club kid
   c. Contemporary, cutting edge, city girl
   d. Avant-garde, experimental, bohemian girl
   e. The mix-it-up, stylish, independent woman who defies categorization

3. Seasons—losing emphasis but still referenced (regional):
   a. Spring/Summer: Can "deliver" up to seven looks a season
   b. Fall/Winter: Same (plus fall more costly than spring) due to fabrics
   c. Fifth season Resort (Regional): All-year-round pieces in lightweight fabrics

4. Design markets—how fashion looks are priced:
   a. Couture day dress: $10,000 (exclusive, established designer)
   b. Demi-couture day dress: $5,000 (younger market, designer label)
   c. Designer day dress: $3,000 (established name or brand)
   d. Young designer day dress: $1,000 (unestablished name, up-and-coming name)
   e. Bridge day dress: $500 (diffusion lines of name-brand "umbrella" labels
   Also: Private Label, Contemporary, Better, Junior, Moderate Categories. Big brand with separate labels, pricing divisions, range or looks

5. Retail venues—where designs are sold:
   a. Designer's own shop, company store e-commerce sites
   b. Department store, all in price point divisions
   c. Boutique, lifestyle shops, catalog, Internet
   Also: Designers, brand names, personalized commercial websites

Attitude in a Pose

Send a message / Make a statement

Attitude is an expression of composure, achieving a balance of look and feeling. How to wear something is just as important as what to wear. Attitude in a pose conveys a fashion point of view, as these examples demonstrate.

1. A narrow, static pose; controlled, classic

2. A slinky, curvy pose; sexy, dressy

3. A bold, more open pose; confident, sporty

4. Another type of open pose; younger, playful

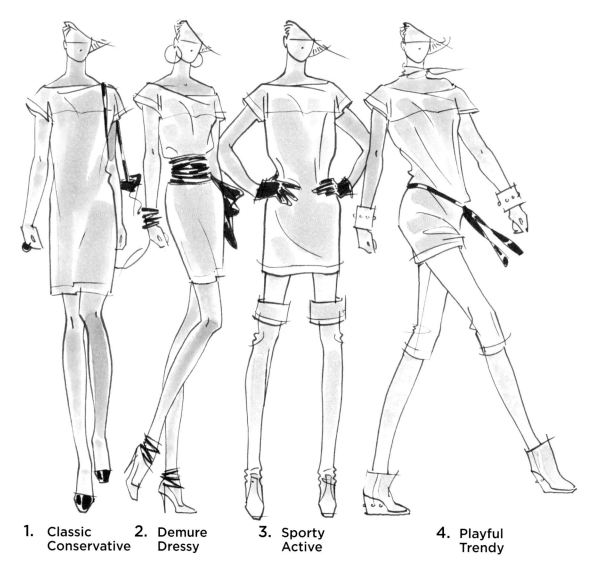

1. Classic Conservative   **2. Demure Dressy**   **3. Sporty Active**   **4. Playful Trendy**

A. Does this pose look playful?

If the design category for this outfit was supposed to be playful, the pose is contradicting its message.

B. Does this pose read as sporty?

A slinky, curvy pose does not optimize the sense and attitude for an active garment's point of view.

C. Does this pose look classic?

Confidence does not contradict classic, but it would help the dress to be in a less aggressive pose.

D. Does this pose appear dressy?

This wide-open, off beat pose fights the fashion image of a sultry, slinky, special-occasion dress.

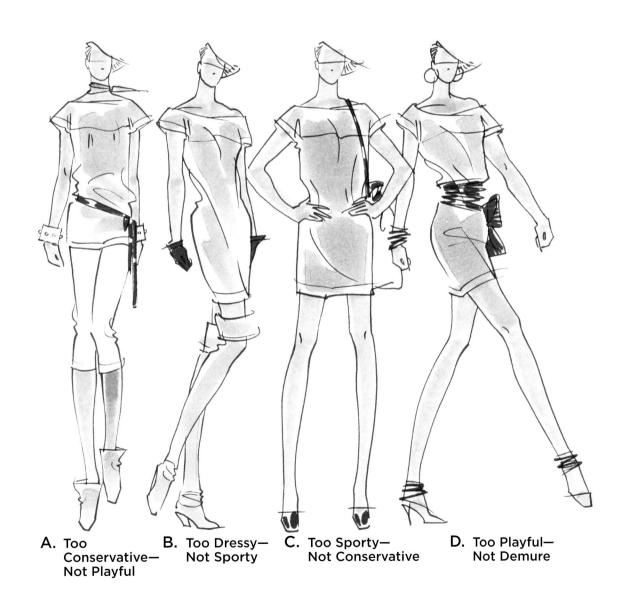

A. Too Conservative— Not Playful

B. Too Dressy— Not Sporty

C. Too Sporty— Not Conservative

D. Too Playful— Not Demure

Design Emphasis

One design goal is to maximize visual impact, to boost the design focus of a garment, emphasize its features—the cut, fit, shape, or fabrication of it. This emphasis is often an exaggeration to heighten the fashion statement in a design collection or in a single garment. One way to create this emphasis is to combine the figure with the flats. Another technique is to exaggerate the details.

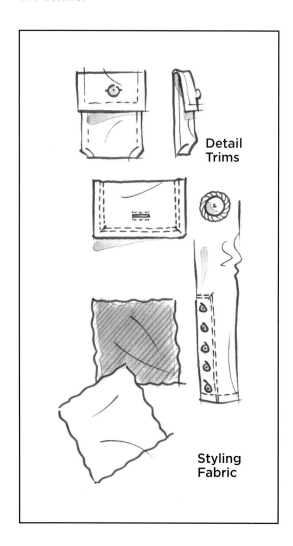

Detail Trims

Styling Fabric

Detailing Emphasis with Front- and Back-View Flats of Same Outfit

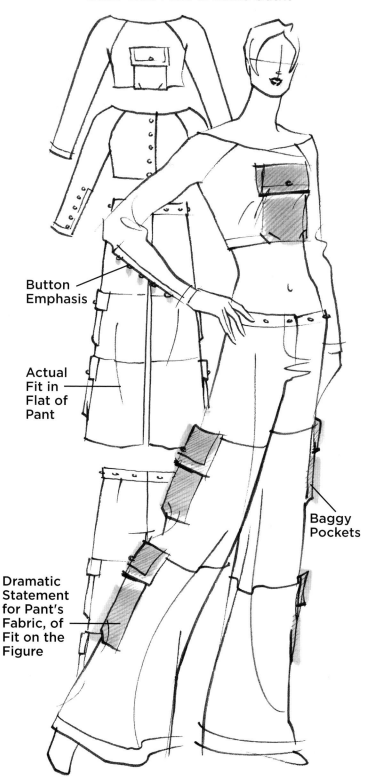

Button Emphasis

Actual Fit in Flat of Pant

Dramatic Statement for Pant's Fabric, of Fit on the Figure

Baggy Pockets

Emphasis on Pant Legs' Fit, Drape, and Oversized Pockets

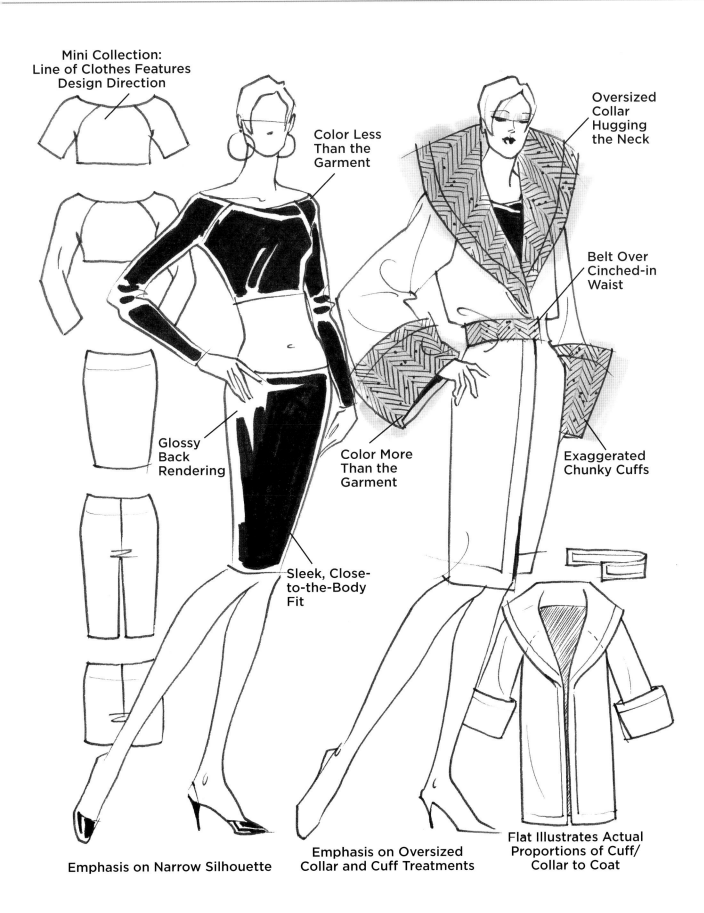

Mini Collection:
Line of Clothes Features
Design Direction

Color Less
Than the
Garment

Oversized
Collar
Hugging
the Neck

Belt Over
Cinched-in
Waist

Glossy
Back
Rendering

Color More
Than the
Garment

Exaggerated
Chunky Cuffs

Sleek, Close-
to-the-Body
Fit

Emphasis on Narrow Silhouette

Emphasis on Oversized
Collar and Cuff Treatments

Flat Illustrates Actual
Proportions of Cuff/
Collar to Coat

Stylization for Designers

 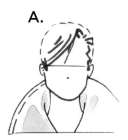 **A.**  **B.**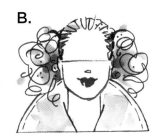

Options: **A.** Head; smaller, less defined, less playful, neutral
B. Head; larger, more playful, more focus on features

Sketching style brings its own point of view to influence a fashion look.

Dressy Trench Coat

Style, beyond attitude and posing, can project different looks, with subtle nuances in the fashion head and rendering choices.

Note:

Compare line quality issues. A tight, clean line can tell a different story from a loose, more spontaneous line.

Note:

Compare coloring options. Two examples of the same coat, both done in partial rendering but with different looks.

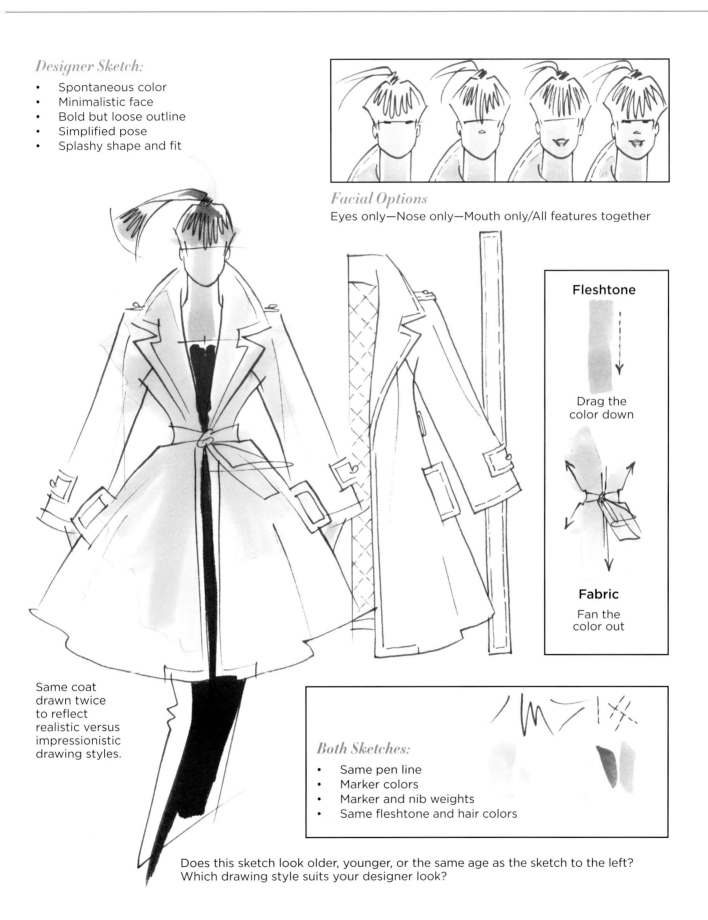

Designer Sketch:

- Spontaneous color
- Minimalistic face
- Bold but loose outline
- Simplified pose
- Splashy shape and fit

Facial Options

Eyes only—Nose only—Mouth only/All features together

Fleshtone

Drag the color down

Fabric

Fan the color out

Same coat drawn twice to reflect realistic versus impressionistic drawing styles.

Both Sketches:

- Same pen line
- Marker colors
- Marker and nib weights
- Same fleshtone and hair colors

Does this sketch look older, younger, or the same age as the sketch to the left? Which drawing style suits your designer look?

Design Objectives

Basic front view poses are the staple posing choice. Simple, direct, easier to draw and dress.

In between basic and dramatic posing is the runway pose. No drama, but creates more styling.

Exaggerated posing creates more visual dynamics, adds dramatic flare and sophistication.

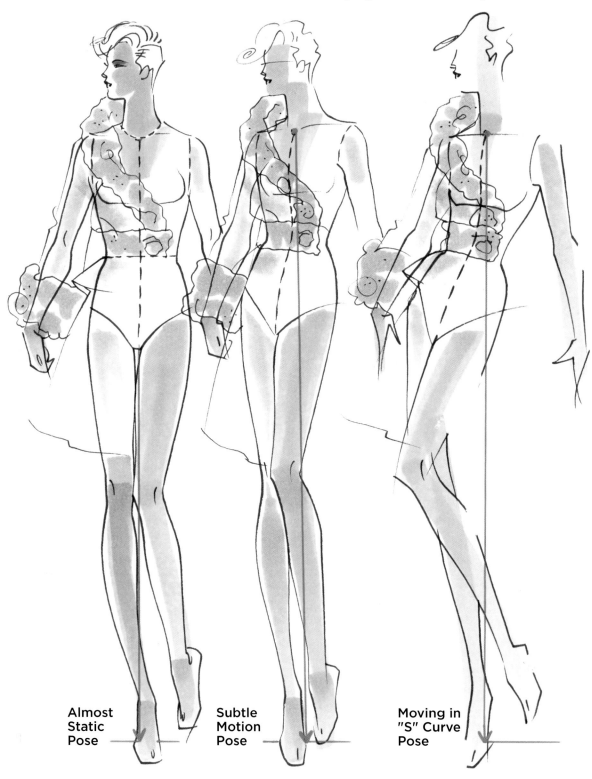

Almost Static Pose

Subtle Motion Pose

Moving in "S" Curve Pose

1. This sketch is informative, a working sketch with all of the important details in place, in focus.

2. This sketch is editorial. It's much more dramatic; less about specifics, and more about its fashion statement.

Focus This Sketch: Tighter rendering, more precision in the design detail

Focus This Sketch: Loose rendering, less precise, more flare, exaggeration

Design Objectives (continued)

The goal of your fashion sketch is to display your ideas, to communicate a design concept. Balance the pose you choose to draw with the shape and construction detail that you have designed. Design takes precedence over the pose. Make sure your pose does not interfere with your garment's features.

No—
Overposed

Losing focus and overstating the design shape of garment; sacrificed to a pose. Too busy.

No—
Underposed

Lost focus on shape and function of this garment in this pose.

No—
Over-illustrated

Too much emphasis on media, not on design.

This is the better example of a working sketch, as explained in the previous spread. The sketch conveys, with clarity, all of its design story. The rendering is loose but is still informative.

Yes—
Balanced Presentation

Runway pose is often the best choice for any outfit. Basic frontal posture keeps focus on design and keeps true to shape and fabrics.

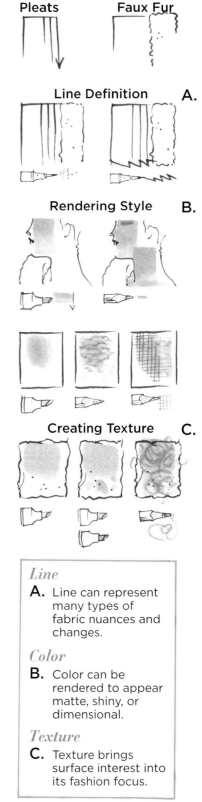

Pleats   **Faux Fur**

Line Definition   **A.**

Rendering Style   **B.**

Creating Texture   **C.**

Line
A. Line can represent many types of fabric nuances and changes.

Color
B. Color can be rendered to appear matte, shiny, or dimensional.

Texture
C. Texture brings surface interest into its fashion focus.

Design Journal Pages

A fashion design croquis book is a visual narrative on design concepts. It includes design direction collages called "storyboards."

Concept
Design inspiration; an original collage of all creative elements in your idea for a fashion project

Customer Profile
Optional yet essential, integral component of target client/audience for each new design concept

Design Story
Documents and combines all of the design concept elements into a visual essay, creating a design story

Design Category
Specific division, line, or grouping of fashion items that will be created by your design concept

Fabric Story
Establishes how your design concept will be constructed/performed in the chosen design category

Color Story
Integrates the fabric choices into a cohesive, coordinated set of colors that become your design palette

Trims and Notions
Practical or decorative, related to the design's form, fit, cut, and function in the design category

Market Research
Rationale for any of the previous headings that validate/contribute to the overall design concept; data on what trends, innovations, or fashion forecasting applies/influenced this design concept

Notes:
Design Collection/Line/Group—Key Elements:
Proportion and fit / construction details or detailing / featuring key pieces
In conjunction with customer projects style, attitude, and possible price points (market)

Fashion Figures and Flats—Artistic Design Focus:
Sketching and rendering technique, dedicated to accentuate customer style and attitude
FIGURES—Informative sketches with artistic license matched to fashion industry standards
FLATS—Precise, accurate, meticulous, self-explanatory sketches. Can be combined with or be separate from the figure work

Croquis Books as a Personal Design Journal
Keep in mind that this is a professional design tool. As such it must be handled with respect.
The croquis book is part of the "job" and is an extension of, a showcase for, your talent for fashion.

This page represents a few fashion journal (croquis or rough sketches) pages this designer created for a single project.

The rough sketches and photo research are combined with written notes on this project to maximize her creative process.

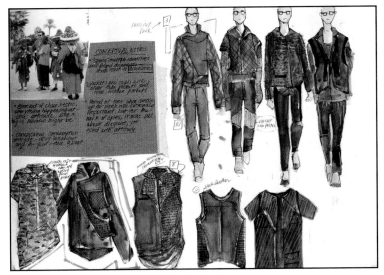

Artwork by Andrea Tsao

This designer uses the walking runway pose mixed with fully rendered flats to accentuate her fabric and design nuances.

Design Journal Thumbnail Sketches

As a designer, the first step, developing a concept, is sketching out your ideas, often mixed with original draping techniques, research, or computer manipulation. You need to draw to communicate your ideas, as seen on this page. This step is as critical to your creative process as the last step—putting finishing touches on your designs right before your fashion show (see the facing page).

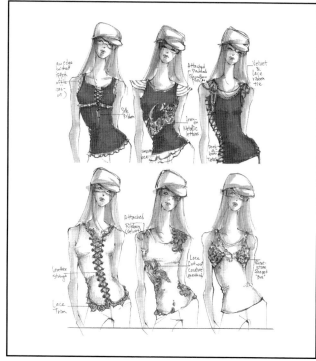

WWD Designer Fittings Photos

Roberto Cavalli

Michael Bastian

Derek Lam

Chanel

Maximizing Design Impact

Mixing figures and flats in a design group doubles your page's fashion potential.

A. *Separates/Flats*

   Flats, separated from what is worn on figures, can define new pieces or display back view of items on the body.

B. *Outfits/Figures*

   Figures define the customer, a garment's fit, its looks; how it's worn and the interplay of colors and fabrics.

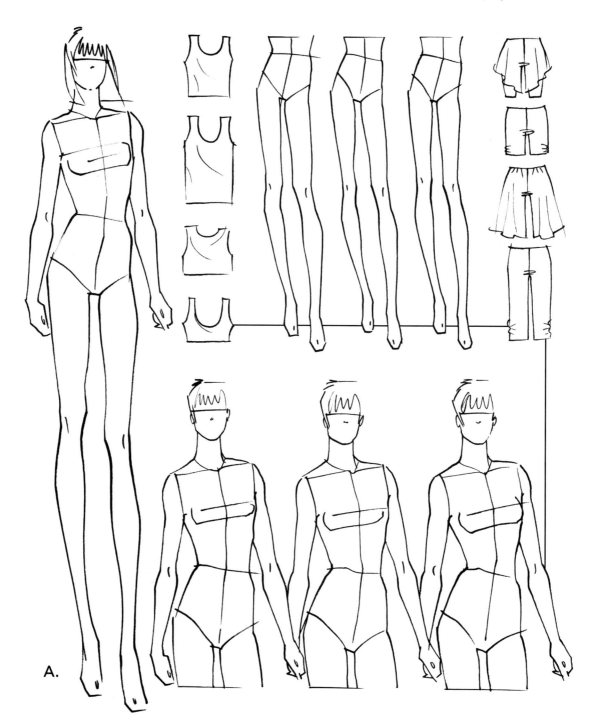

A.

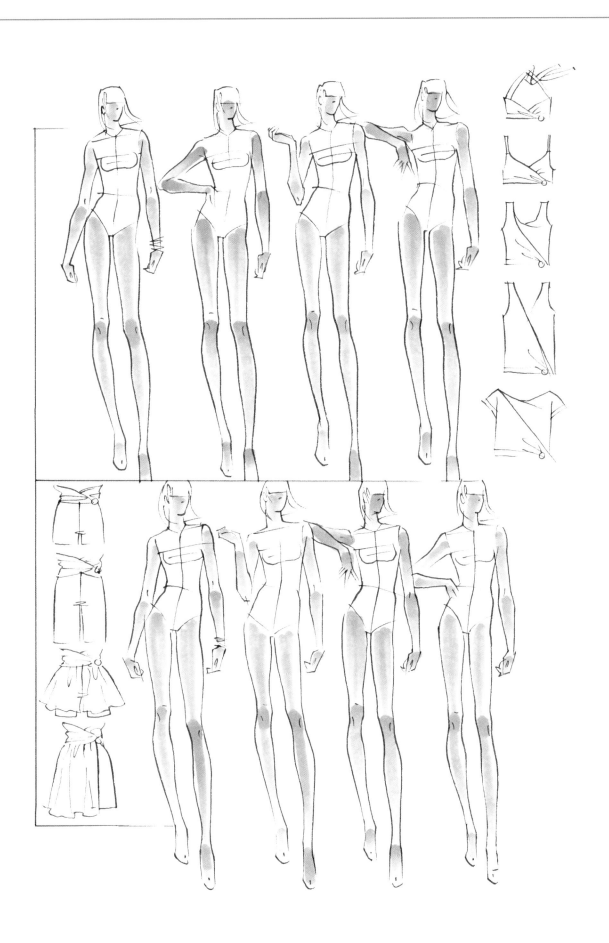

Composition Direction

Composition for layout means having a focus, displaying features and drawing strategies that enhance your art and promote your design content. Pre-planning your layout draws all of the illustrative components for a page together to create a stronger picture. Composition is one of the major factors in the success or failure of a designer's sketch. Here are some of the reasons why layout will help or hurt the visual dynamics on your page.

Layout Focus
- Communicating strengths/concept of your ideas
- Organizing priorities/features within your layout
- Dramatizing visual appeal/style for your sketches

Layout Features
- Presenting your ideas with clarity, brevity, and individuality
- Continuity among design category, customer, season, and price points
- Design progression highlighting construction and focus on detail
- Balance between technique and the technical aspects of illustration and presentation

Layout Strategies
- Design story—communicating information
  1. Lead silhouette—featured element or design focus
  2. Dominant shape or fit story—visual emphasis
  3. Major construction factor or feature—clarity in details
  4. Mix of pieces within collection—play on colors, textures, and line quality

- Color story—strategy for color balance on the page
  1. Lead fabric—which fabric is emphasized
  2. Dominant color—what is the strongest, largest volume of a color
  3. Major print or motif—tonal variations and definition
  4. Texture mix—line quality variations for design specifics

Layout Pitfalls
- Confusing mix of elements or lost focus
- Too much overlapping, which obscures detail
- Overly tiny details, which are too hard to interpret
- Too much empty space dilutes visual impact
- Frayed, wrinkled fabrics that don't look new or fresh
- Too many resources present overwhelming information
- Too many design inspirations that look overdone
- Overworked images that distract from clarity in design message

Combining related units into complex layouts means achieving a balance of content. The units divide the page, and the balance can be achieved through the use of color, line, and shape. A composition can be broken into segments. Balanced segments give a layout pattern, a rhythm.

Layout Breakdown

Composition   Segments   Rhythm

Grouping Figures

Left   *Centered*   *Right*

Layout for the lone figure on a page sets the mass or solid form of the body against the empty volume of space that surrounds the body. The mass of the body is seen as positive space, a solid form. The volume of empty air surrounding the form is seen as negative space. In a layout, the form doesn't change, but the volume surrounding it does. You can balance a layout by placing a figure in the middle of the page, which is called centering. You can create an off-balance effect by shifting the figure to the left or right. This slices the page unevenly, creating a visual impact. Visual impact is the goal for all layouts. Choosing the right or wrong layout will add to or subtract from the visual impact of the design and illustration.

Layout for multiple figures on a page is guided by the same principles but with the added factor of negative space between the various figures. The major decision here is about just how much space you want to leave between each body. The examples on these pages use five figures in six different layouts. Later, these options could be given more shape and color through fashion dressing.

Close Together   +5

All five figures in a tight grouping implies "fashion" connection and is best used for lighter shapes in Spring looks.

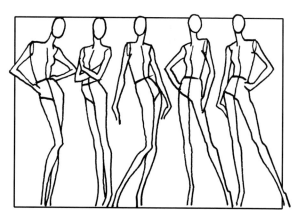

Spread Apart   +5

All five figures in a looser grouping (spread apart) conveys "connectivity" and is best used for heavier silhouettes and Fall looks.

Options

2+3

This layout groups the figures in two separate units. The largest negative space lies between the two groups.

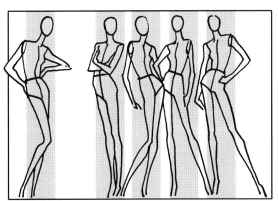

1+4

This layout moves a single figure away from the larger grouping. This is another version of the double unit layout.

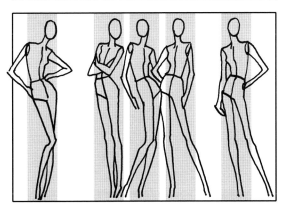

1+3+1

Here the layout moves into three units. The first and last figures are separate from the group in the middle. This creates two large negative spaces instead of just one.

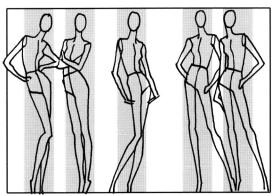

2+1+2

Now the layout reverses itself. The solo center figure is separated from the outside groups of two by a double negative space close to the middle of the page.

Grouping Figures (continued)

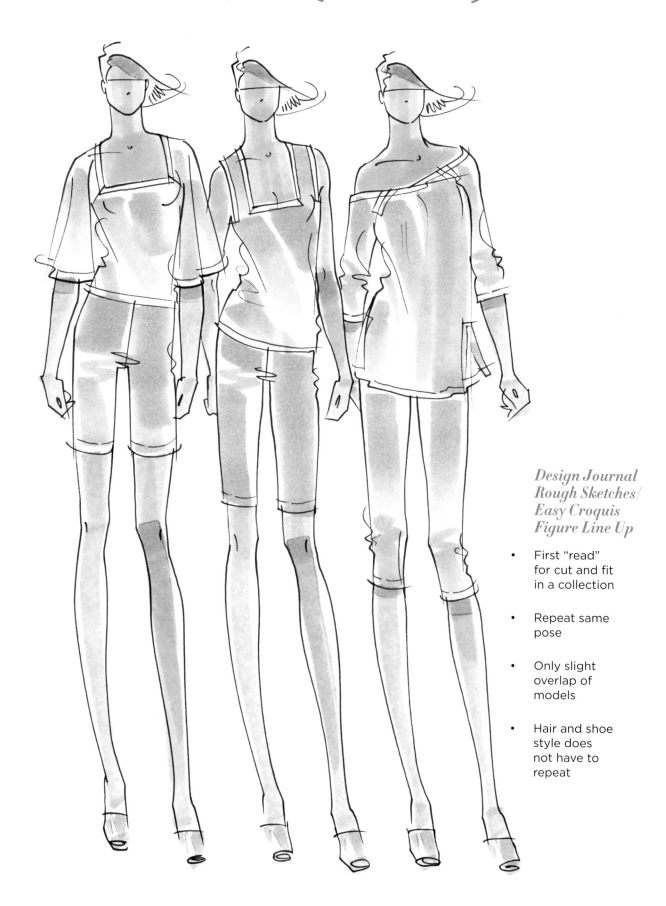

Design Journal Rough Sketches/ Easy Croquis Figure Line Up

- First "read" for cut and fit in a collection

- Repeat same pose

- Only slight overlap of models

- Hair and shoe style does not have to repeat

A group of figures, for fashion design, is usually meant
to convey a collection, a
set of garments in a "line"
(another term for a collection). This figure group-
ing means that each pose
has been selected to display
a garment as well as signal
how each garment relates to
the next.

In both of these example
groups, the figures relate
to each other, connected
and interactive by a fashion
design perspective.

In each example layout,
many poses overlap, covering some part of the next.
This grouping can work
with lightweight fabrics and
simple silhouettes, especially
for resort or spring collections. It becomes harder to
use for fall, due to garment
layering, thicker fabrics, and
more complex silhouettes
that can get lost with too
many overlapping poses.

Sometimes the best solu-
tion for creating a collection
is to set up a repeat pose
with marginal overlapping,
as shown on the facing page.
This kind of grouping works
for any season and still
implies a design connection
that is a lot faster to draw
than all different poses.

Layout or Line Up

Spontaneous versus structured or combination posing is a choice for the figure grouping you make in order to maximize the design potential in your collection.

On the left is the spontaneous grouping of poses. They can be all one size or many, which tend to better focus on outfits. The grouping on the right tends to better focus on separates.

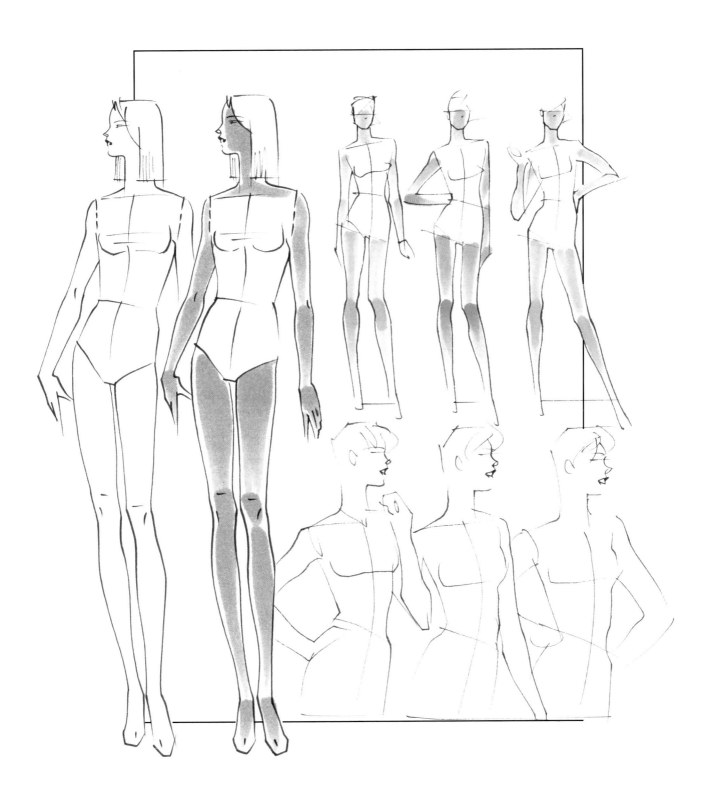

Layout or Line Up (continued)

Your choice of layout could include any of the following:

- **Garment detail:** Accentuating your cut and fit for a design grouping
- **Coordinates:** Maximizing design elements or just use of fabrication
- **Fashion leader:** Featuring the major shape or design silhouette in collection
- **Customer:** Sometimes the mood, attitude, or design category, like Beachwear versus Coats, will dictate a different layout

Note:

The balance of coloring is kept equal among the figures for this grouping; it keeps the focus on the jackets.

Pencil, Pen, Marker, or Paint—these rendering tips apply to all media options.

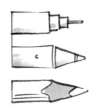

Depending on your media choices, rendering flats in a grouping may need extra steps:

1. 6H pencil shapes for outline
2. Splash of color and textures
3. Now pen or pencil in specific interior detailing that won't smear

Partial Rendering

Shape
Splash the color to accentuate contours of the garment's silhouette.

Shape

Direction
Push the color into folds and bend of the pose.

Direction

Drape
Drag the color down into the fabric.

Drape

Construction
Make the color focus on design detailing and work on cut and shaping to emphasize styling nuances.

Construction

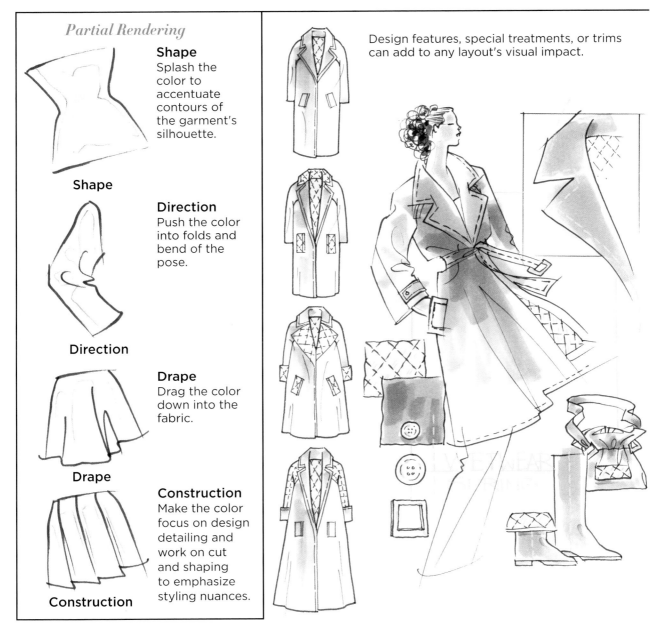

Design features, special treatments, or trims can add to any layout's visual impact.

Note:

Rendering print, patterns, or texture can be done in the same loose, partial coloring techniques. Just use the same type of base color shaping as shown here as your guidelines.

The media mix for this design is gouache and pencil on vellum paper. This spread ties design silhouettes to design inspiration. His finished figures page features his collection's dominant shapes, fabrics, and colorways. His inspiration page presents his sourcing, research, and development. He cleverly integrates text to build on his creative vision.

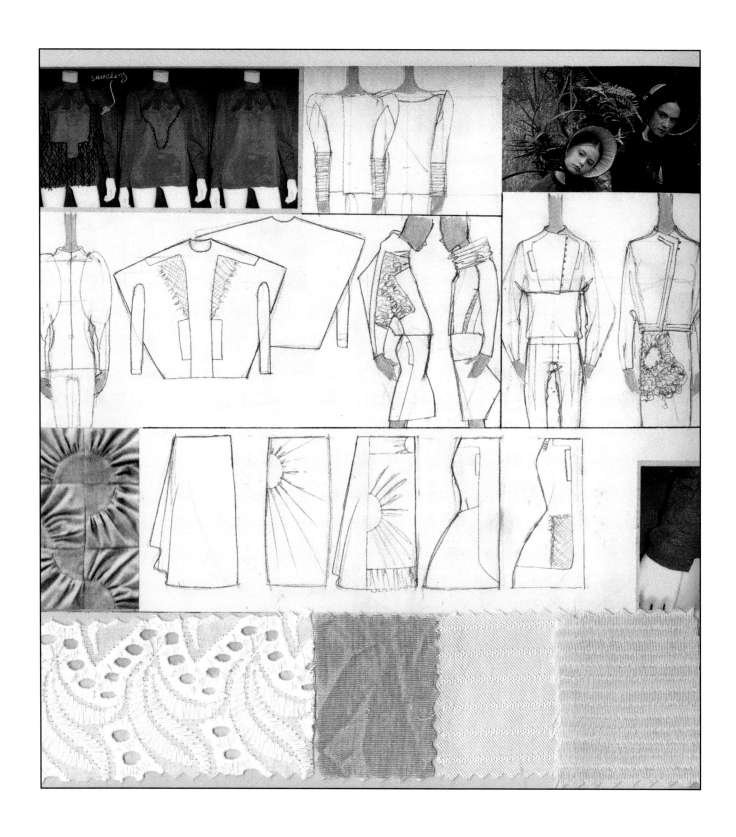

The media mix here is a photographic collage of diverse research and resources. The designer's collage page, mixing it up with working sketches and exploratory draping, is presented with visual clarity and highly focused design structure. His edited, finished figure page features sophisticated fashion art with equally nuanced fashion originality for his collection.

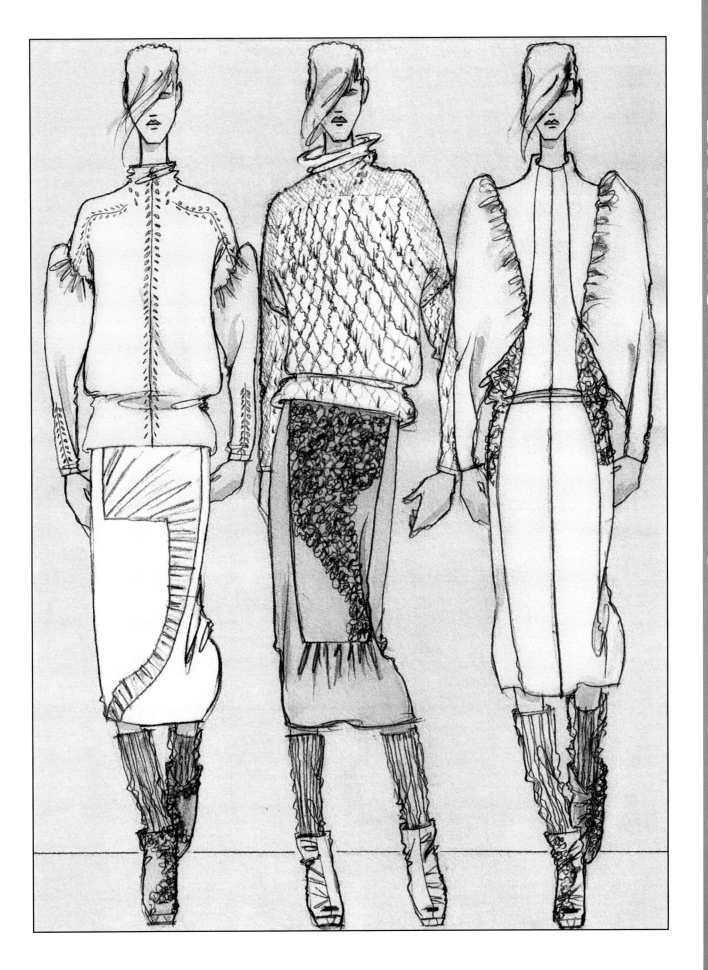

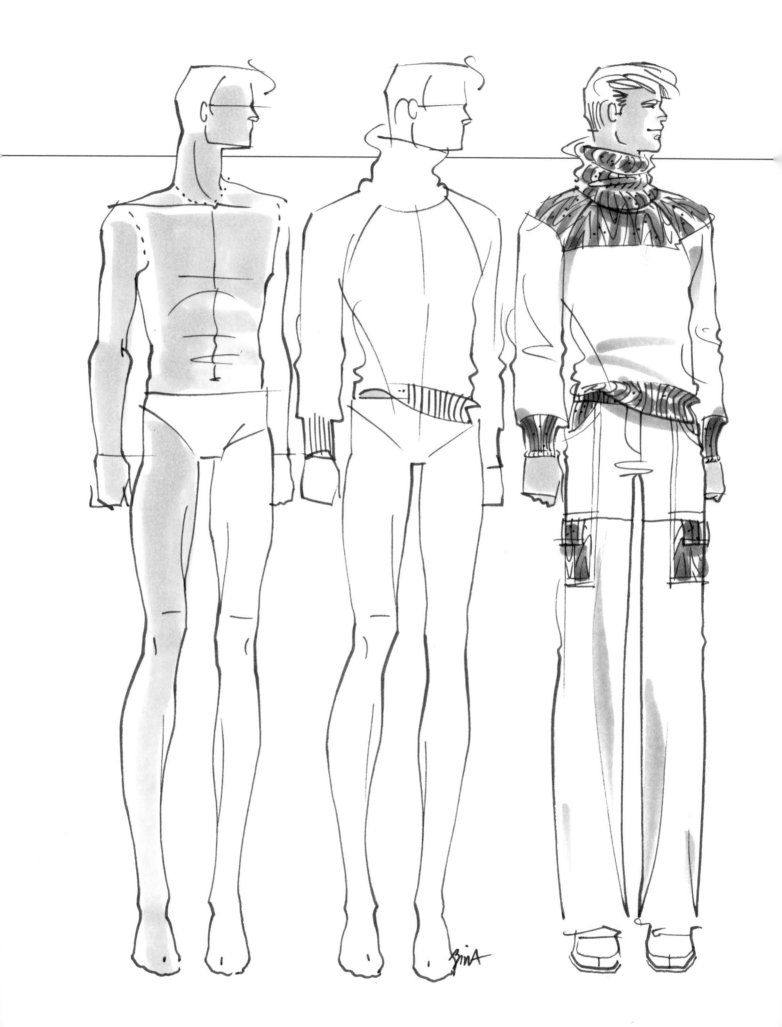

11

Drawing Men

This chapter will direct your attention to proportion and structure for menswear fashion figures. Drawing and dressing the male figure has been simplified to help you master the basics. After learning these basics, you will be equipped to create your own version of the male figure.

To draw the male fashion figure is to work with an idealized body, just as you have done with the female figure. Again, the figure exaggerates or imitates human form, yet it is often devoid of the range of natural human body characteristics. When you have learned how to draw and create a generic type of male figure for fashion, then you can work on drawing a more stylistic figure that suits your needs. You should explore drawing from the complex reality of a life figure and the fashion simplification of the male figure. After you have accomplished this, you can create your own artistic version of the figure with more individual style.

This chapter offers runway and showroom photos from *WWD* for both male figure poses and garment silhouettes. These images offer you another resource of imagery to draw from.

Menswear Figure Basics

Much like the fashion female, the fashion male is an exaggeration. Both forms are elongated and idealized; therefore, they are less true to life and more stylized.

The fashion male's chest makes more of a "V" than the female's. His neck is thicker and his shoulders are broader, but the hips are narrower, without the curve that is drawn on the fashion female.

Heads Tall

0	
1	Chin
2	Chest
3	
3½	Waist
4	
5	Thigh
6	Knees
7	Calf
8	Toes

A. The jawline and the neck are given more emphasis on the male figure.

B. The male figure's shoulders are drawn wide. The waistline is low on the torso. The hipline gets blocky.

C. The arms are drawn with more pronounced curves.

D. The legs are more muscular and more realistic in length.

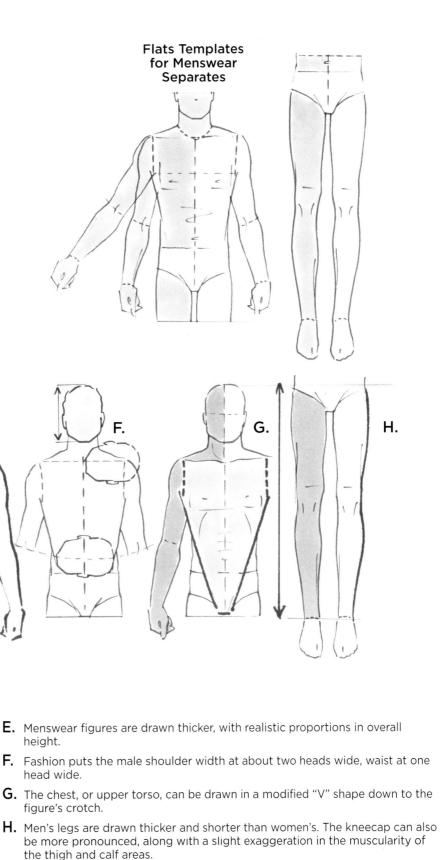

Flats Templates for Menswear Separates

Note:

Flats figure templates for menswear can be split into halves for tops and bottoms, just as is done for womenswear flats. Drawing these templates by hand gives you the option to customize the arms.

E. Menswear figures are drawn thicker, with realistic proportions in overall height.

F. Fashion puts the male shoulder width at about two heads wide, waist at one head wide.

G. The chest, or upper torso, can be drawn in a modified "V" shape down to the figure's crotch.

H. Men's legs are drawn thicker and shorter than women's. The kneecap can also be more pronounced, along with a slight exaggeration in the muscularity of the thigh and calf areas.

Menswear Figure Basics (continued)

Formulas break the figure down into sections that are easier to draw or map out in a sketch. Studying them, you learn to use those pieces to build the figure up again. This drawing process speeds you along until you are confident enough to draw the figure on your own—without referring to a formula. On the other hand, you may invent your own figure drawing formula.

The example on the right cuts the figure directly in half. If you fold over the figure, to touch his toes, at the end of the torso by the crotch, the top of his head would match the level of his feet.

The figure in the middle is cut into thirds, and unlike heads tall formula (also used in womenswear), it is not as clearly defined in natural body bends. It's another method of selective proportions to help your sketching.

Three Figure Formulas—Same Results; Same Proportions

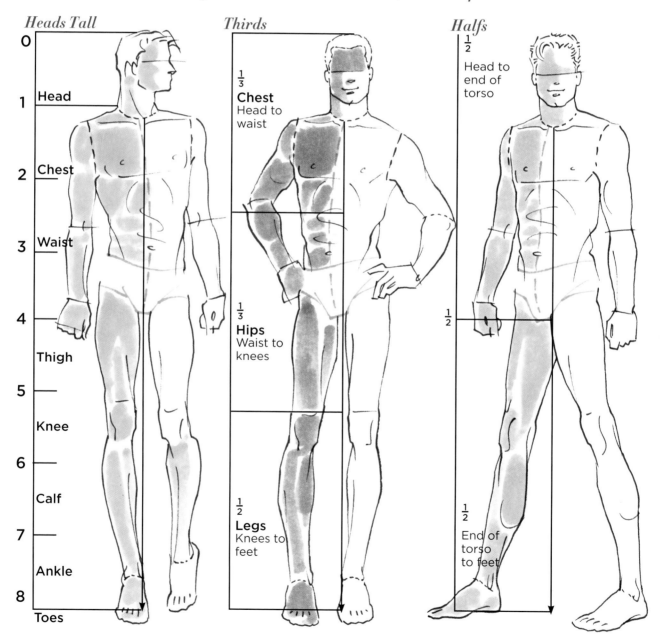

Heads Tall

0
1 Head
2 Chest
3 Waist
4
Thigh
5
Knee
6
Calf
7
Ankle
8
Toes

Thirds

$\frac{1}{3}$
Chest
Head to waist

$\frac{1}{3}$
Hips
Waist to knees

$\frac{1}{2}$
Legs
Knees to feet

Halfs

$\frac{1}{2}$
Head to end of torso

$\frac{1}{2}$
End of torso to feet

The menswear poses on this page turn the figure in three moves to illustrate how the center front on these poses turns with the body. That center front can be a critical line for garment detail and should help you with your design sketching.

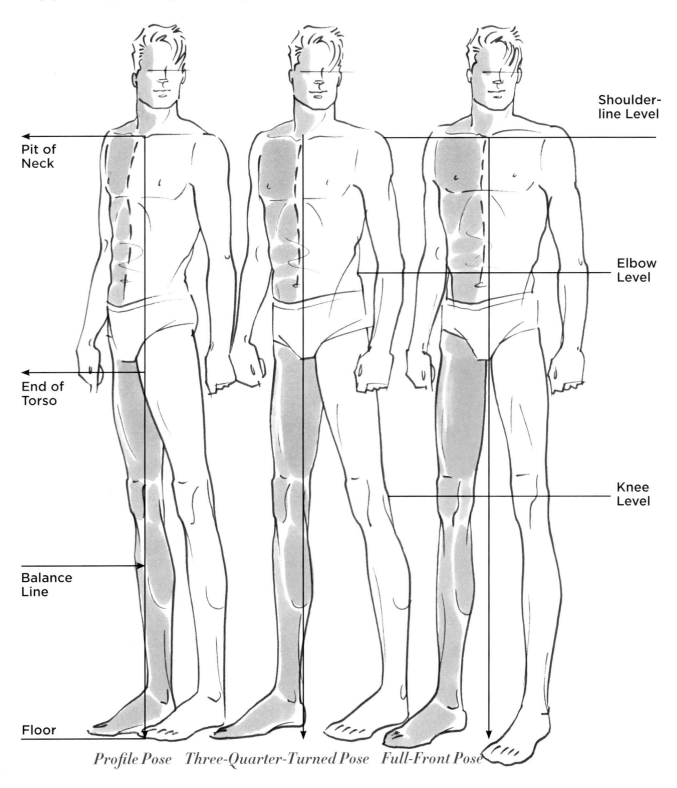

Pit of Neck

Shoulder-line Level

End of Torso

Elbow Level

Knee Level

Balance Line

Floor

Profile Pose   *Three-Quarter-Turned Pose*   *Full-Front Pose*

Proportions for Menswear Figures

In fashion, the menswear figure is not as elongated as the women's figure. The neck is shorter and wider, with a broader shoulder slope. The arms and legs can be thicker, more muscular in appearance. The area just above the ankles is more pronounced and less stretched than on women's legs.

The angles of posing will be more subtle for menswear figures (except for active sportswear). The low shoulder and high hip angles are less dramatic but still active. Center front and center back are still vital to the movement in the pose. The supporting leg with the balance line will always ground the figure on the page.

Smaller Croquis Poses

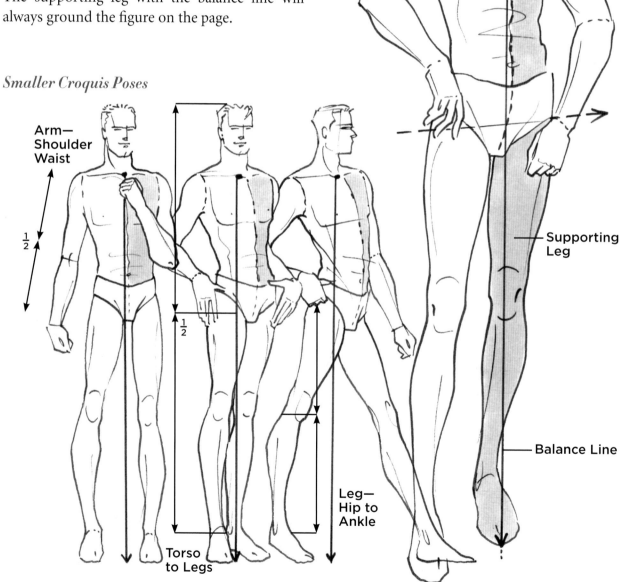

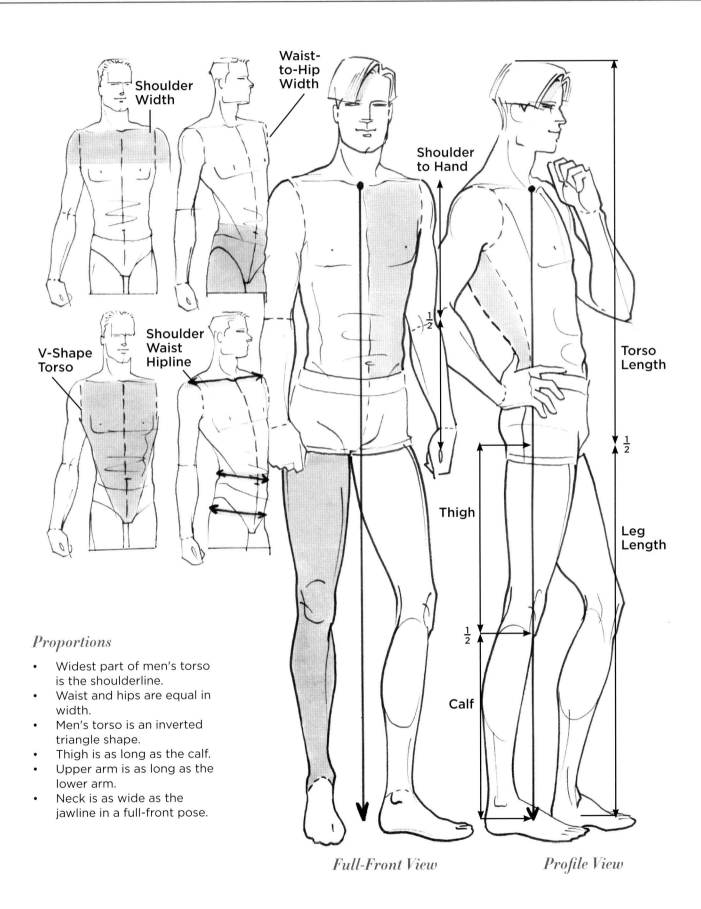

Shoulder Width

Waist-to-Hip Width

Shoulder to Hand

$\frac{1}{2}$

V-Shape Torso

Shoulder Waist Hipline

Torso Length

$\frac{1}{2}$

Thigh

Leg Length

$\frac{1}{2}$

Calf

Proportions

- Widest part of men's torso is the shoulderline.
- Waist and hips are equal in width.
- Men's torso is an inverted triangle shape.
- Thigh is as long as the calf.
- Upper arm is as long as the lower arm.
- Neck is as wide as the jawline in a full-front pose.

Full-Front View

Profile View

Runway Poses for Men

Walking runway poses are pliable. They can be used together and changed enough to look related yet different. Here are the preliminary steps to create this figure.

A. and B. After establishing the head size and neck and shoulder's width, finish the chest.
C. Block in the hipline and draw the crotch so you can complete the torso.
D. Sketch in the arms. They are equal in length to the torso. The elbow is in the middle of the arm.

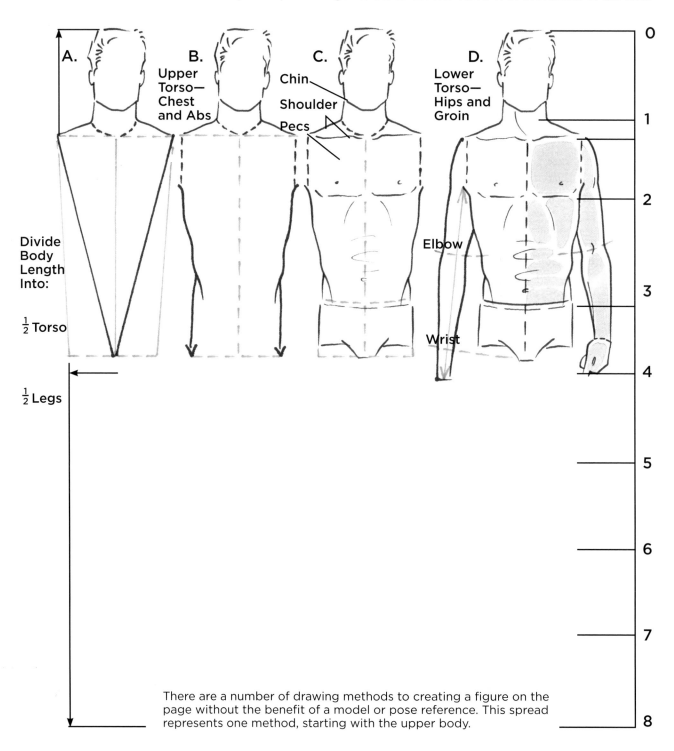

A.

B. Upper Torso— Chest and Abs

Chin

Shoulder

Pecs

C.

D. Lower Torso— Hips and Groin

Divide Body Length Into:

$\frac{1}{2}$ Torso

$\frac{1}{2}$ Legs

Elbow

Wrist

0

1

2

3

4

5

6

7

8

There are a number of drawing methods to creating a figure on the page without the benefit of a model or pose reference. This spread represents one method, starting with the upper body.

E. The legs are going to be equal in length to the length of the head to the crotch.
   Start with the non-bent, supporting leg of the pose.
F. Next is the walking, pulled-back, bent leg that is drawn slightly shorter than the other leg.
G. Complete the figure in what should be close to eight heads tall for easy-to-follow proportions.

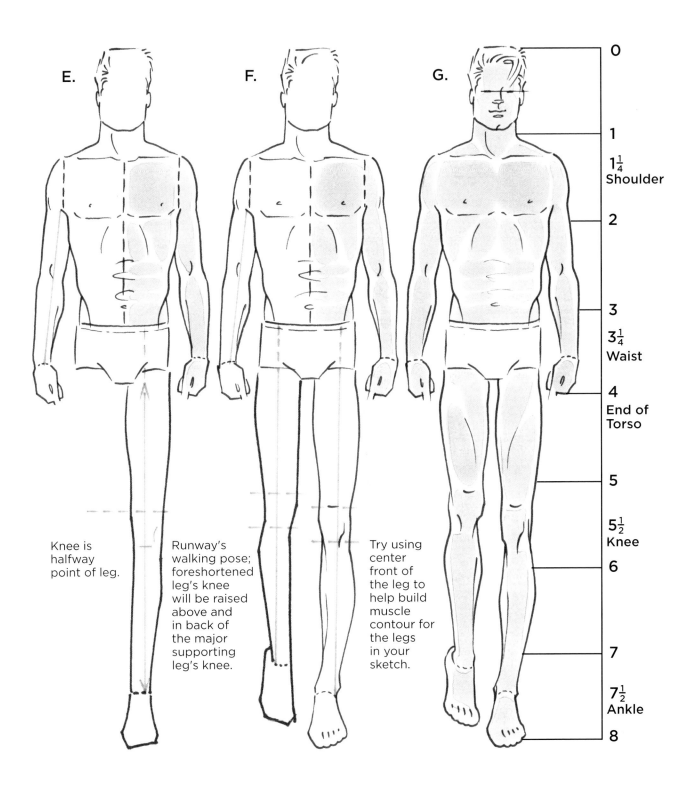

E.

F.

G.

Knee is halfway point of leg.

Runway's walking pose; foreshortened leg's knee will be raised above and in back of the major supporting leg's knee.

Try using center front of the leg to help build muscle contour for the legs in your sketch.

0

1

$1\frac{1}{4}$
Shoulder

2

3

$3\frac{1}{4}$
Waist

4
End of Torso

5

$5\frac{1}{2}$
Knee

6

7

$7\frac{1}{2}$
Ankle

8

Elongation for Menswear

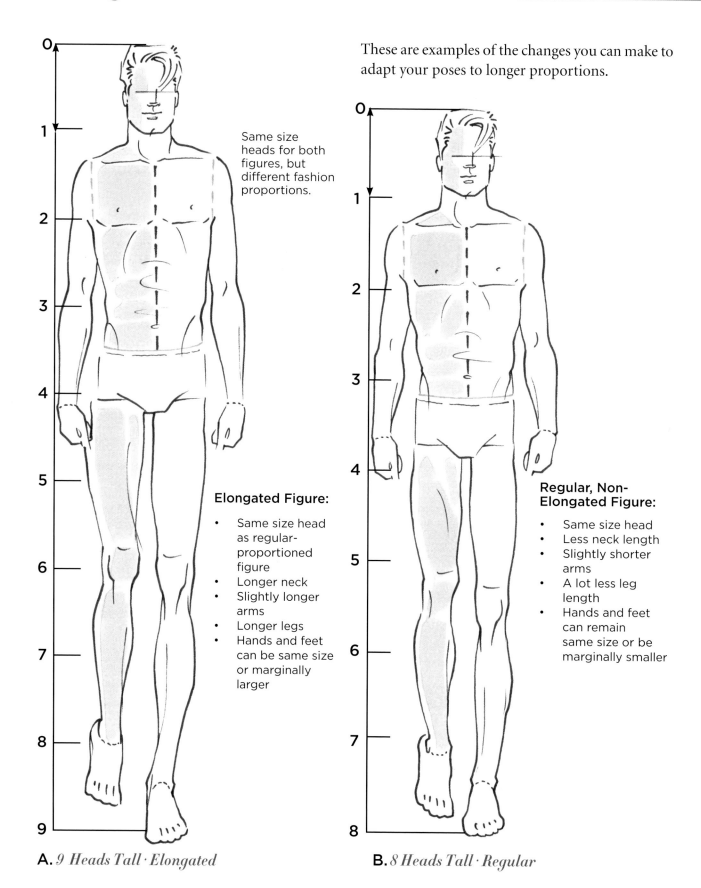

These are examples of the changes you can make to adapt your poses to longer proportions.

Same size heads for both figures, but different fashion proportions.

Elongated Figure:

• Same size head as regular-proportioned figure
• Longer neck
• Slightly longer arms
• Longer legs
• Hands and feet can be same size or marginally larger

Regular, Non-Elongated Figure:

• Same size head
• Less neck length
• Slightly shorter arms
• A lot less leg length
• Hands and feet can remain same size or be marginally smaller

A. *9 Heads Tall · Elongated*

B. *8 Heads Tall · Regular*

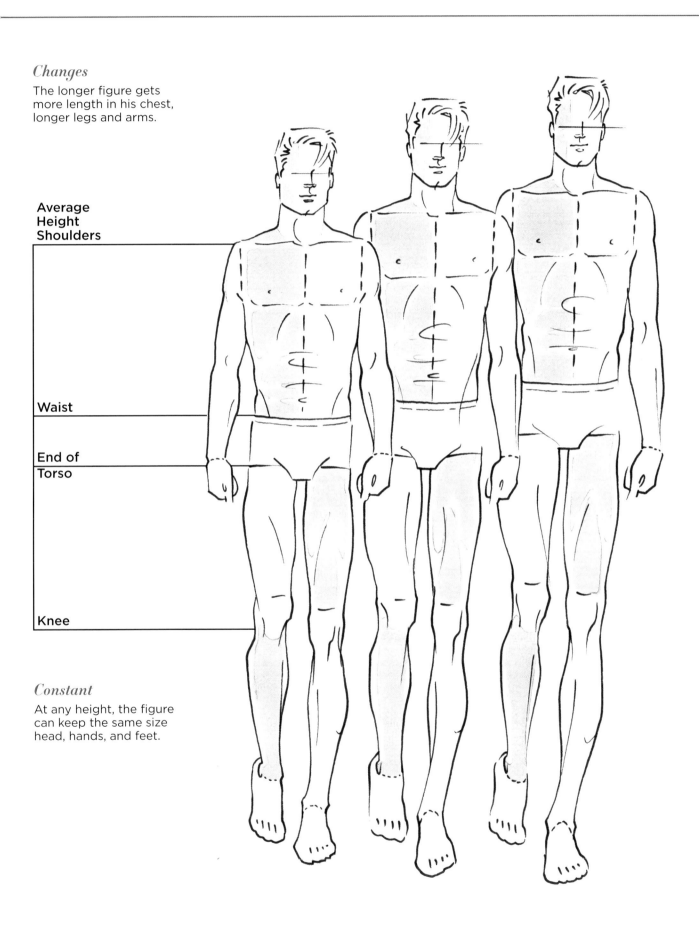

Changes

The longer figure gets more length in his chest, longer legs and arms.

Average Height Shoulders

Waist

End of Torso

Knee

Constant

At any height, the figure can keep the same size head, hands, and feet.

Drawing Men's Legs

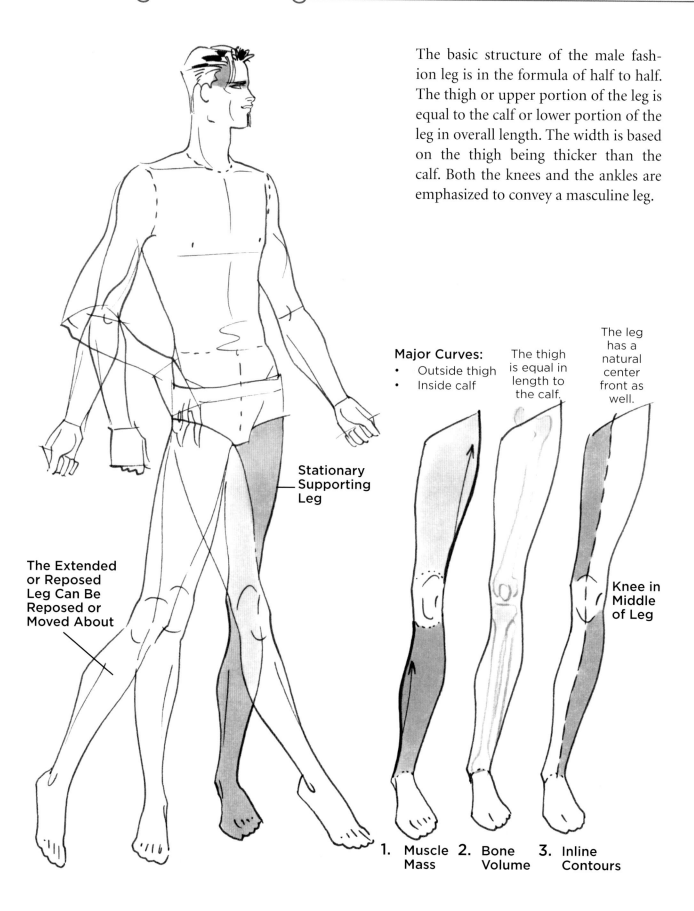

The basic structure of the male fashion leg is in the formula of half to half. The thigh or upper portion of the leg is equal to the calf or lower portion of the leg in overall length. The width is based on the thigh being thicker than the calf. Both the knees and the ankles are emphasized to convey a masculine leg.

Stationary Supporting Leg

The Extended or Reposed Leg Can Be Reposed or Moved About

Major Curves:
- Outside thigh
- Inside calf

The thigh is equal in length to the calf.

The leg has a natural center front as well.

Knee in Middle of Leg

1. Muscle Mass   **2.** Bone Volume   **3.** Inline Contours

Feet

Using the same basic three views for feet, their poses, used for men's footwear, can be simplified.

Legs

The contours of the thighs, knees, and calves, as the leg turns, can be pronounced curves.
.

Feet into Shoes

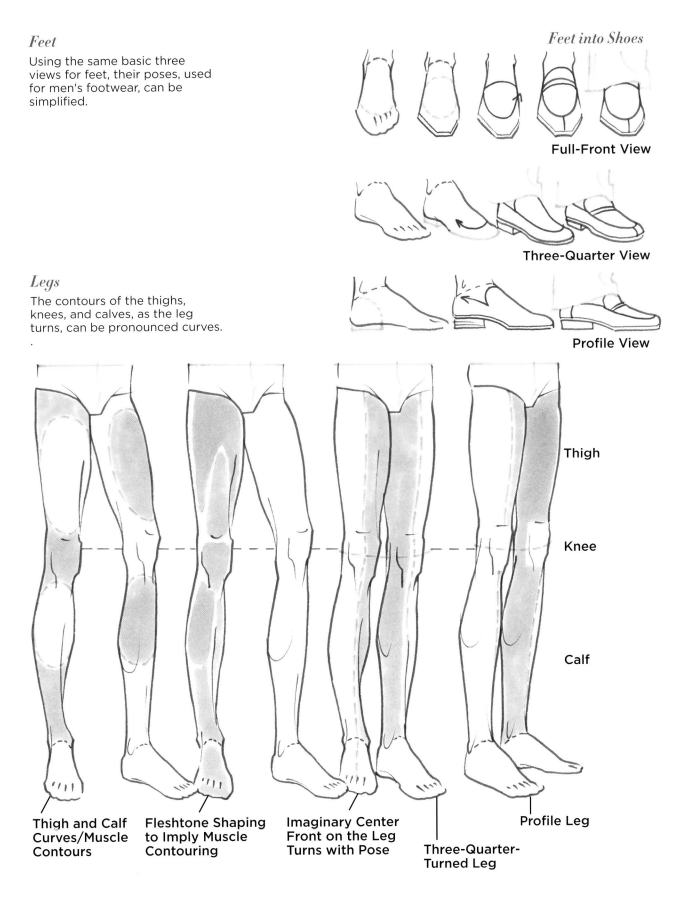

Full-Front View

Three-Quarter View

Profile View

Thigh

Knee

Calf

Thigh and Calf Curves/Muscle Contours

Fleshtone Shaping to Imply Muscle Contouring

Imaginary Center Front on the Leg Turns with Pose

Three-Quarter-Turned Leg

Profile Leg

Drawing Men's Arms and Hands

Masculine arms are drawn slightly heavier and shorter than feminine arms. Whenever you sketch this chunkier arm, you should emphasize the muscular development of the outline contour.

When you practice drawing both the upper and lower curves in the arm, always start at the shoulder. First, draw the upper arm and stop at the elbow, then continue downward toward the wrist.

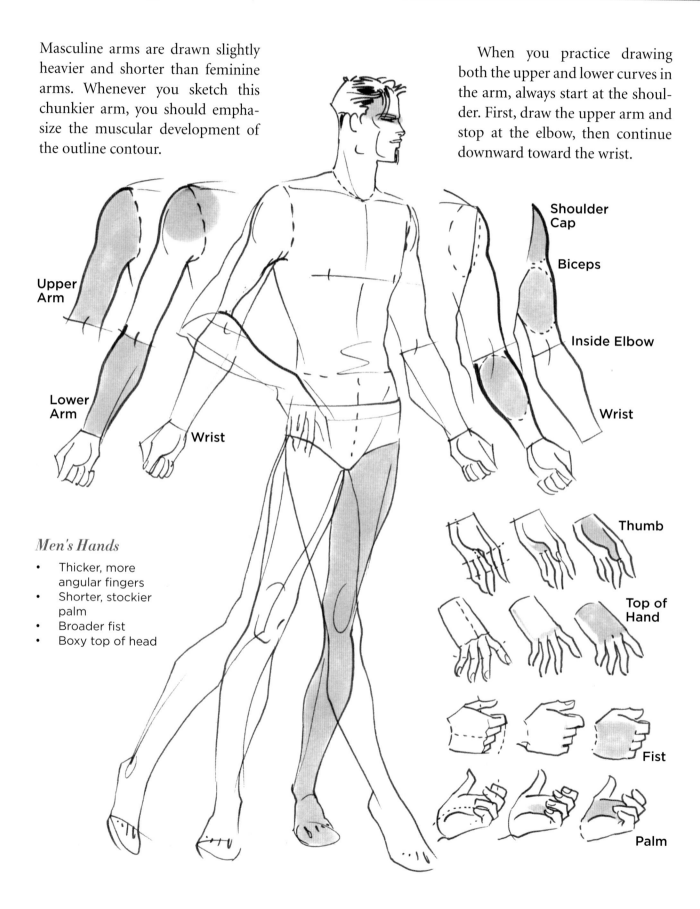

Upper Arm

Lower Arm

Wrist

Shoulder Cap

Biceps

Inside Elbow

Wrist

Men's Hands

- Thicker, more angular fingers
- Shorter, stockier palm
- Broader fist
- Boxy top of head

Thumb

Top of Hand

Fist

Palm

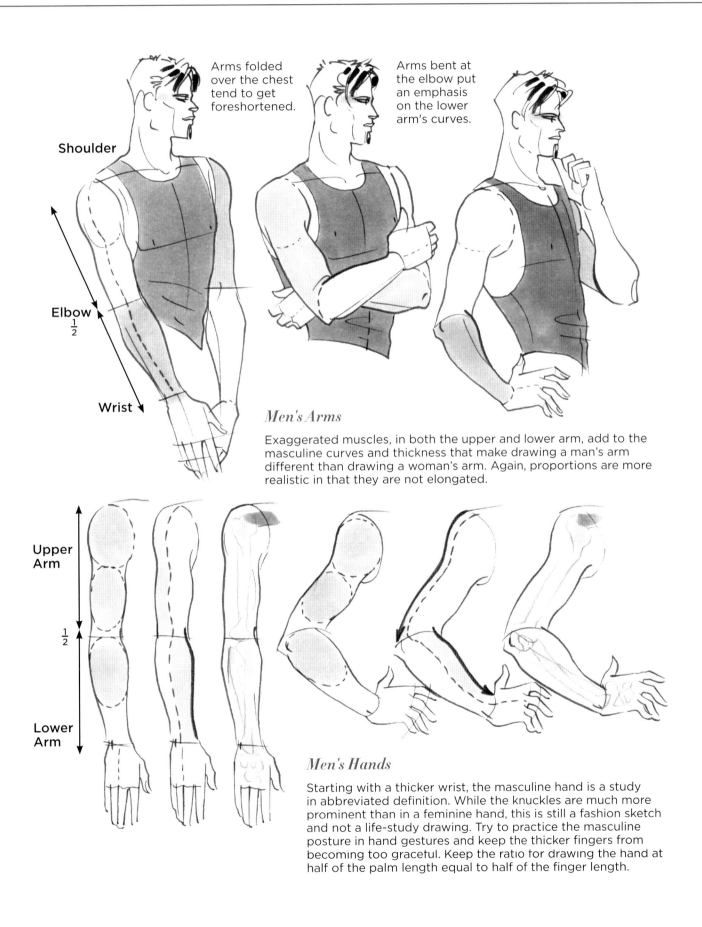

Arms folded over the chest tend to get foreshortened.

Arms bent at the elbow put an emphasis on the lower arm's curves.

Shoulder

Elbow
$\frac{1}{2}$

Wrist

Men's Arms

Exaggerated muscles, in both the upper and lower arm, add to the masculine curves and thickness that make drawing a man's arm different than drawing a woman's arm. Again, proportions are more realistic in that they are not elongated.

Upper Arm

$\frac{1}{2}$

Lower Arm

Men's Hands

Starting with a thicker wrist, the masculine hand is a study in abbreviated definition. While the knuckles are much more prominent than in a feminine hand, this is still a fashion sketch and not a life-study drawing. Try to practice the masculine posture in hand gestures and keep the thicker fingers from becoming too graceful. Keep the ratio for drawing the hand at half of the palm length equal to half of the finger length.

Drawing Men's Heads

Men's fashion heads can be drawn just as stylized and abbreviated as women's fashion heads. Men's fashion heads often have a broader jawline with more emphasis on chin definition. The eyebrows are drawn much closer to the eyes, the nose becomes more prominent, and the male mouth can be both fuller yet subtle. Facial planing and shading help to accentuate the masculine features. While trends dictate hairstyle and attitude—as in what looks casual or formal relative to attire in a design category such as sports clothes versus career clothes—you decide what look fits your drawing style. Study the three basic poses for head: the full-front, the three-quarter turned, and the profile faces.

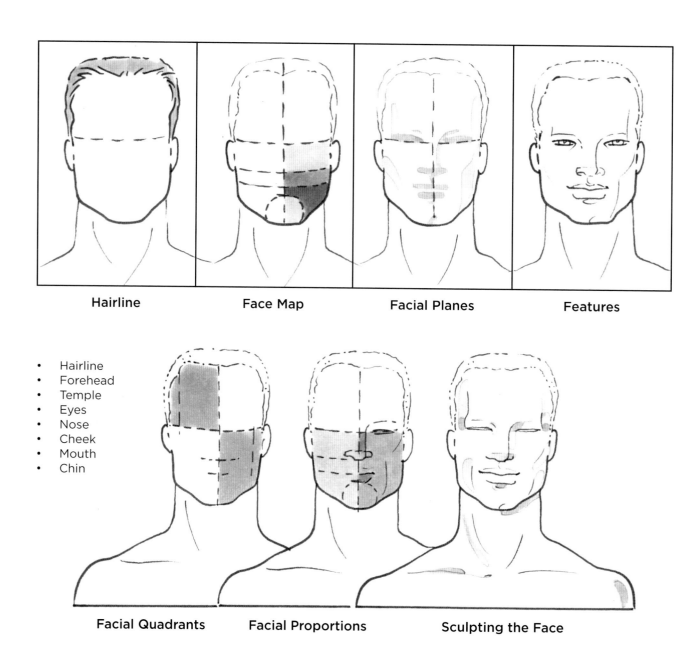

Hairline	Face Map	Facial Planes	Features

- Hairline
- Forehead
- Temple
- Eyes
- Nose
- Cheek
- Mouth
- Chin

Facial Quadrants	Facial Proportions	Sculpting the Face

Drawing Men's Hair

Like all else in fashion, men's hairstyles change with the trends. Long and shaggy is in one season and out the next. Sideburns change from above the ear, to at or below the ear. It is up to you to decide the best look in hair for your male figure—or, of course, to go bald or shaven. For most fashion illustrations, hair is not the focal point, so it's often stylized and more abbreviated. Hair can be drawn with either minimalist shaping, using only a few lines, or modestly realistic, using lots of directional detail. Either version will look right as long as the hairstyle matches your style of drawing.

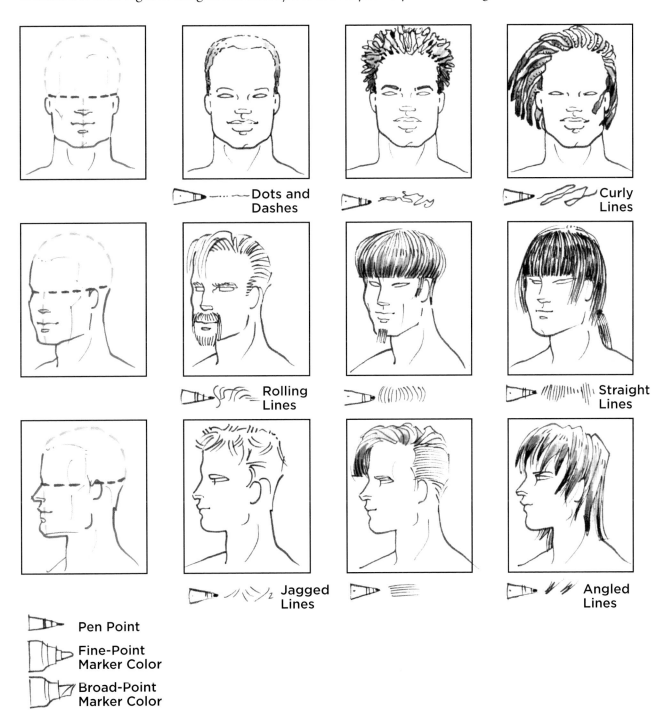

Dots and Dashes

Curly Lines

Rolling Lines

Straight Lines

Jagged Lines

Angled Lines

Pen Point

Fine-Point Marker Color

Broad-Point Marker Color

Clothing the Male Figure

Working up a sketch for menswear requires three basic criteria for a successful image:

A. *Proportions:* Managing to create the right height and weight for your projected customer.

B. *Stance or Pose:* Shows off a garment to its best advantage, creating the right look through the pose, the proportions, and the garment.

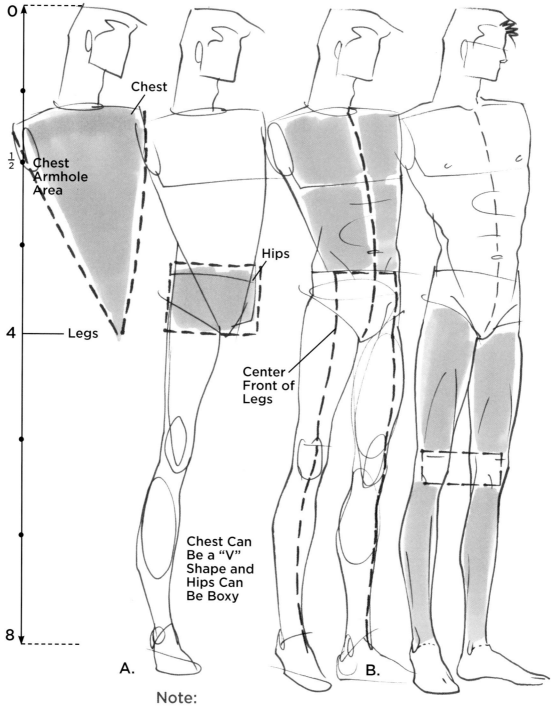

Note:

Center front of the legs help with crease line in pants.

C. Proportions also apply to clothes on the body. They have to be drawn to reflect action in the pose.

D. The pose is drawn to commit the figure to a stance that shows the clothes to their best advantage.

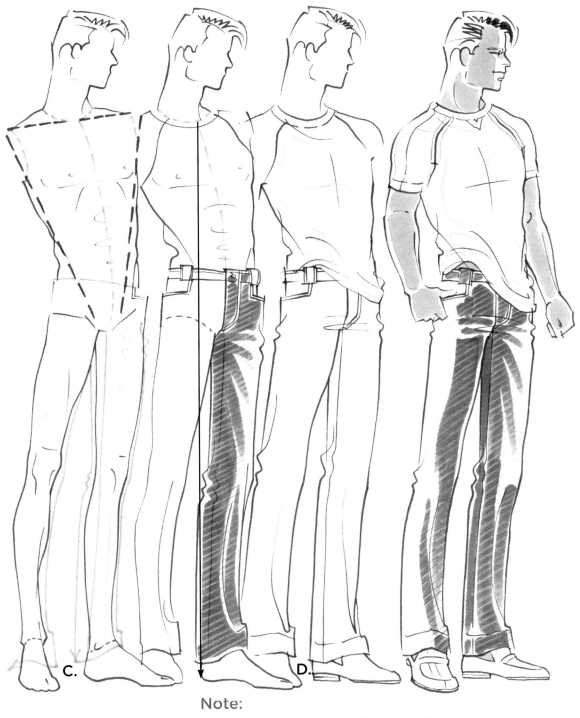

C.   D.

Note:
The balance line keeps the figure from tipping over on your page.

Menswear Pants

Drawing pants for menswear can be a challenge because the male figure's waistline runs evenly into the uncurved outline for his hips, making it difficult to decide where the waist should start. One trick is to consider the point where the elbow would hit on your figure's torso as a good place to locate the waistline. Fashion trends move the waistline all the time, making it harder to draw, but always interesting.

Shorts

Shorts often have a dropped crotch (a loose rise) that adds to the roomy, comfortable fit. Pockets are the design feature that gets the most attention in your sketch.

Trousers

Trousers, either casual or for dress, usually have a straight, slightly wide pants leg. The waistband often has a released pleat, or tow, that falls into the pressed crease down the middle of the leg. Depending on hem length trends, the pants leg may break gently over the shoes.

Jeans

Jeans come in many pant leg styles. This is how to draw a fitted pair: tight and close to the leg. Here you get to crush the fabric a bit at the knees and hug the ankles at the hemline.

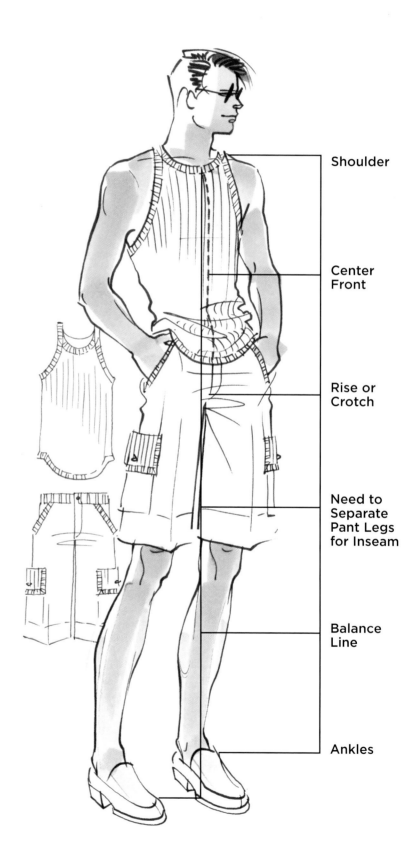

Shoulder

Center Front

Rise or Crotch

Need to Separate Pant Legs for Inseam

Balance Line

Ankles

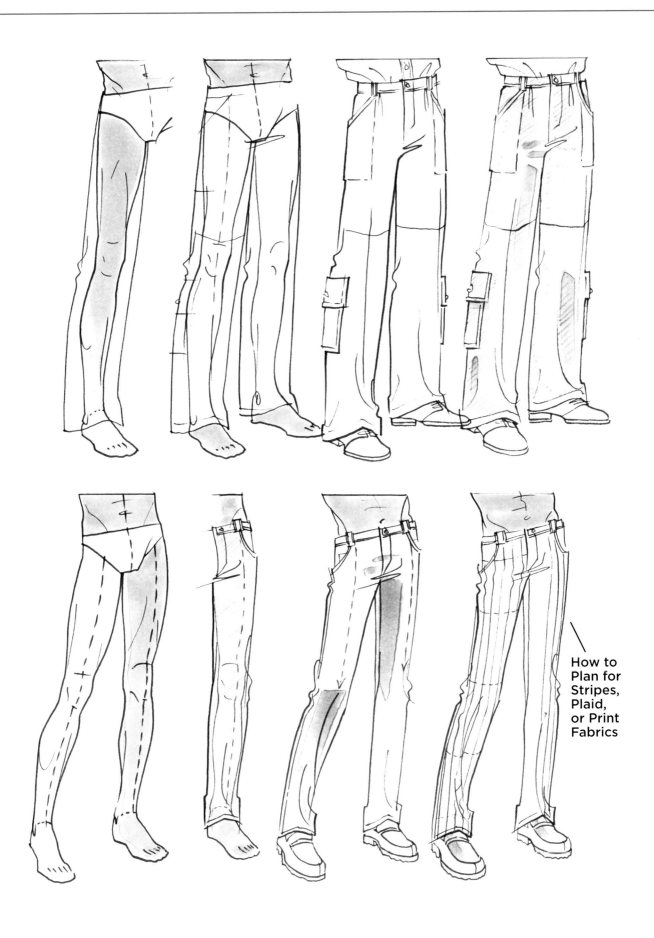

How to
Plan for
Stripes,
Plaid,
or Print
Fabrics

Menswear Tops

Knit Tops

Stretchy knits will reflect more of the body's contours in your pose. Be especially precise about drawing armholes. These seams can roll around the shoulder cap or cling to the collarbone and to the pectoral contours on the chest.

Woven Tops

Crisp shirting fabrics rarely cling, but they do tend to fold and bend in sharp angles with the pose of the body. Keep these folds to a minimum so they do not end up looking like so many wrinkles.

Jackets

Any jacket or blazer worn over woven shirts or knit tops means an excess of layers or fabrics to sketch. The easiest solution to this is to broaden the shoulders to accommodate the extra width of the jacket and to plan for more fabric volume in your sketch.

Adding Volume to the Body for Clothing Layers or Fabric Thickness or Weight

Broader Shoulders, Especially for Men's Outerwear

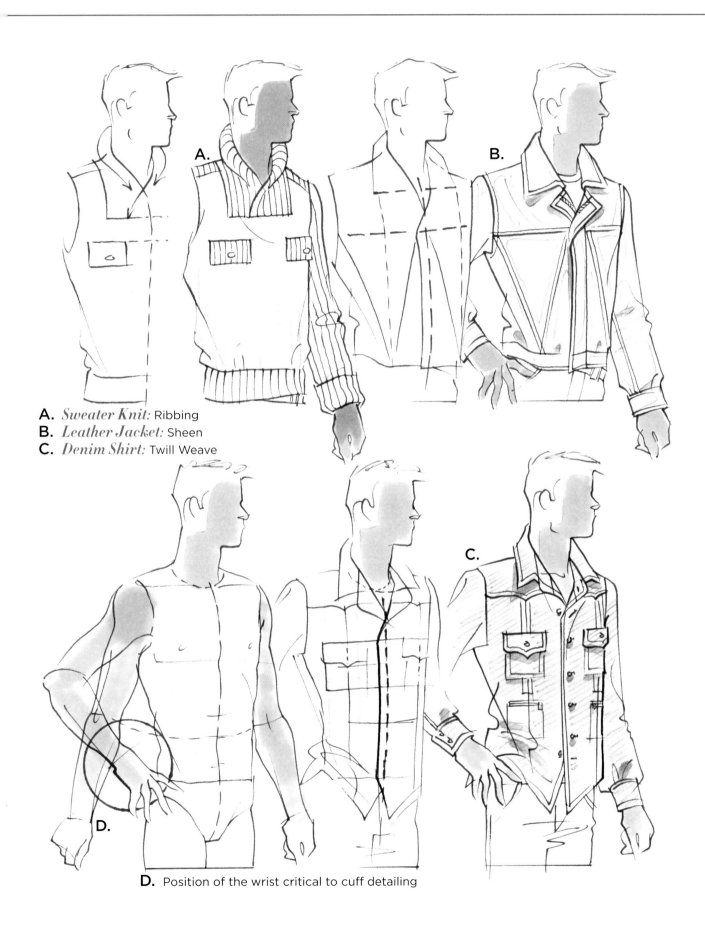

A. *Sweater Knit:* Ribbing
B. *Leather Jacket:* Sheen
C. *Denim Shirt:* Twill Weave

D. Position of the wrist critical to cuff detailing

Sketching a Suit

Before you begin to sketch, visualize what you want to accomplish. Set a goal and plan for it. For example: Picture a man in a business suit. The fabric of the suit looks crisp without being stiff. This is because the suit fabric folds gently on two areas on the figure: the upper right side at the waist, and the opposite lower left side at the back of the knee. These folds of natural creases have been kept to a minimum to avoid looking totally wrinkled. The other smaller demos focus on layering, taking garment detailing to the next level, defining how to maximize complex silhouettes.

Note:

For the clean lines of a suit with some action in the pose, bend the arm or leg on opposite sides of the figure so the sketch does not look too busy or wrinkled.

Details:
Focus on layers

Layers:
• Coat
• Jacket
• Sweater

Jacket Over the Shoulder

Jacket Held in Hand

Jacket Worn Open

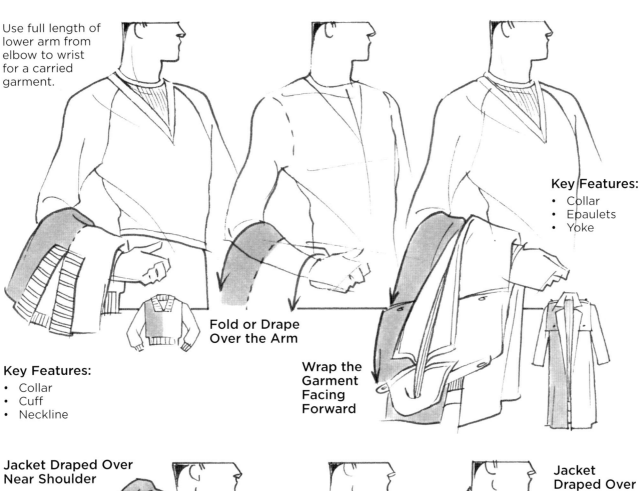

Use full length of lower arm from elbow to wrist for a carried garment.

Key Features:
- Collar
- Cuff
- Neckline

Fold or Drape Over the Arm

Wrap the Garment Facing Forward

Key Features:
- Collar
- Epaulets
- Yoke

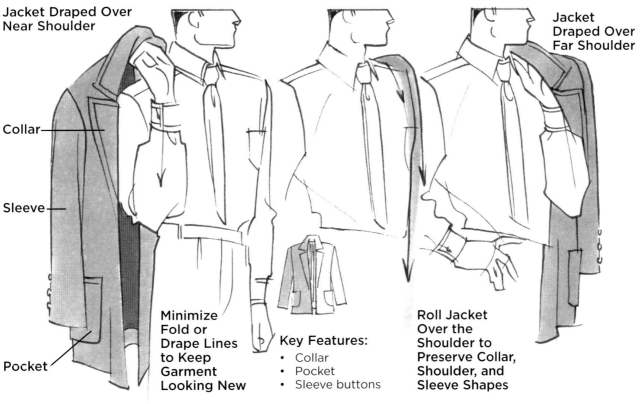

Jacket Draped Over Near Shoulder

Collar

Sleeve

Pocket

Minimize Fold or Drape Lines to Keep Garment Looking New

Key Features:
- Collar
- Pocket
- Sleeve buttons

Roll Jacket Over the Shoulder to Preserve Collar, Shoulder, and Sleeve Shapes

Jacket Draped Over Far Shoulder

Menswear Flats

Sketching flats for menswear means that you need a new set of proportions dedicated to the male fashion figure's template of a flat figure (also called a croquis). You can use the same drawing methods for this flat figure as illustrated on page 330 of this book. Just redirect the width and weight of the body to the male's form. This means a thicker neck, broader shoulders, wider waistline, and narrower hips, compared to the female fashion figure's template.

Men's Flat Template

1. Start your flat figure template with a grid broken into sections that correlate with the natural bends in the body, torso to legs.

2. Draw one complete side of your figure. Sketch in form with angular or realistic outlines, from head to toe.

3. Add on the arm and begin to fill in some of the interior sewing lines on the torso.

4. Trace over your completed side to create two equal halves that are balanced, a mirror image of two sides that make up one body. You can also draw the complete figure freehand, without tracing. Make sure both the left and the right sides of the body match each other.

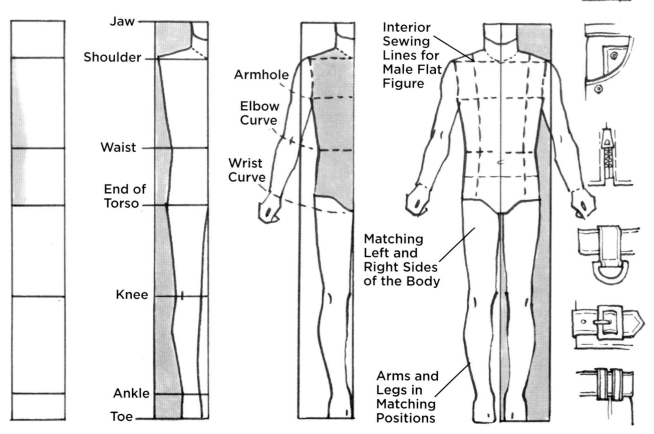

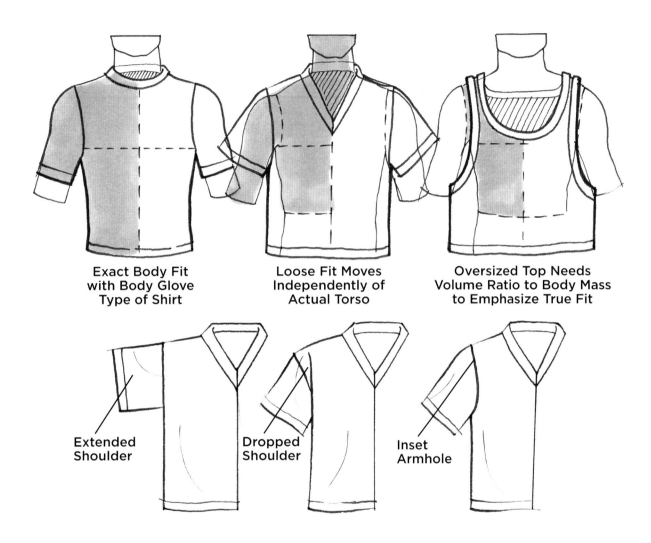

**Exact Body Fit
with Body Glove
Type of Shirt**

**Loose Fit Moves
Independently of
Actual Torso**

**Oversized Top Needs
Volume Ratio to Body Mass
to Emphasize True Fit**

**Extended
Shoulder**

**Dropped
Shoulder**

**Inset
Armhole**

There are options for how much or how to visually explain specific details in a flat. This detail could be in construction, function, or drape. The examples below illustrate the range of options for a functional detail, the detachable leg piece. All three versions are acceptable. Use the one that best suits your needs.

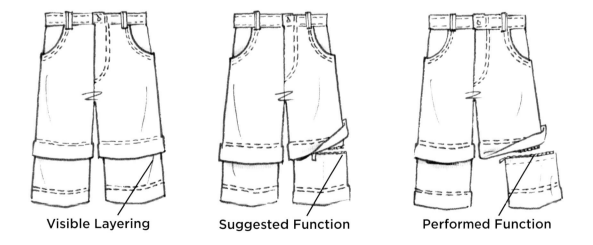

Visible Layering

Suggested Function

Performed Function

Menswear Flats (continued)

Menswear flats, when drawn by hand, will be more accurate if you use a figure template for reference. Your own customized template should include both front and back views, with a few optional arm positions. The examples below provide media and shaping options for the look of basic flats.

Hand-Drawn Flat Templates

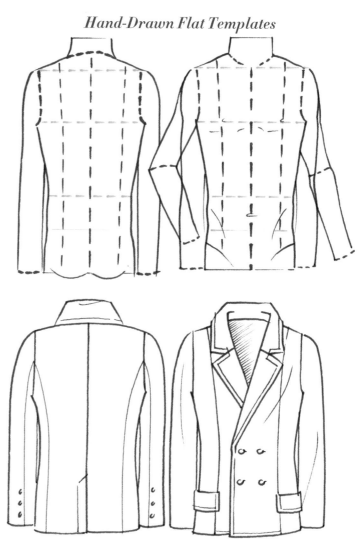

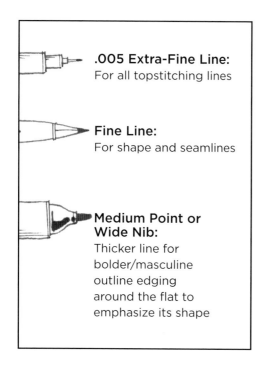

.005 Extra-Fine Line:
For all topstitching lines

Fine Line:
For shape and seamlines

Medium Point or Wide Nib:
Thicker line for bolder/masculine outline edging around the flat to emphasize its shape

Hand-Drawn Flats Using Templates

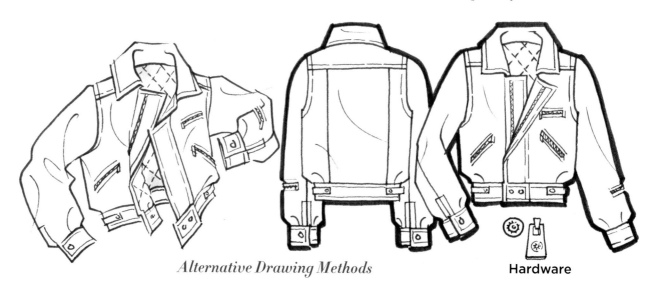

Alternative Drawing Methods

Hardware

Full Front   **Profile**

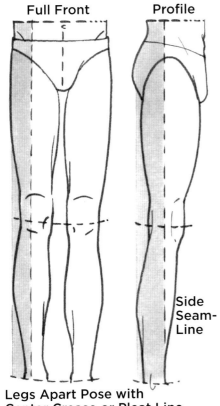

Side Seam-Line

Legs Apart Pose with Center Crease or Pleat Line

Sketch the menswear half figure for bottom flats, starting at the waistline and finishing at the ankles. Pose this partial template with the legs slightly apart to define both pant legs as two units, the critical difference between reading a flat as pants or as a single, joined unit, like a long skirt. Use the profile pants figure template to show important side seam or pocket detailing that gets sliced in the full-front flat.

Full Front   **Profile**

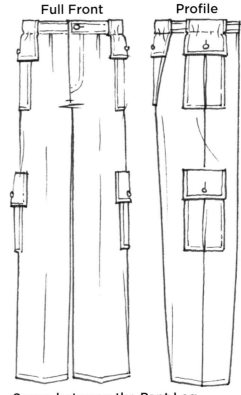

Space between the Pant Leg

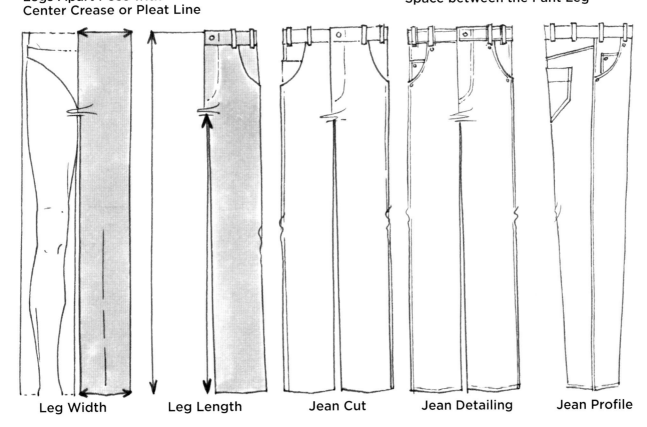

Leg Width   **Leg Length**   **Jean Cut**   **Jean Detailing**   **Jean Profile**

Design Journal Roughs

Here is an example of putting your sketches to work for you. If you find it difficult to work in a specific height or scale and you need another drawing of a different size—larger or smaller—here is an easy solution. Draw in the scale with which you are most comfortable. When the sketches are complete, make reduced or enlarged copies of that page. Then trace your own drawings from that new size. It is that simple. If your original drawing is too large for an average photocopy machine, find a copy shop that makes larger or architectural-sized copies. This is an effective timesaving technique. If you have a model drawing class, you can make sketches of the model in class and then reduce them to thumbnail or croquis book size and use them for your illustration class.

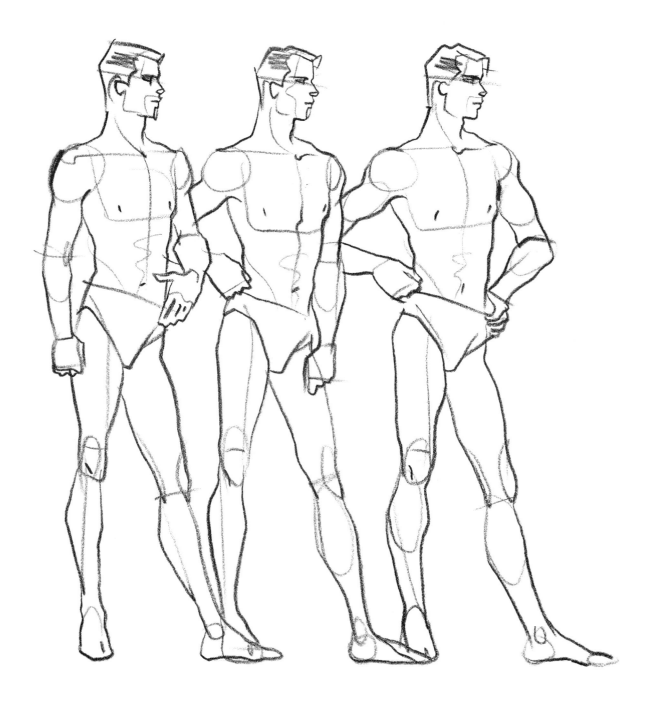

Marker Rendering for Menswear

On this page, the figure has been rendered with lots of highlighting, which is the opposite of shading, but adds the same dimensional look. It creates a sun-drenched fleshtone that picks up on the natural contours in the form of the body. Highlighting is not the same as a loose rendering because it takes planning. It also takes more time than the loose, flat marker strokes used on the croquis figure.

For the garments on this page, fabric color rendering is being introduced in its simplest form: solids and basic prints. Shading has been added to enhance the suggestion of a realistic interpretation in style for the overall sketch. This format is used to illustrate the outfits as if they were worn according to the pose shown. Again, shading is an option; you can practice rendering with or without it.

Stripe,
No Shadow

Stripe,
with Shadow

Print

Solid

Prismacolor Sanford
Cold Gray 30% on
Printed Background

Seersucker Fabric

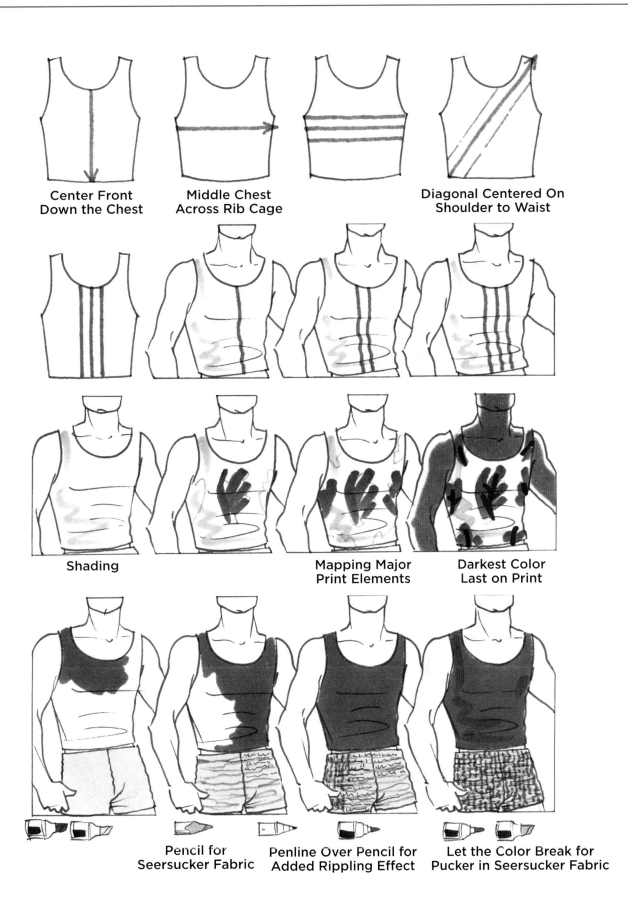

Center Front
Down the Chest

Middle Chest
Across Rib Cage

Diagonal Centered On
Shoulder to Waist

Shading

Mapping Major
Print Elements

Darkest Color
Last on Print

Pencil for
Seersucker Fabric

Penline Over Pencil for
Added Rippling Effect

Let the Color Break for
Pucker in Seersucker Fabric

Fashion Runway and Showroom Poses

These two spreads provide an opportunity to sketch the same walking, runway, or showroom poses for men as shown for women in Chapter 3, Model Drawing. Use the same figure analysis to help inform and support your drawing techniques as you have been studying in this chapter.

Dolce & Gabbana

Dolce &
Gabbana

Ralph Lauren
Purple Label

Ralph Lauren
Purple Label

Ralph
Lauren RLX

Dolce & Gabbana

Ralph Lauren
Purple Label

Ralph Lauren
Purple Label

Ralph
Lauren RLX

This row of menswear figures builds its visual interest through juxtaposition of subtle posing with fashion attitude or power looks. At first glance, you will notice how well these flats are drawn. They are precise and informative, as well as beautiful. Their visual appeal has not sacrificed design detailing. First, this designer took her line quality, her art, seriously enough to ensure that she kept it consistent for the whole collection, making each flat as good as another. She kept her drawing technique even, using the same gouache media for the whole page instead of constantly changing her style. Second, she kept her presentation's format the same, laying out the front- and back-view flats consistently, like mirror images or repeating forms that maximize the use of her page.

Foil w/ Embroidery

Rivets   Foil /Screen Printed Tee

- Option w/ to roll up or keep down.
Closure kept inside Pant.

Foil Printed Tee

Foil Printed Sweater

Designed Buckle and Belt.

This design shows hand-drawn figures with fabric rendering that was digitally manipulated. This is a young, fresh, contemporary take on a casual menswear collection. Her figure work focuses on silhouette, color, and fabrication. Her highly expressive flats, also digitally enhanced, bring detailing to a new level of precision.

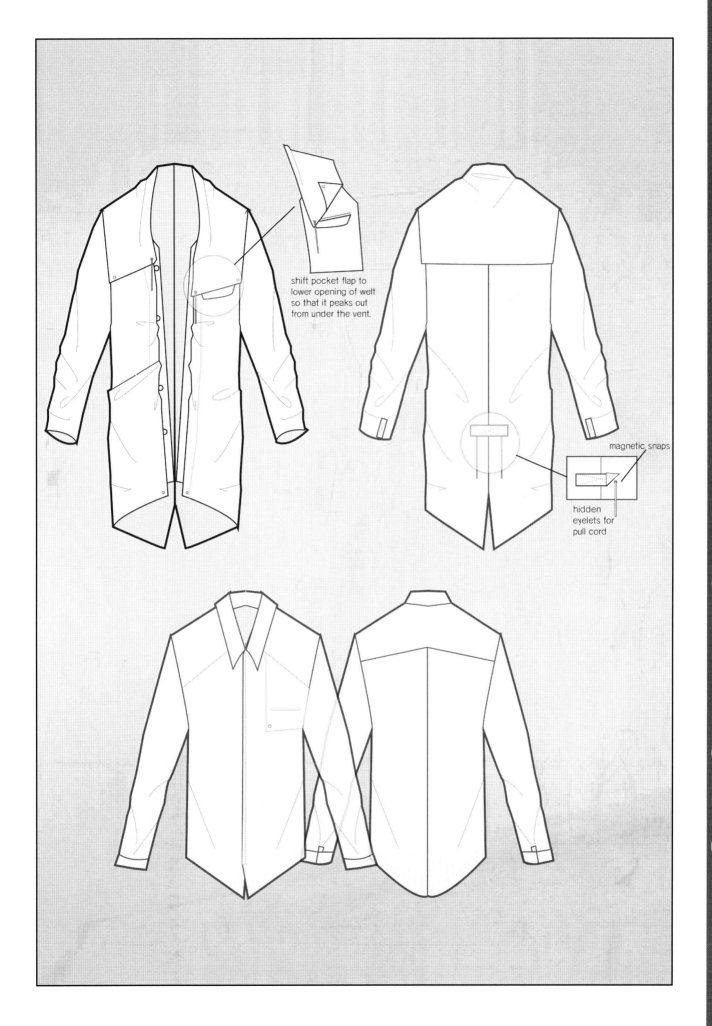

shift pocket flap to
lower opening of welt
so that it peaks out
from under the vent.

magnetic snaps

hidden
eyelets for
pull cord

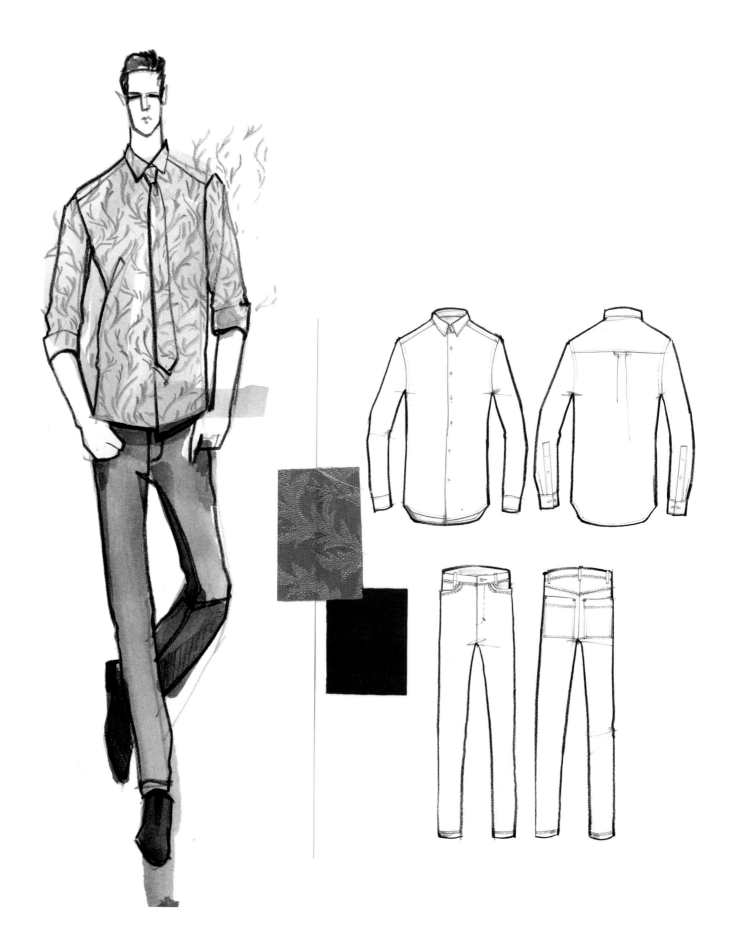

The media mix for this design is gouache, colored pencils, and pencil outline. His menswear pieces are young, sleek, and very modern silhouettes. His relaxed, easy (uncomplicated) poses have a natural look. His artistic subtlety adds authenticity and authority to his presentation.

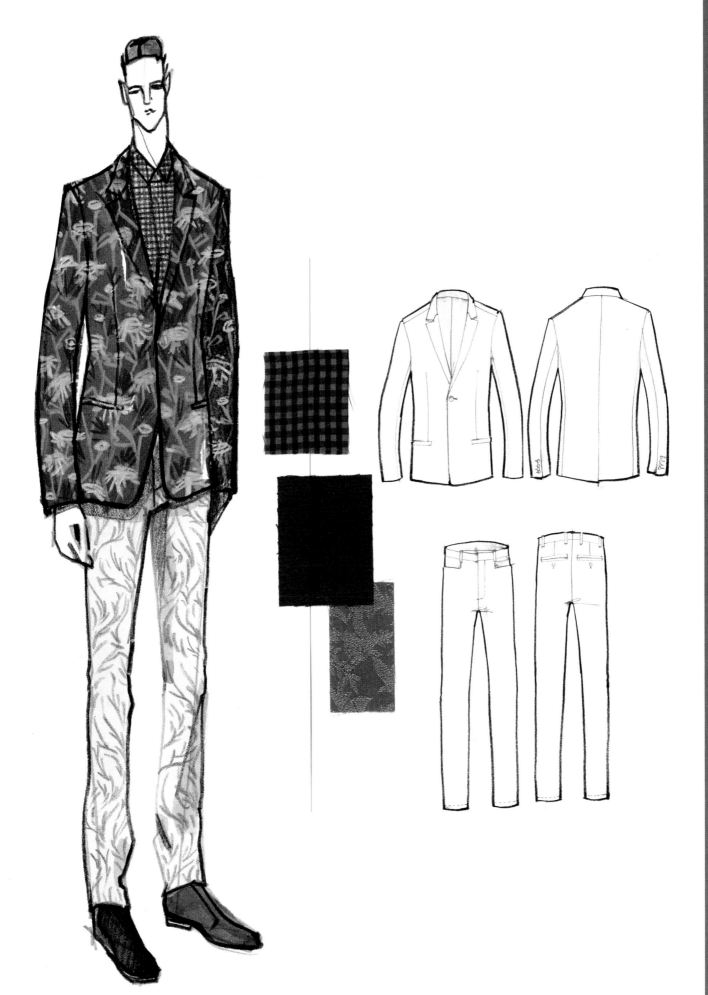

The media mix for this design is gouache and pencil. This designer works in the design journal format. He builds his menswear collection on a foundation of in-depth research, referencing his own cut and draping. His drawings focus on construction and fit. He puts his choice of motif to work across his flat sketches, exploring the potential in his design inspiration.

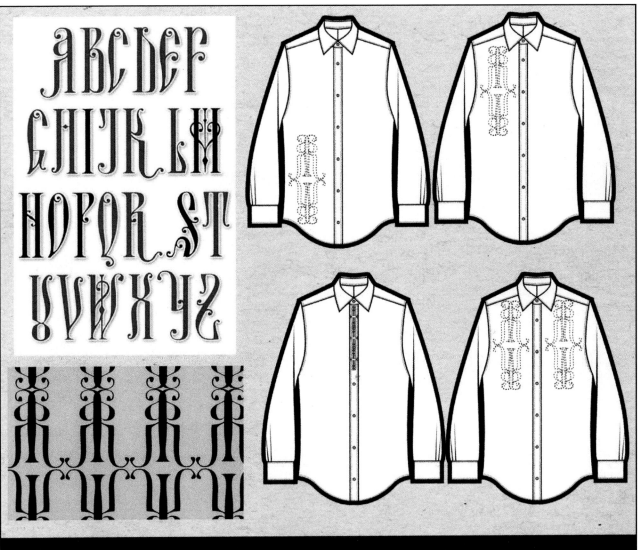

Farquhar

Menswear fashion has always focused on detailing. The detailing represents attention to quality, value, and label, that is, a label or store that was advertising the clothing. In classic advertising approaches for menswear illustration, the cut and fit of the clothes were almost more important than style. If womenswear was based on design attitude, menswear was based on clarifying design facts. During the 1920s, menswear illustration became quite stylized but later reverted back to the dominant realistic version. That realism lent itself to defining precision construction and practical comfort that the menswear industry felt was the duty of the illustration to convey.

Novel tailoring details
from England

Button on thru
S.B. — 2 leather
buttons on thong

sponge rubber
pads prevent slip
— keep shirt
down.

large outside
handy pocket

omission of
left pocket

Zipper closure on
handy pocket

wide spread
blunt vest points
(last button to button)

no breast
pocket
gives jacket
perfect symmetry

Inside utility pocket
for carrying change,
cigarettes, etc.

two buttons for
elastic waistband
adjustment.

12

Drawing Children

Drawing children is the art of capturing playfulness. A designer must skill-fully illustrate children's specific age groups, showing correct size ranges for the retail market.

In this chapter, for the sake of space and time, particular areas such as arms, legs, hands, and feet will be drawn for only one childrenswear age group. Using the basic steps or sketching formulas from these pages should help you draw children of any age. It will only be a matter of larger sizes for older kids and smaller sizes for younger ones. You will learn how to add more dynamic, playful, yet awkward nuances to the full-front, three-quarter turned, and profile poses for children. Unlike adults, kids have almost no neck; they have cute, stubby arms and legs, as well as full, rounded tummies, which presents a nice change in drawing after so much elongation in other chapters. The liberating elements of fun and surprise can be incorporated when you draw kids. Along with the in-depth sketching techniques, this chapter includes a showcase of guest artists and historical references for childrenswear illustration and design. These will introduce you to the diverse possibilities of style choices for drawing children.

Children's Age Groups

Different age groups are defined using basic fashion marketing terms for childrenswear. However, the terms "infant," "toddler," "child," and "young contemporary" (also known as "preteen") are not true indicators of height. An example of this is that a three-year-old can be as tall as a five-year-old. But these children's clothing terms, from a business point of view, serve the purpose of suggesting the range of size changes between one age group and another.

Note:

With head sizes, exaggeration is the key factor. In sketching childrenswear, head sizes are going to be relative to your drawing style. Kids' heads often are drawn larger than their body size might dictate. Big heads are part of making kidswear fun and they add that extra sense of playfulness to your sketches.

- This mix of kids represents the range in sizes for childrenswear.
- Kids' heads can be drawn proportionally larger than their bodies, like in anime sketching.

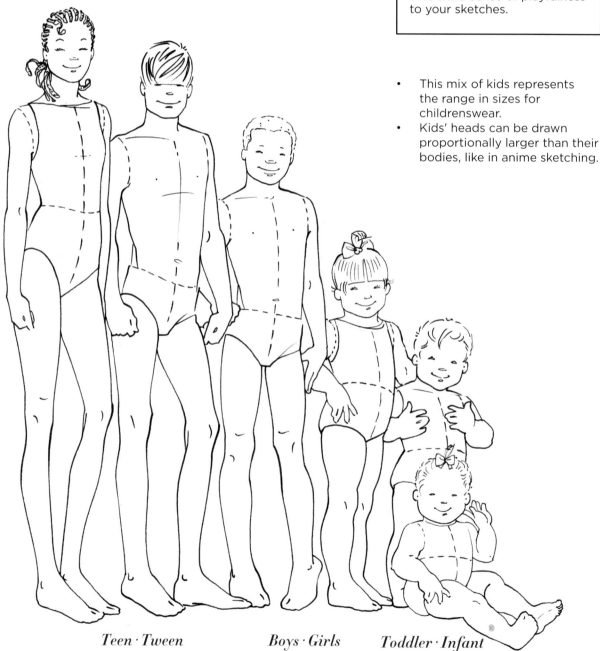

Teen · Tween   *Boys · Girls*   *Toddler · Infant*

Figures A, B, and C exaggerate those differences in size and height by defining the proportion. All three figures are lined up at the shoulder. After that one connection, you can see that is all they have in common. The head, arms, and length of legs vary; so do the waistlines and end of torsos.

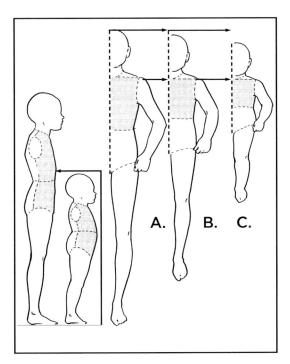

A. B. C.

When drawing kids of different ages, a less exaggerated method for evaluating their height is to line them up at floor level, in profile. This kind of size reference will make drawing kids easier.

It will also help to remember childrenswear sizes:

Infants: 3 to 26 months
Toddlers: 1T to 4T
Young Girls/Boys: 2 to 6 single sizes
Girls: 6x
Preteen: 7 to 14 single sizes

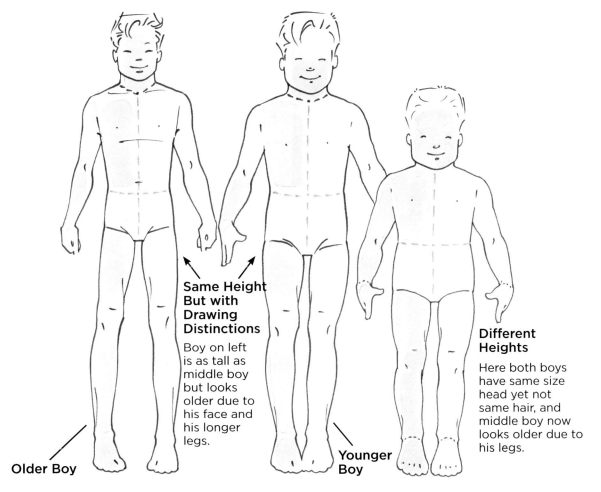

Same Height But with Drawing Distinctions

Boy on left is as tall as middle boy but looks older due to his face and his longer legs.

Older Boy

Younger Boy

Different Heights

Here both boys have same size head yet not same hair, and middle boy now looks older due to his legs.

Childrenswear Proportions

The easiest set of proportions for drawing infants is to use the head's width and length to measure the torso's segments. The infant's torso is two heads long. Childrenswear proportions seem tiny, almost abbreviated. Often there is so much to draw in such a condensed space, even though their figures can be drawn larger and wider to show off all of your design details. Drawing flats for their clothes is more of a challenge. For childrenswear tops watch the neck and shoulderline for easy access openings. Note that armhole to side seam lengths can change by age group. The side seam, inseam lengths will be critical for bottoms.

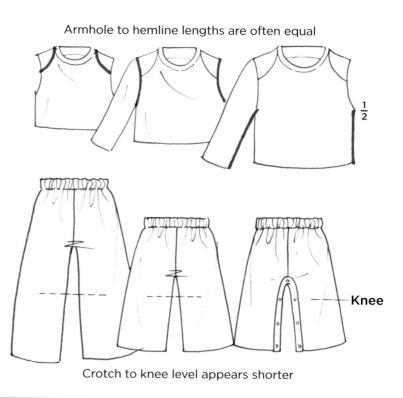

Armhole to hemline lengths are often equal

$\frac{1}{2}$

Knee

Crotch to knee level appears shorter

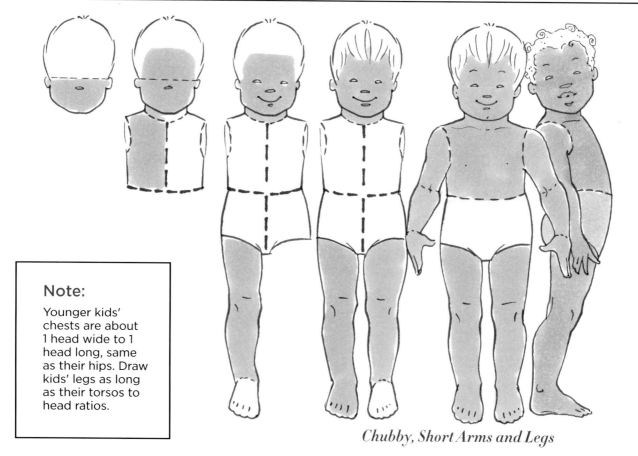

Note:
Younger kids' chests are about 1 head wide to 1 head long, same as their hips. Draw kids' legs as long as their torsos to head ratios.

Chubby, Short Arms and Legs

Infant

The distinction between infants and toddlers, in fashion, is that toddlers stand and infants do not. The fashion focus on babies' clothing is often on diaper access on the legs or crotch of a garment. For this reason infants are drawn in seated poses. The seated pose is a convenient fashion pose for specific inseam garment details.

Ages: Birth to 2 years
Infant Sizes in Months: 3 to 6 mo., 6 to 9 mo., 9 to 12 mo., 12 to 18 mo., 18 mo. to 24 mo.

Babies: Two Heads Tall and One Head Wide

Tip:
Remember that infants do not stand.

Seated Poses for Diaper Access Treatments on Your Garments

Toddler

Toddlers, at ages two to four years, are finally standing. This separates them from infants, who only sit in your sketches. Toddlers, like infants, still have babyish large heads, hidden necks, and chubby torsos with cute, rounded tummies. Drawing toddlers upright and walking in your sketch, plus keeping them short and stocky, will establish them as no longer infants but not quite young children either. These proportion changes are a challenge, but also fun to practice.

Ages: 2 to 4 years
Toddlers: 2T to 4T

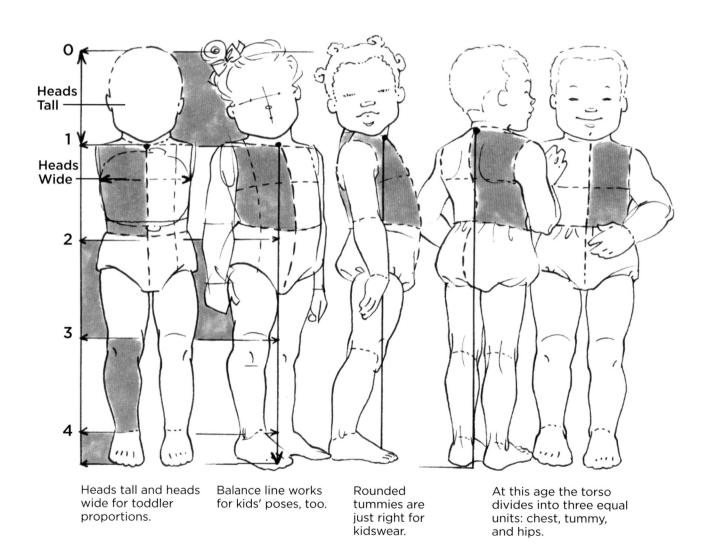

Heads tall and heads wide for toddler proportions.

Balance line works for kids' poses, too.

Rounded tummies are just right for kidswear.

At this age the torso divides into three equal units: chest, tummy, and hips.

Younger Child

The younger child, ages four to six years, is sketched somewhere between not babyish (no more need for diaper access) but still really childish. "Childish" is conveyed by a playful, awkward look in your figures. A head taller than the toddler, the younger child has slightly longer arms and legs, while retaining the rounded tummy of a small child. Choose a pose that is playful, fun, but awkward, and a bit off balance for this child, so that the age variation can be distinguishable in your sketching.

Ages: 4 to 6 years
Toddlers: 4 to 6x

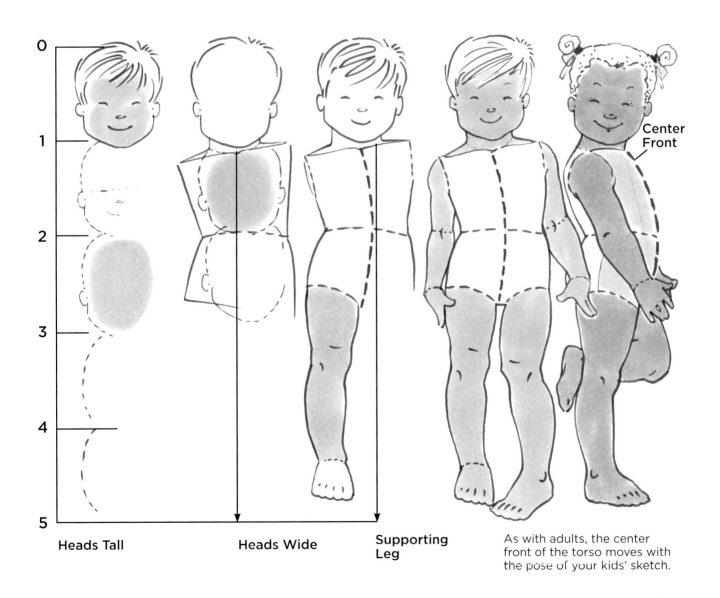

Center Front

Heads Tall

Heads Wide

Supporting Leg

As with adults, the center front of the torso moves with the pose of your kids' sketch.

Child

A boy or a girl child, at ages seven to nine years, has to be drawn taller than a younger child. The head is sketched more in proportion with the rest of the body, and finally, there is some neck to draw. Posing for this age group becomes less awkward, more dynamic, and very active according to your fashion category, design silhouette's fabrication, and drawing style.

Ages: 7 to 9 years
Sizes: 7 to 14

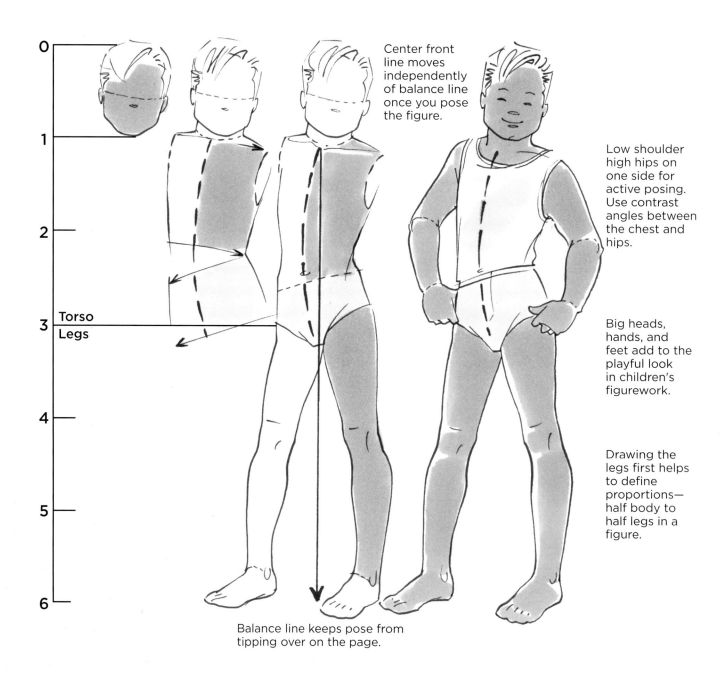

Center front line moves independently of balance line once you pose the figure.

Low shoulder high hips on one side for active posing. Use contrast angles between the chest and hips.

Big heads, hands, and feet add to the playful look in children's figurework.

Drawing the legs first helps to define proportions—half body to half legs in a figure.

Balance line keeps pose from tipping over on the page.

Tween Boy

The boy or girl tween, at ages 10 to 12, is certainly more mature looking than a child, yet still not as grown up as a teenager in your sketches. (Tween is short for that in-between age.) In real life a tween's height can greatly vary. To keep your age groups distinct, draw them shorter than your teenager's market of Young Contemporary, so you have room for age variety in your childrenswear design repertoire.

Ages: 10 to 12 years

Heads Tall

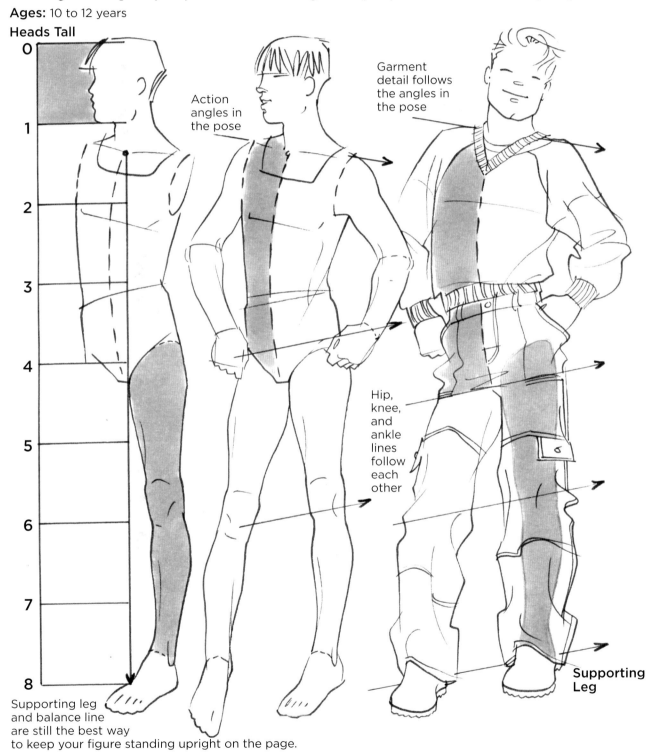

Action angles in the pose

Garment detail follows the angles in the pose

Hip, knee, and ankle lines follow each other

Supporting Leg

Supporting leg and balance line are still the best way to keep your figure standing upright on the page.

Tween to Teen

Subtle changes, beyond just growing taller, separate the tween from a teen in your sketching. Most of these changes are reflected in the torso you draw. Hint at the budding curves for the girl teen's torso (still not as mature as a woman's torso), and broaden the shoulders for the teen boy while still keeping him long and lanky. All teens get the elongated fashion neck, and their bodies stay chunky, not so grown up yet.

Ages: 10 to 12 years
Tween Girl

Ages: 13 years and up
Teen Girl

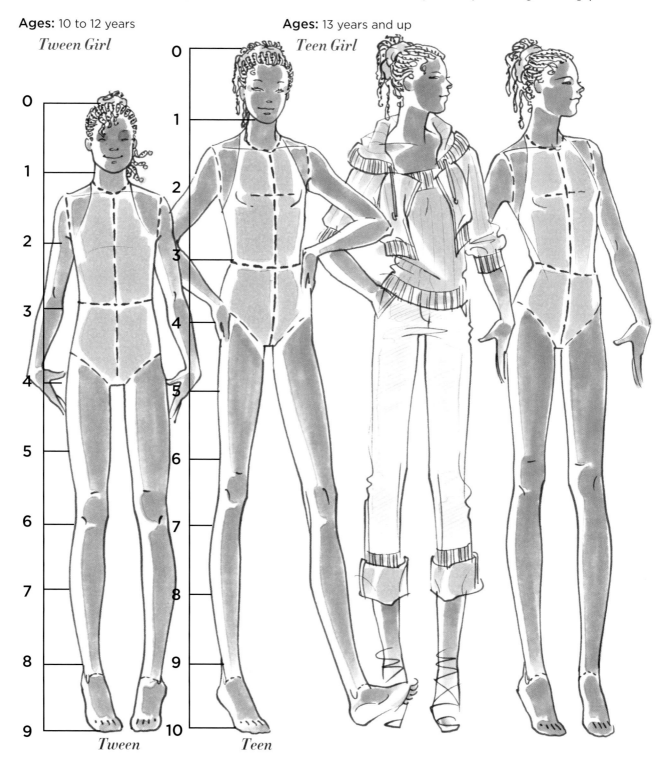

Tween

Teen

Teen Boy

The teen boy or girl, at ages 13 to 16, is still not drawn like an adult. This age group has stores dedicated to their own fashion taste and style. Even though, in real life, teens can wear adult-sized clothing, the fashion industry treats teens as a separate business category. To keep the teen youthful, stay with a rounded face, chunky hands, and big feet. Keep the teen's torso immature or boy's shoulders understated and draw him in gawky or playful poses.

Age: 13 years and up

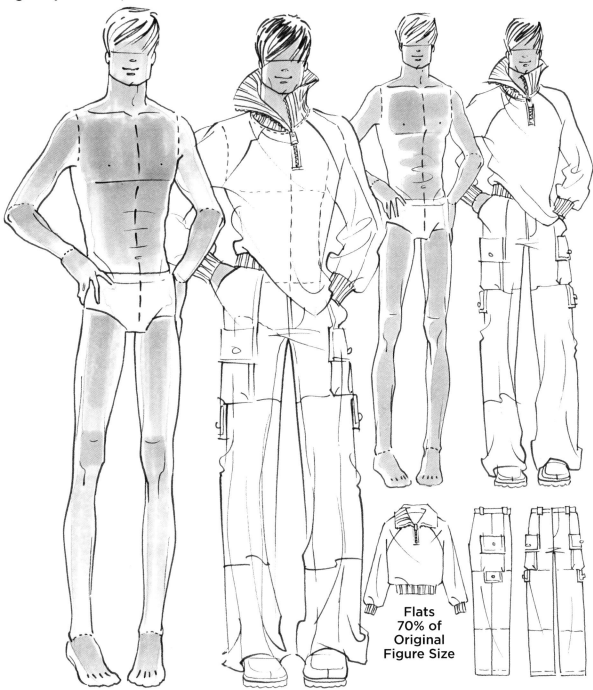

**Flats
70% of
Original
Figure Size**

Drawing Children's Heads

Full-Front Pose

Three-Quarter-Turned Pose

Profile Pose

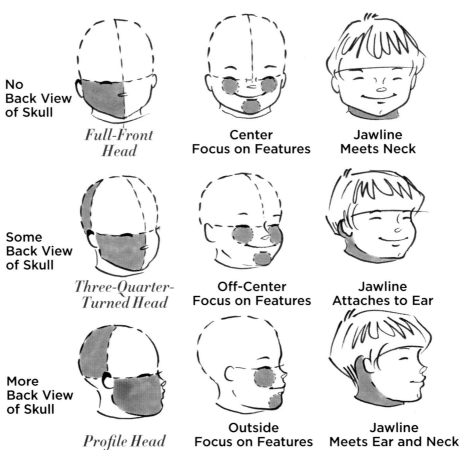

No Back View of Skull

Full-Front Head

Center Focus on Features

Jawline Meets Neck

Some Back View of Skull

Three-Quarter-Turned Head

Off-Center Focus on Features

Jawline Attaches to Ear

More Back View of Skull

Profile Head

Outside Focus on Features

Jawline Meets Ear and Neck

While all of the basic principles of drawing the head have been covered in the sections on women's and men's heads, there are unique qualities about the head of a child. Beyond gender, cuteness, and style interpretations, a child's face seems to have more forehead and a more condensed area of feature placement. These two factors, plus the not-quite-fully-developed eyes, nose, and mouth, make drawing a child's face more fun. Illustrated below are three stylized formulas for creating a child's face.

Round

Square

Heart

Drawing Children's Arms and Hands

In fashion sketching, arms on children mimic the same adult formula: The upper half and the lower half of the arm are equal in length. The elbow remains in the middle. The main difference between the adult's arm and the child's arm is that the child's arm is drawn with much less exaggeration.

Easy Drawing Formulas

1. Upper arm is same length as lower arm.
2. Draw the elbow in the middle of the arm.
3. The arm's width is just about half of a hand's width.
4. The arm's length can be four hands long.

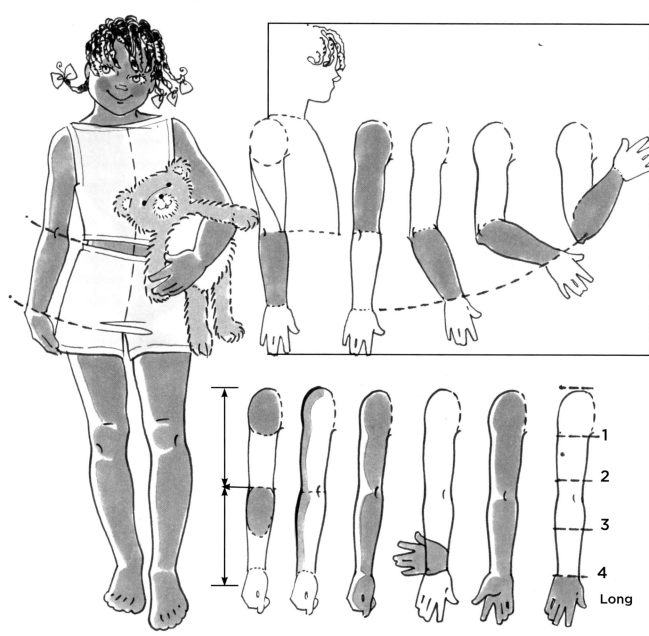

- Their arm width is about half of a hand wide.
- Kids' arm length is about 4 "hands" long.

Hands, when drawn at this reduced size, tend to look like cartoon caricatures. The stubby little fingers get very rounded. This is the opposite of the tapered, elongated female fashion hand, or the bulky male fashion hand with its exaggerated knuckles. All of the detail in a child's hand is lost due to its smallness in your sketch. As you draw hands for any age child, practice hand positions that are playful. Focus in on the fingers, the inside of the palm, or the back of the hand.

Elbow Arc

Drawing Children's Legs and Feet

The adult fashion leg formula states that the upper half of the leg (the thigh) is equal in length to the lower half of the leg (the calf). This formula is the same for children. The difference lies in the short stocky legs of children versus the exaggerated leg length of the adult fashion figure. While adapting this formula to children, it helps to focus in on the knee and the ankle, as the leg turns. Remember, practice drawing both the right and the left leg.

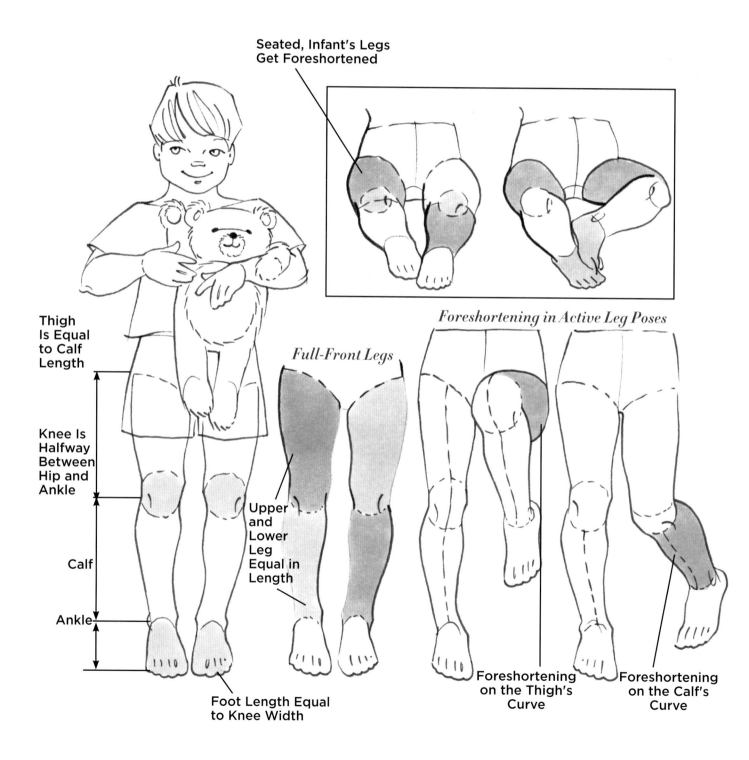

Seated, Infant's Legs Get Foreshortened

Foreshortening in Active Leg Poses

Full-Front Legs

Thigh Is Equal to Calf Length

Knee Is Halfway Between Hip and Ankle

Upper and Lower Leg Equal in Length

Calf

Ankle

Foot Length Equal to Knee Width

Foreshortening on the Thigh's Curve

Foreshortening on the Calf's Curve

After you have learned the formulas for drawing children's legs, you will be ready to pose the legs in a manner that reflects the age group you are portraying. Although the examples on these pages represent both child and infant, you should choose the age you want to practice. The point is to find the right amount of playfulness or awkwardness that best depicts the attitude of the child in the age group you want to sketch. Keep in mind that infant legs need to be drawn in a sitting position because infants rarely can stand on their own.

Infant Legs
Emphasis on closure seams

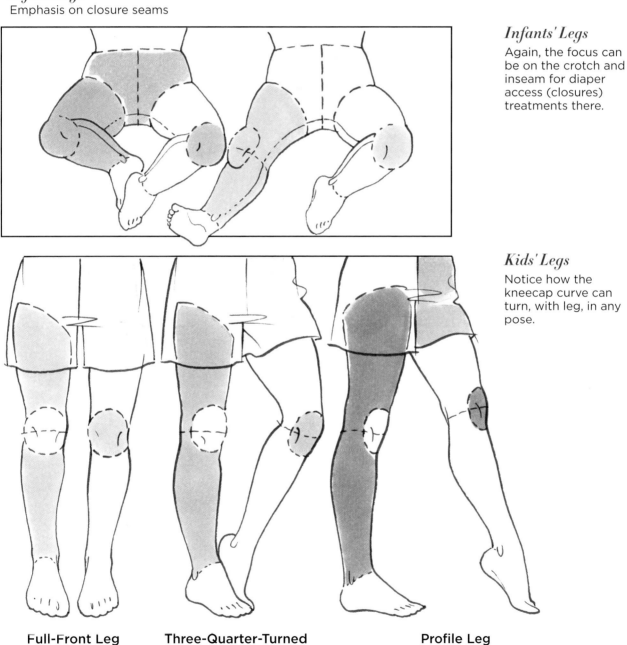

Infants' Legs
Again, the focus can be on the crotch and inseam for diaper access (closures) treatments there.

Kids' Legs
Notice how the kneecap curve can turn, with leg, in any pose.

Full-Front Leg and Knee

Three-Quarter-Turned Leg and Knee

Profile Leg and Knee

Design Roughs for Childrenswear

A loose and spontaneous technique is perfect for drawing children's fashion because this portrays the constant motion of a child. This animation easily translates into a group of figures that can be used in croquis for childrenswear. Croquis for fashion illustration or design often focus on the clothes, which are clustered together for shape, color, and layers. Childrenswear croquis can line up easily across the waistline. Line the figures up in a row, with the same floor and the same ceiling for a group look. It is often easier and faster to sketch them in the same body size, which represents the clothing size of a certain age group. If a drawing places taller kids together with shorter kids, it will seem to be representing two different clothing sizes or two different age groups, rather than just one.

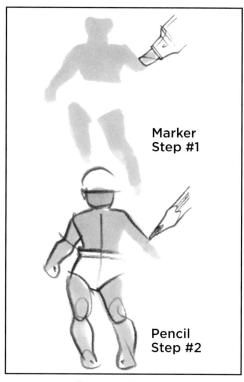

Marker
Step #1

Pencil
Step #2

Gesture Croquis

Gesture Sketching to Create Rough Croquis Posing

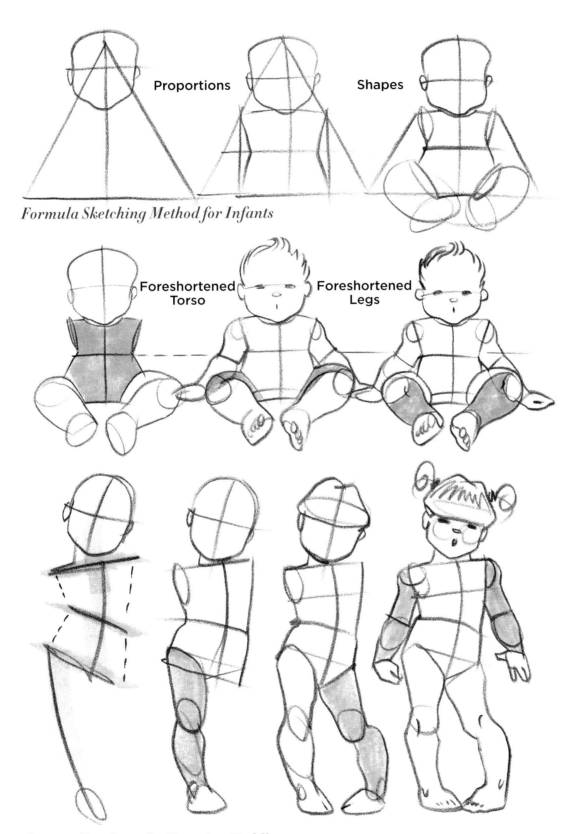

Proportions

Shapes

Formula Sketching Method for Infants

Foreshortened
Torso

Foreshortened
Legs

Gesture Sketching for Drawing Toddlers

Rendering Childrenswear

Rendering faces and hair in color on adult and child fashion figures is also divided into loose and tight looks. The looser look in rendering goes best with your croquis. The tighter look makes the most sense with your finishes.

You can mix any technique with another to convey a sense of style. For instance, the hair of the red-headed girl has been rendered in a free-form style, while the black hair has been done in a tighter, more detailed manner. In contrast, the boy's hair (the middle head) hasn't had any marker color applied at all. The brown pencil shading gets the message across just as well for hair coloring.

Notice that for kids, the face can be sketched in the same shape for boys or girls. In a fashion illustration, it is the hairstyle that usually defines gender at younger ages. This does not hold true for the adults.

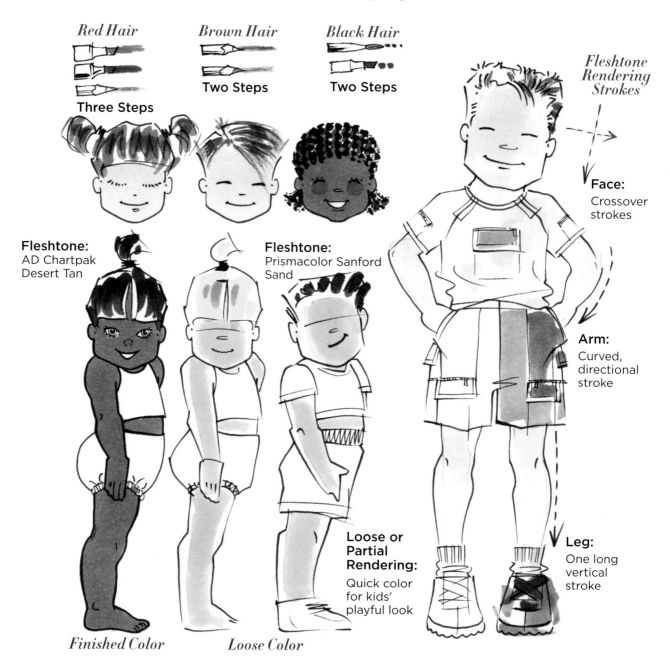

Red Hair

Three Steps

Brown Hair

Two Steps

Black Hair

Two Steps

Fleshtone Rendering Strokes

Face: Crossover strokes

Fleshtone: AD Chartpak Desert Tan

Fleshtone: Prismacolor Sanford Sand

Arm: Curved, directional stroke

Loose or Partial Rendering: Quick color for kids' playful look

Leg: One long vertical stroke

Finished Color

Loose Color

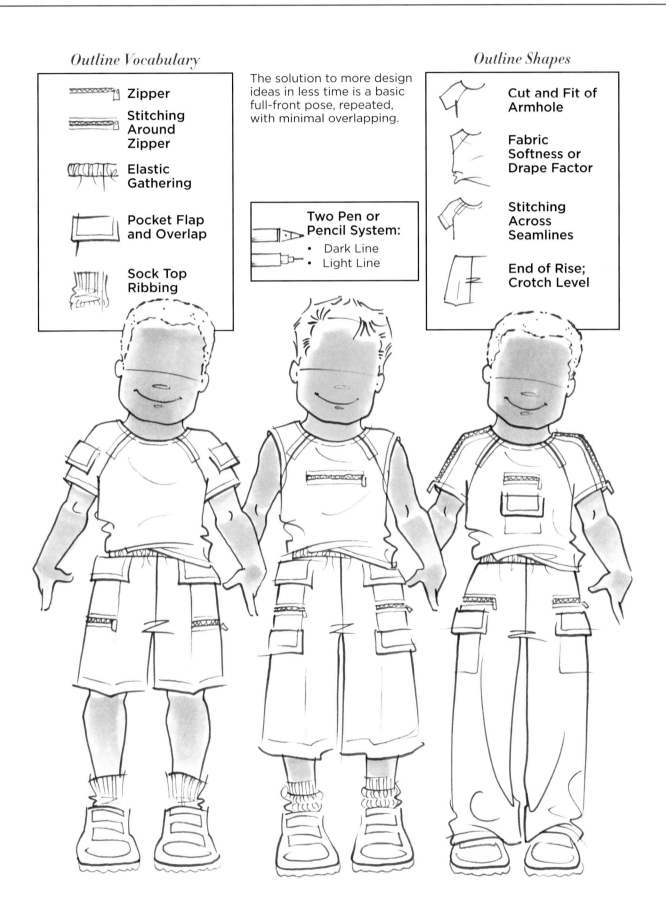

Outline Vocabulary

- *(zipper icon)* Zipper
- *(stitching icon)* Stitching Around Zipper
- *(elastic icon)* Elastic Gathering
- *(pocket flap icon)* Pocket Flap and Overlap
- *(sock top icon)* Sock Top Ribbing

The solution to more design ideas in less time is a basic full-front pose, repeated, with minimal overlapping.

Two Pen or Pencil System:
- Dark Line
- Light Line

Outline Shapes

- *(armhole icon)* Cut and Fit of Armhole
- *(drape icon)* Fabric Softness or Drape Factor
- *(seamline icon)* Stitching Across Seamlines
- *(rise icon)* End of Rise; Crotch Level

Flats for Children

Children's clothing is often tops and bottoms, mix-and-match garments, or one-piece dressing like onesies, overalls, or jumpers (as on the facing page). It helps to break the children's figure into two units to facilitate working on these flats. In drawing children's flats you want to focus on the differences in detail of a garment's front and back. The terms "inside back" and "inside front" are part of your flat sketching vocabulary.

Back and Front Detailing

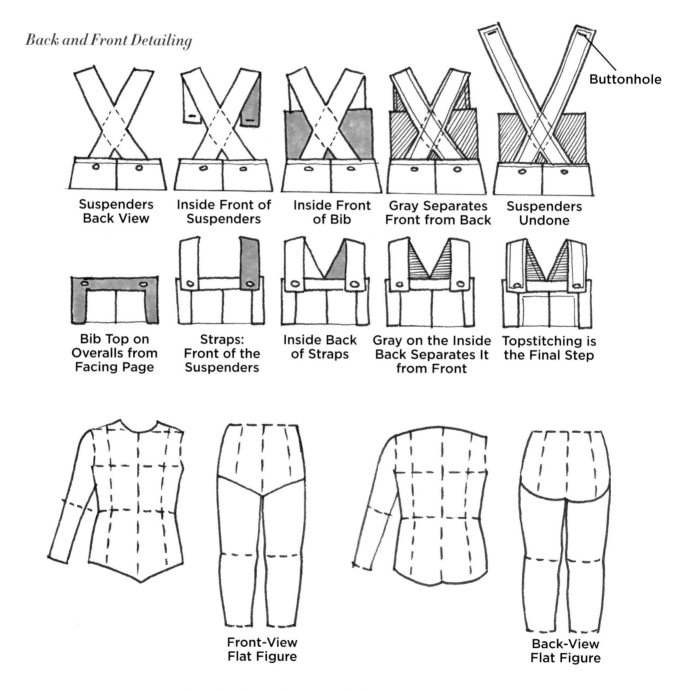

Buttonhole

Suspenders Back View	Inside Front of Suspenders	Inside Front of Bib	Gray Separates Front from Back	Suspenders Undone
Bib Top on Overalls from Facing Page	Straps: Front of the Suspenders	Inside Back of Straps	Gray on the Inside Back Separates It from Front	Topstitching is the Final Step

Front-View
Flat Figure

Back-View
Flat Figure

These front- and back-view flat figures are for toddlers.

Kids' garments are often more decorated or have more elaborate closures than other kinds of clothing to provide easy access to dress or undress a child quickly. This is a lot of specific detail on a small piece of clothing displayed on your flat. Strive for accuracy and clarity in the information you put into flats. Here are some examples of how to make front- and back-view flats connect with each other.

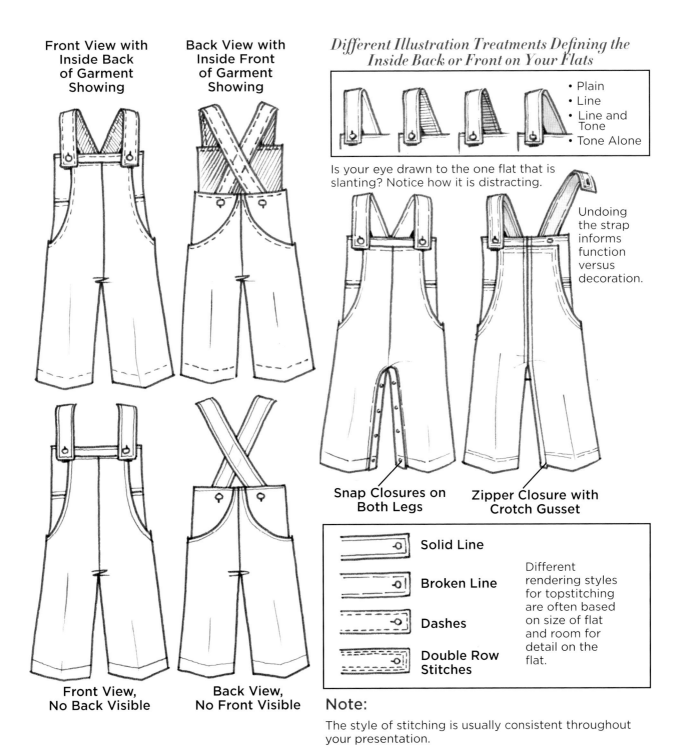

Front View with Inside Back of Garment Showing

Back View with Inside Front of Garment Showing

Different Illustration Treatments Defining the Inside Back or Front on Your Flats

- Plain
- Line
- Line and Tone
- Tone Alone

Is your eye drawn to the one flat that is slanting? Notice how it is distracting.

Undoing the strap informs function versus decoration.

Snap Closures on Both Legs

Zipper Closure with Crotch Gusset

Front View, No Back Visible

Back View, No Front Visible

Solid Line

Broken Line

Dashes

Double Row Stitches

Different rendering styles for topstitching are often based on size of flat and room for detail on the flat.

Note:

The style of stitching is usually consistent throughout your presentation.

This artist designed her collection around some of the classic elements of the 1960s British pop icons and mixed it with details from the 1920s newsboy look. With these two influences, she has created a clever hybrid of past and present in her clothes yet kept her drawing style completely contemporary. She worked on vellum-finished watercolor paper and used an H-pencil, Prismacolor pencils, a #4 sable brush, and gouache.

The media mix for this group of illustrations is gouache, marker, pen, and pencil. The designer accentuates her range in childrenswear with drawing and rendering skills, which focus on the differences between the fashion perspectives in her collections. A sense of humor permeates her figure work, adding to the youthful, animated attitude in her fashion silhouettes.

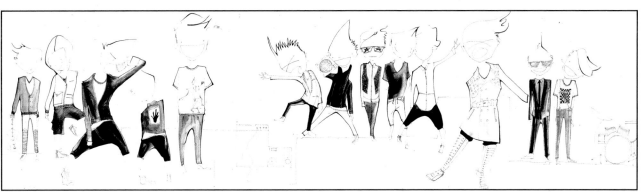

The media mix the designer uses is gouache and pencil. The cute factor in her fall collection, driven by creative choices in trims, enhances the arty playfulness in both her figures and fashion silhouettes. Decorative borders around her art pages complement her trims and create a signature "frame" for her color story.

The media mix for this illustration is gouache, pen, and pencil. Referencing a children's book character as design inspiration, the designer ties into the dark and moody color palette, which adds to the character-driven figures with their own built-in narrative as design inspiration. The boys' casual sportswear was inspired by the clever word play between roadside billboards (as seen through a car's rearview mirror) and classic music billboards.

NOTE: SIZES ON ALL THESE DRESSES ARE CUT FULL. SIZE 2 WILL FIT BETTY EVEN THOUGH SHE "IS LARGE FOR HER AGE"

For the readers of CLOTHES who have asked for
A MAIL ORDER PAGE

HOW TO ORDER

Order by number. Mail to Filene's, in care of the Mail Service Department. Be sure to note the size you wish, and the color, and mention your second choice of color if you have one. A charge account is of great convenience in ordering by mail. If you do not charge, send check or money order

The CHILDREN'S SHOP

1
Bloomer dresses, $2. Pink, blue and green checked gingham. Ruffled collar and cuffs are white. "Kindergarten" pocket has appliqued leaves. 2, 4 and 6 years

2
Poplin rompers, $2. Pink, blue and white poplin of a fine grade. White or self collars and cuffs. Colored embroidery and smocking. 1, 2, 3 and 4 years

3
Poplin trouser suits, $3. Frilled white poplin blouses on to which button colored poplin trousers (pink, blue and white). Buttons all around. 2, 4 and 6 years

The WOMEN'S SHOP

4
Women's linen dresses, $7.50. These dresses are from the shop where we have sold a thousand dresses by telephone-order in one day. An overhead style, with adjustable tie-belt. Blue, orchid, green, gray, brown, rose, and white Irish linen, hand drawn and machine hemstitched. Venetian pattern lace medallions, as durable as linen. Sizes 36, 38, 40, 42, 44 and 46

The GIRLS' SHOP

5
Girls' pongee dresses, $4. All silk, natural color. Blouse buttons a few inches in back. The skirts have pleats at the sides, and long tie-belts. Necktie is two-tone ribbon. Hand embroidery in brown silk on tie-slot, collar and cuffs. 8, 10, 12 and 14 years

6
Juniors' two-piece Balbriggan jersey dresses, $15. The most fashionable dress in the world at the moment. Skirt is on an elastic band. Note the kick pleat in front. French blue, jade green, rose, tan and cinnamon. The huge tie is printed silk in a variety of designs. 13, 15 and 17 years

The MISSES' SHOP

7
Misses' flannel dresses, $15. One of those tremendously simple dresses that button down the front. It has THE RIGHT COLLAR. Poudre blue, green, rust and tan flannel, with contrasting bands of natural color kashmir. 14, 16, 18 and 20 years

From the beginning, illustration for childrenswear in the fashion field was divided into two separate illustrative styles: realistic or stylized. The realistic artists developed the interior, working on shading and sculpting the form within their illustrations. The stylized artists developed the exterior, working on the pure shapes created by the outline edge of their illustrations. As you can see on these pages, both versions are equally successful for fashion.

THE SPRINGTIME FAMILY SEWING

The Little Boy and the Little Girl

In Their Best Clothes and Their Playtime Clothes

SUITABLE to wear in the hot summer days, the attractive suit below could be made without the long, full sleeves. The arrangement of the stripes is effective in the panel.

Patterns (No. 6737) come in three sizes: 4, 6 and 8 years. Size 6 years requires four yards of 27-inch material.

THE suit below, although made on plain boyish lines, is equally adaptable for a girl. The one-piece sleeves are set in at the armholes and gathered into band cuffs.

Patterns (No. 6739) for this suit come in three sizes: 4, 6 and 8 years. Size 6 years requires four yards of 30-inch material.

FOR morning wear the peasant dress below would be serviceable if made of small-checked gingham, striped percale or plain-color chambray.

Patterns (No. 6709) come in five sizes: 4 to 12 years. Size 8 years requires four yards and three-quarters of 30-inch material.

WHEN mother has time for dainty handwork she may make a dress like the one below, for which a suitable material would be sheer batiste, longcloth or fine linen.

The box-plaits and yoke band are embroidered with dots, which would be pretty in light blue. No patterns can be supplied.

6721
14055

6737
14406

6739

6709

6717-14125

PICTURED above is a little tunic dress with the skirt attached to an underbody gathered at the neck. It may have either full-length or shorter sleeves.

Patterns (No. 6721) come in five sizes: 4 to 12 years. Size 8 years requires two yards and three-quarters of 30-inch material.

ST below, the well-cut sailor suit furnishes a good example of a "first-trousers" suit for the boy who has outgrown his Russian blouse and knickerbockers.

Patterns (No. 6733) come in four sizes: 4, 6, 8 and 10 years. Size 8 years requires two yards and three-quarters of 36-inch material.

BRAIDING in simple border designs is always pleasing when used on dresses for the younger children, and a charming suggestion of well-executed work is shown above.

Patterns (No. 6717) come in five sizes: 4 to 12 years. Size 8 years requires three yards and three-quarters of 30-inch material.

ANY little fellow who wants to dress like a true sailorman will be pleased with the suit below. This is made with full-length trousers, wide at the ends; and the blouse is a typical "middy."

Patterns (No. 6731) come in four sizes: 4, 6, 8 and 10 years. Size 8 years requires five yards of 27-inch material.

6735

6733

6729

6731

THIS manly little Russian suit is made with straight trousers, which many boys prefer to the full knickerbockers.

Patterns (No. 6735) come in four sizes: 2, 4, 6 and 8 years. Size 6 years requires three yards and a half of 27-inch material and five-eighths of a yard of 27-inch contrasting material.

A PRETTY variation in cut is shown in the above dress for a little girl. It is made with a panel front and separate side sections, with short sleevecaps in one piece.

Although no patterns can be supplied this dress could be cut over a one-piece peasant foundation by adding the separate panel to the front and back, buttoning in the back.

HERE is a real boy's suit made with a big sailor collar and worn with a silk tie and a patent-leather belt. Then there is a pocket to be crammed with all kinds of things.

Patterns (No. 6729) for this one-piece blouse suit come in three sizes: 4, 6 and 8 years. Size 6 years requires four yards and a quarter of 27-inch material.

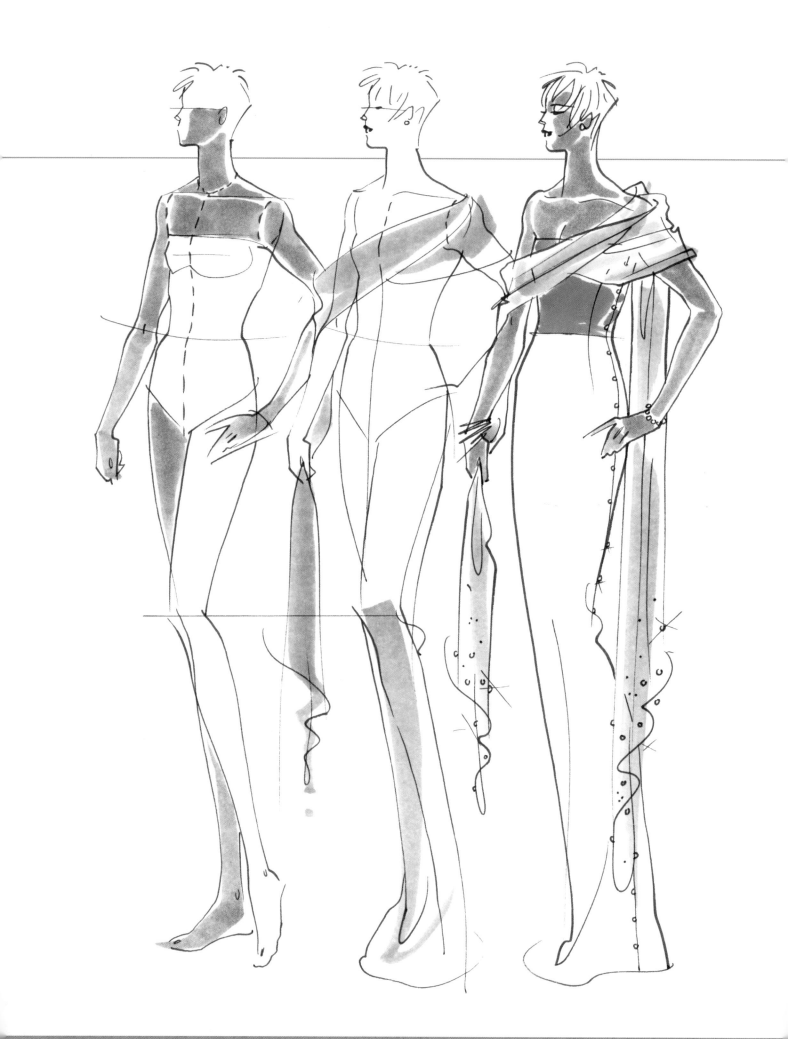

13

Accessories

Accessory design can be its own dedicated field of study and is an integral component of fashion. This chapter will help you work on some of the preliminary sketching methods that accessory design requires. Accessories have become their own source of style—classic, provocative, and imaginative. This chapter covers a few categories—jewelry, sunglasses, hats, belts, handbags, and shoes—giving you a base of drawing skills to build upon. Trends favor one category or the other, season after season, but if you plan ahead and practice them all, you will always be prepared for the changes in demand.

You have to learn to sketch the basic shapes of jewelry before you learn to illustrate design detail or its gemology. Sunglasses are a fabulous mix of fun and function. Belts and hats ride the wave of style, as do all of their trims and notions. Handbags enjoy the coveted position of favorite accessory. Shoes are a driving force in the market, and new design techniques have increased their fashion value.

The market for accessory fashion has grown. The demand for designer licensing and branding has taken almost every category of accessories to a new level of importance in the industry and with the public as fashion consumers. These are just more reasons to learn how to draw them.

Jewelry Croquis

These accessories are drawn in a freehand style. Jewelry design sketching can be done in a more formal style on graph paper in order to control size and placement or can be drawn on a form to display fit and proportion. Here are some basic guidelines for drawing jewelry:

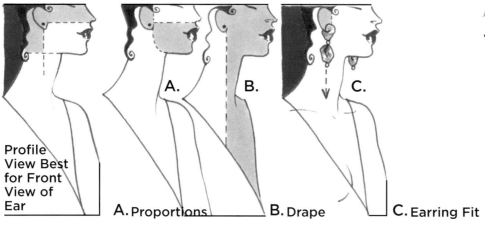

Profile View Best for Front View of Ear

A. Proportions

B. Drape

C. Earring Fit

Drawing Earrings

- Some earrings hug the earlobe, level to the mouth on the face. Some earrings dangle below the jawline.

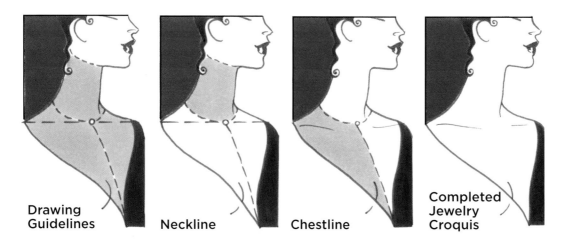

Drawing Guidelines

Neckline

Chestline

Completed Jewelry Croquis

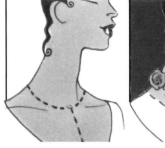

Fashion Elongation for Necklaces

Jewelry Design on the Neck

Jewelry Design on the Chest

Drawing Necklaces

- Chokers, pendants, and necklaces start at the base of the neck. They can fit high on the neck, rest below the neck, on the shoulder's slope, or follow center front down the middle of the chest.

Hippie or Love Beads   **Opera Length: 48" Plus**   **Rope Length**

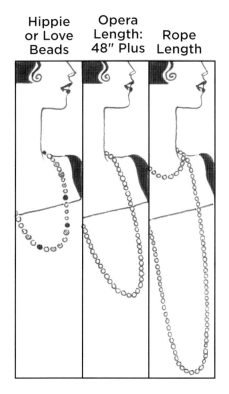

An accessory can be drawn on the form to show its fit and function in actual size. Stylize or simplify the form on the part of the body on which the accessory is worn. Sketch the body form lightly and draw the accessory with more emphasis.

Stick Pin   **Brooch**   **Cameo Pin**

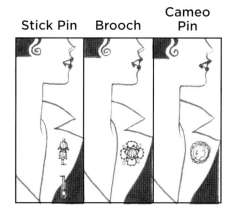

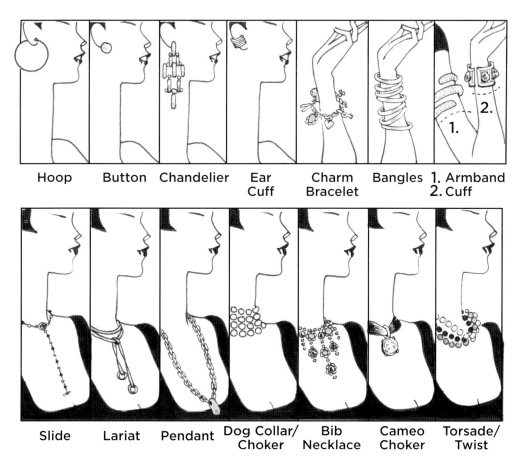

Hoop   **Button**   **Chandelier**   **Ear Cuff**   **Charm Bracelet**   **Bangles**   **1. Armband 2. Cuff**

Slide   **Lariat**   **Pendant**   **Dog Collar/ Choker**   **Bib Necklace**   **Cameo Choker**   **Torsade/ Twist**

Jewelry Templates

Minimalistic fashion heads, arms, wrists to hands, or ankles to feet can be showcases for jewelry design sketches. Staging or posing a jewelry item demonstrates its size, fit, and function. Drawn on simple, stylized body shapes, laid out flat in an aerial view, or posed alone, these jewelry positions can be modified to fit your design process.

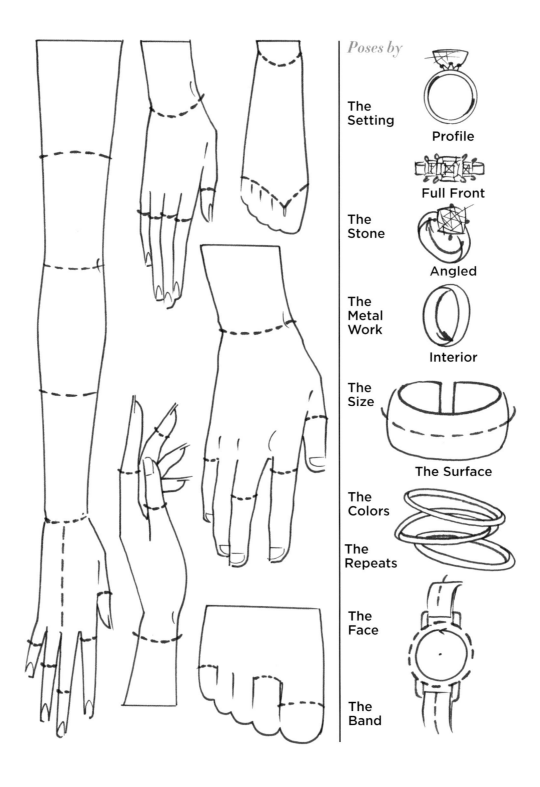

Poses by

The Setting — Profile

The Stone — Full Front

The Metal Work — Angled

The Size — Interior

The Surface

The Colors

The Repeats

The Face

The Band

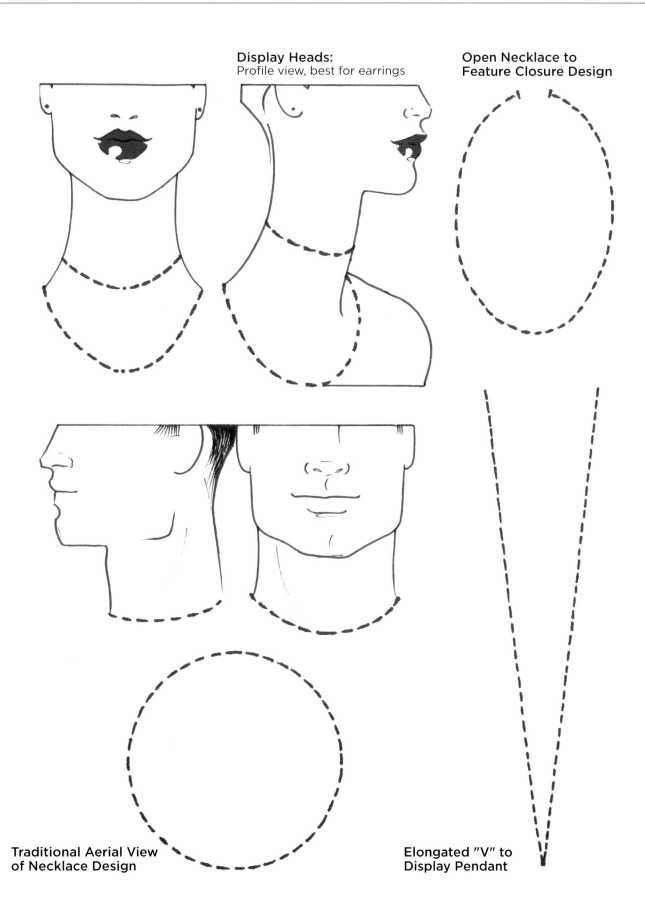

Display Heads:
Profile view, best for earrings

**Open Necklace to
Feature Closure Design**

**Traditional Aerial View
of Necklace Design**

**Elongated "V" to
Display Pendant**

Sunglasses

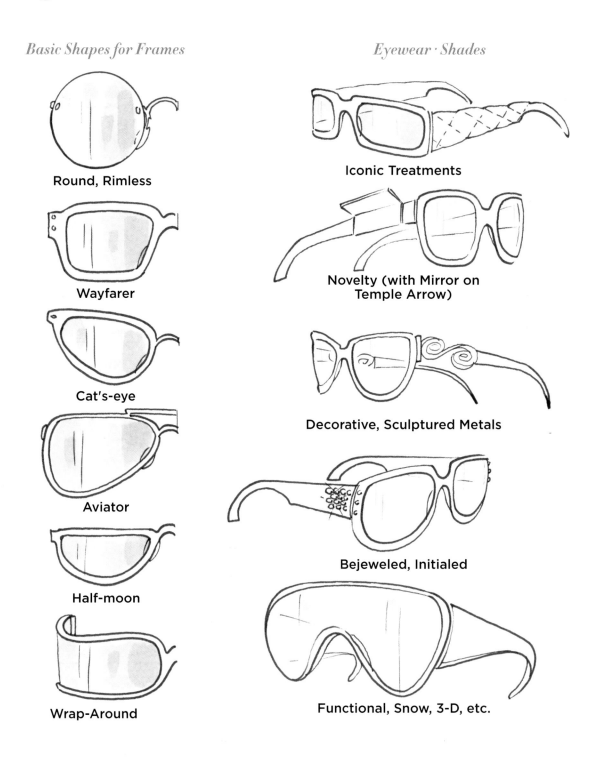

Basic Shapes for Frames

Round, Rimless

Wayfarer

Cat's-eye

Aviator

Half-moon

Wrap-Around

Eyewear · Shades

Iconic Treatments

Novelty (with Mirror on Temple Arrow)

Decorative, Sculptured Metals

Bejeweled, Initialed

Functional, Snow, 3-D, etc.

Sunglasses can have their own distinct shapes, functions, and names that can be repeated any season. Beyond that, their materials, wide or narrow shaping, and their bridge, nose, and arms are based on trend. Any type of eyeglass frame, on or off the face, like jewelry, can be posed at any angle that will maximize its design features.

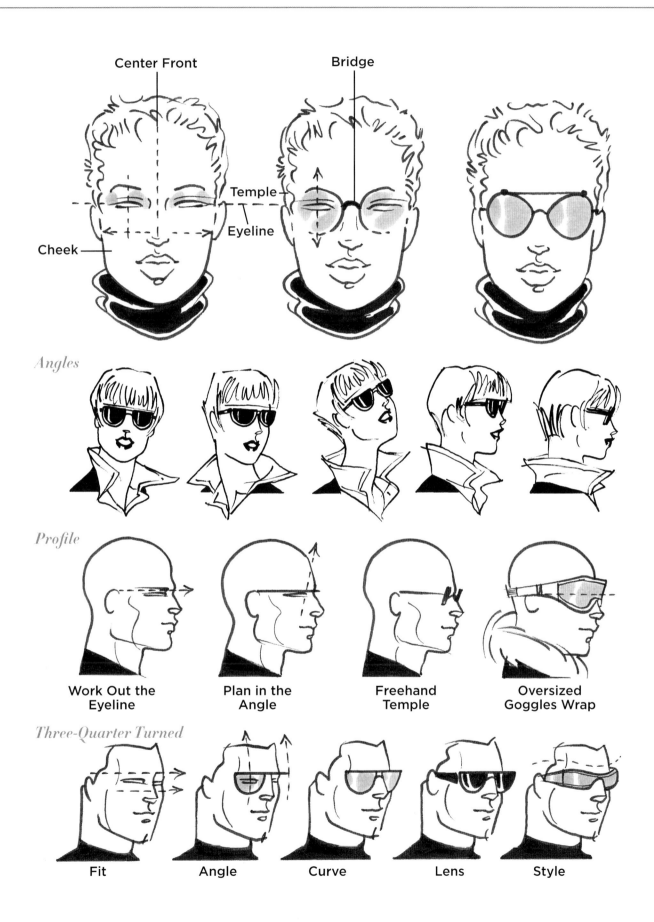

Center Front

Bridge

Temple

Eyeline

Cheek

Angles

Profile

Work Out the
Eyeline

Plan in the
Angle

Freehand
Temple

Oversized
Goggles Wrap

Three-Quarter Turned

Fit

Angle

Curve

Lens

Style

Hats and Gloves

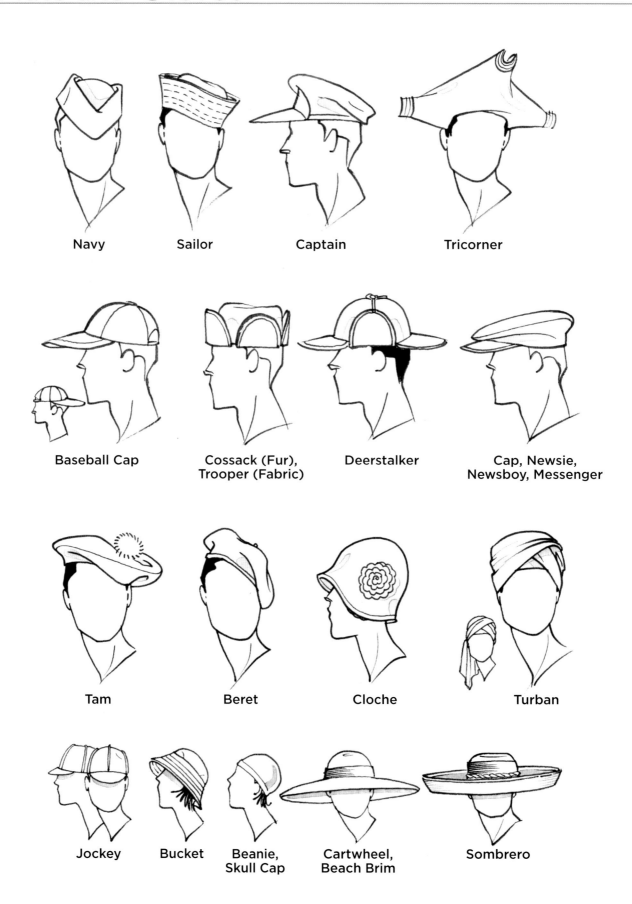

Navy   Sailor   Captain   Tricorner

Baseball Cap   Cossack (Fur), Trooper (Fabric)   Deerstalker   Cap, Newsie, Newsboy, Messenger

Tam   Beret   Cloche   Turban

Jockey   Bucket   Beanie, Skull Cap   Cartwheel, Beach Brim   Sombrero

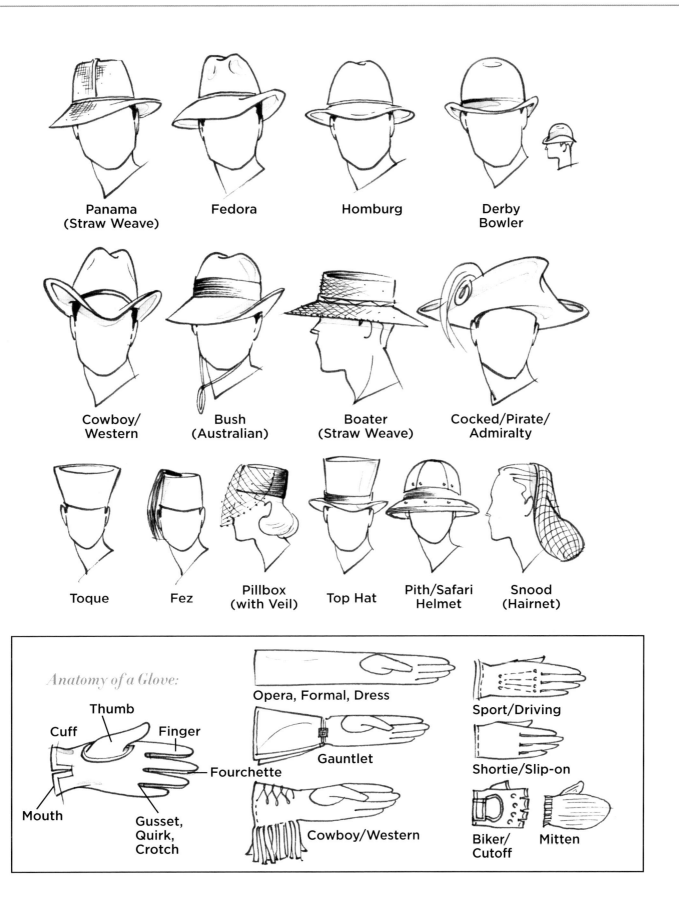

Panama
(Straw Weave)

Fedora

Homburg

Derby
Bowler

Cowboy/
Western

Bush
(Australian)

Boater
(Straw Weave)

Cocked/Pirate/
Admiralty

Toque

Fez

Pillbox
(with Veil)

Top Hat

Pith/Safari
Helmet

Snood
(Hairnet)

Anatomy of a Glove:

Thumb

Cuff

Finger

Fourchette

Mouth

Gusset,
Quirk,
Crotch

Opera, Formal, Dress

Gauntlet

Cowboy/Western

Sport/Driving

Shortie/Slip-on

Biker/
Cutoff

Mitten

Drawing Men's Hats

Drawing hats requires a balance among the fit, type of hat, and the style in which it's worn—posing on the head. The crown of the hat should fit over the top half of the head. The brim usually cuts across the face near the eyeline, curled or flipped according to trend.

Cowboy-Style Widest Brim

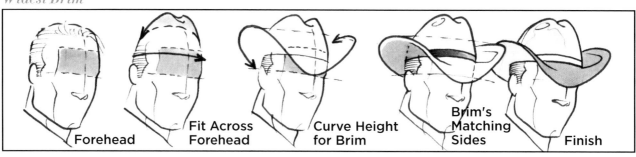

Forehead | Fit Across Forehead | Curve Height for Brim | Brim's Matching Sides | Finish

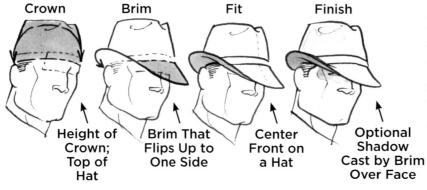

Crown | Brim | Fit | Finish

Height of Crown; Top of Hat | Brim That Flips Up to One Side | Center Front on a Hat | Optional Shadow Cast by Brim Over Face

Drawing a hat's brim in this double position—flipped up and then down again—gives you the opportunity to accentuate fit, cut, and different materials.

Brim Fit

The brim of a hat may be sketched covering both the eyes as well as some of the nose.

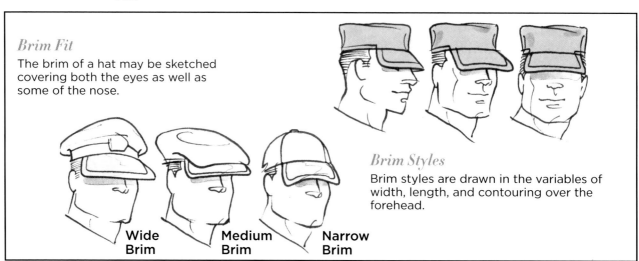

Brim Styles

Brim styles are drawn in the variables of width, length, and contouring over the forehead.

Wide Brim | Medium Brim | Narrow Brim

Drawing Women's Hats

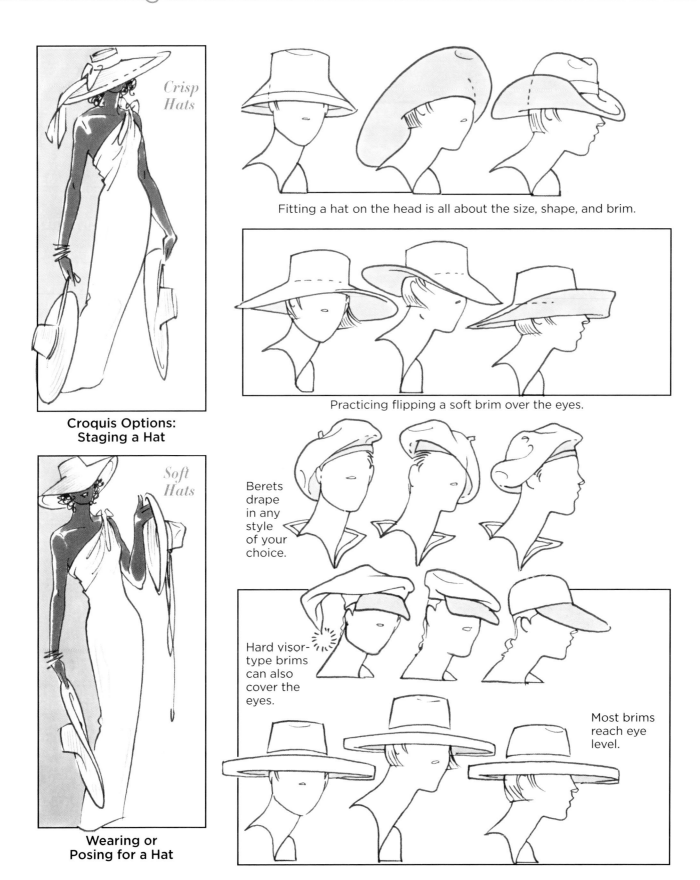

Crisp Hats

**Croquis Options:
Staging a Hat**

Soft Hats

**Wearing or
Posing for a Hat**

Fitting a hat on the head is all about the size, shape, and brim.

Practicing flipping a soft brim over the eyes.

Berets drape in any style of your choice.

Hard visor-type brims can also cover the eyes.

Most brims reach eye level.

Belts

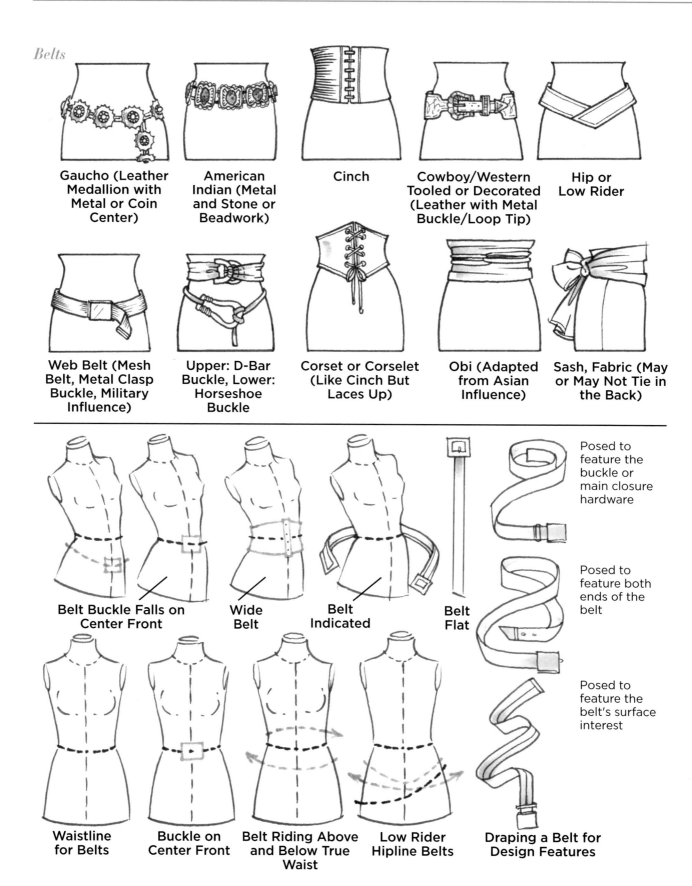

Belts

Gaucho (Leather Medallion with Metal or Coin Center)

American Indian (Metal and Stone or Beadwork)

Cinch

Cowboy/Western Tooled or Decorated (Leather with Metal Buckle/Loop Tip)

Hip or Low Rider

Web Belt (Mesh Belt, Metal Clasp Buckle, Military Influence)

Upper: D-Bar Buckle, Lower: Horseshoe Buckle

Corset or Corselet (Like Cinch But Laces Up)

Obi (Adapted from Asian Influence)

Sash, Fabric (May or May Not Tie in the Back)

Belt Buckle Falls on Center Front

Wide Belt

Belt Indicated

Belt Flat

Posed to feature the buckle or main closure hardware

Posed to feature both ends of the belt

Waistline for Belts

Buckle on Center Front

Belt Riding Above and Below True Waist

Low Rider Hipline Belts

Draping a Belt for Design Features

Posed to feature the belt's surface interest

Hardware for Belts and Bags

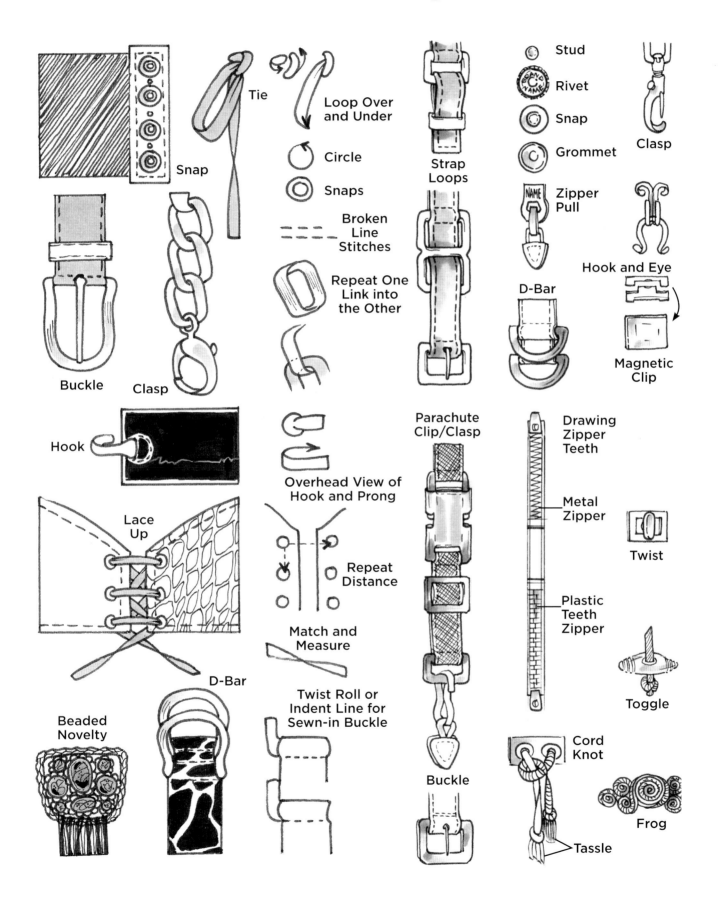

Snap

Tie

Loop Over and Under

Circle

Snaps

Broken Line Stitches

Repeat One Link into the Other

Buckle

Clasp

Hook

Lace Up

Overhead View of Hook and Prong

Repeat Distance

Match and Measure

Twist Roll or Indent Line for Sewn-in Buckle

Beaded Novelty

D-Bar

Strap Loops

D-Bar

Parachute Clip/Clasp

Buckle

Stud

Rivet

Snap

Grommet

Clasp

Zipper Pull

Hook and Eye

Magnetic Clip

Drawing Zipper Teeth

Metal Zipper

Plastic Teeth Zipper

Twist

Toggle

Cord Knot

Tassle

Frog

Handbags and Purses

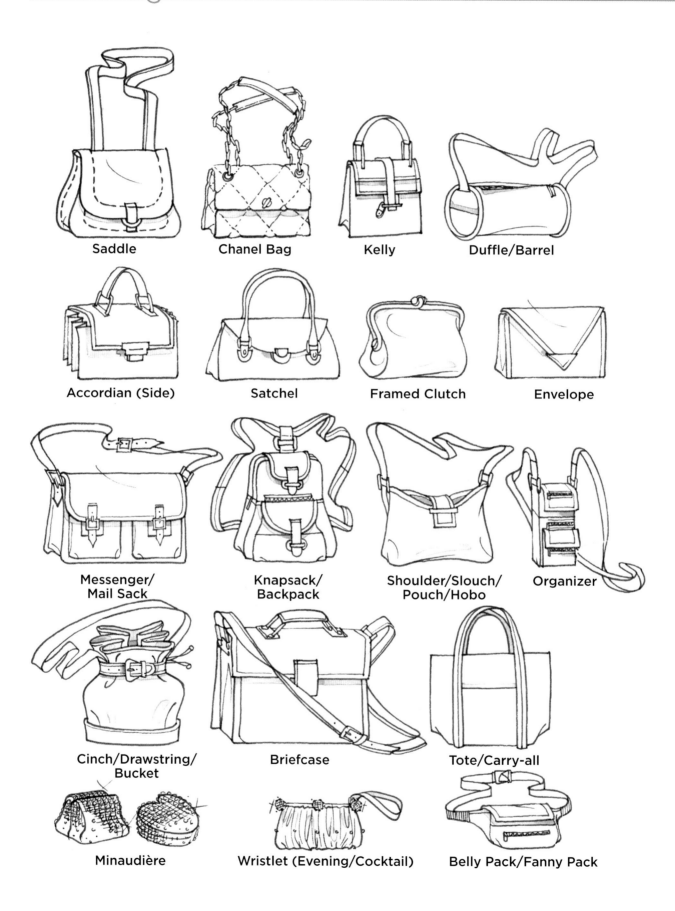

Saddle

Chanel Bag

Kelly

Duffle/Barrel

Accordian (Side)

Satchel

Framed Clutch

Envelope

Messenger/
Mail Sack

Knapsack/
Backpack

Shoulder/Slouch/
Pouch/Hobo

Organizer

Cinch/Drawstring/
Bucket

Briefcase

Tote/Carry-all

Minaudière

Wristlet (Evening/Cocktail)

Belly Pack/Fanny Pack

Shoes

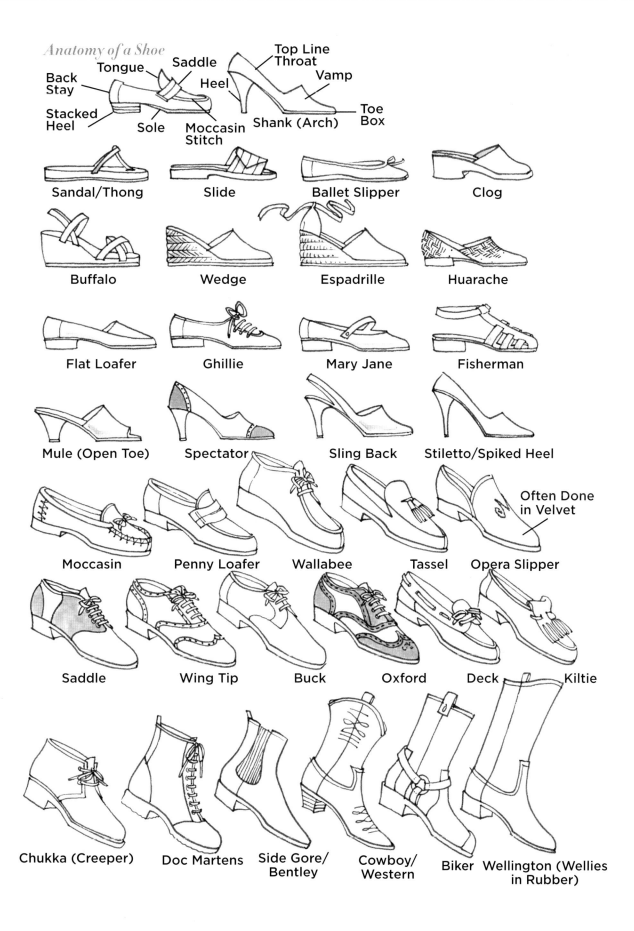

Anatomy of a Shoe

Back Stay · Tongue · Saddle · Heel · Top Line · Throat · Vamp · Stacked Heel · Sole · Moccasin Stitch · Shank (Arch) · Toe Box

Sandal/Thong · Slide · Ballet Slipper · Clog

Buffalo · Wedge · Espadrille · Huarache

Flat Loafer · Ghillie · Mary Jane · Fisherman

Mule (Open Toe) · Spectator · Sling Back · Stiletto/Spiked Heel

Moccasin · Penny Loafer · Wallabee · Tassel · Opera Slipper · Often Done in Velvet

Saddle · Wing Tip · Buck · Oxford · Deck · Kiltie

Chukka (Creeper) · Doc Martens · Side Gore/ Bentley · Cowboy/ Western · Biker · Wellington (Wellies in Rubber)

Footwear Design Roughs

The red line on these shoe templates defines the shape or placement of the innersole or the outside border of the tread/sole.

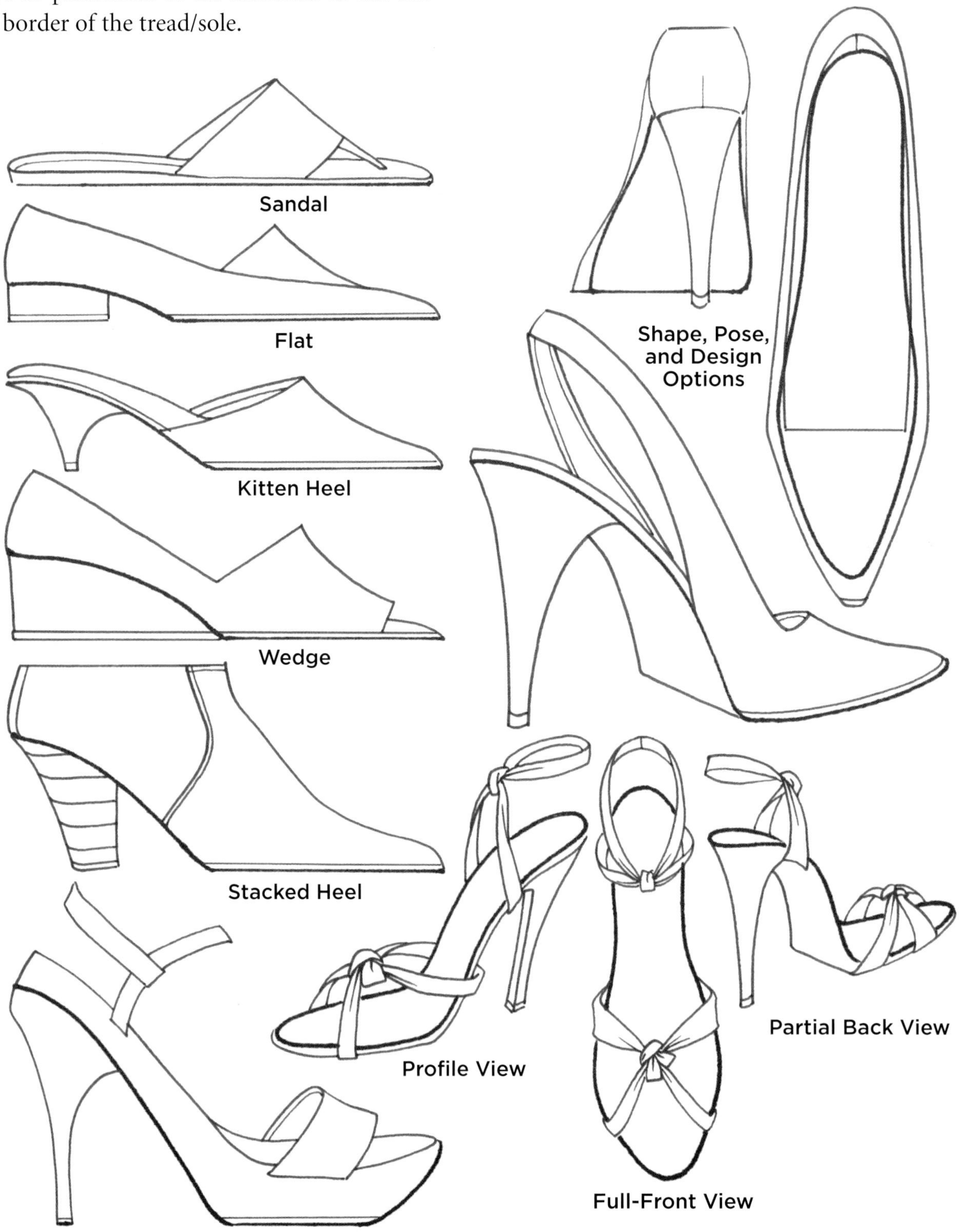

Sandal

Flat

Kitten Heel

Wedge

Stacked Heel

Platform

Shape, Pose, and Design Options

Profile View

Full-Front View

Partial Back View

Here are examples of the five classic types of heels. Historically each type has been done in a variety of heights, widths, and materials, from leathers to plastics, each decorated to fit the trends for all types of shoes. Active sportswear shoes make up another category of heels, from golf to ski to skating. That's when heels and soles or treads of shoes start to get specialized. More recently, bowling shoes were adapted to mass market in a trend that defied specialization, so it is wise to practice drawing any and all shoes that you find interesting.

Front or Top View of Foot Has No Visible Heel

Flat Heel

High Heel

Wedge

Platform

Boot Heel

Sporty Shoes

Sporty footwear design is expanding into new design territory every season, blurring the distinctions between work and play shoes, casual and formal. Shoe design is blending performance and function factors with technology and decoration. This mix is creating hybrids between shoes and sneakers (like heelies) that go beyond specialty shoes in the golf, ski, or skating categories. What's next? The sole of a shoe is now a design focus. Shoe prints (footprints) run from licensed images and brand signatures to pop culture iconography. On the flip side, inside the shoe, the inner sole is being given images for the wearer's eyes only. Here, the styling signals a secret status or private satisfaction in color or print. This means that you need to know how to draw a shoe from the inside out, front to back, top to bottom, and side to side. If the interest in shoes is huge, so should be your sketches of them.

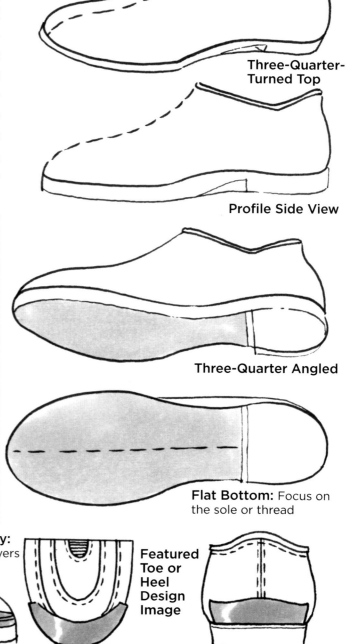

Flat Top

Three-Quarter-Turned Top

Profile Side View

Three-Quarter Angled

Flat Bottom: Focus on the sole or thread

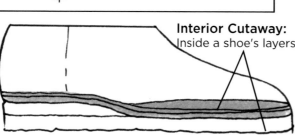

Casual Lace-Up Grid

Interior Cutaway: Inside a shoe's layers

Featured Toe or Heel Design Image

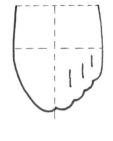 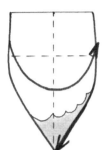 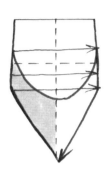 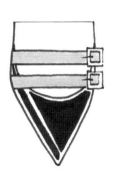

- When designing the shape of a shoe, the toe is just as critical as the heel.
- Drawing shoes as stylized versus realistic adds more dramatic license to their design, fit, and decorations.

Sportswear footwear often needs preliminary grid lines to map out the webbing or lacing details to emphasize trims and stylistic nuances.

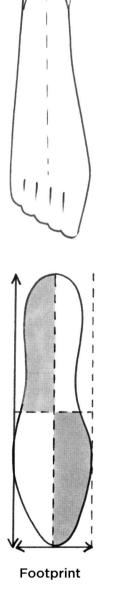 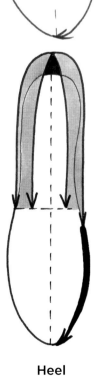 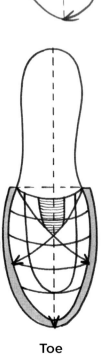  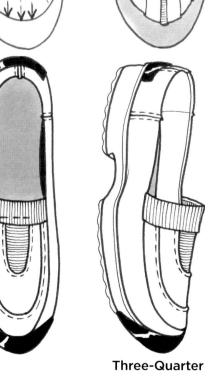

Footprint **Heel** **Toe** **Topside** **Three-Quarter Turned**

much clutch

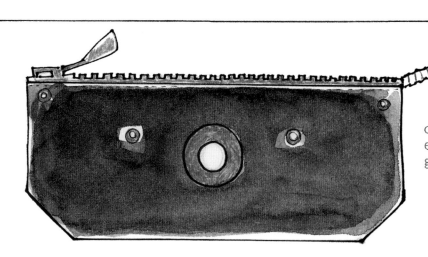

chocolate brown clutch
embellished with brass
grommets and hardware.

solid and striped canvas clutch
with hidden magnetic closures
and grommet detail.

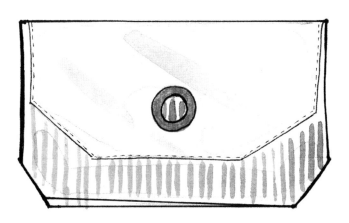

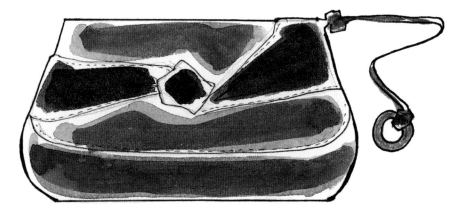

round shaped clutch with stitched
knotted detail on front flap.
knotted strap detail at corner.

With a rendering that looks fresh and loose, the designer's work has that spontaneous sense of style. She was inspired by sun-faded, muted colors and knotted, scrunched, pulled leather looks for her roomy totes and sleek, strappy sandals. She used a size #8 pointed tip brush, gouache in light washes, Sharpie marker, brown Prismacolor pencil, and a ruler.

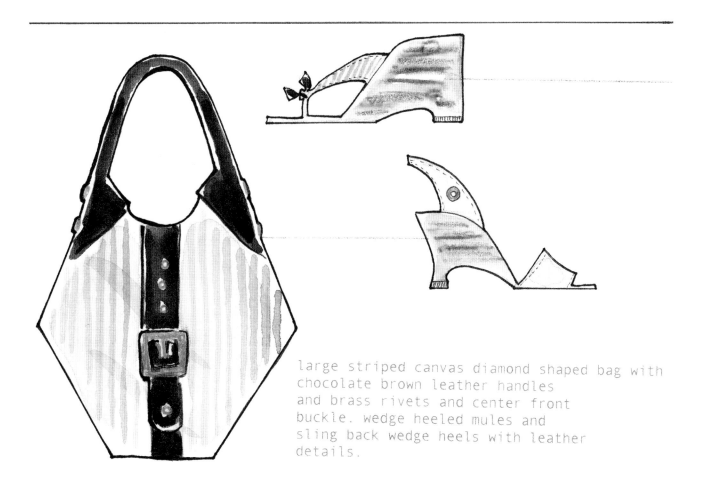

large striped canvas diamond shaped bag with
chocolate brown leather handles
and brass rivets and center front
buckle. wedge heeled mules and
sling back wedge heels with leather
details.

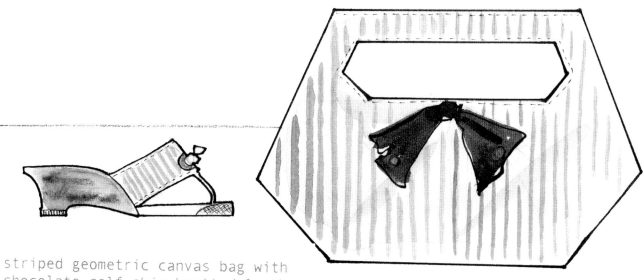

striped geometric canvas bag with
chocolate calf skin knotted leather
detail. slide on wedge with striped
canvas upper and knotted toe piece.

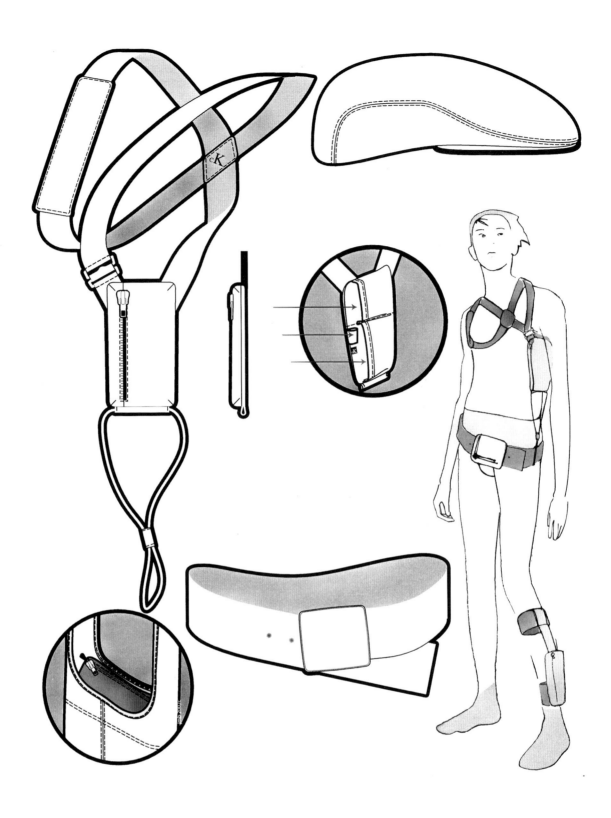

The finished accessories page is a computer-aided drawing (CAD) design. It was created using raster and vector software, pencil, pen, paper, and digitizing hardware. The designer's products are unique, and he creates items that fill the gaps in the market.

After he sketched the ideas, he prepared them to be imported into a raster program by redrawing the sketches in ink. The figure on the page is the only part brought in from outside the computer. After the figure is digitized, it needs to be cleaned and exported as a path to a vector program. In the vector program the figure is used as a reference of proportion for the technical drawings. Once the figure was drawn and composed on the page, Jason used a PMS print to match the fabrics for output.

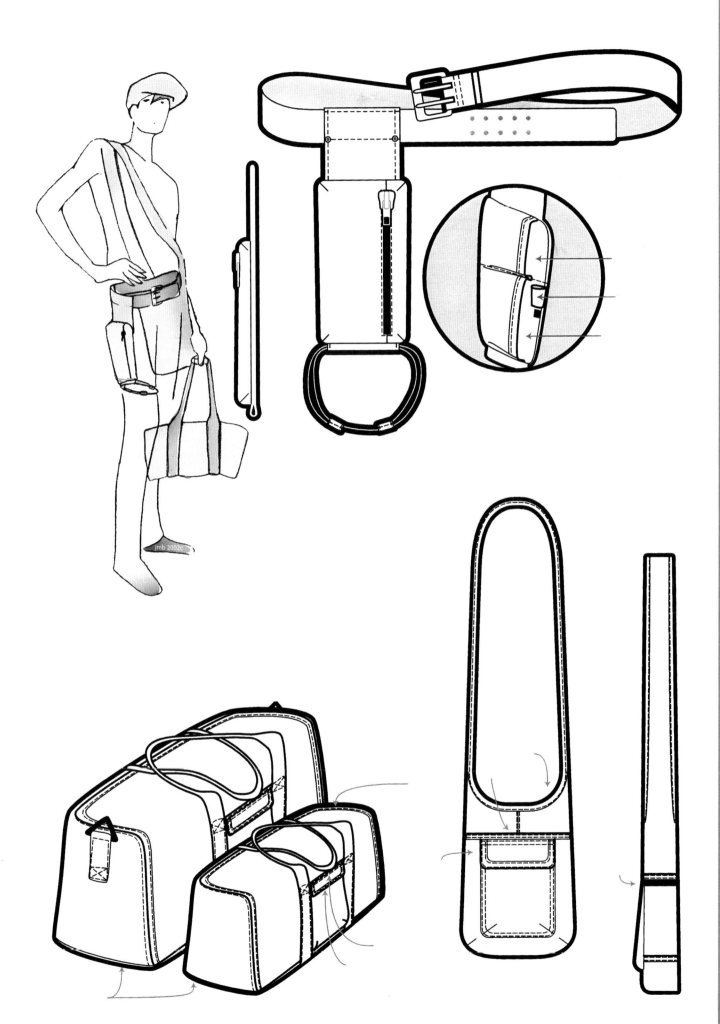

jmb 2002c

The media mix here is a collage of research and resources combined in a journal format. This designer's sketchbook of ideas is a storyboard of his talent and imagination at work, conveying his unique approach to accessory design. The designer's products are unique, and he creates items that fill the gaps in the market.

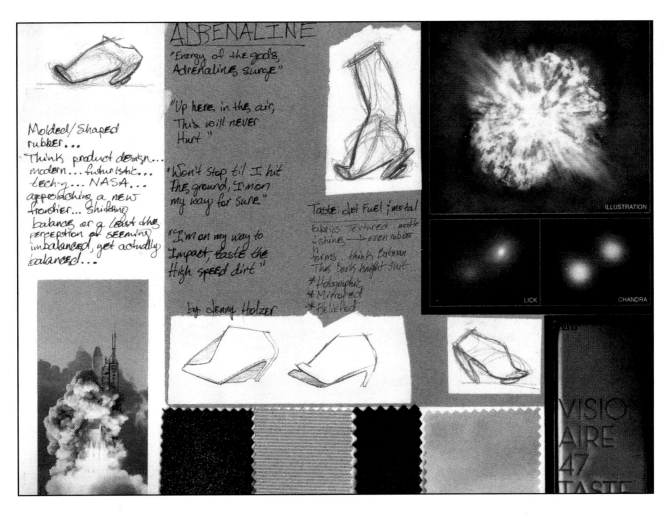

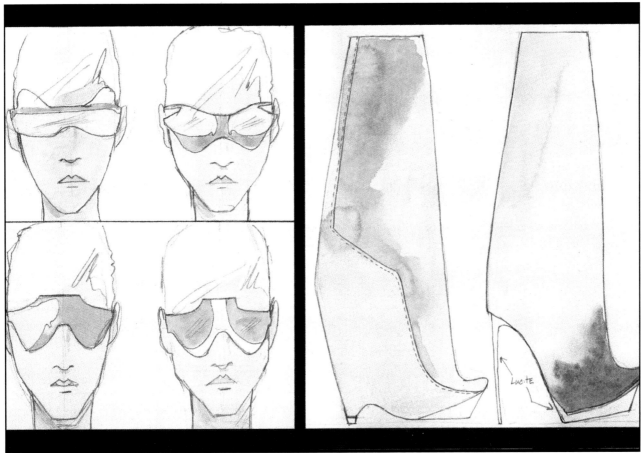

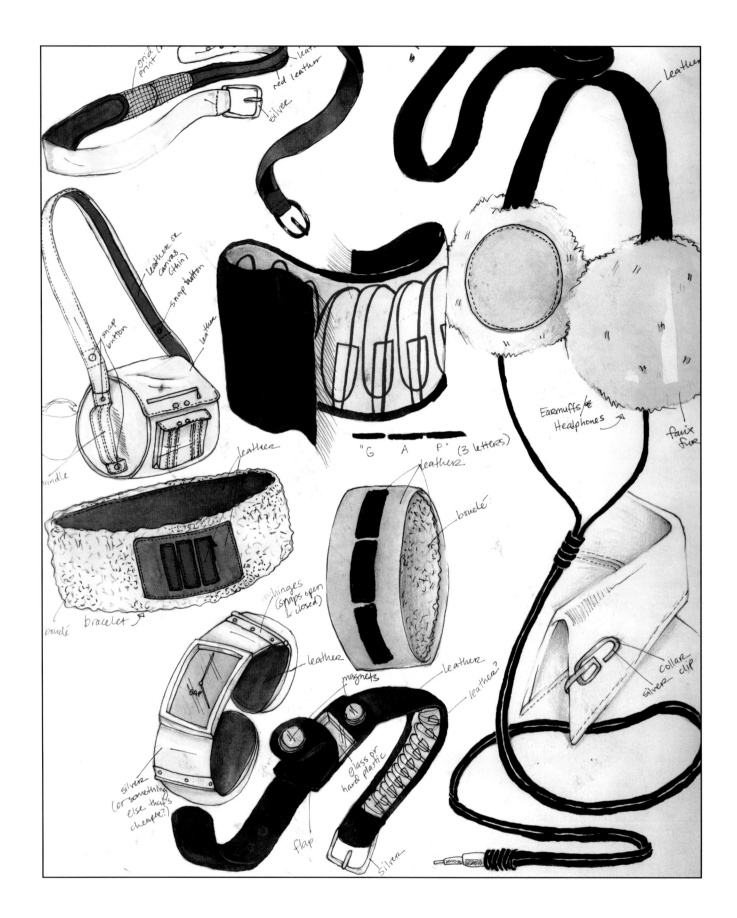

The media mix for this designer is gouache, marker pens, and pencil. These accessory rough sketches, or croquis, are unedited design ideas, part of her larger contemporary menswear collection. The menswear figure work preceded and influenced the design inspiration for her accessories as a natural extension of her customer's lifestyle.

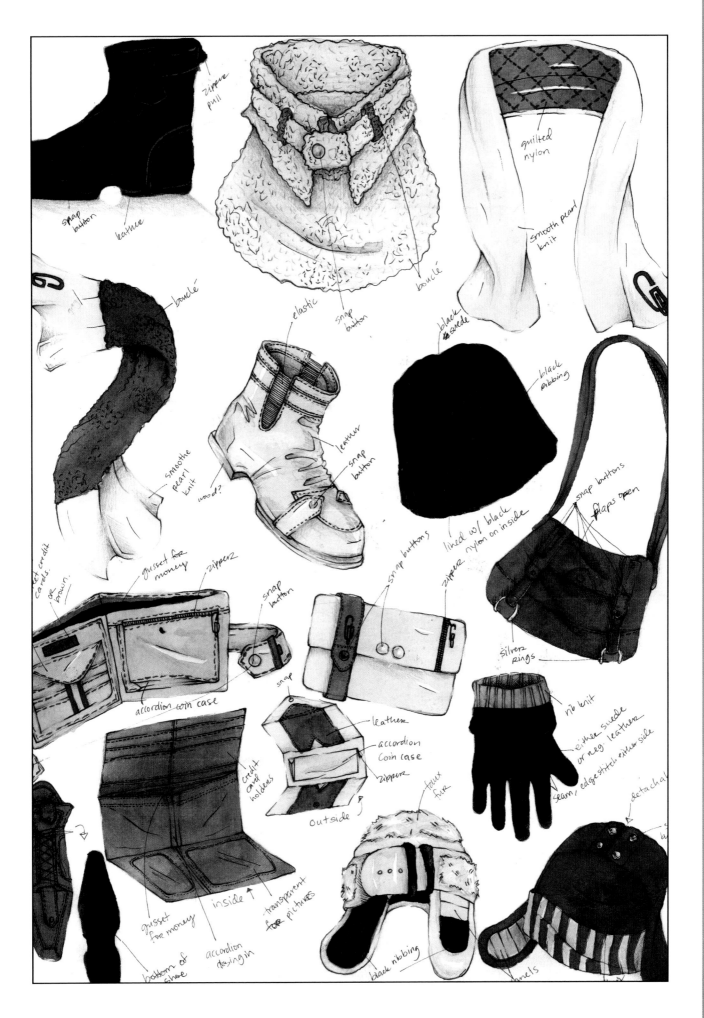

WWD Photo References

The media mix for this design is pen line and Sumi ink. These necklace sketches are a fusion of fine arts with precision drawing skills, done for an accessories catalog. Imagination and talent make these jewelry sketches elegant. These same sketches, drawn and rendered in full color, would be on par with professional designer quality, finished sketches.

This spread provides historical context for how accessory trends were covered and featured in *Women's Wear Daily*, the industry trade paper. Before glossy imagery, illustrators were hired to create sketches of the hottest new accessories for all relevant categories. The layouts included customers' projections, trade commentary, and some static photographic images—the precursors to the branding imagery in today's marketplace advertising.

Main Floor Accessories

Handmade Laces, White Embroidery In Fine Neckwear

Hand-embroidered organdie and hand-worked laces from France make extravagantly feminine collars and jabots at Boue Soeurs.

A wide Puritan collar of Cluny lace is featured in the lace group which include shapes for square and batteau necklines. Most collars lie loosely over organdie undercollar cut wider than the lace. White cotton organdie embroidered in white fine floral designs make assorted collar styles. There are over-sized Peter Pan types and collars cut low and wide for deep necklines. A tiered silk organdie jabot with scattered embroidery on each flounce has a narrow pointed collar.

Colors for silk and cotton organdie are blue, pink, green and cocoa. Green and brown tones are reminiscent of popular colors of the 1930's.

Fall Through Holiday

A Little Touch of Fur

Early buyer response to fur-trimmed accessories gives impetus to new fur items, or new ways of applying the fur touch.

1. White velveteen Peter Pan collar is demurely accented with swirl or ermine, around pearl stud. Tucker collar by Fran and Lou. $15 dozen.

* * *

2. Natural mink cluster on red velveteen leaves centered with gold kid and pearl dots. From Natural Mink Flower Corp. $2.50

4. Little mink orchid and matching stud buttons to be worn on anything. Silver kid leaves and gray sparkle are added to flower. At Paris-Fleur Cie. Flower, $3.50 each, buttons $4.80 dozen.

* * *

5. Opulent fox collar and cuffs in newsy red on red cashmere, cherry tones. By Goodman Bros. and Stamler. $47.50 complete. Collar $16.50, cuffs $12.50 set.

* * *

6. Dramatic satin stole edged with dramatic fox black, or

rows of tawny colored stones, $26.50 each wholesale at Midtown Belts Co.

* * *

8. Strands of rhinestones give this white pony contour belt a new "hip" look. By Mickey Belts, Inc. $30 each.

* * *

9. Leopard belt fob on gold-plated clip fits any belt. From a group of fur novelties at Singer-Cohen, Inc. $1 retail.

* * *

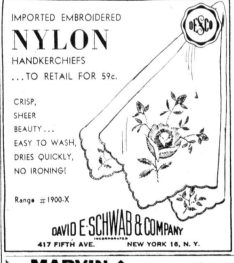

Fashion Archive

Because fashion is quickly blurring the boundaries between all categories and constantly renaming the garments, this Fashion Archive will help you identify the basics. Much of the related design detailing has been placed on simple silhouettes for layout reasons. Because design shapes, construction, and detailing have an unlimited range of images, for the sake of time and space, this section explores the fundamentals and uses the traditionally accepted names for the shapes, construction, and detailing of garments. Each page presents either a category for design labeling or a core of related design detailing. For the categories, it is common practice to imagine that the items are unique to that category and, therefore, are given names that might otherwise be different for the same shape (of a garment) in another category. For example, the pajama top that is called a sleepshirt in the innerwear category might be called a campshirt in the sportswear category.

Problem Spots is a great catch-all for common drawing glitches. For the artist who is just starting out, it is a relief to know what not to do as well as what is right for a drawing. The premise behind these Problem Spots is to minimize the possibility of errors and to encourage success with all your fashion drawing.

Necklines

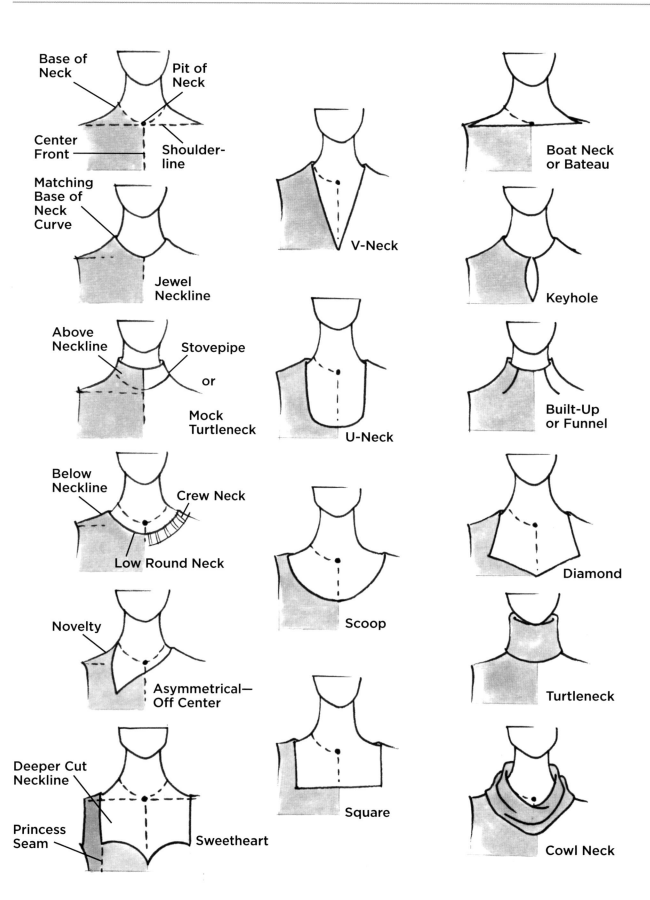

Base of Neck

Pit of Neck

Center Front

Shoulder-line

Matching Base of Neck Curve

Jewel Neckline

Above Neckline

Stovepipe

or

Mock Turtleneck

Below Neckline

Crew Neck

Low Round Neck

Novelty

Asymmetrical—Off Center

Deeper Cut Neckline

Princess Seam

Sweetheart

V-Neck

U-Neck

Scoop

Square

Boat Neck or Bateau

Keyhole

Built-Up or Funnel

Diamond

Turtleneck

Cowl Neck

Collars

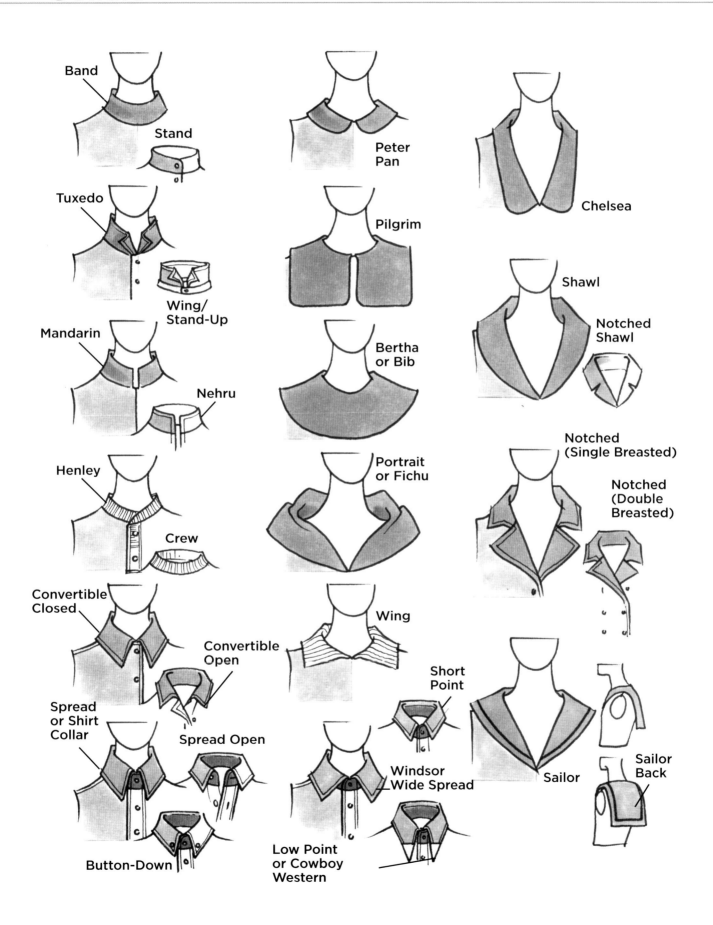

Band

Stand

Peter Pan

Tuxedo

Wing/Stand-Up

Pilgrim

Chelsea

Mandarin

Nehru

Bertha or Bib

Shawl

Notched Shawl

Henley

Crew

Portrait or Fichu

Notched (Single Breasted)

Notched (Double Breasted)

Convertible Closed

Convertible Open

Wing

Spread or Shirt Collar

Spread Open

Short Point

Windsor Wide Spread

Sailor

Sailor Back

Button-Down

Low Point or Cowboy Western

Collars and Lapels

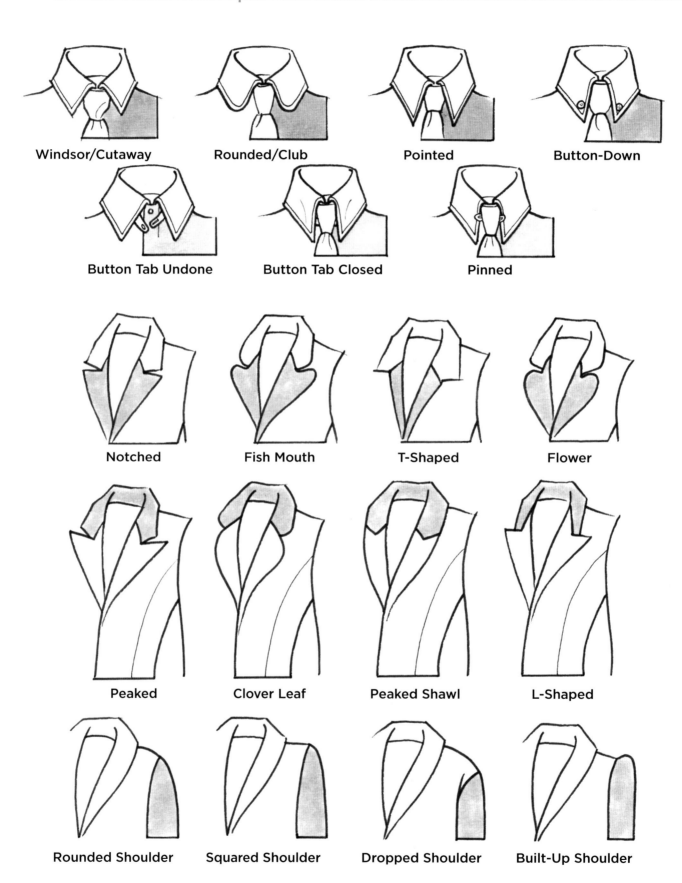

Windsor/Cutaway   Rounded/Club   Pointed   Button-Down

Button Tab Undone   Button Tab Closed   Pinned

Notched   Fish Mouth   T-Shaped   Flower

Peaked   Clover Leaf   Peaked Shawl   L-Shaped

Rounded Shoulder   Squared Shoulder   Dropped Shoulder   Built-Up Shoulder

Cuffs

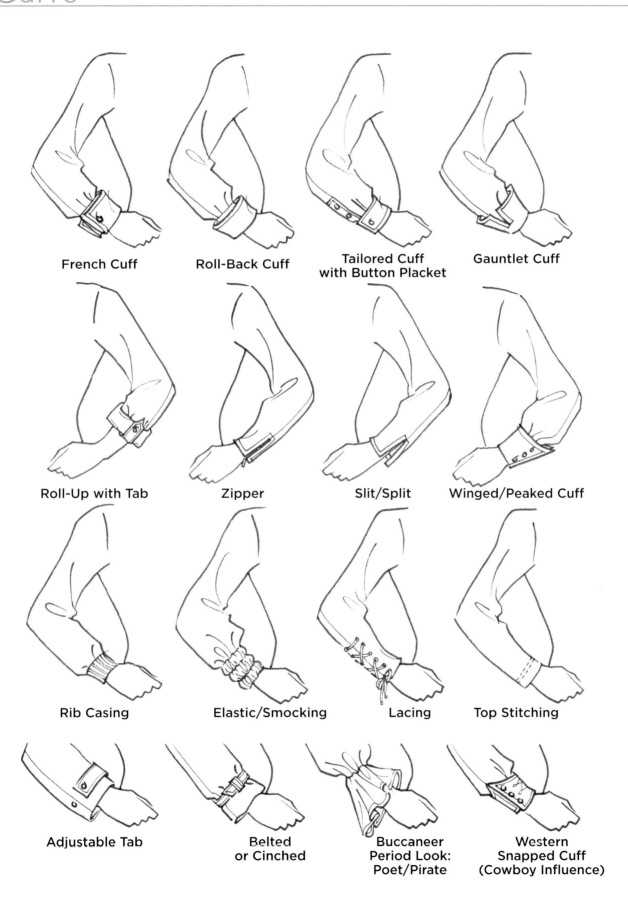

French Cuff

Roll-Back Cuff

Tailored Cuff
with Button Placket

Gauntlet Cuff

Roll-Up with Tab

Zipper

Slit/Split

Winged/Peaked Cuff

Rib Casing

Elastic/Smocking

Lacing

Top Stitching

Adjustable Tab

Belted
or Cinched

Buccaneer
Period Look:
Poet/Pirate

Western
Snapped Cuff
(Cowboy Influence)

Armhole Treatments

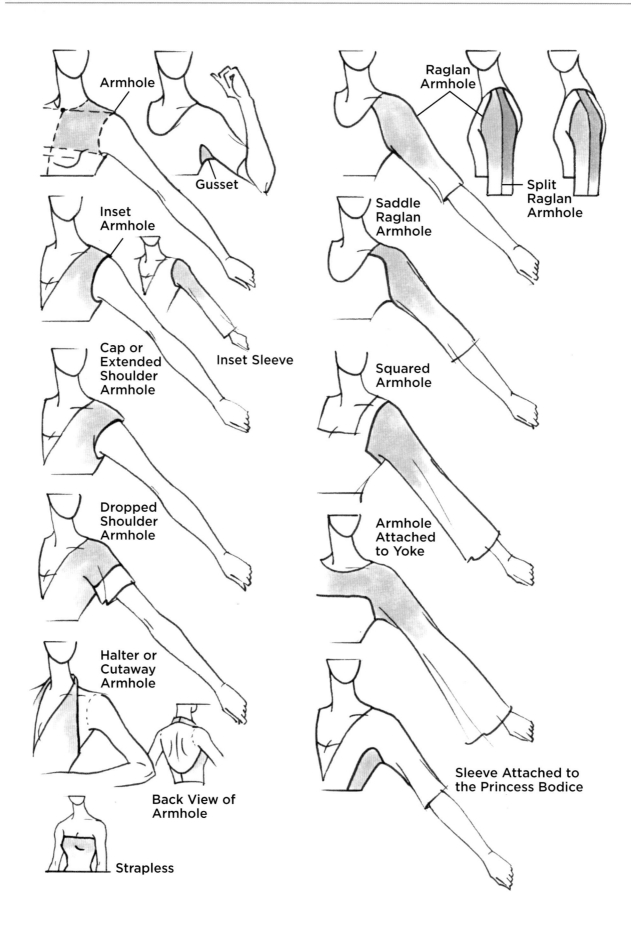

Armhole

Gusset

Inset Armhole

Inset Sleeve

Cap or Extended Shoulder Armhole

Dropped Shoulder Armhole

Halter or Cutaway Armhole

Back View of Armhole

Strapless

Raglan Armhole

Split Raglan Armhole

Saddle Raglan Armhole

Squared Armhole

Armhole Attached to Yoke

Sleeve Attached to the Princess Bodice

Sketching Smocking and Shirring

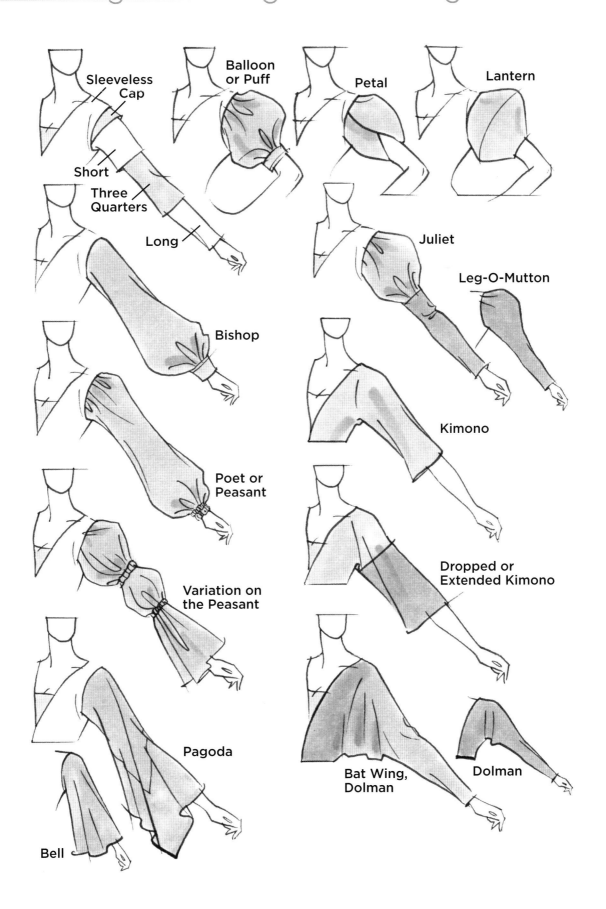

Sleeveless Cap

Short

Three Quarters

Long

Balloon or Puff

Petal

Lantern

Bishop

Juliet

Leg-O-Mutton

Poet or Peasant

Kimono

Variation on the Peasant

Dropped or Extended Kimono

Pagoda

Bell

Bat Wing, Dolman

Dolman

Neckline Treatments (Bows and Ties)

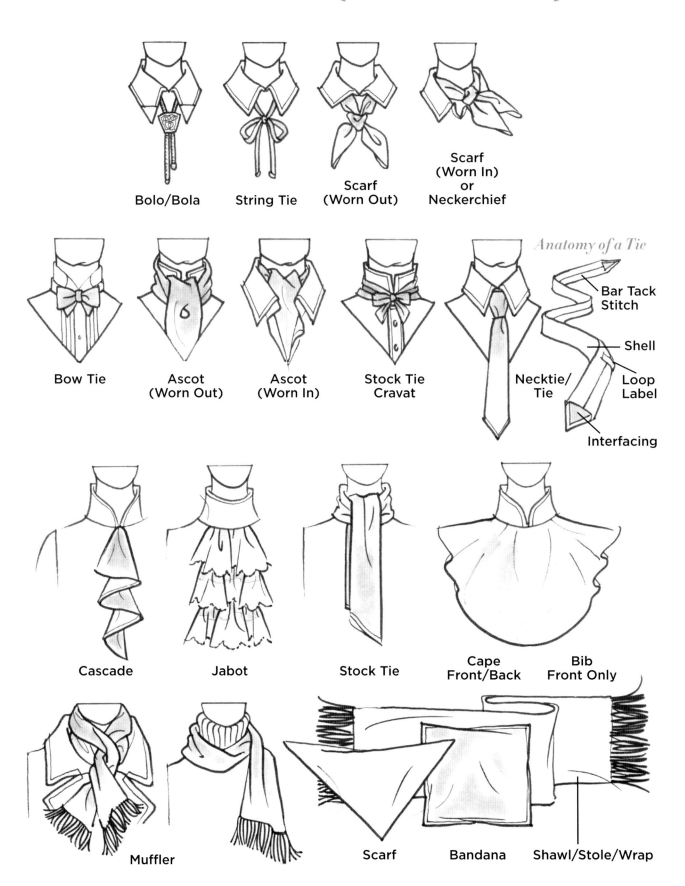

Bolo/Bola

String Tie

Scarf (Worn Out)

Scarf (Worn In) or Neckerchief

Bow Tie

Ascot (Worn Out)

Ascot (Worn In)

Stock Tie Cravat

Necktie/Tie

Anatomy of a Tie

Bar Tack Stitch

Shell

Loop Label

Interfacing

Cascade

Jabot

Stock Tie

Cape Front/Back

Bib Front Only

Muffler

Scarf

Bandana

Shawl/Stole/Wrap

Hemline Treatments

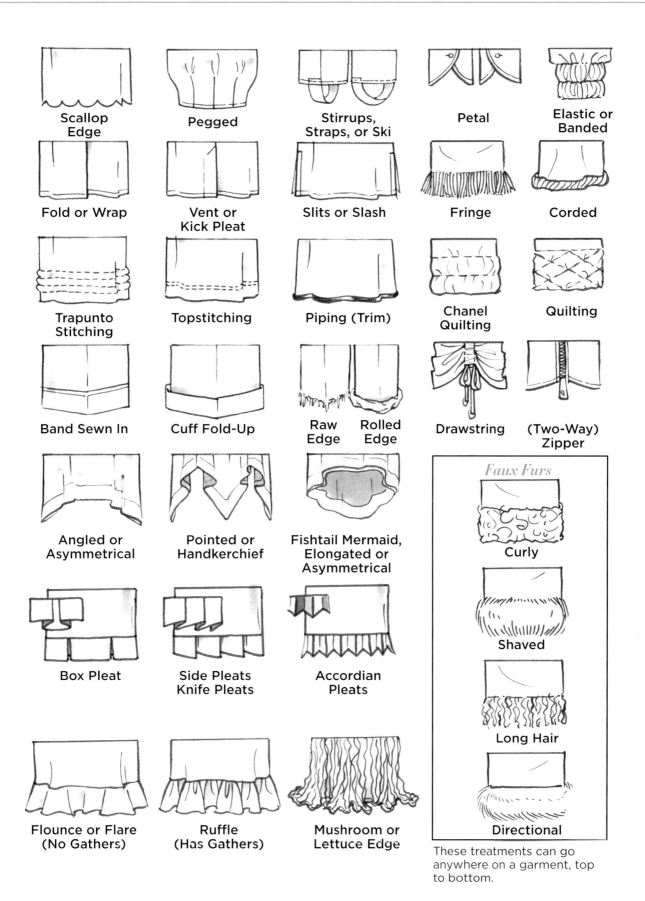

Scallop Edge

Pegged

Stirrups, Straps, or Ski

Petal

Elastic or Banded

Fold or Wrap

Vent or Kick Pleat

Slits or Slash

Fringe

Corded

Trapunto Stitching

Topstitching

Piping (Trim)

Chanel Quilting

Quilting

Band Sewn In

Cuff Fold-Up

Raw Edge   Rolled Edge

Drawstring

(Two-Way) Zipper

Angled or Asymmetrical

Pointed or Handkerchief

Fishtail Mermaid, Elongated or Asymmetrical

Box Pleat

Side Pleats Knife Pleats

Accordian Pleats

Flounce or Flare (No Gathers)

Ruffle (Has Gathers)

Mushroom or Lettuce Edge

Faux Furs

Curly

Shaved

Long Hair

Directional

These treatments can go anywhere on a garment, top to bottom.

Tops and Details

Tube Top

Bandeau

Bustier

Cami/Camisole

Halter Top

Cropped Top (Shorter Cut)

Vest

Weskit (Longer Waist)

Polo (Banded Cuffs)

Rugby (Striped)

Camp Loose Fit/Single Pocket

Cutaway Tee "Wife Beater" (Skinny/Cling Knit)

Tank

Tee

Henley (Winter Underwear)

Epaulet

Button Tabs

Button Placket

Button Loop

Loop for Toggle   Button

Toggle

Frog

Loop for Frog   Button for Frog

Blouses and Shirts

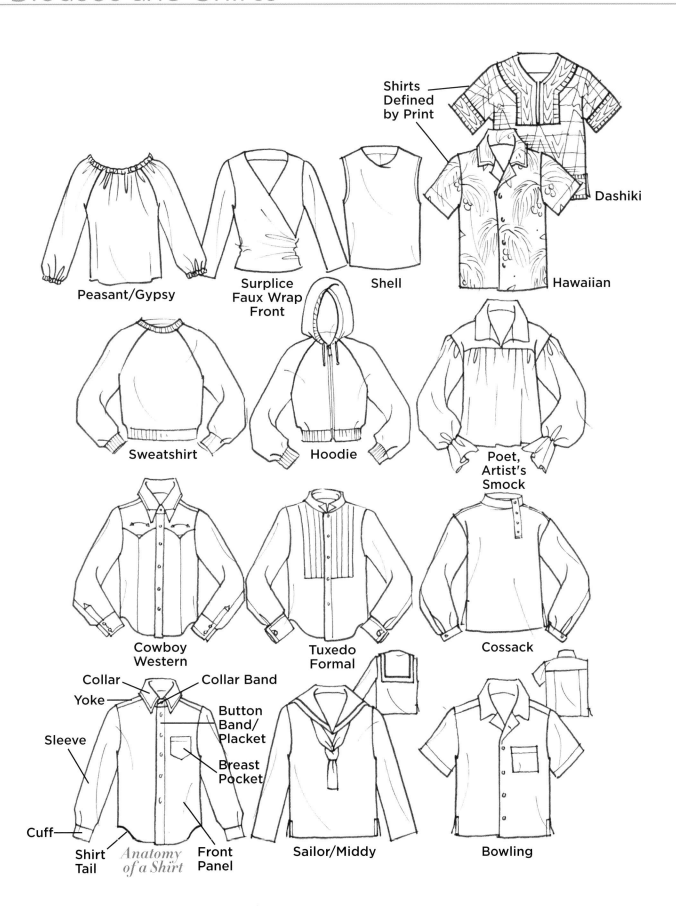

Shirts Defined by Print

Dashiki

Hawaiian

Peasant/Gypsy

Surplice Faux Wrap Front

Shell

Sweatshirt

Hoodie

Poet, Artist's Smock

Cowboy Western

Tuxedo Formal

Cossack

Collar

Collar Band

Yoke

Button Band/ Placket

Sleeve

Breast Pocket

Cuff

Shirt Tail

Anatomy of a Shirt

Front Panel

Sailor/Middy

Bowling

Bathrobe

Nightgown

Peignoir Set

Caftan-Djellabah

Caftan, Open

Muumuu

Kimono

Catsuit

Union Jack

Duster

Sleepshirt

PJs/Pajamas

Baby Doll Set

Sleep Set/ Shorties

Foundations and Innerwear

Leg Garter

Bodysuit

Teddy

Cami/ Camisole

Bustier

Merry Widow

Corset

Garter Belt

Underwire

Soft Cup

Padded, Uplift

Contour Cup, Shaped

Bandeau

Strapless

Crinoline Petticoat

Half Slip

Slip

Sports Bra

Shelf

Full Slip

Tap Panty

Boxer

Girdle

Body Slimmers, Shapers, Spanx, and Girdles

High Cut, Thigh Highs, Thigh Riders

Briefs

Bikini Hipster

Thong

Boy Cut

Shorts and Pants

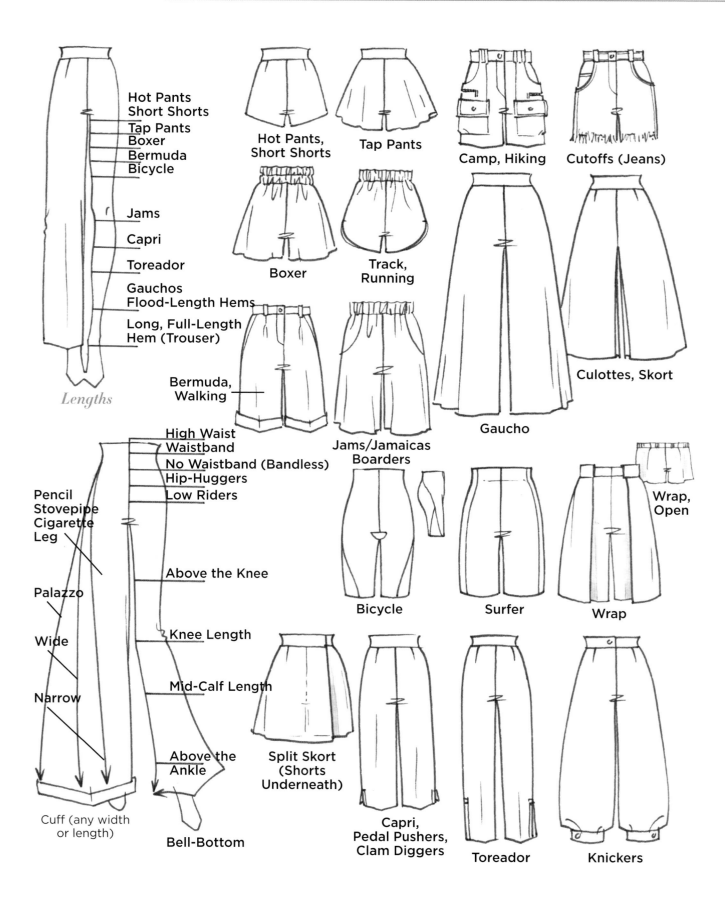

Hot Pants
Short Shorts
Tap Pants
Boxer
Bermuda
Bicycle

Jams

Capri

Toreador

Gauchos
Flood-Length Hems

Long, Full-Length
Hem (Trouser)

Lengths

Hot Pants,
Short Shorts

Tap Pants

Camp, Hiking

Cutoffs (Jeans)

Boxer

Track,
Running

Bermuda,
Walking

Jams/Jamaicas
Boarders

Gaucho

Culottes, Skort

High Waist
Waistband
No Waistband (Bandless)
Hip-Huggers
Low Riders

Pencil
Stovepipe
Cigarette
Leg

Palazzo

Wide

Narrow

Above the Knee

Knee Length

Mid-Calf Length

Above the
Ankle

Cuff (any width
or length)

Bell-Bottom

Split Skort
(Shorts
Underneath)

Bicycle

Surfer

Wrap

Wrap,
Open

Capri,
Pedal Pushers,
Clam Diggers

Toreador

Knickers

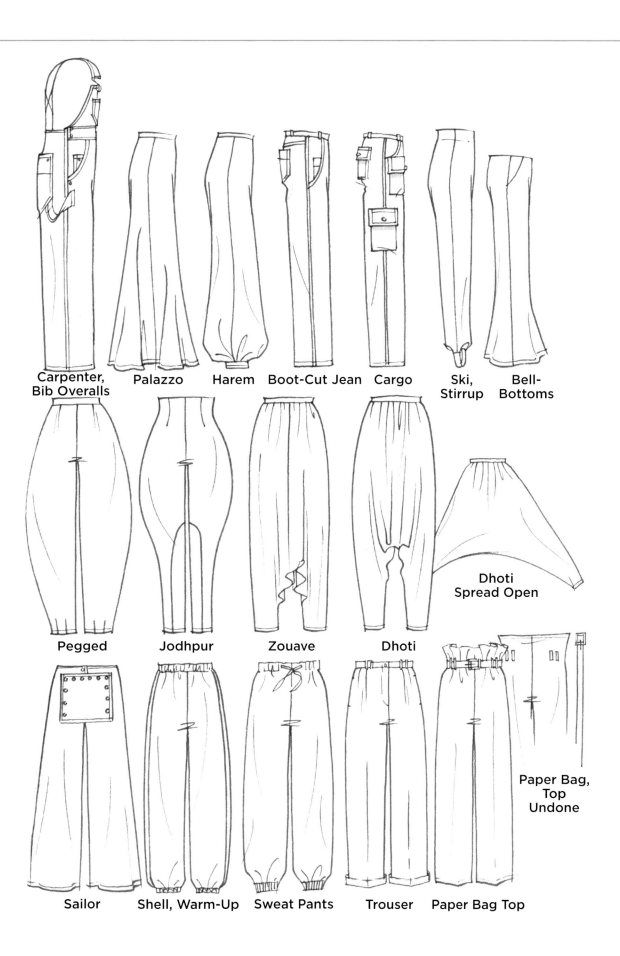

Carpenter, Bib Overalls

Palazzo

Harem

Boot-Cut Jean

Cargo

Ski, Stirrup

Bell-Bottoms

Pegged

Jodhpur

Zouave

Dhoti

Dhoti Spread Open

Sailor

Shell, Warm-Up

Sweat Pants

Trouser

Paper Bag Top

Paper Bag, Top Undone

Waistline Details

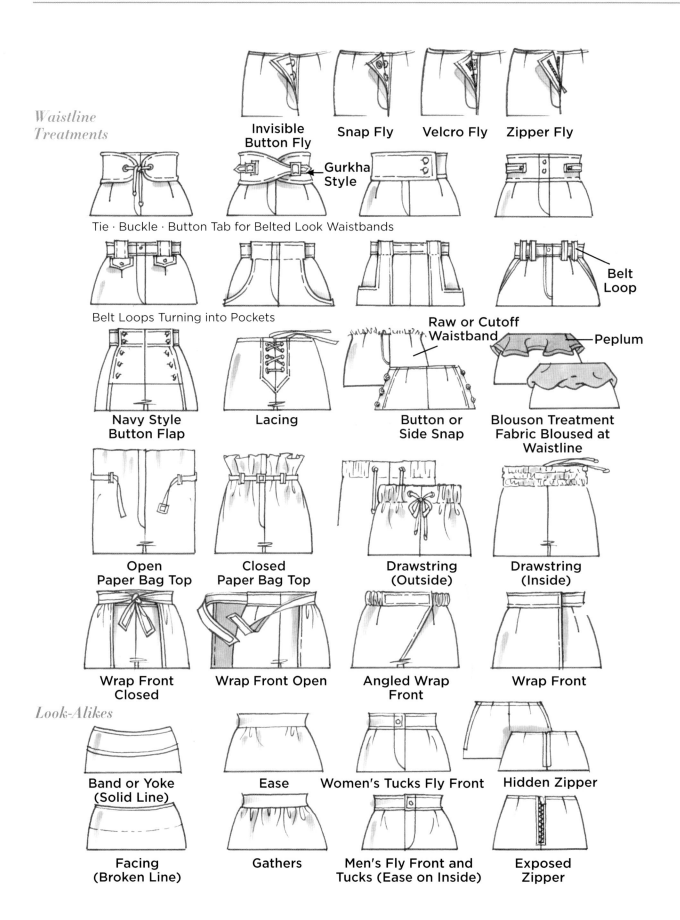

*Waistline
Treatments*

**Invisible
Button Fly** **Snap Fly** **Velcro Fly** **Zipper Fly**

Gurkha
Style

Belt
Loop

Tie · Buckle · Button Tab for Belted Look Waistbands

Belt Loops Turning into Pockets

Raw or Cutoff
Waistband

Peplum

**Navy Style
Button Flap** **Lacing** **Button or
Side Snap** **Blouson Treatment
Fabric Bloused at
Waistline**

**Open
Paper Bag Top** **Closed
Paper Bag Top** **Drawstring
(Outside)** **Drawstring
(Inside)**

**Wrap Front
Closed** **Wrap Front Open** **Angled Wrap
Front** **Wrap Front**

Look-Alikes

**Band or Yoke
(Solid Line)** **Ease** **Women's Tucks Fly Front** **Hidden Zipper**

**Facing
(Broken Line)** **Gathers** **Men's Fly Front and
Tucks (Ease on Inside)** **Exposed
Zipper**

Pockets

Size and placement for a pocket on a garment depend on both fabrication and trend. Pocket styling can be layered or combined in many variations.

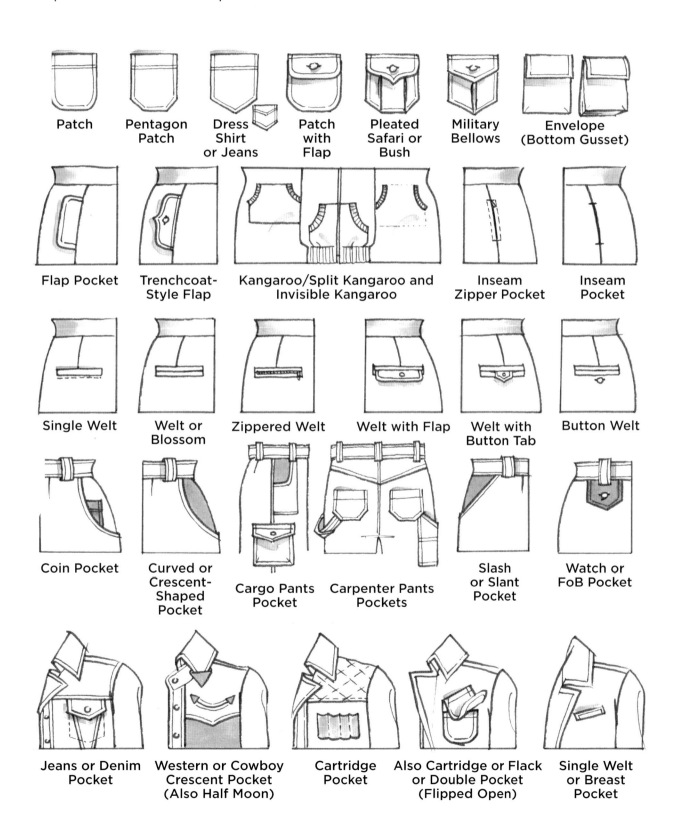

Patch

Pentagon Patch

Dress Shirt or Jeans

Patch with Flap

Pleated Safari or Bush

Military Bellows

Envelope (Bottom Gusset)

Flap Pocket

Trenchcoat-Style Flap

Kangaroo/Split Kangaroo and Invisible Kangaroo

Inseam Zipper Pocket

Inseam Pocket

Single Welt

Welt or Blossom

Zippered Welt

Welt with Flap

Welt with Button Tab

Button Welt

Coin Pocket

Curved or Crescent-Shaped Pocket

Cargo Pants Pocket

Carpenter Pants Pockets

Slash or Slant Pocket

Watch or FoB Pocket

Jeans or Denim Pocket

Western or Cowboy Crescent Pocket (Also Half Moon)

Cartridge Pocket

Also Cartridge or Flack or Double Pocket (Flipped Open)

Single Welt or Breast Pocket

Skirt Lengths

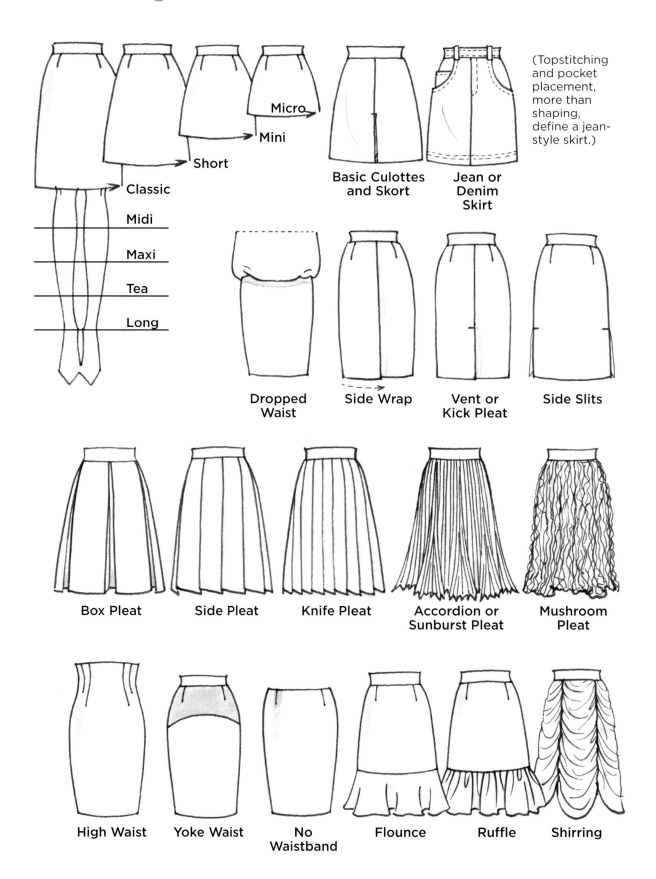

Micro

Mini

Short

Classic

Midi

Maxi

Tea

Long

Basic Culottes and Skort

Jean or Denim Skirt

(Topstitching and pocket placement, more than shaping, define a jean-style skirt.)

Dropped Waist

Side Wrap

Vent or Kick Pleat

Side Slits

Box Pleat

Side Pleat

Knife Pleat

Accordion or Sunburst Pleat

Mushroom Pleat

High Waist

Yoke Waist

No Waistband

Flounce

Ruffle

Shirring

Skirts

Pegged

Fitted or Straight

A-Line

Dirndl or Bell

Trumpet

Flare/Full

Gathered

Prairie

Tiered

Layered

Parachute

Six-Panel Gore

Eight-Panel Gore

Godet with Seams

Godet without Seams

Wrap

Kilt

Handkerchief

Asymmetrical—
Longer at the Sides
Fishtail—
Longer in the Back

Cowl

Sarong

Pareo/Scarf
(Swimwear
Accessory/Scarf)

Dressmaker Darts (Bodice)

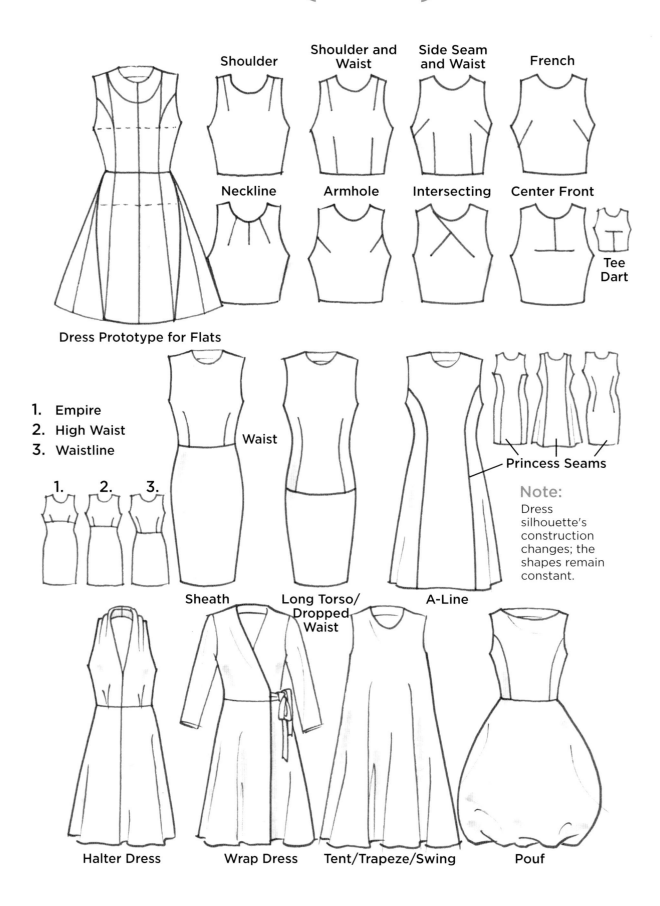

Shoulder

Shoulder and Waist

Side Seam and Waist

French

Neckline

Armhole

Intersecting

Center Front

Tee Dart

Dress Prototype for Flats

1. Empire
2. High Waist
3. Waistline

1.   2.   3.

Waist

Princess Seams

Note:
Dress silhouette's construction changes; the shapes remain constant.

Sheath

Long Torso/ Dropped Waist

A-Line

Halter Dress

Wrap Dress

Tent/Trapeze/Swing

Pouf

Dresses

Slip Dress,
Lingerie
Influence

Sundress,
Usually
Sleeveless

Apron Dress, Real
or Faux Two-Piece

Apron,
Backless

Coat Dress, Often
in Fall Fabrics

Cheongsam,
Qípáo, Asian Influence

Chemise
Shift

Tunic or
Faux Two-Piece

Empire, High
Bustline Seams

Shirt Dress, or Shirt
Waist, Usually Belted

Blouson, Usually
Drop Waisted

Jumper, Real or
Faux Two-Piece

Jumper,
Goes
Over a
Top or
Blouse

Jackets and Blazers

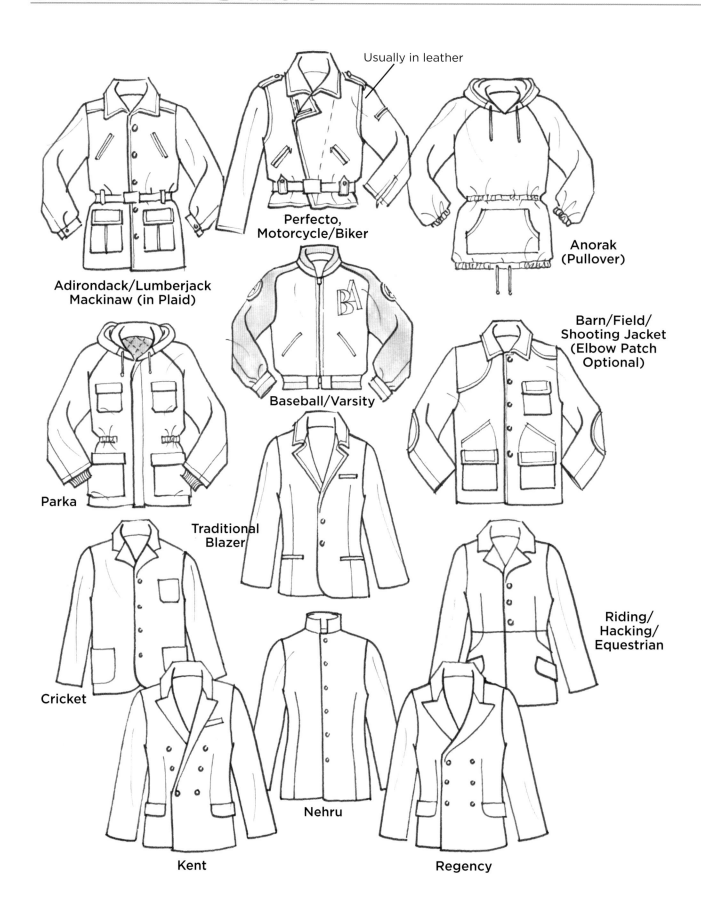

Usually in leather

Perfecto,
Motorcycle/Biker

Anorak
(Pullover)

Adirondack/Lumberjack
Mackinaw (in Plaid)

Barn/Field/
Shooting Jacket
(Elbow Patch
Optional)

Parka

Baseball/Varsity

Traditional
Blazer

Cricket

Riding/
Hacking/
Equestrian

Nehru

Kent

Regency

Jackets

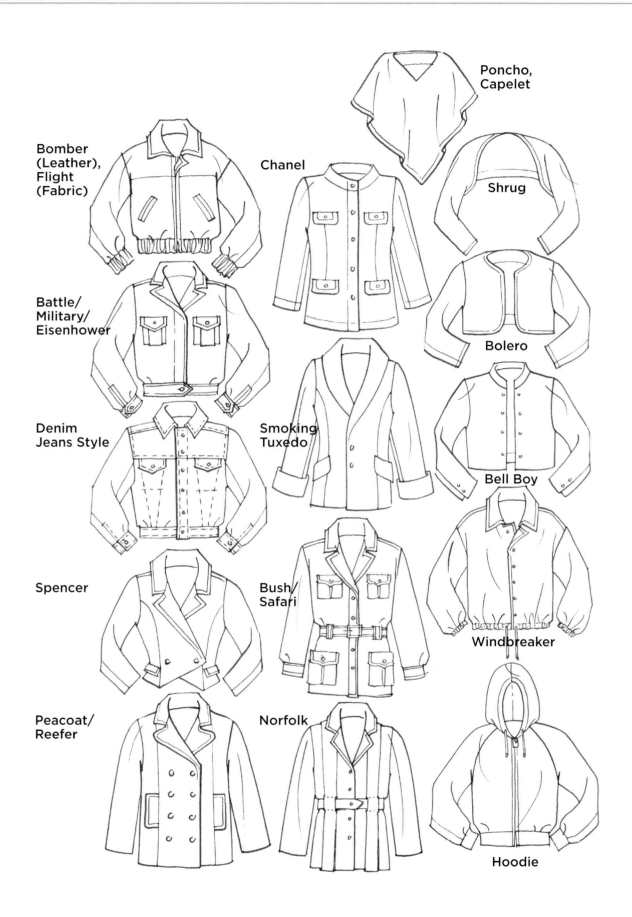

Bomber (Leather), Flight (Fabric)

Chanel

Poncho, Capelet

Shrug

Battle/ Military/ Eisenhower

Bolero

Denim Jeans Style

Smoking Tuxedo

Spencer

Bush/ Safari

Bell Boy

Windbreaker

Peacoat/ Reefer

Norfolk

Hoodie

Coats and Outerwear

Redingote   Coachman   Princess Seam   Tent/Trapeze/Swing

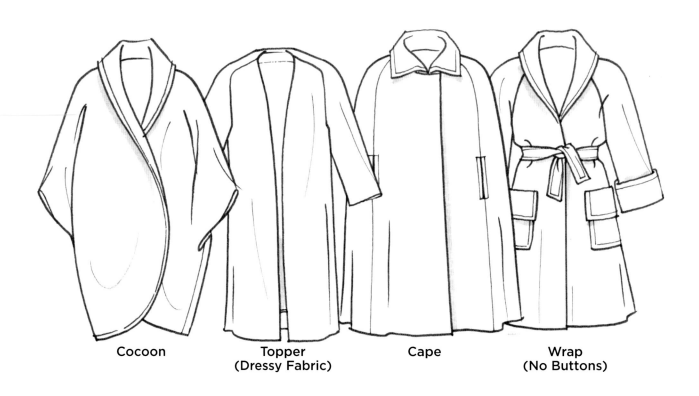

Cocoon   Topper (Dressy Fabric)   Cape   Wrap (No Buttons)

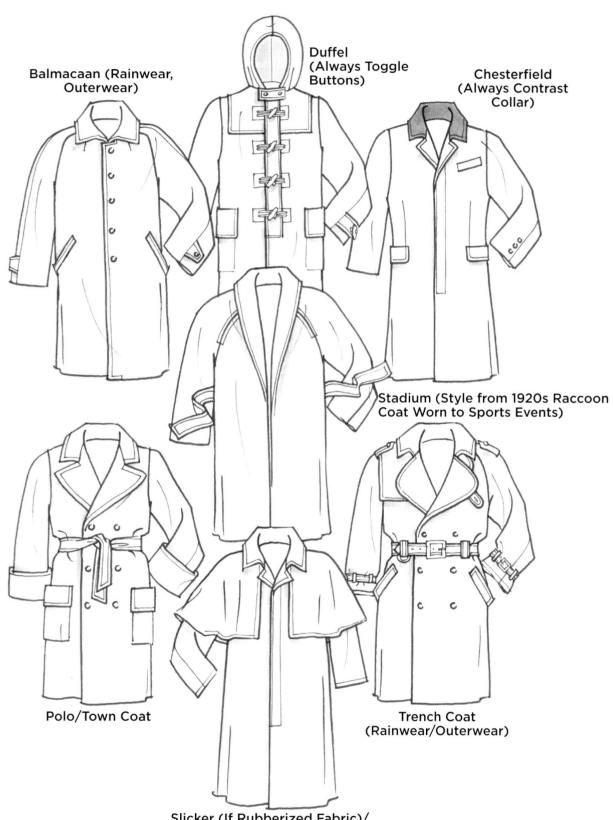

Balmacaan (Rainwear, Outerwear)

Duffel (Always Toggle Buttons)

Chesterfield (Always Contrast Collar)

Stadium (Style from 1920s Raccoon Coat Worn to Sports Events)

Polo/Town Coat

Trench Coat (Rainwear/Outerwear)

Slicker (If Rubberized Fabric)/ Mackintosh (Due to Shoulder Cape) (Rainwear)

Problem Spots

Shoulder Width

Shoulder width can be close to or double the length of the figure's neck. This width has to be balanced within the figure's pose to properly display garment details.

Neck Width to Shoulders

The neck can be drawn tubular, from below the chin, fanning out slightly into the base of the neck where it meets the shoulder slope in subtle contours.

Bustline Contours

Bustline contours are usually minimal, and fall just below the armpit, leaving room for, not crowding out, design detail on the upper chest area.

Fashion Hands

Hands in a designer sketch are often drawn in subtle, minimizing poses so as not to interfere with any design details.

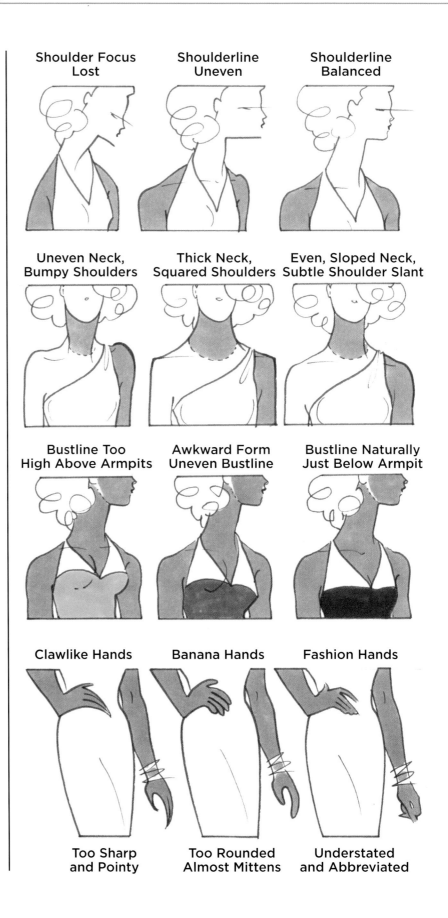

Shoulder Focus Lost — Shoulderline Uneven — Shoulderline Balanced

Uneven Neck, Bumpy Shoulders — Thick Neck, Squared Shoulders — Even, Sloped Neck, Subtle Shoulder Slant

Bustline Too High Above Armpits — Awkward Form Uneven Bustline — Bustline Naturally Just Below Armpit

Clawlike Hands — Banana Hands — Fashion Hands

Too Sharp and Pointy — Too Rounded Almost Mittens — Understated and Abbreviated

Shoulder Slope

Shoulder slope can be critical to design detail. Fit and shape have to be balanced between the neck and over the shoulder slope.

Garment Shoulders

Design detail across the shoulders has to look balanced. Uneven, mismatched, or droopy shoulders can distract from your fashion statement.

Upper Chest

In between the neck, the shoulders, and the bustline contour is the middle of the upper chest area. It can be a critical spot for design detail.

Bustline Level

The natural bustline level is in the middle of the torso, balanced halfway between the shoulderline and the waistline.

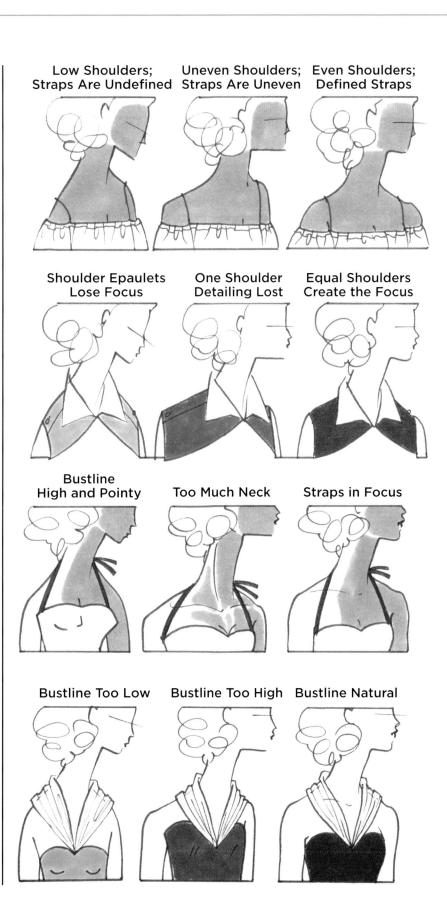

Low Shoulders; Straps Are Undefined   **Uneven Shoulders; Straps Are Uneven**   **Even Shoulders; Defined Straps**

Shoulder Epaulets Lose Focus   **One Shoulder Detailing Lost**   **Equal Shoulders Create the Focus**

Bustline High and Pointy   **Too Much Neck**   **Straps in Focus**

Bustline Too Low   **Bustline Too High**   **Bustline Natural**

Problem Spots (continued)

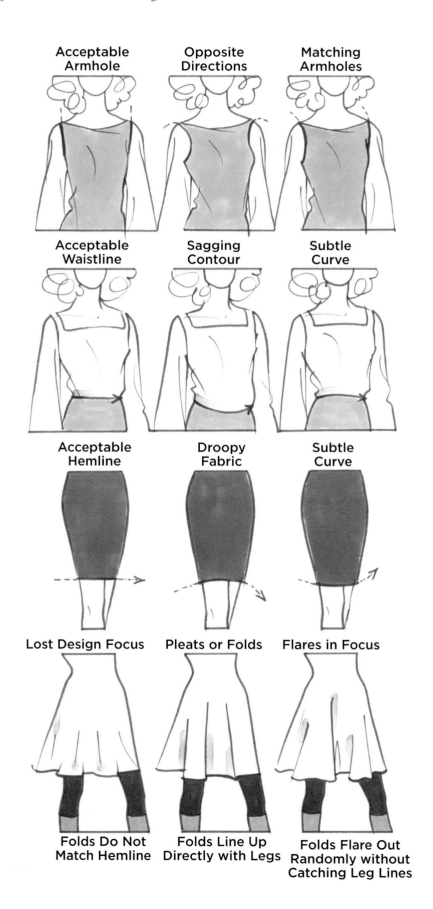

Armholes

Armholes look more natural with parallel curve lines. Lines that mirror the curve of center front in most poses (unless armhole cut specifically unmatched).

Acceptable Armhole   **Opposite Directions**   **Matching Armholes**

Waistlines

Waistlines can be drawn with a straight line but look more natural with a curved line. The wrong curve suggests a tummy sag where it should be a minor tummy tuck.

Acceptable Waistline   **Sagging Contour**   **Subtle Curve**

Hemlines

Hemlines circle the figure. This circle is usually an ellipse. Unless specifically designed to droop, keep the hemlines in subtle, curving contours.

Acceptable Hemline   **Droopy Fabric**   **Subtle Curve**

Lost Design Focus   Pleats or Folds   Flares in Focus

Flares and Folds

This type of drape creates slightly conal-shaped contours. To look natural, these sloped folds fall randomly and do not cling to the legs in a pose.

Folds Do Not Match Hemline   Folds Line Up Directly with Legs   Folds Flare Out Randomly without Catching Leg Lines

Collar Treatments

Unless designed differently, draw a collar with equal volume, shaping, and tips (or points) that reflect and match the shoulderline angles in a pose.

Waistbands

To tuck in or "blouse" fabric wherever it falls on the figure, use random ease lines into the waistband area, according to fabric type.

Pants Inseam / Crotch

A tight "V" drawn across the crotch or inseam on your design suggests a bad fit. The better fit over the crotch or inseam is drawn as a looser, broken line like a "Z."

Pleats and Hemlines

Pleats usually require precise delineation in their location, with specific repeats and coordinated hemline treatments.

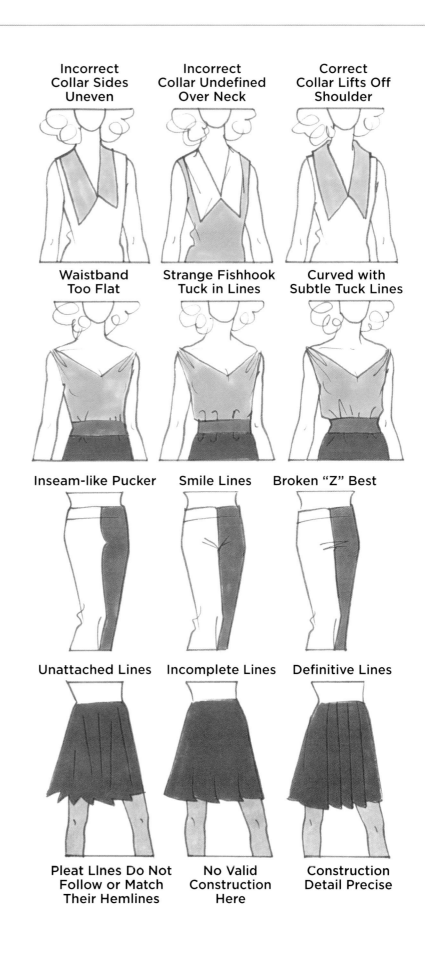

Incorrect Collar Sides Uneven　**Incorrect Collar Undefined Over Neck**　**Correct Collar Lifts Off Shoulder**

Waistband Too Flat　**Strange Fishhook Tuck in Lines**　**Curved with Subtle Tuck Lines**

Inseam-like Pucker　**Smile Lines**　**Broken "Z" Best**

Unattached Lines　**Incomplete Lines**　**Definitive Lines**

Pleat LInes Do Not Follow or Match Their Hemlines　**No Valid Construction Here**　**Construction Detail Precise**

Problem Spots (continued)

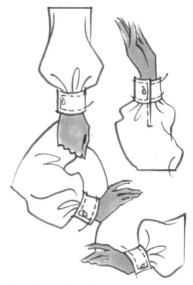

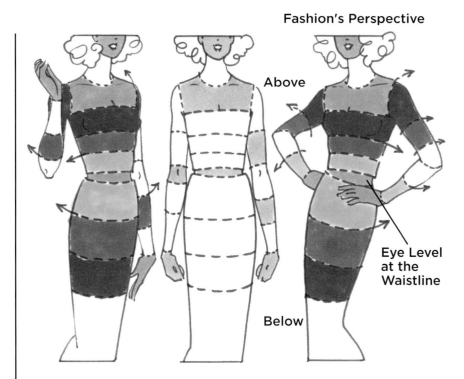

Above

Eye Level
at the
Waistline

Below

Sketching Contours to Round off Seams and Hems

Circling the Arm

The hem of a sleeve or cuff, if fitted, has to rotate around the arm or wrist, suggesting a circular fabric form.

Circling the Leg

Hemlines usually fall around the leg or ankle in a circular form. They are drawn with subtle rounded contours, keeping the fabric from looking flat or stiff.

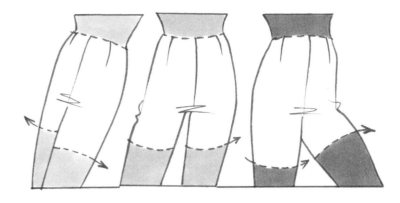

Using Leg Curves to Contour Hemline and Fit

Front / Back Inseams

Unlike the front view crotch or inseam's "Z" lines, the back view's lines, if fitted, can get a hint of snug bottom curves.

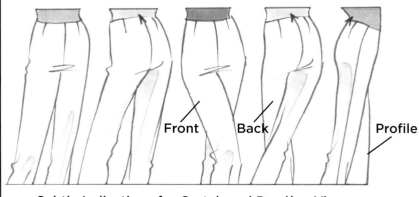

Front   Back   Profile

Subtle Indications for Crotch and Derrière Views

Detail in Pencil or Pen Line

Pinched: Too tight lines
Wrinkled: Too much lines
Optimal: Subtle hint of lines

Sleeves, Elbow to Wrist

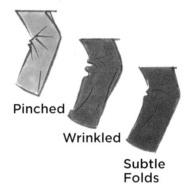

Pinched

Wrinkled

Subtle Folds

Bending Fabric

Fabric over the legs (pants, shorts, etc.) will look unnaturally flat or stiff unless drawn with a few simplified folds corresponding to the natural bends in the body, in a pose.

Design Detail

A. Don't let drawing style compromise design information.

B. Don't overstate fabric folds that compromise design function.

C. Balance drawing style with fabric type to accentuate design detail.

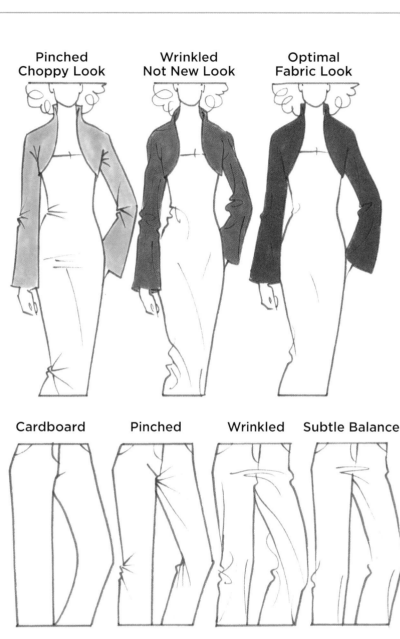

| Pinched Choppy Look | Wrinkled Not New Look | Optimal Fabric Look |

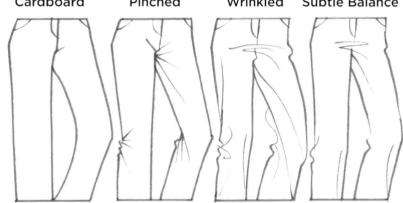

Cardboard   Pinched   Wrinkled   Subtle Balance

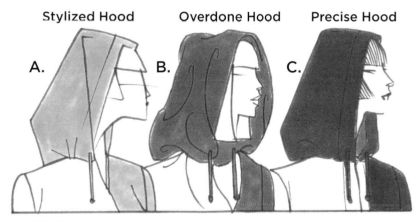

Stylized Hood   Overdone Hood   Precise Hood

A.   B.   C.

Lost/Minimized Detail   Obscured Detail   Obvious Detail

Credits

All photos below courtesy of WWD

CHAPTER 1
Pg. 14: Pasha Antonov

CHAPTER 3
Pg. 72: Marc Serota (left/right)
Pg. 74: Marc Serota
Pg. 76: George Chinsee (left), Donato Sardello (right)
Pg. 78: John Aquino

CHAPTER 4
Pg. 102: Kyle Ericksen
Pg. 103: Kyle Ericksen (top left), Delphine Achard (top right),
    Kyle Ericksen (bottom left), Kyle Ericksen (bottom right)

CHAPTER 5
Pg. 121: Giovanni Giannoni (top left), Giovanna Pavesi (top
    middle), John Aquino, Talaya Centeno and Thomas Ian
    naccone (top right), John Aquino (bottom left), Davide
    Maestri (bottom middle), Davide Maestri (bottom right)
Pg. 127: Kyle Ericksen (top left), John Aquino (top right), John
    Aquino (middle), Kyle Ericksen (bottom left), Giovanna
    Pavesi (bottom right)
Pg. 135: Giovanni Giannoni (top left), Kyle Ericksen (top
    middle), John Aquino (top right), Todd Matarazzo (bottom
    left), Giovanni Giannoni (bottom middle), George Chinsee
    (bottom right)

CHAPTER 7
Pg. 190: Thomas Iannaccone
Pg. 196: Davide Maestri (all)
Pg. 197: John Aquino (left/middle), Giovanni Giannoni (right)
Pg. 202: Giovanni Giannoni (left), John Aquino (middle/right)
Pg. 203: Mauricio Miranda (left), Thomas Iannaccone
    (middle), Robert Mitra (right)
Pg. 206: Thomas Iannaccone (left), Giovanni Giannoni (right)

Pg. 207: Mauricio Miranda (top left), Stuart Tyson + Solange
    Sandstrom (top right), Mauricio Miranda (bottom left),
    Robert Mitra (bottom right)
Pg. 208: Giovanni Giannoni (all), Giovanni Giannoni (middle)

CHAPTER 8
Pg. 231: George Chinsee (top left), Thomas Iannaccone (top
    right), Giovanni Giannoni (middle/bottom left/bottom
    right)
Pg. 246: John Aquino
Pg. 248: Giovanni Giannoni (top), Mauricio Miranda (bottom)
Pg. 249: Giovanni Giannoni (top), John Aquino (bottom)
Pg. 250: Giovanni Giannoni (top left/top right/bottom left/
    bottom right), George Chinsee (middle)
Pg. 252: Thomas Iannaccone (left), Stephane Feugere (middle),
    Giovanni Giannoni (right)
Pg. 253: Mauricio Miranda (top), Thomas Iannaccone (bottom)

CHAPTER 9
Pg. 282: Robert Mitra (left), Dominique Maitre (top right),
    Giovanni Giannoni (bottom right)

CHAPTER 10
Pg. 311: Isabella De Maddalena (top left), Thomas Iannaccone
    (top right), Pavel Antonov (bottom left), Dominique
    Maitre (bottom right)

CHAPTER 11
Pg. 362: Davide Maestri
Pg. 363: Giovanni Giannoni (top left), John Aquino (top right/
    bottom left), George Chinsee (bottom right)

CHAPTER 13
Pg. 438: Stuart Tyson + Solange Sandstrom (top left), Stuart
    Tyson (top right/bottom left), Cathy Crawford (bottom
    right)

Index

Accessories, 410–41
    belts, 422–23
    guest artists, 430–31
    handbags and purses, 424, 430–33
    historical illustrations, 440–41
    jewelry, 412–15, 438–39
    menswear, 436
    shoes, 425–29, 434
    sunglasses, 416–17
Anatomy, interpreting, 70–71
Angles, in model drawing, 64–65
Animal prints, 208–9
Argyle pattern, 283
Armhole treatments, 448, 470
Arms and hands, 10, 50–55, 468
    children's, 390–91
    foreshortening, 52–53
    gloves, 419
    men's, 342–43
    sleeves, 110–11
Attitude, in pose, 298–99

Balance line, 22–23, 63, 347
Basic figure forms, 38–59
    arms, 50–53
    feet, 46–49
    flats mixed with, 162–65
    foreshortening, 44–45
    hands, 54–55, 59
    legs, 40–45, 58
    tips for drawing, 56–59
    torso definition, 38–39
Basic rendering. See Rendering
    techniques, basic
Beene, Geoffrey, 214
Belts, 422–23, 458
Bhatia, Neha, 368–69

Black fabric, 246–49
Blazers, 128–29, 464
Blouses, 112–13, 120–21, 453
    templates for, 146–47
Bodice darts, 462
Bottoms. See Pants; Shorts; Skirts
Bows and ties, 450
Bridal looks, 233–38
    trains, 236–37
Buchanon, Jason, 432–33
Bustline, 468–69

Cascades and ruffles, 224–27
Chang, Serena, 402–3
Checks, ginghams, and plaids, 200–201
Children's wear, 377–409
    age groups, 378–79, 383–87
    arms and hands, 390–91
    design roughs for, 394–95
    flats for, 178–79, 398–99
    guest artists, 400–407
    heads, 388–89
    historical illustrations, 408–9
    infants, 381
    legs and feet, 392–93
    older boys, 385, 387
    proportions, 380
    rendering, 396–97
    toddlers, 382, 395
    tween to teen, 385–87
    younger child, 383–84
Chi Lo, Yuen, 256–59
Clements, Raya, 216–17
Coats and outerwear, 132–35, 466–67
    See also Jackets
    flats, 156–57
    stylization, 302–3

Collars and necklines. See Necklines and
    collars
Color rendering, 194–97
    designer challenges, 210–15
    nuances, 196–97
    testing, 194–95
    watercolor and gouache, 185–87
Composition, 295, 314–15
Conmy, Matt, 370–71
Courrèges, André, 211
Cowls, 228, 230–31
Croquis (Design Roughs)
    children's wear, 394
    footwear, 426–27
    jewelry, 412–15
    templates, 14–15, 160–61
Cuffs, 447

Dacosta, Felice, 438
Designer color challenges, 210–15
Design focus, 295–327
    attitude in pose, 298–99
    composition and layout, 295, 314–15
    direction, 296–97, 314–15
    emphasis, 300–301
    grouping figures, 316 19
    guest artist, 308, 324–27
    journal pages, 308–10, 358–59
    layout or lineup, 320–23
    maximizing impact, 312–13
    objectives, 304–7
    stylization, 302–3
    thumbnail sketches, 310
WWD fittings photos, 311
Details. See Fashion archive; Garments
    and garment details
Drape and volume, 240–43

Drawing technique. See Rendering technique

Dresses, 112–13, 120–21, 462–63
See also Gowns
bodice darts, 462
designer challenges, 212–15
gowns and, 238–39
hemline treatments, 243, 451, 471
templates for, 146–47

Dressmaker darts, 462

Elongation
See also Figure proportions
for menswear, 338–39
and stylization, 2–3

Emphasis, in design, 300–301

Fabric rendering
black, 246–49
fall, 204–7
luxe, 244–45

Faces. See Heads and faces

Fashion archive, 442–73

Feathers, fringe, and lace, 252–53

Feet, 46–49, 341
See also Legs; Shoes

Figure forms. See Basic figure forms

Figure proportions, 1–35
back views, 26–27
balance line, 22–23
center front, 24–25
changing, 232–33
children's wear, 380
consistent proportions, 10–11
croquis templates, 14–15
elongation and stylization, 2–3
fashion objectives, 12–13
figure map, heads tall, 8–9
freehand drawing, 16–17
fuller figure, 30–31
guidelines, 4–5
heads tall, figure grid, 6–7
maternity fashions, 32–33
menswear, 334–35
posing dynamics, 20–21
profile pose, 28–29
subjective height, 18–19

Flares and gathers, 116–17, 230–31, 470

Flats, 141–65
analyzing garment for, 170–71
bottoms (shorts, pants, and skirts), 148–49
children's wear, 178–79, 398–99
comprehensive, 154–55
croquis mixed with, 160–61
dress and gown, 238–39
figure formulas for, 144–45
figures mixed with, 162–65
figure templates, 142–43
guest artist, 176–77
knitwear, 268–69
menswear, 354–57
presentation/portfolio, 158–59
specs and, 141, 166–73
structure for, 150–51
swimwear and lingerie, 152–53
tops (shirts, blouses, and dresses), 146–47
women's outerwear, 156–57

Fleshtones, 100, 182–83

Flowers, Sascha, 366–67

Footwear. See Shoes

Foreshortening
arms, 52–53
legs, 44–45

Formal wear. See Gowns

Foundations and innerwear, 455
lingerie, 152–53

Franklin, Malinda, 436–37

Freehand drawing, 16–17

Fuller figure proportions, 30–31

Galanos, James, 214

Garment flats. See Flats

Garments and garment details, 107–39
blazers, 128–29
blouses and dresses, 112–13
coats, 132–35
emphasis and, 300
flares and gathers, 116–17
guest artists, 136–39
jackets, 128–31, 134–35
necklines and collars, 108–9
pants, 122–27
pleats, 118–19
shorts, 126–27

skirts, 114–21
sleeves, 110–11
in specs, 169
tops, 453–54

Gathers and flares, 116–17, 230–31, 471

Geometric patterns, 202–3

Gernreich, Rudy, 213

Gesture components, 68–69

Gingham, 200–201

Gloves, 420

Gores, 230, 231

Gouache, 184

Gowns, 254–55
bridal looks, 233–38
changing proportions, 232–33
flats, 238–39

Gupta, Anika, 406–7

Guthrie, Julian, 324–27, 372–73, 434–35

Hair and hair color, 98–99
men's, 344

Handbags and purses, 424, 430–33

Hands, 54–55, 59, 468
See also Arms and hands
children's, 391
gloves, 420
men's, 342–43

Hats, 418–21
and gloves, 419
men's, 418–20

Heads and faces, 81–105
See also Hats
children, 388–89
diamond technique for, 86
facial features, 90–91, 94–95
fleshtone and pencil, 100
full-front, 84, 85, 87
hair and hair color, 98–99, 344
men's, 344–45
period looks, 101
posing the head, 92–93
profile head, 84, 85, 89
runway looks, 102–5
stylizing face, 96–97
sunglasses, 416
three-quarter-turned, 84, 85, 88

Hemline treatments, 243, 451, 470

Herrera, Carolina, 212

Historical illustrations, 34–35
    accessories, 440–41
    children's wear, 408–9
    menswear, 374–75
    period heads, 101

Intarsia knit patterns, 283

Jackets, 128–31, 134–35, 464–65
    blazers, 128–29, 464
    men's, 350, 351
Jewelry, 412–15, 438–39
Journal pages, 308–10
    menswear, 358–59

Kennedy, Elizabeth, 254–55
Knits, drawing, 265–83
    basic stitches, 270–71
    cables and combinations, 276–77
    complex, 278–81
    essentials for, 266–67
    flats, 268–69
    guest artists, 284–93
    intarsia pattern, 283
    men's, 350, 351
    repeat patterns, 272–75, 283
    WWD photo reference, 282–83
Kwon, Christina, 176–77, 288–89

Lace. See Feathers, fringe, and lace
Lapels, 446
Lau, Jodie, 178–79, 286–87
Layout
    composition and, 295, 314–15
    or lineup, 320–23
Leflore, Latoya, 434
Legs, 10, 40–49
    children's, 392–93
    feet, 46–49, 341
    foreshortening, 44–45, 392
    knees, 58
    men's, 340–41
Lingerie, 152–53
Loungewear, 455
Luxe fabric, 244–45

Manfredonia, Anthony, 284–85
Maternity fashions, 32–33

Measurements, 166–68
    See also Specs (specifications)
Men and menswear, 329–75
    accessories, 439–40
    arms and hands, 342–43
    clothing the figure, 346–47
    design journal roughs, 358–59
    elongation for, 338–39
    figure basics, 330–33
    flats, 354–57
    guest artists, 366–73
    hats, 419, 421
    heads and hair, 344–45
    historical illustrations, 374–75
    legs and feet, 340–41
    marker rendering for, 360–61
    pants, 348–49
    proportions for, 334–35
    runway and showroom poses for,
        336–37, 362–65
    suits, 352–53
    tops, 350–51
Mikami, Eri, 400–401
Model drawing, 61–79
    angles, 64–65
    balance line, 63
    gesture components, 68–69
    interpreting anatomy, 70–71
    poses, 62
    runway and showroom poses, 72–79
    torso, 66–67
Necklines and collars, 108–9, 445–47, 472
    bows and ties, 451
    cowls, 228
    lapels, 446

Outerwear. See Coats and outerwear

Pants, 122–27, 457–58
    inseam crotch, 472
    men's, 348–49, 357
    shorts, 126–27, 148–49, 346, 457
    templates for, 148–49
Pantsuit, 211
Patterns, 198–203
    animal prints, 208–9
    checks, gingham, and plaids, 200–201
    geometric, 202–3

in knits, 272–75, 283
    stripes, 198–99
Pereira, Eduarda, 218–21
Pin tucks, 230–31
Plaids and checks, 200–201
Pleats, 118–19, 472
Pockets, 460
Poses, 62, 304
    attitude in, 298–99
    head, 92–93, 102–5
    legs, 42–43
    menswear, 346–47
    posing dynamics, 20–21
    profile, 28–29
    runway and showroom (See Runway
        and showroom poses)
Presentation or portfolio flats, 158–59
Prints, reducing, 188–89
Problem spots, 469–74
Proportions. See Figure proportions
Pucci, Emilio, 212
Purses and handbags, 424–25, 433–36

Rendering techniques, basic, 181–221
    animal prints, 208–9
    cascades, 226–27
    checks, gingham, and plaids, 200–201
    children's wear, 396–97
    color nuances, 196–97
    color testing, 194–95
    designer color challenges, 210–15
    fabric practice templates, 192–93
    fabric rendering, 186–87
    fall fabrics, 204–7
    finished vs. partial, 190–91
    fleshtones, 182–83
    geometric patterns, 202–3
    gouache, 184
    guest artists, 216–21
    reducing prints, 188–89
    stripes, 198–99
    watercolor, 185–87
Rendering techniques, high-end, 223–63
    beading, satin, chiffon, crystal
        pleating, and tulle, 250–51
    black fabric, 246–49
    bridal looks, 233–38
    cascades, 226–27

changing proportions, 232–33
children's wear, 396–97
cowls, 228
drape and volume, 240–43
feathers, fringe, and lace, 252–53
gathers, gores, cowl drape, and pin
    tucks, 230–31
guests artists, 254–63
luxe fabric, 244–45
menswear, 360–61
ruffles, 224–25, 230
smocking and shirring, 228, 449
Ruffles and cascades, 224–27, 230
Runway and showroom poses, 72–79
    fashion heads, 102–5
    menswear, 336–37, 362–65

Salgado, Jose Toffy, Jr., 292–93
Scaasi, Arnold, 215
Shirring. See Smocking and shirring
Shirts, 453
    templates for, 146–47
Shoes, 425–30, 434, 438
    croquis, 427–28
    sporty, 429–30
Shorts, 126–27, 346, 456
    templates for, 148–49

Shoulders, 468–69
Showroom poses. See Runway and
    showroom poses
Singh, Joseph, 290–91
Skirts, 114–21, 460–61
    flares and gathers in, 116–17
    hemline treatments, 243, 451, 471
    lengths, 456, 460
    pleats in, 118–19
    templates for, 148–49
Sleepwear, 454
Sleeves, 110–11
    armhole treatments, 448, 470
    cuffs for, 447
Sloper, 167
Smocking and shirring, 229, 447, 449,
    453
Spec sheets, 174–75
Specs (specifications), 141, 166–73
    analyzing garment for, 170–71
    flats and, 170–73
    measuring and detailing for, 168–69
Stripes, 198–99
Stylization, 302–3
Suits, men's, 352–53
Sung, Aram, 136–37
Sunglasses, 416–17

Swimwear, 152–53

Templates
    croquis, 14–15, 160–61, 414–15
    fabric practice, 192–93
    flat figure, 142–43
    jewelry, 412–15
    menswear flats, 354, 356
    skirts, pants, and shorts, 148–49
    for tops, 146–47
Ties and bows, 450
Tops and details, 452
    See also Blouses
    menswear, 350–51
    shirts, 146–47, 453
Torso, 66–67
    definition, 38–39
Tsao, Andrea, 308

Waistlines
    belts, 422–23, 458
    problems with, 470, 472
Watercolor rendering, 185–87
Wolff, Callista, 404–5
Wu, Carmen Chen, 138–39, 260–63
WWD designer fittings photos, 311